AMERICA'S SAILORS IN THE GREAT WAR

THE AMERICAN MILITARY EXPERIENCE
John C. McManus, Series Editor

The books in this series portray and analyze the experience of Americans in military service during war and peacetime from the onset of the twentieth century to the present. The series emphasizes the profound impact wars have had on nearly every aspect of recent American history and considers the significant effects of modern conflict on combatants and noncombatants alike. Titles in the series include accounts of battles, campaigns, and wars; unit histories; biographical and autobiographical narratives; investigations of technology and warfare; studies of the social and economic consequences of war; and in general, the best recent scholarship on Americans in the modern armed forces. The books in the series are written and designed for a diverse audience that encompasses nonspecialists as well as expert readers.

AMERICA'S SAILORS IN THE GREAT WAR

SEAS, SKIES, AND SUBMARINES

Lisle A. Rose

UNIVERSITY OF MISSOURI PRESS
Columbia

ISBN: 978-0-8262-2105-6
Library of Congress Catalog Number: 2016957560

∞™This paper meets the requirements of the
American National Standard for Permanence of Paper
for Printed Library Materials, Z39.48, 1984.

Typefaces: Bembo and Trajan

In memory of Charles Crooks, Gunner's Mate First Class, US Navy, 1917–18

Contents

Illustrations

Figures

Maps

Acknowledgments

I HAVE INCURRED A number of debts in the time it has taken to research and write this book. The staff at the Government Documents desk at Suzallo Library, University of Washington, were unfailingly helpful, especially in tracking down pertinent maps, which proved a surprisingly frustrating job. Mary Ryan at the Naval Submarine Museum, Keyport, Washington; Megan Churchwell of the Puget Sound Naval Museum; Nancy Miller, Stacie Peterson, and Jonathan Casey of the National World War I Museum in Kansas City; and Paul Marlow of the Puget Sound Maritime Historical Society provided assistance at key moments. No one who writes a history of the US Navy in World War I can do so without acknowledging the signal scholarly contribution that Todd Woofenden has made to our understanding of the subchasers and Geoffrey Rossano to the naval war in the air.

Clair Willcox at the University of Missouri Press suggested I undertake this project as part of the American Military Experience series. As always, he has been a stout supporter and acute critic. Mary Conley provided invaluable assistance and insights in the production process. John Rose once again stepped forward to prepare the maps for publication. As always, my wife, Harriet Dashiell Schwar, has contributed her own perspective and insights into the shaping of the manuscript while enduring the inevitable stresses and tensions of living with an author under full steam. I thank all of these individuals, understanding full well that any and all errors of fact or interpretation are mine alone.

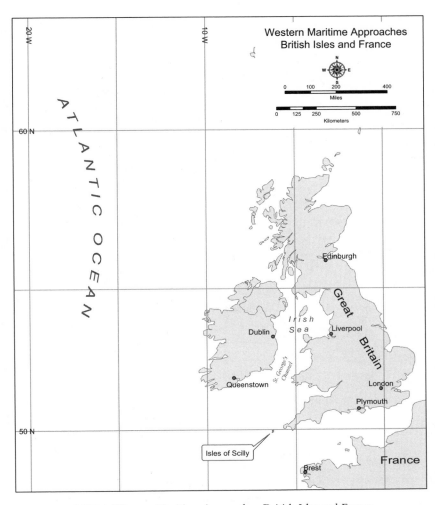

MAP 1. Western Maritime Approaches: British Isles and France

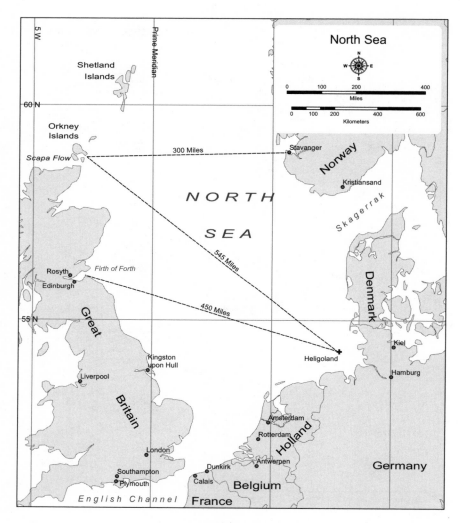

MAP 2. The North Sea

MAP 3. The Adriatic Sea and Strait of Otranto

AMERICA'S SAILORS IN THE GREAT WAR

Introduction

Wнат was it like for Americans fighting the naval war of 1917–18? What challenges did the professionals, the reservists, and the thousands of enlistees face from the enemy and from often cruel seas and stormy skies? What innovations were they forced to make, and what discomforts did they endure? How well did they do? These are the questions taken up in the following pages. *American Sailors in the Great War* is not a formal history of US naval operations in European waters in World War I. William N. Sill recently fulfilled that formidable task admirably and in exhaustive detail. Nor does it emphasize naval administration and Anglo-American cooperation and conferences beyond the essentials of setting the policy background and context within which America's sailors fought the 1917–18 war at sea. Over the years, David F. Trask and Mary Klachko have addressed the "captains and cabinets" administrative issues in detail. Paul G. Halpern, Arthur J. Marder, Robert K. Massie, Norman Friedman, and Lawrence Sondhaus have explored the American naval story a century ago as part of broader or related studies, and I have benefited from both their insights and their research.[1]

Nonetheless, much remains to be told about a fleet and its sailors who believed that they stood on the cutting edge of steadily advancing technology and who trained to fight within that context only to find themselves suddenly confronted with a new kind of war.

Space and cost restrictions dictate the exclusion of tangential areas of US naval activity both during and immediately after the war. The prior dispatch of US Marines to the Dominican Republic, Nicaragua, Honduras, and Haiti to enforce the Roosevelt Corollary to the Monroe Doctrine is a separate tale, one not closely intertwined with American naval preoccupations during the "Great

3

War." Given the limited range of German U-boats and the virtual disappearance of German surface raiders after 1916, naval activities in the Caribbean and off the Pacific coast of Mexico centered on prudent patrolling by subchasers and a handful of other small vessels either to detect the unanticipated presence of German surface raiders (none were found) and a possible German naval filibuster against Cuba (none was ever contemplated, much less carried out) or to keep a wary eye on the machinations of our ostensible Japanese ally, who, it was widely alleged and feared, clearly had an eye on a possible naval base or bases on the Mexican west coast. In 1915 the presence of a Japanese naval squadron, including battle cruiser *Asama*, off Baja California allegedly hunting German raiders known to have been in the area ignited hysterical reactions across the southwest tier of American states, including California. Washington sent an armored cruiser to look into matters, and the Japanese quickly departed. Like the phantom German filibusterers and raiders in the Caribbean, no Japanese base was ever found because none was built. But in 1917–18, prudence seemed to dictate the assignment of most of the West Coast–built subchasers to patrol duties from San Diego to Panama and on into the Caribbean.[2]

An early critic of the story I have written dismisses it as a tale of "Yankee triumphalism." I cheerfully plead guilty. As in any successful enterprise, whatever follies, confusions, and personal rivalries gripped those on high were redeemed by those below who dedicated themselves to the grinding discipline of daily work. There are times when what men do in a decent cause must compel respect and appreciation, and the United States Navy at sea and in the air during the First World War more than won the accolades bestowed upon it.

For the most part, the ocean war was a "small boys" conflict of destroyers, subchasers, armed yachts, and even submarines—ships that could not function with cowardice and incompetence stalking their crews. Those who could not measure up were quickly weeded out, either before their ships left American shores or immediately after arrival in combat zones. The mistakes and tragedies inherent in brand-new forms of warfare (convoying and antisubmarine operations) were dealt with on scene professionally and with remarkably little hysteria. Subchaser sailors, for example, simply refused to admit the patent unsuitability of their vessels and carried on their war against the U-boats with touching faith that success in the form of a "kill" was perpetually imminent.

With little thought to consequences, the Navy Department rushed massive battleships and tiny subchasers alike to European waters in the winter of 1917–18 through some of the stormiest seas on earth. Crews battled mountainous waves, freezing winds, and chaotic conditions belowdecks, whose grimness can scarcely be imagined. Yet they came through, ready for duty. Once there America's sailors manned destroyers during long, frigid gray days and cold, foggy nights in the Atlantic, perpetually stressed by the burden of responsibility that convoy escorting fastened upon them with a rigidity that never relaxed. They experienced the ordeal of manning new weapons of war like the submarine that behaved erratically, including unlooked-for plunges to murky depths. Several hundred turned to the skies, where some routinely flew and fought at dangerous heights never before achieved, save by the most daring pioneers, while others spent long hours droning through clouds several hundred feet above tossing seas, looking for U-boats that seldom materialized.

One hundred seventy-eight German submarines were destroyed by Allied action in the First World War. The United States Navy is generally credited with sinking but one of them. The service participated in none of the major surface actions such as Dogger Bank or Jutland that kept Kaiser Wilhelm's vaunted High Seas Fleet at bay. The navy neither initiated nor participated in any amphibious operations. But what it did do in helping guarantee the safe passage of a two-million-man American Expeditionary Force (AEF) to France, in assisting in the suppression of the U-boat menace, and in bolstering the Royal Navy during its time of quiet crisis after Jutland contributed signally to the eventual victory. These achievements, in turn, laid the foundations of a great maritime service whose powers would be fully realized in an unimaginably bigger war to come.

After the Armistice, some of the subchasers lingered in northern European waters for a time, assisting Allied forces in their ultimately feckless support of the anti-Bolshevik forces in Russia. But this is another separate tale, tangential at best to America's naval history in the Great War and one that deserves someone's separate story elsewhere. The narrative thus closes with the return of nearly all the elements of the battle fleet to home waters at the end of 1918.

CHAPTER ONE

State of Play

MARCH 1917, A hundred miles west-southwest of Ireland. Under hazy skies, a steamer perhaps four hundred feet long, displacing five to six thousand tons, plows through lightly choppy seas toward Liverpool or one of the Channel ports. Its holds are crammed with vitally needed grain for the English people and critical supplies for the British army on the western front. Officers and crew are apprehensive; they know they have entered the zone of unrestricted submarine warfare declared the month before by the German Admiralty in Berlin. But despite a steady rise of U-boat sinkings, the odds of their getting through remain better than 60 percent. Together with their brother merchant sailors, they insist upon steaming alone, without the protection and support that a convoy could provide. They believe that convoys take too long to assemble and thus are not cost-effective. Port authorities fear that clusters of convoyed vessels entering harbor and docking all at once would create chaos. At sea, the constant changes in course and speed required for zigzagging in massed formation to frustrate a submerged U-boat attack increase costs even more and demand a level of seamanship that few claim to possess. And the very fact that merchantmen would be "huddled" together in a heavy cluster of ships would make the U-boat's task even easier. Perhaps two or three escorted ships could do a successful convoy run, but no more.[1] The British Admiralty agrees. Convoying belonged to the Age of Fighting Sail when merchant vessels carrying the wealth of new worlds in America and Asia required protection against pirates and enemy fleets. Convoying would be ineffective against the modern U-boat, and neither the French nor the British navies could spare from their precious battle fleets more than a handful of the destroyers required for escort

7

and screening of merchantmen. So the thousands of ships required to keep Britain and thus France and their combined armed forces in the war continue to sail alone toward and through the ever-narrowing funnel of the Western Approaches where lurk the kaiser's submarines.

On this particular day, as so often, even a moderate sea state successfully masks the narrow ribbon created by a U-boat periscope and the wake of its torpedoes. Without warning, the steamer is rocked by an enormous explosion on the starboard side amidships. As the cold waters of the Atlantic rush into the hull, the engine room becomes an inferno of scalding steam escaping from ruptured boilers and flying hunks of red-hot steel from blasted coal furnaces and grates. Men not immediately boiled or burned to death soon drown from the inrushing waters, while above them the rapidly heeling hull renders all the port-side lifeboats useless; many on the starboard side have been reduced to splinters by the torpedo blast. A host of panicky crewmen and the few civilian passengers on board erupt on deck, while the radio operator sends a hasty SOS before rushing to the rails; the distress call might or might not be picked up ashore. Quickly the vessel capsizes, the shattered hull remaining afloat for a brief time before disappearing beneath the waves, carrying down with it many of those who could not swim or failed to get far enough away. A few are able to reach the several lifeboats that had somehow been launched.

Having made its kill, the submarine cautiously surfaces after its commander first sweeps the horizon with his periscope for telltale signs of smoke that might mark one of the few British destroyers on antisubmarine patrol. Satisfied that no enemy vessels are about, the German crew might in a relatively few instances toss some of their meager stores of food, or water, to the steamer's survivors or point them in the direction of the nearest land, far away. Then the U-boat, engines clanking, foams off, remaining on the surface in hypervigilance for the several hours required to recharge its batteries. Now alone on a vast ocean, the survivors are more likely than not doomed to die slowly of exposure, hunger, and thirst.

Such is life at sea in the third year of the First World War: underhanded, brutal, pitiless.

A century later, it is difficult to measure the revulsion with which the German air and submarine campaigns of 1915–18 were greeted among the peoples of the West. Even as the world's great navies began slowly stocking their inventories with "Undersea Boats" in the years before the war, the submarine, along with the "Zeppelin" airship, was widely perceived as an unprecedented violator of basic human decency and fair play. "Before 1914," an American naval officer wrote eight years later, "nobody knew what a naval war would be like with the new weapon introduced: *the submarine*. Of course, through numerous exercises, its offensive power had been revealed, but as to the means of meeting the danger, the Admiralties were out of wits, for there had been no war experience to throw any light on the subject. When some young officer happened to succeed in attacking, his admiral barely acknowledged the fact—when he did not receive the report with a rebuke."[2] Training exercises on the Continent and in the waters around the British Isles in the years just prior to the "Great War" reflected a century of general peace in which warfare was perceived in the "highly ritualized and idealistic" terms of a medieval jousting tournament, encouraging "the participants to play out their understanding of" combat, "without having to reconcile it to an unsavory and very dangerous reality (in the case of medieval warfare) or a culturally unimaginable future (in the case of submarine warfare)." Near the end of 1913, a memorandum was prepared in the highest levels of the British Admiralty "in which it was prophesied that the Germans would use their submarines for attacking commerce. So utterly repugnant was this novel idea that both the First Lord [of the Admiralty, Winston Churchill] and the First Sea Lord [Admiral Louis Mountbatten] declared that the paper was fatally 'marred by this suggestion.'"[3]

But at sea and in the air as on the western front, the Great War generated its own momentum. Before the horror of the trenches was the terror of the sea. At first German and British submarines confined their campaigns to attacks against each other's fleet units, which caused mild panic and some significant losses within the Royal Navy but no disruption of its operations to keep the kaiser's High Seas Fleet penned up in its several North Sea ports. The British naval blockade of Germany announced early in 1915 and firmly if not ruthlessly pursued with frequent interceptions of neutral shipping not only caused anger and dismay among neutral nations—most especially the United States—but also induced the German Admiralty to counter with the only effective weapon it could muster, unrestricted submarine warfare, conducted by means of not only the gun and the torpedo, but also the laying of minefields in the North Sea and adjacent waters.

Perhaps characteristically, the Germans all too soon outdid themselves. In the process, they seemed to confirm and conform to the notion of the bestial "Hun" who violated Belgian neutrality while executing innocent civilians (including nurse Edith Cavell) and deliberately destroying the lovely medieval city and cathedral of Louvain. Declaring a "war zone" around the British Isles, the Imperial German Navy soon enforced it in the most awful fashion. On the early afternoon of May 7, 1915, a single torpedo from the submerged U-20 sank the great Cunard passenger liner *Lusitania*. In the next hour or so, more than twelve hundred people, including more than one hundred Americans, drowned in the chilly waters off Queenstown (now Cobh), Ireland. Just twenty-four days later, as world opinion continued to seethe with outrage, a single German naval airship—a "Zeppelin"—carried out the first nighttime raid on London, killing seven and wounding thirty-five. In September, in another single Zeppelin raid, LZ-13 floated over central London unmolested, dropping bombs that killed twenty-two and caused more than a half-million pounds in damage.

Suddenly, there seemed no place to hide from an enemy who used whatever medium was at hand to spread indiscriminate terror wherever and whenever possible. The unrepentant, indeed publicly joyful, reaction to the sinking of *Lusitania* by the German Admiralty and people (who convinced themselves that the great liner carried large stocks of munitions and thus got what it deserved) only intensified the general revulsion elsewhere. In Allied eyes, the German U-boat campaign confirmed the submarine's sinful status as a silent marauder, an "underwater pirate," an "undersea serpent," who killed without warning from ambush beneath the waves, a pitiless, barbaric warrior who "ravaged" the sea lanes and for whom there was no place in modern warfare. Germany's employment of submarines "covered the new weapon with infamy." Behind this widespread outrage in both the British Isles and the United States was the naive belief that "sea power" in and of itself "is essentially pacific in its aims and workings." It thus stood to reason that the evil Hun was prosecuting a submarine war "to bring military tyranny to bear upon the seas and to carry it to the uttermost parts of the Earth where sea power has planted freedom." Allied naval authorities at the time convinced themselves that the U-boat was at best an annoyance to both war fleets and merchant traffic so long as it adhered to the laws of war. Only "by resorting to unscrupulous methods" had it "become a dangerous commerce destroyer and as such has taken a prominent part in the war."

As the conflict ground on and five British hospital ships and their people perished before German torpedoes, feelings became, if possible, even more inflamed. Incidents real and alleged included the British steamer *Belgian Prince*, whose crew was rescued by the U-boat that sank their ship, only to be kept on deck as the submarine skipper closed his hatches, ran several miles, and then submerged deliberately, drowning all but three of his hapless prisoners. By 1918 Britons viewed the submarine war in apocalyptic terms as "the main battlefield of our spiritual crusade." Antisubmarine war sailors had become "our champions in the contest of ideals . . . the defenders of human nature against those who preach and practice barbarism. . . . Between the old chivalry, and the new savagery, there can be no truce; one of the two must go under." The bestiality of the German people was beyond question: "Everything that could be charged against them has been already proved by their own words and actions. They have sunk without warning women and children, doctors and nurses, neutrals and wounded men, not by tens or hundreds but by thousands. They have publicly rejoiced over these murders with medals and flags, with songs and school holidays." American opinion swung decisively behind this view. On the eve of his departure for European waters, young subchaser skipper George Dole wrote that "the Kaiser's deep sea monsters represent the most perfect engines of evil genius man has been able to devise."[4]

The sinking of the *Lusitania* had outraged President Wilson, who promptly dispatched a stiff note to Berlin, demanding no more such incidents and insisting that U-boat crews be held to "strict accountability" for any future violations of traditional international law of the sea that protected peaceful shipping from harm. Should Berlin fail to take these steps, the United States would break off diplomatic relations—often, though not invariably, a prelude to war. The kaiser's government reacted grudgingly. As Wilhelm and his people saw it, the British blockade not only flagrantly impoverished an innocent German people but also positively rewarded American business and industrial interests, which, while kept from dealing directly with Germany, could find ready markets and investments in the Allied war effort. Germany responded to Wilson's demands accordingly. While there was to be no more flagrant destruction of neutral vessels or of passenger ships, the Imperial Navy refused to suspend its U-boat war against British and French merchant shipping in the face of a continuing Allied blockade. The few neutrals who continued to book passage on smaller British passenger vessels, like the cross-Channel steamer *Sussex* torpedoed by a U-boat in early 1916 with the loss of several Americans, not only took their lives into their hands, but also forced Wilson to make impossible demands on Berlin. These included a German promise—the so-called *Sussex* Pledge—to order its U-boats to surface, determine the nature of the ship to be attacked, and, if it was a ship carrying passengers, to guarantee the safety of these innocents and the crew before sinking. Once again, the president had threatened to break off diplomatic relations if Berlin failed to accede to his demands. The kaiser and his immediate entourage became in turn outraged by Wilson's behavior, which Foreign Minister Arthur Zimmerman characterized as hypocritical. The president, he exclaimed, "feels and thinks English." Late in 1916, Zimmerman began carefully probing the Mexican government for an alliance that might allow German submarine bases on the Gulf coast.[5]

The British had already nullified the kind of hard-to-enforce policy embodied in the *Sussex* Pledge by countering the Submarine Menace, as it was known in Allied circles, with the introduction of "Q," or "mystery," ships. These apparently innocent but heavily armed cargo steamers and even some sailing schooners (which to German U-boat skippers might be carrying civilian passengers in addition to cargo), traveling alone, had orders to throw open their gun ports and blaze away the moment a U-boat surfaced to determine their nature. To submarine crews, the Q ships represented the essence of British perfidy; their U-boat had suddenly become as much the hunted as the hunter. Indeed, some British Q-ship commanders relished their role quite as keenly as if they'd been riding to hounds in an English field. To hard-pressed Britons, the barbarity of the U-boat war rendered all previous questions of international law null and void. In Whitehall's view, it was "only necessary to state as a fact that Germany decided to use her submarines to attack and sink our commerce, the life-blood of the British Isles and the source of supply not only to the Army in France but the Grand Fleet that was successfully keeping its German opposite under thumb." But their very nature limited the number of Q ships that could be deployed. Each converted merchant steamer or sailing vessel was one more removed from Britain's steadily dwindling inventory of ships vital to national survival. Q ships always faced the prospect of heavy damage if not outright destruction in battle with U-boats. Clearly, they were of limited utility in the antisubmarine war that raged with ever-accelerating intensity in 1915–16.[6]

Further German folly escalated Wilson's growing outrage. Shipyards at Kiel, Bremen, and Hamburg had begun to produce the first of eight monster (for the time) eighteen-hundred-plus-ton "merchant" U-boats designed to circumvent the British blockade through long-range underwater passage to markets in the New World.[7] In the summer of 1916, one of these huge vessels, *Deutschland*, made two voyages from Germany to the United States and back. A postwar American naval report concluded that their purpose "must remain a matter, more or less of conjecture," though both were probably purely commercial voyages. "That feat changed everyone's mind." Should any one of the merchant U-boats be converted to "cruisers" or should the normal U-boat in fact possess a longer cruising range than believed, Germany could take its frightful brand of warfare straight to the American coast should the United States choose to enter hostilities. In September Germany dramatized this fear when U-53 under the command of Lieutenant Hans Rose, an Iron Cross pinned to his chest, suddenly appeared in Narragansett Bay, not far from the US Naval War College and the basic training center for entering naval recruits. This voyage, the American report concluded, "assumes more a character of a path-finding expedition. This vessel was a strictly combative vessel. It is interesting to note that on the arrival of this vessel at Newport, the commanding officer stated to the American submarine that he did not need or want a pilot to enter Newport, and that he wanted no supplies or provisions or materials of any kind." Rose boldly came ashore to call on authorities, informing them in no uncertain terms that his vessel was an armed warship. The German *kapitän* then took his boat to sea, the crew ostentatiously cheering American fleet units on their way out. Within a few short days, Rose managed to sink no fewer than five merchant vessels (three British, one Norwegian, and one Dutch). All were in international waters, but within view of the Nantucket Lightship. The British steamship *Stephano* carried American passengers.

Rushed to sea to search for survivors, the US Navy experienced the horrors of the U-boat war directly as the destroyer *Benham* fished the wretched survivors of the Dutch steamer SS *Blommersdijk* from the frigid waters of the Atlantic. "The man in the street" became sensibly "scared." Already alarmed by the potentials of a vast surface war in Atlantic waters suggested by the Battle of Jutland at the end of May, as well as a growing naval rivalry with Japan in the Pacific, Congress and the Wilson administration promptly set to work constructing "a Navy second to none." The Navy Department itself began to quietly compile a register of civilian-owned vessels—motorboats, yawls, schooners, harbor tugs, and, perhaps most important, privately owned and commercial steam yachts—that might be expropriated for future antisubmarine warfare both along the American Coast from Maine to Florida and in European waters in the case of the bigger ships. The inventory was large and impressive, for in earlier years "many" a yachtsman who was at once wealthy and patriotic had his substantial pleasure craft "built specifically for use" as a navy patrol boat in wartime. By the time the program concluded in 1918, more than four thousand vessels had been requisitioned.[8]

The German submarine issue was part of a complex tapestry of competing interests, memories, and decisions that at once stayed American entry into the Great War for many months, yet in the end made it inevitable. The country was but a century removed from the last British effort to destroy it and its Revolution. In 1813, a British force had burned Washington, DC, sending President Madison ("Little Jemmy"), his family, and the US government flying like partridges into the northern Virginia countryside. Thereafter, Anglo-American tensions flared over rights to what is now the US Pacific Northwest, outright British sympathy and support for the Confederacy during the early years of the Civil War (the Confederate steam raider *Alabama* was built in a British yard), and the current rigidly enforced British naval blockade of Germany. Memories were long and resentments died hard. Anglophobia remained entrenched in the upper reaches of the US armed forces. As late as 1911–12, games at the Army War College, of which navy officials were certainly aware, if not outright observers to, were based on "War Plan Red," in which British forces ("Red") attacked the United States through Canada after neutralizing "Blue" (US) naval forces in Caribbean and Atlantic waters. "In this war game, RED completely overcame any resistance that BLUE could offer." As Wilson pondered taking the country to war in the early months of 1917, the new (and first) chief of naval operations (CNO), William S. Benson, told Admiral William Sowden Sims, the designated naval representative to the British Admiralty, not to "let the British pull the wool over your eyes. It is none of our business pulling their chestnuts out of the fire. We would as soon fight the British as the Germans." Later Benson admitted to a congressional committee that "I might put it this way. I thought that there were certain things going on that we ought to be prepared for in an emergency. Our ships were being held up" by the Royal Navy enforcing the blockade, "and certain things were going on that might make it necessary for us to take a definite stand."[9]

At the same time, certain circles within Britain's naval establishment and media harbored a distinct attitude toward the American cousins that mingled outright contempt with underlying anxiety. In early 1916, the British Navy League claimed that proposed military and naval preparedness programs in the United States suffered from "a fundamental and very grave defect, namely that they represent not the matured plans of the naval and military experts who alone are qualified in the matter, but rather the proposals of the purely civilian minds of the Secretary of the Navy and the Secretary of War." The "New American Naval Programme" came in for particular condemnation as "*the political design of an ephemeral politician, Mr. Josephus Daniels, the present United States Secretary of the Navy.*" Lurking not far beneath John Bull's ostentatious dismissal of American plans, however, was an obvious concern owHHowthat when it appeared in a half decade or so, "'America's New Armada' might be employed against British interests in retaliation for the clear violation of neutral rights by the Royal Navy as it maintained its wartime blockade of the Continent. Such fears could not have been swept away completely by Wilson's request for a declaration of war against the Central Powers since the president accompanied his call with a pledge to the nation that it would enter the conflict not as an outright ally of Britain and France, but as an 'Associated Power.'"[10]

In the end, three decades of German-American rivalries and suspicions proved decisive. The two fledgling industrial fleets had first tested each other's mettle in a far-off Samoan harbor twenty-eight years before, as each sought to bend a local civil war to their advantage while a lone British gunboat looked on. A decade later, German warships appeared in Manila Bay shortly after Dewey's victory over the Spaniards, obviously hoping to capitalize on whatever weaknesses or hesitation American sailors might display in guiding the fortunes of the native population. Characteristically, the British also appeared, but it was the Germans who seemed the more passively aggressive. In the earliest years of the new century, Anglo-American naval relations warmed dramatically. Following the Spanish-American War, both services were active on the China Station, and the 1900 Boxer Rebellion brought them into close alliance. Sims forged friendships with senior Royal Navy officers, including John Jellicoe, who would lead the Grand Fleet at Jutland before becoming Britain's first sea lord. Joseph Taussig, then a lowly ensign, found himself thrown in with Jellicoe as both suffered wounds at the hands of the Boxers. In 1917, Jellicoe would send a personal word of welcome to Taussig when he brought the first contingent of American destroyers to Queenstown.[11]

No comparable bonds were forged between American sailors and their German opposites. To the contrary, Germany appeared to be the most determined European power to meddle in the financial and internal affairs of bankrupt Latin American and Caribbean island nations. Despite Theodore Roosevelt's 1904 "Corollary" to the Monroe Doctrine stating that henceforth the United States would, if necessary, intervene in the affairs of miscreant Western Hemisphere nations to supervise their relations with European governments and bankers, German intervention continued right on to 1914. Meanwhile, planning for an outright naval war with the United States, including an invasion of points along the East Coast, became, for a time, part of German naval policy, grounded in a growing contempt for ostensibly lax or nonexistent American moral standards and fiber. A German Admiralty staff memorandum of January 1902 "recommended an assault on Puerto Rico, followed by a blockade of American Atlantic and Gulf of Mexico seaports and eventual operations against . . . Boston and New York."[12]

How much American political and naval authorities knew of specific German plans is unclear. After 1905, however, they exhibited little interest in challenging Britain's continued dominance of the world's sea lanes but a growing interest in maintaining parity if not supremacy over the rapidly expanding German fleet. Looking back on the years immediately preceding the First World War from the perspective of the Second, an American naval historian wrote that the Anglo-German naval race of 1906–14 "held the greatest interest" for Washington policy makers. "Fearing a German challenge in South and Central America, American political and naval leaders regarded every German ship as a threat to American security. Having laid claim to second place in the hierarchy of naval powers, we found that the German [construction] program placed heavy obligations on American naval appropriations." Through strenuous building efforts during the first years of the new century, the US Navy maintained a clear preponderance of tonnage over its German rival. Theodore Roosevelt and Alfred Thayer Mahan together "with a whole host of individuals in Congressional and naval circles saw security for America's place in the world only behind a fleet that could accept with confidence a German naval challenge." "We must recognize," George T. Davis concluded in 1940, that paralleling Europe's naval race in the years before World War I "ran the course of a German-American naval rivalry. Less intensely than for the British, but no less effectively, German sea power remained the cardinal standard of American naval needs." The crux of the matter was this: the United States could not allow any nation with a great standing army such as Germany to surpass American naval power.[13]

The submarine—the *Unterseeboot*, or "U-boat"—was in many ways the culmination of a broad-based Industrial Revolution in sea power. Remarkable advances in naval construction, propulsion, and ordnance filled the half century following the American Civil War. Mastery and proficiency of ever-advancing technologies were mandatory as wooden sailing ships gave way to steel-clad, steam-powered vessels; hand-signaling gave way to long-range wireless communications; and weapons systems expanded from simple broadside batteries to long-range armaments capable of firing heavy ordnance more or less accurately up to twenty miles, while torpedoes were perfected to provide a dramatic new element to war at sea.[14] Toward the end, oil began to replace coal, while turbines provided the power required to expand the speed and size of warships to hitherto undreamed-of dimensions. There was little room for old-fashioned Marlinspike seamanship in this new world of power. Ever more intelligent and imaginative sailors were required from the bridge to the new engine rooms and radio shacks.[15]

Hugh Rodman, who would command the Sixth (American) Battle Squadron of the Grand Fleet during its eleven-month service in European waters during 1917–18, later wrote with pardonable pride that no era in his navy's history had seen more "gigantic strides in improvement and efficiency" than in the nineteen years following the 1898 Spanish-American War. At the time of the conflict with Spain, America's "New Navy," comprising a handful of steam-powered, steel-clad, big-gunned warships, was little more than a decade old and still a negligible force in world affairs. At the Battles of Santiago and Manila Bay, the Americans were able to muster a total of but four small "predreadnought" battleships, several cruisers, and (at Manila Bay) a single gunboat. By 1917, the American battle fleet had grown to become the world's second or third largest. As for the ships themselves, "Not only have the battle-ships grown nearly two and a half times as large, increased their speed and the number and caliber of their guns, but endless modern inventions and improvements have been installed. Gunnery practice has been all but revolutionized, so great is its relative efficiency in comparison with former days." Moreover, "a new spirit has been instilled in both the commissioned and enlisted personnel; undesirables have been weeded out and a basic policy introduced whose object is the professional education of officers and men to the highest degree."[16]

Successful exercise of sea power is a complex business involving many elements, not the least of which is mastery of the world ocean. To know the seven seas intimately, to operate upon all of them with confidence and skill, elevates a sea service to a unique status. Throughout the first half of the twentieth century, the great battle fleets of Japan, France, Italy, czarist and communist Russia, and Imperial and Nazi Germany largely exercised regional influence; only occasionally did Berlin, Paris, Rome, St. Petersburg, or Tokyo dispatch a handful of large or small units to the far corners of the earth. The navies of Britain and the United States, on the other hand, operated routinely on a global scale. Britain had long attained and practiced the art of international naval mastery, and the United States expressed its own aspirations as early as the Barbary Wars that began in 1801. Forty years later, a handful of American warships could be found routinely cruising off Brazil and West Africa, in European waters, and in the Pacific off South America. In 1854, Perry would open Japan. Thirty-plus years on, America's handful of new steel and steam warships successfully contested German and British pretensions at Samoa. But it was the rush of industrial American naval power after 1898 that gave a hint of global mastery. In the decade following the Spanish-American War, the size of the US fleet expanded dramatically both in numbers and in diversity. The round-the-world voyage in 1907–9 of the Great White Fleet comprised no fewer than sixteen predreadnoughts, and the subsequent routine appearances of ever-larger and more powerful US battleships in European and Mediterranean waters thereafter have tended to obscure the remarkable activities of more modest elements of the nation's emerging industrial navy.[17] The history of one ship and one flotilla of new small torpedo boats dramatized the American Navy's growing reach and capability.

USS *Brooklyn* was a ninety-two-hundred-ton, four-hundred-plus-foot armored cruiser commissioned in 1896. Capable of twenty knots, it carried a main battery of eight eight-inch guns and a crew of 561. Following its first overseas assignment carrying government representatives to Queen Victoria's 1897 Diamond Jubilee, the graceful warship with its three large stacks and tumble-home hull played a key role the following year in the Battle of Santiago that destroyed the Spanish squadron in Cuban waters. Within the year, the cruiser was on its way to the Far East via the Suez Canal to support America's new imperial responsibilities in Philippine and Chinese waters. To ensure a successful voyage, Washington had to make arrangements with the Royal Navy for the refueling of the big coal burner at various stations along the route. Arriving in Manila, *Brooklyn* promptly became the flagship of the Asiatic Squadron, participating in the North China Relief Expedition that suppressed the Boxer Rebellion and supporting the army in its ultimately successful effort to subdue the Philippine insurrectionists. During its brief time in the Far East, *Brooklyn* made cruises to Australia and the Dutch East Indies before sailing in 1902 back to the United States via Suez. For the next several years, it made a number of cruises to European and Mediterranean waters as part of the navy's Atlantic Squadron. Placed out of commission in 1908, it emerged seven years later to serve on Neutrality Patrol around Boston Harbor before again making the long sail to Asian waters, where it served once more as flagship, cruising to China, Japan, and Russia. In 1920, *Brooklyn* briefly became flagship of the newly created Pacific Fleet's destroyer squadrons before sailing to California the following year for final decommissioning.[18]

Nine-thousand-ton armored cruisers were not the only American warships to routinely undertake long voyages in the years prior to the Great War of 1914–18. As *Brooklyn* sailed back and forth between the Atlantic and Far Eastern waters, a contingent of the navy's smallest combatants—"torpedo boat destroyers"—sailed halfway around the world with little incident. By the late 1890s, waterborne propulsion technology in the form of fast boats and torpedoes had become prominent among the industrial inventions that were destabilizing traditional naval power. To protect their fleets from these new threats, the great navies devised torpedo boat destroyers. In May 1898, Congress authorized sixteen such "fast and agile" vessels, the first thirteen of which were the

Bainbridge class, 400-ton vessels with coal-fired steam engines armed with two torpedo tubes and two three-inch guns. Twenty-six 740-ton "destroyers," as they quickly became known, soon followed, their still modest tonnage earning them the nickname "flivvers." The last was commissioned in 1912 as the US Navy steadily advanced the design. The "broken deck" *Cassin* class of the following year and four other classes to follow displaced a full 1,000 tons (giving them the name "one tonners"), possessed high fo'c'sles and oil-fired steam-turbine engines, and carried eight torpedo tubes and four four-inch .50-caliber guns. As the Great War came on and developed, the comparatively spacious deck space of these first truly modern destroyers allowed for an easy addition of antisubmarine gear, most notably depth-charge racks and Y-guns (heavy mortars designed to simultaneously hurl two depth charges one on either side of the ship).[19]

In December 1903, the First Torpedo Flotilla, five tiny ships led by *Bainbridge* and escorted by the auxiliary cruiser *Buffalo*—set sail from Hampton Roads to Manila via Key West, Puerto Rico, the Canary Islands, Gibraltar, the Suez Canal, Bombay (Mumbai), Colombo, and Singapore. At one point, the small flotilla had to wait a week in Malta, where *Barry* was dry-docked to have damaged propellers repaired. As with *Brooklyn* and all later global voyaging, assured coaling was a key feature of the flotilla's long journey, and at another point in the journey, miscalculations as to fuel consumption forced *Buffalo* to recoal *Chauncey* directly in the middle of the Indian Ocean rather than at one of the numerous British coaling stations that stretched across the route from Gibraltar to Hong Kong. Four months after leaving Virginia, the small fleet at last reached Manila in April 1904. The successful completion of the journey "from the East Coast to the Orient did much to prove torpedo-boat destroyers capable of extended operations at sea with the fleet." Subsequent operations on the Asiatic Station over the next dozen-plus years in which the flotilla alternated between summer duty in Chinese waters and winters in the Philippines further emphasized the usefulness and "ultimate versatility" of America's ever-growing and more powerful destroyer fleet.[20]

In the spring and summer of 1914 as Europe tottered toward war, the navy and its marines engaged in a brief little conflict supporting rebel forces during the Mexican Revolution. By the time a German steamer loaded with arms for the Huerta government arrived at Veracruz in April, the United States had assembled a formidable fleet offshore, including a half-dozen battleships. Four thousand marines and sailors from that fleet stormed ashore to seize the customs house and were promptly engaged by "desperate street fighters." Seventeen

Americans and well over a hundred Mexicans were killed in the fighting; the arms never reached Huerta, who was soon overthrown while Germany's long-standing interest in a New World adventure was abruptly overwhelmed by the needs of a two-front European war.

While the Mexican intervention provided the navy and marines with an opportunity to test their combat skills, the most striking aspect of the venture was in the air. Upon President Wilson's call for action, the fledgling naval air station at Pensacola was ordered to provide the expedition with several first-generation flying craft, both seaplanes and flying boats. Stowed aboard battleship *Mississippi* and armored cruiser *Birmingham* where they were lowered to the water for takeoff, the aircraft, especially AH-3, set a number of records. Pilot Patrick Bellinger and observer Richard Saufley aboard that "hydroaeroplane" were fired upon by "a group of Mexican Army stragglers." Though riddled with bullets, the aircraft returned safely to the battleship, was hoisted aboard, and was swiftly repaired by dedicated mechanics from Pensacola. Shortly thereafter, Bellinger took his plane down to barely two hundred feet over enemy lines "to take some of the Navy's first aerial photographs during wartime." Exhaustively deployed in the skies over Veracruz and adjacent areas, AH-3 soon "suffered chronic engine problems," requiring never-ending work on valves, exhausts, and the magneto. Staggering aloft on one of its final missions, AH-3 with the dedicated Bellinger and Saufley on board came under enemy fire. Infuriated by his orders not to use his revolver in retaliation, Bellinger was given a bar of soap by one of the mechanics, and on his next mission Saufley hurled the "weapon" upon Mexican heads, thereby constituting "the first ordnance dropped from a U.S. plane on an enemy.[21] However briefly, the US Navy, its fliers, and its marines had tasted combat. (In one of the very last gestures of international goodwill before the outbreak of World War I that August, American sailors invited colleagues from British, French, Spanish, Dutch, and German naval vessels observing the Yankee invasion to come aboard *Pennsylvania* and other warships to help drink up the last reserves of alcohol before the US Navy officially went "dry" at the order of Navy Secretary Daniels. "Small launches" proceeded "from ship to ship to help eliminate the soon-to-be contraband" in a series of often raucous parties.)[22]

By this time, battleships with single-caliber main batteries had become the standard capital ship within the world's great sea services. While the Royal Navy's *Dreadnought* had been the first to appear in 1906, its ostensibly "revolutionary" design had already been anticipated by other great powers. Dreadnoughts USS *Michigan* and Japan's *Satsuma* followed closely behind. While twenty-three "predreadnoughts" from 1898 to 1905 remained in commission, the US Navy by 1917 boasted no fewer than fifteen dreadnoughts of steadily progressive design, many with names that would resonate down the years—*Pennsylvania, Arizona, Oklahoma, Texas, Nevada.* Splendid brutes all, they were the match of any capital ships in the world, save for Britain's latest *Royal Sovereign* and *Queen Elizabeth* classes. Massive and heavily armed, all except the first two were more than five hundred feet long, displacing upwards of and then more than thirty thousand tons. They carried powerful batteries of eight to twelve twelve- and fourteen-inch guns. Manning each of these monsters efficiently required crews well in excess of a thousand men. The very month that Woodrow Wilson carried the country to war, another massive battleship, *New Mexico,* came into being, to be followed two months later by its sister ship *Idaho.* A "train" of supply and repair vessels supported this battle fleet that was screened by some sixty-odd destroyers of varying sizes, capabilities, and ages running back to the turn of the century. Like the newest battleships, all but the oldest "tin cans" were oil rather than coal burners; unlike their huge brethren whose armored hulls and underpowered engineering plants labored to make twenty knots through the water, the slim, highly maneuverable little vessels could dash about at thirty knots or more.[23]

On the eve of the Great War in 1914, a portion of the American fleet visited Kiel, Germany, and other Baltic ports. Once the European conflict broke out, the fleet restricted its operations to Western Hemispheric waters. The exceptions were the old "protected cruiser" *Des Moines* and predreadnought *North Carolina,* which Wilson promptly dispatched to the eastern Mediterranean "to protect Americans in the Near East." *Des Moines* was the first US warship on the scene in May 1915, where it "protected American citizens and interests threatened in the Middle Eastern theater of war, carrying missionaries and other refugees out of Turkey and Syria, delivering relief funds, carrying United States officials, and serving on exercises which took her to ports in Italy, France, Spain, and Algeria." Among the passengers the ship's captain unwittingly took aboard at Beirut were two aspiring Jewish secret agents bound for Cairo to contact British authorities on the state of Turkish defenses in Palestine.[24]

Following port calls in England and France, *North Carolina* slipped through the Straits of Gibraltar and for the next nine months cruised the watery triangle between Jaffa, Beirut, and Alexandria, its presence a reminder of the might of the still neutral United States. It did not return to Boston until the following June after a brief stay in Egypt that gave the crew opportunity to visit the Pyramids.[25]

The rest of the fleet engaged in more prosaic activities, including a series of exercises both in the winter drill grounds of the Caribbean and in the summer grounds that stretched from Maine to the Chesapeake. There great battleships and small destroyers maneuvered day and night and engaged in frequent target practice and steaming trials. Battleship and destroyer divisions engaged in spirited competition that led to a high state of professionalism, but also a need for frequent upkeep and repairs, especially among the smaller vessels. One exercise involved defense of the East Coast against an invasion fleet from Europe (a persistent bugaboo among eastern residents since the Spanish-American War). Unfortunately for the state of public opinion, the invading fleet evaded the defenders and thus theoretically bombarded Boston and New York Harbors.[26]

Shaping the steady growth of such a formidable force demanded constant advances in administration. Although the navy lacked a general staff, it did possess after 1900 a General Board that made recommendations on a wide variety of matters from ship design to overall strategy. Its semiautonomous, often feuding bureaus that had vexed and flummoxed a succession of service secretaries finally prompted Wilson and Congress to create the position of chief of naval operations in 1915 so that authority and decision making could be centered on a single senior officer.[27]

From the US Naval Academy at Annapolis to the postgraduate War College at Newport, Rhode Island, and the adjacent drill fields and service schools where enlisted recruits received their basic and advanced training, ongoing professional development was the touchstone of an American naval career—one practically open to whites only. The virulent prejudice against African Americans and other minorities that marked the half century after Appomattox reached its apogee within the ranks of the US Navy where "black applicants" for enlistment "were almost as unwelcome as convicts." The service only grudgingly accepted a relative handful of such recruits, the overwhelming majority of whom were quickly shunted to work as servants in the officers' wardrooms.[28]

Training of junior and senior commanders emphasized the grounding of doctrine in team-work and experience, the sharing of experience by all those involved, and the coordination of experience and observation through frequent conferences, "for the purpose of progressively modifying and amending the doctrine as additional practical experience is gained." Pragmatic response to immediate demand was the only consideration. The objective was to drill each ship's company from captain to seaman in what was expected of them so that in battle, each ship "would fall into a preassigned place" to carry out its assignment. Split-second maneuvering was key: "how to change in nothing flat from

'column' or line ahead . . . to line abreast and back again" as conditions warrant-
ed. Much emphasis was placed on the realities of vessel and crew capabilities.
In 1913 then captain William Sowden Sims, the newly appointed commander
of the Atlantic Fleet Destroyer Flotilla, gathered his captains together aboard his
flagship and "made them a little speech," the gist of which was that collective
judgment trumped individual judgment every time. Sims, who impressed one
of his captains, Bill Halsey, as a "crisp and decisive" speaker "with an air of benign authority," added that "conclusions based upon maximum knowledge and
experience could only be reached after a full and frank discussion by all members of the organization." Frequent conferences, like those conducted at the
Naval War College, were mandatory, and Sims, as commanding officer, would
act as moderator, not dictator. Once a theoretical doctrine was developed, Sims
recalled to a college audience years later, he sent his destroyers to sea to test it
out, where it was usually "found, as we expected, to be half wrong." Back to sea
the destroyers went, maneuvering usually in the Caribbean off Guantánamo,
occasionally moving as far north as the Massachusetts coast, where the doctrine
was honed through repeated activity involving endless steaming drills, target
practices, and mock torpedo attacks. "The conditions of wind and weather
worked constantly against success," Sims's biographer later wrote of those incessant peacetime exercises between 1913 and 1916. "One can guess at the despair
of the individual commander as the hours wore on. Each was alone in the black
night unable to see because of spray and the occasional rain, unable to stand"
on narrow bridges crammed with crude navigation and steering equipment
"without clinging for long hours" to narrow rails for support, "dependent for
knowledge of the degree to which he was playing his part as a team member upon the few laconic messages which were addressed to him." A jocular,
pleasant man with a genius for converting grinding work to challenging play,
Sims in his three years made the destroyer flotilla his own. "It was his organization, body and soul," a subordinate remembered, "principally in soul." Unwittingly, Sims had prepared his destroyermen with the tools needed—stamina,
self-confidence, trust in their fellow commanding officers—to prevail in the
U-boat war to come, while bringing vast wartime convoys safely across vast
and dangerous seas.[29]

American naval officers exhibited keen interest in maintaining close contact
with their civilian counterparts in the engineering and scientific fields, so that
advances in industrial technology could be quickly applied where appropriate.
The navy was represented on the standards committees of various engineering
societies, and naval designers and developers routinely called on "engineering

societies and recognized civilian experts along certain lines for help in the solution of special problems." The formation of a Consulting Board reflected the navy's recognition of the importance of having available the nation's "scientific engineering talents for consultation and advice" on an ongoing basis. The development of long-range radio communications both on ship and ashore consumed much of the navy's attention in the prewar years. As early as the summer of 1907, "radio equipment had been installed on all naval surface vessels and most of the low-powered shore radio stations had been in operation for four years." Thereafter, naval officers maintained close contacts with early commercial pioneers, including Marconi and Lee De Forest, in a common, if not always friction-free, enterprise to improve and expand this revolutionary communications system. By 1916, a US Naval Radio Service was in existence, and the service expanded its interest to the skies, establishing an Aircraft Radio Laboratory at Pensacola.[30]

The training of enlisted personnel was no less dedicated or intense. A growing war fleet possessed of ever-elaborating advanced technologies needed youngsters who could think and do. After 1900, the navy actively sought out sober and responsible boys from midwestern and southern towns and farms where what would later be known as "family values" were strong. City lads were dismissed as "riffraff," potential troublemakers whom the navy did not need. In part, recruitment policy was based on sincere prejudice, but it was also grounded in a shrewd appreciation that the more white boys recruited from the nation's heartland, the easier it would be to gain appropriations from Congress. Even so, only 20 to 25 percent of the boys who applied at recruiting offices in Ohio, Illinois, Missouri, or Alabama were accepted. Officers might complain then, as in many decades to follow, that the service was "more of 'a big training school' than anything else" for the young men in their care. A relative handful of youngsters entered the service with the intention of pursuing a career, "but the vast majority of sailors were 'one enlistment men' who signed on for four years and then returned to civilian life," having slaked their thirst "for a man's cup of adventure before settling down to the prosaic task that gives daily bread."[31]

Whatever the boys' motives, Josephus Daniels was determined to make his navy "the greatest educational institution in America." In his eight-year stewardship after 1913, he convinced Congress to set aside a modest number of slots at Annapolis to be filled by sailors from the fleet, and he ordered a crackdown on hazing at the academy. In their few brief weeks of boot camp at Newport, Hampton Roads (Norfolk), Great Lakes (forty miles north of Chicago), or Yerba Buena Island in San Francisco Bay, recruits were taught not only basic seamanship and the rhythms, responsibilities, and expectations of shipboard life but also swimming, geography, mathematics, algebra, geometry, and navigation. An hour a day of "Swedish Gymnastics" in addition to constant marching and boat drill were designed "to develop in the young men muscular strength, alertness, and power to think and act quickly in any emergency." At a time of increasing fleet expansion in response to the European war, the service accepted a few functional illiterates who were promptly given intensive courses in reading and writing before undertaking the usual training curriculum. With basic training completed, the lowest minority from each graduating company were sent directly to the fleet, where they became deckhands or "coal passers" in the engine rooms of the older warships. The majority, however, were sent to service schools, where they could "strike" for a rating awarded after graduation. Concentrated largely in the Northeast, with a handful at Norfolk or on the West Coast (and some contracted out during World War I to private-sector corporations and even a handful of colleges and universities, including Harvard), the navy's schools ran the gamut of contemporary technology, from yeoman (clerk), storekeeper, electrician, carpenter's mate, and musician to radio-electrician, machinist mate, gunner's mate, torpedo man, signalman, quartermaster (navigation), hospital and pharmacy, "commissary" (cooking and baking), "artificer" (shipfitting, painting, damage control, and the like), and various engine-room technologies. Once out in the fleet or on stations ashore, enlisted men were encouraged to pursue professional development within their rates. Aboard the bigger ships, men who had not already served two years were given from 1:30 to 2:45 each afternoon for study, "some students thus to prepare for warrant rank, and there are some who hope to enter the Naval Academy."[32]

Not everyone was enamored of the reforms. Bernhard Bieri, a junior officer at the time, insisted that "most of the enlisted men weren't about to be educated. They came into the Navy to get away from book education. So the plan never worked out very well" and "finally fell through." Indications are, however, that whatever falling away there was from Daniels's commitment occurred after the war.[33]

By 1915, many in the navy, including Daniels himself, viewed aviation as "an indispensable adjunct" of fleet operations, especially long-range scouting of enemy fleets and the spotting of submarines and minefields close inshore. The pilots themselves were determined to exploit the modest capabilities they and their handful of planes had demonstrated over Veracruz. No matter the cost, they would continue to fly higher, faster, farther. In the process, these pioneers pushed multiple envelope edges. Leading them all was Lieutenant Richard

Saufley, who had flown frequently with Bellinger over enemy lines at Veracruz. Saufley's enthusiasm for aviation prompted him to publish no fewer than four articles in the US Naval Institute *Proceedings* between 1914 and 1916. The first was "Naval Aviation: Its Value and Its Needs"; the last one was ironically titled "Aeroplane Accidents: Causes and Remedies." In the early spring of the latter year over Pensacola, Saufley drove his Curtiss "hydroaeroplane" just beyond sixteen thousand feet. Three days later, he slightly exceeded that altitude. By June he was dead, crashing in the bright waters off nearby Santa Rosa Island after being in the air on an endurance test for eight hours and fifty-one minutes.[34]

No naval technology demanded greater expertise than that of the submarine, largely the invention of American John Holland. As early as May 1907, USS *Octopus*, a 105-foot "Holland type" submarine with an estimated undersea cruising radius of eighty miles at five knots, sank beneath the waters of Narragansett Bay and settled on the bottom for twenty-four hours before surfacing easily and with no effect on the crew. This feat was understandably applauded, because the French submarine *Lutin* had recently been found "wrecked with her crew dead, 137 feet" down in the harbor at Bizerte, Tunis, after a seventeen-hour dive. But while the size and operating capabilities of American submarines continually grew in the first years of the twentieth century, the United States lagged somewhat behind Britain's Royal Navy and the Imperial German Navy. The first boats truly meant and built for long-range cruising rather than purely coastal defense did not appear until 1913. The "F" class was capable of a surface range of two-thousand-plus miles. Two years later, the first modestly impressive 450 tonners of the "L" class hit the water, capable of a submerged speed over ten knots and a surface radius of action between two and three thousand miles. At that time, the navy possessed thirty-seven undersea craft (many of them totally unfit for war, others confined to coastal defense activities), and a submarine school had been established to educate both officers and men at New London, Connecticut, adjacent to the Electric Boat Company.[35]

These undersea boats were the extreme exemplification of the darker side of enlisted service in all the world's navies in 1917, a universally crude, gritty, and isolated experience that would appall the modern seaman. In submarine hulls little more than 150 feet long and 17 feet wide, twenty-five to thirty officers and men existed with "ballast tanks, oil tanks, storage batteries, motors, torpedoes, and an operating compartment in which are grouped the devices for controlling ballast tanks, periscopes and rudders." Conditions in the surface navies were far better and more relaxed for officers, who enjoyed perks and shared living quarters and wardroom facilities with fewer and fewer colleagues as they moved up the promotion ladder. Life for the enlisted man, however, was never cushy. As David Colamaria observes, "In some cases, life on board warships of the New Steel Navy was worse than it had been in the time of wooden ships. New engine technology put off tremendous heat, and ventilation equipment had not yet been perfected. Additionally, ship designers struggled to fit all of this new equipment on board warships which needed to achieve high speeds, carry tremendous firepower, and still retain seagoing agility. In this battle for space, sailors were often on the losing end."[36] The contrast between officer and enlisted sleeping quarters was "stark," helping to reinforce ancient lines of authority and subordination even as the new industrial technologies operated by ever more talented enlisted men were beginning to demand the opposite.

One officer observed that the average American "gob" was a "rough customer" who aboard ship was forced to abandon whatever ties he had ashore "for a new society in a new world." Life was "shockingly point-blank. It permits no luxuries, few comforts. There is a struggle for survival that lasts through twenty-four hours each day." The resultant "manhood" was "without veneer, hard inside and out, fearing nothing, hoping everything, and ready to work, work, work." Aboard destroyers—and later subchasers—enlisted men necessarily slept in "racks" stacked three or four high, which was the only way to give some guarantee of safe sleeping in those heavy seas where "small boys" pitched and rolled unmercifully, throwing their crewmen about like corks in dark, narrow, cramped, overheated spaces. Each rack was composed of a piece of canvas stretched tightly on a metal frame upon which the sailor placed his thin mattress encased in a sheeted cover (commonly referred to as a "fart sack") together with a rough blanket and small pillow. Today's metal-frame bunks in which sailors sleep on deep mattresses with separate sheets, individual lighting, and a privacy curtain (with pullout laptop computer shelves aboard more recent vessels) would have elicited jaw-dropping disbelief and no little contempt from America's sailors a century ago. Eating was an adventure, washing nearly impossible.

Ironically, living compartments on America's most advanced battleships as late as the 1920s were even worse. Men were forced to share compartments often filled with machinery. Low bars were built from which hooks were fitted for slinging hammocks. Small spaces were made for petty officers to stow folded sleeping cots during daylight hours. Most sailors, especially those cursed with restless sleep, hated their narrow hammocks out of which nasty falls to steel decks some feet below were all too common. Hammock lashings served as storage areas for shoes and underclothing, making petty theft attractive. Seamen and petty officers also ate here, the tables and benches stowed away on ceilings (overheads) when not in use. Mandatory bathing and washing of clothes took place in adjacent washrooms using a bucket issued daily that the men filled with freshwater and heated at a steam outlet. "With practice," a sailor "would be able to wet himself, soap up, rinse down, brush his teeth, and, finally, wash his underwear . . . with only that single allotment of water." However, if the captain chose to cut the freshwater ration to a half bucket or less per day in order to preserve oil or coal power, many a crewman was forced to turn to always available cold saltwater showers. All of this took time in the precious morning moments between breakfast and ship's muster or in the evening hours before or after dinner. "It was not unusual to see men lined up, waiting for access to the washroom" or to a shipmate's bucket if there were an insufficient number to go around. Toilet facilities on all warships large and small were primitive. Often positioned forward—hence the name "head"—on the battleships, they comprised "54-foot-long troughs," one serving as an open urinal, the other as a privy with holes cut at intervals in boards placed over the trough. Practical jokers loved to construct toilet-paper rafts and set them afire "to drift beneath the unsuspecting sailor sitting downstream." Human waste was carried away from the toilet areas by a stream of saltwater that sluiced the excrement off the ship and into the ocean or bay, as the case might be.

Only America's newest battleships in 1917 contained individual lockers for crewmen; on the older capital ships and smaller vessels, the men lived as sailors had for centuries past— out of their seabags—and were allowed to stow a few personal possessions in what were called "ditty bags," open at any moment to inspection by condescending division officers who were prone to claim that their contents revealed the "overgrown pocket of the small boy." In only one measure had the lot of the enlisted man materially improved over earlier centuries. Authorities had at last begun to recognize the connection between food and health. Galleys had been moved up onto the main deck compartments, close to fresh air and sunshine, "immaculately clean and with the latest cooking equipment." The food itself was necessarily plain, but hearty and reasonably tasty.

Periodic replenishment of the warships' fuel supply added yet another level of discomfort to a sailor's strenuous life. Oil was just coming into wide use in the US Navy in 1917; the newest modern battleships, like *Arizona* and *Pennsylvania*, burned it as a fuel. So did most destroyers. But the majority of capital ships and the older small boys remained prodigious consumers of coal. "Recoaling" was, in the words of one officer, an "ordeal" of "dirt and exhaustion."

Another remembered it as "a relic of barbarism." Coal was carried to the fleet wherever it was by "colliers," who passed it over heavy bagful by heavy bagful to the receiving battleship, cruiser, or destroyer, where dozens or scores of seamen—"deck apes" in their dirtiest clothes—manhandled each bag to chutes connecting the deck with storage bunkers below. Coaling had to be done as quickly as possible, and on many occasions the collier's booms swung coal bags over faster than the crew of the receiving vessel could handle them. Great mounds of coal with the inevitably accompanying clouds of dust accumulated on a battleship's or destroyer's deck. As soon as the latest round of coaling was completed and the last filthy chunks of black had been shoveled off the decks and down the chutes, "tired and . . . worn" sailors were expected to immediately transform the "filthy, sooty mass of grime" that was their battleship, cruiser, or destroyer into a "scoured, holystoned, [freshly] painted," and sparkling clean man-of-war manned by a spotless, polished crew.

Life at sea thus remained marginally sanitary at best, and the almost constant heavy smoke generated by all the navy's ships at sea further compounded the problem, to say nothing of complicating ships' gunnery and navigation. The sanitation problem was met by a determination to ensure the personal hygiene of every enlisted man, from chief petty officer to common seaman. Each recruit from the day he enlisted was "drilled" in the habits of cleanliness. Awakened at 6:30 each morning, he spent the hour before breakfast clearing away his sleeping gear (hammock or cot), bathing, scrubbing clothes, cleaning the decks, and shining the brightwork. Throughout the day, as the yeomen, bridge gangs, and engine-room people went about their business, the deck force continued to scrub and clean, chip, paint, and polish. Periodic "scrubbing days" sent the entire crew to clean "every possible thing" aboard.[37]

As the navy continued to expand during the first thirty-two months of Europe's Great War, it received, in addition to the growing flood of recruits, another source of already modestly trained officers and seamen in the form of reservists from across the nation, many of whom were enrolled in state or regional naval militias on both coasts and in Ohio. The militias had provided men for the Spanish-American War and in 1917 stood ready to do so once more. And as the war in Europe progressed and the German Submarine Menace became ever clearer, other, informal, groups of enthusiasts sprang to action. Hundreds of young Americans had already been sucked into action on and above the western and Italian fronts as ambulance drivers, flyers for the Lafayette Escadrille and the British Royal Flying Corps, even the French Foreign Legion. At home, thousands joined the state national guards or drilled informally at one of several "businessmen's training camps" in Plattsburgh, New York. No group more eagerly awaited "the government's call to service" than "the First Yale Unit," whose members enlisted in the US Navy Reserve several weeks before Wilson made his famous plea for a crusade to make the world safe for democracy. The college boys learned to fly at their own (or their father's) expense, with wealthy businessmen picking up the tab for equipment. The Yalies would become famous as "the nucleus" of the navy's formidable "overseas aviation efforts."[38]

By the spring of 1917, 197 US warships led by a dozen and more powerful steam and steel battleships of the latest design were in commission. Six years earlier, the navy had been manned by slightly more than 50,000 officers and men. Now, 65,777 enlisted men filled the service's ships and shore establishments commanded by roughly a tenth that number of officers. The army, by contrast, comprised 212,000 men, 85,000 of whom were either national guard or reserves in national service. Both services would prove to be hollow shells in relation to the wartime demands soon to be placed upon them: transport of an efficient 2-million-man army across the Atlantic to tip the scales of combat decisively in favor of the Allies. With the country fully behind them, the army and navy responded impressively. In the nineteen months of war between April 1917 and November 1918, the army grew well over tenfold to 3,764,000 men, nearly 1,340,000 of whom were counted "in action." The navy's warship inventory swelled to more than 2,000 vessels, the vast majority small antisubmarine vessels of various types, while its ranks grew to over half a million sailors. Accustomed to training 1,200 to 1,600 recruits at a time, the stations at Norfolk, Great Lakes, Newport, and San Francisco Bay found themselves flooded at any given moment with up to 40,000 young men who had to obtain at least a rudimentary naval education through hasty drills, classes, and dutiful perusal of *The Bluejackets Manual*. Pressed to man a fleet in unprecedented expansion, the navy recruited its first women as "yeomanettes" to provide clerical and typing services in the department and at various bases around the country.[39]

Yet on the eve of Wilson's declaration of war, all was not well within America's sea service. A midlevel officer later admitted the service was not psychologically ready for combat.[40] Its most glaring professional deficiency was lack of experience in handling great numbers of warships—large or small—under battle conditions. Santiago and Manila Bay had provided no such opportunities and, in fact, were of a different time. So was the Great White Fleet, whose battleships were obsolete and which for all their impressive performance cruised under peacetime conditions.

A handful of critics had long recognized that the battle fleet was also grossly imbalanced. During the Taft presidency (1909–13), the White House and Capitol Hill had bickered steadily over the issue, and the navy suffered. "A balanced fighting fleet should have included not only first-class battleships, but also fast scout cruisers, destroyer flotillas to protect the capital ships, and various other classes of vessels in certain recognized proportions. Forced to make compromises at every turn" with a parsimonious Congress, "the Administration had sacrificed cruisers, destroyers, and the other essential components of a fighting fleet in its desperate but futile attempts to keep pace with capital-ship construction abroad." When Josephus Daniels became navy secretary under Wilson in 1913, he refused to confront the issue, choosing to "squander his time and energy on relatively trivial matters." Another recent critic has charged Daniels with being "forceful and opinionated," but as a "journalist by trade quite ignorant of the operating Navy" at a time when Europe stood on the brink of war. In a time of rapid changes in naval technology and operations, all of the navy's twenty-odd armored and first-class cruisers were at least a decade old. Moreover, they ranged in size from under four thousand tons with just two five-inch gun main batteries to more than fourteen thousand tons with ten-inch-gun main batteries. Their speed (at least twenty-two knots) and, with a few exceptions, their size (ten to fourteen thousand tons, 425–500 feet) might be sufficient to remain within a modern battle line, but the firepower of even the largest vessel was that of the obsolete predreadnought era—four ten-inch guns at best and a secondary battery of six-inchers.[41]

While defenders of the battleship after 1914 remained smitten by naval theorist Alfred Thayer Mahan's insistence that great navies demanded great capital ships, most of what naval action there was during the European war revealed that combat at sea was speeding up and dramatically diversifying. Jutland demonstrated that an effective battle fleet required a screen of truly modern destroyers—fast, nimble, and well-armed oil burners—far more than the thirty-odd such vessels that the US Navy then possessed. Above all, Dogger Bank and Jutland together had demonstrated the need for a raft of speedy scout cruisers—four- to seven-thousand-ton ships carrying six-inch guns and capable of making twenty-five knots—to seek out the enemy and to further screen the main British and German battle fleets in defensive depth. Germany had also employed a handful of its small light-cruiser force together with armed merchant raiders in a *guerre de course*—commerce war—against British trade worldwide. The Royal Navy contained no fewer than thirty-nine light cruisers built since 1908. Germany's High Seas Fleet—a name reflecting aspiration rather than reality—contained thirteen built in the same period.[42] The United States had no such vessels.

Finally, the Americans had disdained to develop the battle-cruiser type that had distinguished the naval race between Britain and Germany in the decade before the Great War. Britain's battle cruisers—her "big cats," to use Winston Churchill's phrase—had not distinguished themselves in any of the few sea fights with Germany, and at Jutland no fewer than three had blown up under enemy heavy gunfire; German battle cruisers, on the other hand, fought well while absorbing a substantial amount of punishment. Despite its melancholy recent history, the battle cruiser with its heavy armament and high speed (achieved through a drastic reduction in hull armor) was still widely perceived as an essential element in any modern battle fleet, and the US Navy had none.

The 1916 legislation meant to create a maritime force second to none would correct deficiencies within the battle fleet (with provisions soon added to build more destroyers), while a "Flying Corps authorized in 1916 had not yet been established." Despite relatively few training planes and a handful of dirigibles, naval aviators had developed no expansion plan.[43]

The most important challenge to US sea power, however, would prove to be the navy's patent inability in April 1917 to wage—indeed to adequately understand the nature of—effective antisubmarine warfare. The US and Royal Navies had come to realize by this time the submarine's formidable advantages; they simply had no clear idea how to respond.

> Whenever it decries danger from afar, the submarine can disappear under the water in anywhere from twenty seconds to a minute. And its great advantage is that it can detect its enemy long before that enemy can detect the submarine. A U-boat riding awash, or sailing with only its conning tower exposed, can see a destroyer at a distance of about fifteen miles if the weather is clear; but under the same conditions, the destroyer can see the submarine at a distance of about four miles. Possessing this great advantage, the submarine can usually decide whether it will meet the enemy or not; if it decides that it is wise to avoid an encounter, all that it has to do is duck, remain submerged until the destroyer has passed on, entirely unconscious of its presence, and then resume its real work which is not that of fighting warships, but of sinking merchantmen.

Moreover, the U-boats possessed a submerged radius of more than one hundred miles. British experience had shown that "even if located" underwater, a U-boat could usually "escape with great facility." The U-boat's natural enemy (beyond the Q ship) seemed to be the destroyer. But were destroyers, or indeed any surface vessel large or small, really capable of defeating the kaiser's submarines? Destroyers were fine if they could be deployed in very large numbers "in confined waters" near the coasts of Britain or France. But as waters broadened appreciably, so did their effectiveness decline in equal measure.[44]

Critics discovered another basic flaw in America's overall maritime posture. Beyond the reality of a currently unbalanced fleet lay "the lack of sea transportation to embark our troops in case of hostilities." Few citizens in 1914 and 1915 envisaged, much less relished, the prospect of sending a great army to Europe. War with Japan, on the other hand, seemed possible and would surely entail the loss of the Philippines and Guam, perhaps even Hawaii. A series of expeditionary forces would be required to retake these possessions. Such an endeavor might prove impossible without an adequate sealift of men and supplies in place.[45] Yet little had been done to build up a formidable merchant marine.

Last but by no means least, the navy suffered from administrative confusion at its highest levels. Rather than clarifying existing arrangements, the first chief of naval operations complicated matters further. Ernest King, who could have written the book—and later did—on how to succeed in the navy without really liking anyone, saw matters up close as an officer on the staff of Admiral Henry T. Mayo, commander of the Atlantic Fleet. From King's dyspeptic perspective, Secretary Daniels and CNO William Benson shared a "predilection . . . for retaining in Washington the detailed control of matters that might more properly have been dealt with in the fleet." Benson compounded the felony by a tendency toward "vacillation" during times of crisis that would infect overall Navy Department policy.[46]

So, despite the 1916 naval legislation, the United States would bring a flawed cutlass to any war at sea fought in the near future. Not until 1925 would its anticipated plethora of new, ultramodern battleships and battle cruisers, handful of scout cruisers, fifty destroyers, and sixty-seven submarines be able to stand up to Japan or to whatever sea power emerged largely unscathed from the European war. The implications surrounding the appearance of *Deutschland* and U-53 in American waters shortly after the legislation was enacted forced a quick shift in both tactical and strategic thinking. Not only did the Navy Department begin to register privately owned vessels for possible antisubmarine patrol, but it also began "hasty preparations to build submarines and a destroyer fleet." The shift was almost too late, for Germany was indeed about to unleash its growing flotilla of submarines on Atlantic and Mediterranean sea lanes without restriction.

After the spring of 1917, the First World War at sea would become a battle against the kaiser's finest and most implacable sailors.[47]

As early as the opening of that year, the war's outline had become heart-breakingly obvious. After twenty-nine months of indiscriminate carnage on both eastern and western fronts, together with campaigns at the Dardanelles and in the adjacent Middle East, neither side saw victory in sight. Any sane person could see that the conflict must end, that the passionate prodigality in blood and treasure—more than two million lives in all—was serving no purpose except itself. Trench warfare had become meaningless beyond its own immediate realm. "Several million men lived like moles," and casualty lists defied belief. After five months, the campaign on the Somme alone had claimed more than a million lives, but the belligerents could not bring themselves to betray the sacrifices they had made in order to accept the kind of less than perfect peace that Wilson offered. Britain's lord president of the council, Lord Curzon, wrote mournfully that "well into another year, perhaps longer, must we continue the dreadful tragedy that is turning the world into hell."[48]

The German high command, however, glimpsed a sun break of hope. Russia was in extremis. Should it fall out of the war—as, indeed, it soon would—the kaiser and his generals could anticipate freeing up at least a half-million German soldiers for action in the West. Suddenly, the U-boat became an irresistibly attractive component of a fresh policy initiative. His military stymied and bled white after Verdun, the kaiser allowed his navy to talk him into a bold and, as it ultimately became clear, fatal policy. Systematically employed since the previous October as a riposte against the British blockade, yet restrained by adherence to internationally recognized prize rules, the submarine could be a war-winning weapon if fully unleashed. And as it happened, German submarine and wireless technologies were in the midst of dramatic leaps forward. For the first time, brand-new boats, "larger and more powerful" than any others in the German arsenal and staging out of the Flanders ports of Zeebrugge and Ostend, were capable of extending the submarine war far out into the Atlantic to longitude 17'W and beyond—roughly 240 to 300 miles, where the "Western Approaches" to Britain and the Continent began to bend and narrow, more readily defining commercial shipping lanes. Here lay the choicest hunting ground that any U-boat skipper could dream of. An increase in wireless wattage allowed U-boats to pick up messages from home out to thirty-two hundred miles, even to depths of one hundred feet. In October 1916, the first month of restricted warfare, German submarines sent 185 enemy ships to the bottom. One hundred more ships followed in November. In December, 197 merchantmen totaling nearly 330,000 tons were victims of fatal U-boat attacks. Numbers and aggregate tonnage of victims maintained the pace into the new year.[49]

The argument for reinstituting all-out submarine warfare against world shipping became irresistible to Admiral Henning von Holtzendorff and members of his Admiralty staff in Berlin. While its army held Germany's earlier conquests on both the eastern and the western fronts, the navy would assume the offensive with "an illegal campaign of unrestricted submarine warfare." Unleashing the U-boats on neutral shipping in the Channel, Irish Sea, Mediterranean, and, now, on the Atlantic approaches to Europe could starve England into submission within six months. And with that linchpin of the Allied cause removed and a half-million more battle-hardened German soldiers from the east appearing in the western trenches poised to strike, France would have no choice but to surrender as well. Of course, Wilson would probably use the issue of unrestricted submarine warfare to bring the United States into the conflict, but all Europe, east and west of the Elbe, would belong to Germany long before American forces could arrive in sufficient numbers to make a difference.

The vision was too intoxicating to reject. On January 31, 1917, the announcement went out from Berlin: all-out submarine warfare would recommence immediately. Any and all ships found by the kaiser's undersea sailors would be sunk on sight. America's sailors as well as politicians and a divided public realized a Rubicon had been crossed: "From this day on, Germany made herself an outlaw among nations." The U-boat decision followed by just two weeks the interception, decoding, and prompt dispatch to Washington by British intelligence of a top-secret telegram from German foreign minister Arthur Zimmerman to the ambassador in Mexico, offering America's neighbor return of lands in the Southwest lost to the United States seventy years before if Mexico would come into the war on Germany's side. The German ambassador was to remind Mexican president Venustiano Carranza that "the ruthless employment of our submarines now offers the prospect of compelling England in a few months to make peace." Carranza was asked to approach Japan to see if that nation, too, would like an alliance with the Central Powers. The Zimmerman Telegram goaded Wilson and the nation beyond endurance, not least because the threat of continued unrestricted, indeed "ruthless," submarine warfare (in Zimmerman's own words) was clearly the chief guarantee that a German-Mexican and perhaps Japanese alliance would work. Zimmerman's subsequent decision not to repudiate the telegram merely added fuel to America's patriotic bonfire.[50]

Wilson promptly severed diplomatic relations and soon reluctantly agreed to the arming of American merchantmen. But he—and Congress—anguished for ten weeks over the question of outright war, while leading British officials fumed that the president had no stomach for battle. In fact, American society in 1917 was as unsettled as any in the Western world. A civil war half a century earlier had destroyed a largely agrarian order, and the Industrial Revolution that followed hard upon it had created enormous economic, political, and social dislocations. A "progressive" reform movement meant to ameliorate conditions had emerged after 1900 and was reaching its peak when war broke out in Europe fourteen years later. Inevitably, the matter of taking the nation into that war generated questions and doubt. For many in the American West, entry "represented what the gold standard had signified to William Jennings Bryan's supporters in the 1896 election: a conspiracy by eastern plutocrats to fasten suffering on the common people for the benefit of big capital." To cries of "treason," "treason," George Norris of Nebraska told his Senate colleagues that "we are going to war on the command of gold.... I feel that we are about to put the dollar sign on the American flag." Southerners were terrified that a mass citizen army would require putting guns in the hands of African Americans, encouraging if not igniting an upsurge of egalitarian sentiments that could not be suppressed. Overall hung questions of the plight and place of twelve million so-called hyphenated Americans, chiefly Germans and Irish.[51]

Inevitably, the U-boat campaign and the Zimmerman Telegram forced everyone's hand. The kaiser's captains not only began sinking neutral ships at will, but also began their deliberate and "murderous vendetta" against clearly marked and illuminated British hospital ships that forced medical personnel and litter patients to conduct hasty evacuations into stormy seas. Where they were not drowned along with their patients, doctors and nurses performed heroically. Other hospital ships fatally struck mines in fields lain by enemy submarines off the English coasts and in the Mediterranean.[52] Germany was clearly practicing a kind of barbaric conflict that had not been seen since the Thirty Years' War swept over that cursed land three centuries earlier. The president anguished, but the direction of his thinking in those long weeks of ever-rising tension was clearly articulated by his navy secretary. Addressing the Naval Academy graduating class on March 2, Daniels told the new graduates that they were living in a time when "great issues stir the depths of men. Small questions are shriveled. Life, death, liberty, valor, justice, immortality are the themes that alone grip us in this hour. Questions big with the fate not alone of nations, but the world, may be decided by you." Wilson had determined that the new ensigns be commissioned three months early because "nearly all the world is in the vortex of war and no people can feel that they may not be drawn into it. . . . I summon you to your high calling."[53]

Sixteen days later, on March 18, 1917, German submarines cold-bloodedly sank three American steamers. The president dared not ignore the gauntlet thrown at his feet. On the twenty-first he at last polled the cabinet and found solid support for a declaration of war. Daniels, it was said, agreed with tears in his eyes. Walter Hines Page, the ambassador to the Court of St. James, had sent several cables across the Atlantic, urging that a senior naval official be sent to London to represent American interests and to cooperate closely with the Admiralty. Within hours of the cabinet meeting, Sims was detached from his post as director of the Naval War College and ordered to London. The battle fleet had gone to its winter training grounds in the Caribbean, "but we didn't stay long," a junior officer recalled. "We came back up and went into the York River . . . behind the submarine nets, in early 1917." There, at "Base 2," an antisubmarine boom "was thrown across the river; outposts and pickets were posted," while "a destroyer patrol extending from Eastport [Maine] to Key West was placed in operation."[54] Wilson called an absent Congress back into session, and once it gathered in a dramatic evening session on April 2, the president asked for a declaration of war against the "Central Powers"—Germany and its ally, the Austro-Hungarian Empire. Four days later, shortly after noon, and following bitter debate, Vice President Thomas Riley Marshall from his raised chair in the Senate of the United States signed a Congressional Resolution declaring that a state of war now existed between the United States and Germany. An hour later, Wilson added his signature, making the declaration national law.

As the president finished, Daniels's aide Byron McCandless rushed out of the executive office and "wigwagged" the news to his fellow lieutenant commander Royal Ingersoll, standing in a window at the Navy Department across the street. Ingersoll raced down the corridor to the communications office and had "Sixteen Alnav"—All Navy Radio Message number 16 for that still young year—sent from radio towers across the river in Alexandria, Virginia, to fleet units scattered from the Atlantic Coast to Alaska and the Philippines. Almost immediately, a similar message was flashed to Mayo, who was presumably as aware of the irony of the situation as was his secretary, for the "secret rendezvous" on the York River of a battle fleet now pledged to fight alongside the Royal Navy was at precisely the point where 136 years earlier, the appearance of a French fleet had spelled the doom of Britain's increasingly strenuous efforts to retain their American colonies.[55]

Over the next eighteen months, the United States Navy would employ ever-expanding resources and manpower to help ensure the security of those Atlantic and Mediterranean sea lanes so vital to the war effort. Thousands of youngsters would eagerly volunteer for sea duty "to fight the Hun" (and, doubtless, to avoid the trenches). Naval service came as a shock, but the vast majority who survived the war weathered often harsh and even terrifying experiences to, in their own estimation, become better men. Young John Langdon Leighton, an intelligence officer on Sims's London staff, doubtless summed up the opinions of many when, directly after the war, he wrote:

> Those of us who joined the ranks of the Navy in this War found ourselves playing a new role in the comedy or drama of life. We left a universe of freedom and entered a world in which hours for smoking, shore leave, uniforms to be worn, and the adjustment of our lives were prescribed by autocratic law and regulations. We chafed under our restrictions and blamed those who enforced them in their tyrannical attitude. We did not realize that in an Officer's orders, or the manner in which we were addressed, there was nothing of the personal; these men were but enforcing that splendid institution, the code of discipline. But as I now look back and see before me the characters of those Officers with whom I came in contact, I doubt whether any finer or more manly group of men exists. They were educated and trained to know the true meaning of duty, responsibility, and devotion; they were brisk in their manner, quick to act, severe in their judgments, and, at heart, human.[56]

With "splendid cooperation" from the army, which "organized and developed an efficient system for loading and unloading" vessels "at the terminal points," the navy would in the next eighteen months either transport or safeguard a substantial portion of an American Expeditionary Force—more than two million men strong—across the Atlantic to France together with many times that amount of tonnage needed to construct great staging bases, airfields, and cantonments behind the western front. At the same time, destroyers by the scores—nearly every one the navy possessed—together with armed yachts and subchasers by the hundreds, and the planting of a vast minefield in the upper North Sea helped British and French comrades suppress the German U-boats. The navy's influence even reached ashore with participation by its fledgling bomber aircraft in raids against German submarine facilities in Belgium, the employment of a fourteen-inch long-range naval battery against German artillery positions, and the "massive construction" of new aviation facilities on either side of the English Channel—"entire autonomous towns and villages three thousand miles from home."[57]

If the American Army that landed in France in 1917–18 failed to perform optimally, as some have argued;[58] if the formation of an American Expeditionary Force in France entailed constant struggle for influence between "fractious Bureaus" at home and headquarters overseas; if endless bickering between American and Anglo-French naval authorities ignited "command rivalries and resentments at the highest levels," American sea, air-, and land power nonetheless provided the decisive margin of force that checkmated and finally overwhelmed the kaiser's soldiers after four years of stalemate and bloodshed.[59] In the process, the United States Navy became a truly modern service, sufficiently blooded and oriented toward a second, even more massive, global conflict that would see it dominate the world ocean from that day to this.

Beat to Quarters

Wilson's declaration of war provided the Allied Powers with the prospect of a massive replenishment of men and ships from across the Atlantic. It was almost too late. On all fronts from Flanders to Mesopotamia, "there was no prospect of victory over the Central Powers" unless and until "heavy American forces could be sent to Europe to turn the scale. . . . The sending of an American army to France would necessitate the safeguarding of the lines of communication across the Atlantic; in other words, the result of the war was seen to hang upon whether or not the Allies and the United States could obtain and hold the mastery of the sea. As in all wars in which maritime nations have been engaged, sea power was to prove the decisive factor."[1]

Neither the French nor the British proved hesitant to exploit their new-found fortune. In April 1917, the Great War remained very much in the balance both on the western front and in its adjacent waters. Yet with a single critical exception—the convoy system—the Anglo-French Allies had developed the template for victory at sea. Germany's U-boat arm would be eventually suppressed by a mass of small antisubmarine vessels ranging from destroyers at the high end to armed yachts, trawlers, large motorboats, and even submarines, dirigibles, kite balloons, and seaplanes. They would employ such weapons as the depth charge, the hydrophone, and the "Y-gun."[2] All of these weapons had come into the Anglo-French arsenals by the end of 1916; the problem was that there were simply not enough of any one of them, and in the case of the depth charge, improvements were required. The American contribution, including Sims's vigorous advocacy of the convoy system, the elaboration of better depth charges, and the laying of a majority of the mines in the Northern

Barrage between the Orkneys and Norway, provided the critical tipping point to ensure victory.

Literally within hours of the president's request to Congress and while Sims was still at sea on his way to London, an Anglo-French mission composed of top-level military and naval officials stationed in the Western Hemisphere was pulled together under instructions from Paris and London and sailed toward the United States. By April 11 the Allied representatives were in conference at Norfolk with Daniels, Benson, Mayo, and other senior naval officials. A few days later, the meeting moved on to Washington. The Americans "possessed only the vaguest notion of the military and naval situation in Europe." Wilson had wanted it this way in order to maintain his self-defined status as grand mediator of a world war, should events come to that. The strategy dovetailed neatly with both the Allies and the Central Powers, neither of whom had any wish to make the peoples across the sea privy to their mutually desperate straits. Now with the United States in the war, it was time to lay cards on the table.

What the besieged Allies wanted most and immediately from their new associate were destroyers. The Americans were initially cold to the plea, for they did not wish to weaken the battle-fleet screen. Strenuous winter maneuvers in the Caribbean training grounds had left the destroyer divisions in a weakened matériel state that only prolonged docking could rectify. But Royal Navy representative Vice Admiral Montague Browning would not be put off, pressing hard for at least a few such vessels to demonstrate an American presence in European waters.

His hosts might have been pardoned for raising eyebrows. According to one semiauthoritative twenty-first-century source, the Royal Navy in August 1914 possessed no fewer than 221 destroyers. Admittedly, they were of all types, ranging back to the most primitive commissioned two decades before. Forty-two of the best of the type operated with the Grand Fleet out of Scapa Flow. Over the next three years, the total number of British destroyers may have reached 300. Throughout the war, however, the Admiralty worked the ships in all kinds of weather and conditions. As a consequence, a great number were lost to collision, mines, enemy torpedoes, and running aground from the English coast to Gallipoli.[3]

When the Americans continued to stand firm, Browning pleaded for just one ship "to have a great moral effect." It was Mayo who broke the logjam that Daniels and Benson had created. When Daniels turned to his Atlantic Fleet commander and asked if at least one destroyer could be spared, Mayo replied, "We can send a division [six ships] and should not send less than that." On April

13, "specific terms of an agreement were drafted in Admiral Benson's office." The Americans agreed to patrol in both North and South Atlantic waters and to maintain their Asiatic Squadron. Six destroyers were to be sent posthaste to Europe. Some small craft—steam- and wind-powered yachts swiftly requisitioned from civilian owners—were designated for service on the French coast. Beyond these points, Daniels and Benson would not go. They and most of their subordinates were steeped in the Mahanian dictum that "the United States should not divide its battle fleet" and that the navy's primary function was to guard the American coastline.[4] Destroyers were an integral part of both considerations. Soon enough, however, events forced a dramatic turn.

Sims reached Liverpool on the ninth, where a special Admiralty train rushed him to London. The following day he began intense conversations with Admiral Sir John Jellicoe, commander of the Grand Fleet at Jutland and now, as first sea lord of the Admiralty, Benson's practical opposite. The American envoy had landed in the midst of a flaming row within and beyond the Admiralty over the question of convoys. According to Sims, "The fear of German submarines was not disturbing the London season which had now reached its height; the theatres were packed every night; everywhere, indeed, the men and women of the upper classes were apparently giving little thought to any danger that might be hanging over their country." As historian Arthur Marder later discovered, this false sense of security, if in fact it existed, was due to the fact that the British were underestimating the extent of their shipping losses "by over 50 per cent."[5]

The government, however, *was* aware of the ever-mounting crisis at sea, as were shipowners and maritime insurance companies on both sides of the Atlantic who were "being thrown almost into a panic." A man of instinctive caution and no little pessimism, Jellicoe had long recognized the enormous difficulties in waging an effective antisubmarine campaign. He had been making dark predictions even before he stepped into the Admiralty building off Trafalgar Square as first sea lord in January 1917. Two months before, as Germany reintroduced restricted submarine warfare against Allied commerce, he expressed his fears to the Admiralty from his Grand Fleet flagship, the battleship *Iron Duke* lying in the fleet anchorage at Scapa Flow. "There appears to be a serious danger that our losses in merchant ships, combined with the losses in neutral merchant ships, may by the early summer of 1917 have such a serious effect upon the import of food and other necessaries into the allied countries as to force us into accepting peace terms, which the military position on the Continent would not justify and which would fall far short of our desires." He proceeded to outline the ineffectiveness of destroyers as U-boat killers in those

"open waters" far from shore in which the German submarines were beginning to operate in ever-larger numbers. Promptly invited to London to air his
views further before the War Committee, Jellicoe stated that he had no plan
afoot to fight the Submarine Menace beyond deploying the handful of armed
Q ships that he deemed essentially powerless, as "these could not act offensively
because they could not see the submarines." Admiral Sir Henry Oliver, chief
of the Admiralty's War Staff, supported him. A small man with a tight face and
turned-down mouth, he told the meeting that a convoy system employing a
single merchantman and a naval escort was being tried in the Mediterranean,
but it was a major drain on resources and any group larger than one-on-one
had proved fatal: "The French tried more, and lost two or three of their ships."
Jellicoe added that a larger formation would invite chaos in trying to keep so
many ships together, and others at the meeting, reflecting widespread belief
within the fleet, emphasized that in terms of tonnage, a large convoy "was most
wasteful."[6]

In his initial address as first sea lord, Jellicoe tried to strike a balance between
anxiety and resolve. The Submarine Menace was "far greater now than at any
period of the war. . . . All our energy" would be required to combat it. But "it
must and will be dealt with. Of that I am confident."[7]

For a time, he had Fleet Street and the country behind him. But shipping
losses continued to mount alarmingly. By May, a "reptile press" (in the words
of one high Admiralty official), led by Lord Northcliffe's *Daily Mail*, had begun
mounting a spirited campaign against the navy's antisubmarine war, or, rather,
lack thereof. Back in March, Cabinet Minister without Portfolio Sir Edward
Carson, himself no friend of the antisubmarine convoy idea, had reemphasized
the price being paid by the Royal Navy as long-standing ruler of the global
ocean. "In all the theatres of war the world over, the Navy" had had to provide
patrols, convoys (to protect the Australian–New Zealand Army Corps from
German surface raiders in the Indian Ocean), "mine-sweepers and -layers, air
[power], mine carriers, fleet messengers," and so on. "Recollect," he added, that
"if you criticize us for not doing enough . . . we have to fight with the weapons
which are there, because you cannot improvise ships as you would a gun or
a rifle." To First Lord of the Admiralty Sir Eric Geddes, the Submarine Menace had by this time become as "inconceivable" as it was "insoluble." Britain's
mighty merchant marine "was being sunk at a rate which would soon have
brought us to the point of inability to continue the war." The fourth volume
of the official British history of the war at sea, which appeared a decade later,
confirmed the alarming situation: "Everything, indeed, combined to show that

the Allies were really within sight of disaster." Thanks to increasing use of underwater attack by torpedo as a supplement to sinkings by their deck guns, the
U-boats were on a rampage, while their own losses declined. "Only a change in
our system of defence could turn the tide." A singular source of the crisis had
been the inaction of British shipbuilders during much of the war. "Virtually all
construction of new merchant ships had been stopped in 1914" on the assump-
tion that the conflict would be brief and naval construction must take priority.
Not until the horrendous monthly losses in the spring and summer of 1916
were priorities reversed "and urgent measures of conservation [that is, repair of
torpedo-damaged ships] were put in hand."[8]

Yet others, most notably Admiral David Beatty, who had "fleeted up" to
command the Grand Fleet after Jellicoe's posting to the Admiralty, "kept urging" that a convoy system be tried. No less a personage than Prime Minister
David Lloyd George would later put himself forward, with some justification,
as father of the convoy idea. The prime minister's disgust with the Admiralty
on this, and other, issues was characteristically loud and without equivocation.
"Watching the shipping losses soar, he . . . poured contempt on the 'palsied and
muddle-headed Admiralty' with its 'atmosphere of crouching nervousness,' its
'condition of utter despair' and its 'paralytic documents.' The 'fear-dimmed eyes
of our Mall admirals' reflected a 'stunned pessimism.'" Cabinet War Committee
secretary Maurice Hankey presented a paper that spring cautiously supporting
convoys "if practicable," and naval officers in the Trade Office also championed
the idea. Rear Admiral Alexander Duff, new head of the Admiralty's antisubmarine office, was another supporter. Nonetheless, the Admiralty Board, with
Sir Henry Oliver in full cry, continued to oppose the convoy idea "with all the
passion of the bigoted.[9]

After Sims and Jellicoe exchanged greetings that April day in 1917, the latter reached into a desk drawer and withdrew a document indicating that in
February—the first month of unrestricted submarine warfare—U-boats had
sent 536,000 tons of British and neutral shipping to the bottom of the Atlantic.
The figure had increased to 603,000 tons in March and, if projections for April
held true—as they did—close to 1 million tons of desperately needed shipping
and supplies would perish at sea. ("During that month, 430 British, Allied and
neutral merchantmen" were "sent to the bottom by submarines, an average of
over 14 a day.") Sims "was fairly astounded" by the news. "'Yes,'" Jellicoe replied
quietly, "as if he were discussing the weather and not the future of the British
Empire, 'it is impossible for us to go on with the war if losses like this continue.'" Well, Sims asked, what was being done about it? "Everything that we

can," Jellicoe replied. Small craft that could be used "to fight submarines" were being rounded up; British yards had taken on crash programs to build as many destroyers, trawlers, "and other like craft as fast as we can." But the "situation was very serious," Jellicoe concluded, "and we shall need all the assistance we can get."

With its highly effective counterblockade by U-boat, it looked like Germany was winning the war, Sims replied bluntly. "They will win," Jellicoe responded, "unless we can stop these losses—and stop them soon." Sims pressed: Was there no solution? "Absolutely none that we can see now," Jellicoe allegedly replied. Despite strenuous patrolling by destroyers and other antisubmarine craft, Jellicoe "showed no confidence that they would be able to control the depredations of the U-boat."[10]

Recalling his conversation with Sims, Jellicoe remembered the conclusion of discussions in less apocalyptic terms. What he did say, the former first sea lord recalled in 1934, was not that there were "absolutely" no successful resolutions to the Submarine Menace but that "the counter measures being devised could not be immediately successful as time was required for their production." To avoid immediate catastrophe, help from the United States was essential, especially destroyers and other small antisubmarine craft.[11]

A young intelligence officer on Sims's staff wrote soon after the war that "at a rough estimate the British Navy" in early 1917 "was handling 80%" of the antisubmarine war in the North Sea, English Channel, "all waters west of Ireland," and the west coast of France. To cover this responsibility, it could muster at best "a meager two dozen" destroyers stationed at Milford Haven, Plymouth, and Holyhead. The great majority of Britain's two hundred–odd destroyers were concentrated in the Home Fleet, protecting His Majesty's capital ships and providing an offensive punch through torpedo attacks during fleet actions. After three years of constant steaming and intermittent warfare, the destroyer crews were overwhelmed and exhausted, and the vessels themselves were often badly in need of repair. The Admiralty had "theoretically" marked off the Western Approaches—those waters south, west, and east of Ireland—"into large squares or areas," each the responsibility of a single patrol destroyer. The paucity of these vessels, however, meant that the patrol areas were unmanageably large. "This put the destroyer in a position of little value, for as the submarine could see the destroyer long before the destroyer could see the submarine, and as submarines were looking for merchant ships, not for destroyers, the submarine could very easily avoid the anti-submarine vessels." In practice, the system was "disastrous," and early in 1917 a new one was put in place. "All incoming ships were now directed to come into the Western British Ports, along any one of four or five different and designated lanes, which the destroyers were to keep as free from submarines as possible. An incoming or outgoing ship, while passing along one of these lanes, would be picked up by a destroyer and escorted for some distance, and then left alone until she was picked up again." But as John Langdon Leighton observed, the new system "was successful only in that while one escorted ship arrived safely at its port, probably another two or three were unescorted, and therefore open to attack. It worked out better than its predecessor, but there still was very much to be desired."[12]

Nor was the then celebrated "mine barrage" of nets, mines, and trawlers that stretched the twenty miles or so between Dover and Calais as effective as thought and claimed. While the barrage did much to keep U-boats from harming cross-Channel shipping lanes at their narrowest, it "was not particularly effective" in deterring the Germans from using this quickest passage to the open Atlantic. This was due in part to the murky waters of the Channel but largely to the British disinterest in and distaste for mine warfare as a weapon of weaker naval powers. In the first three years of the war, British mines were "so defective that oysters and other sea growth, which attached themselves to their prongs made many of them harmless." Many others, together with the submerged nets designed to snare U-boats, were simply blown away by the storms and gales that often lashed the Channel waters. "In 1918, Admiral Sir Roger Keyes reconstructed this barrage with a new type of mine and transformed it into a really effective barrier." But in the spring of 1917 and for many months thereafter, German U-boats "had little difficulty in slipping through, particularly in the night time." British efforts to mine German waters, particularly the Helgoland Bight, were consistently frustrated by the enemy's efficient minesweeping efforts.[13]

Sims struggled to fully grasp the dimensions of the submarine problem, and he soon discovered what he thought—erroneously—was a major cause. Ironically, it seemed that a paucity, not a plethora, of U-boats operating between 20–17 degrees W longitude and Brest—an area roughly four hundred by two hundred miles "densely infested" with Allied merchantmen—was making detection almost impossible. Hunting U-boats involved the proverbial search for a needle in a haystack among a mass of shipping. The Imperial German Navy had possessed relatively few submarines when in 1915 it determined to throw a counterblockade against the British Isles. Although the shipyards in Hamburg and elsewhere turned to building U-boats at the expense of all other warship construction, subsequent operations would prove that only about 10 percent of

German submarines could be deployed at a single time. This was as true when Germany reinstituted unrestricted submarine warfare in February 1917 as it had been earlier. In 1921 Sims speculated that had Germany been able to deploy fifty U-boats at sea in 1917, more might have been lost, but Britain would have seen at least several million tons of shipping per month sent to the bottom and would have had to sue for peace. As it was, he believed, the Germans were usually able to put six to ten submarines on patrol at any given time, sometimes as few as four, occasionally as many as a dozen. At one point, they were able to muster fifteen, but no more. A careful 1931 study of the German submarine war essentially supported Sims's figures: freeze-framing one moment, the authors found that twenty-one North Sea U-boats were out, either returning from, setting out for, or on station. Eight "Flanders boats were in the Channel or south Irish waters." Meanwhile, thirteen other submarines were busily ravaging commercial traffic in the Mediterranean. The only way to defeat these potentially fatal maritime pests was to throw masses of antisubmarine vessels at them.

The analysis was as faulty as the proposed solutions. Later research indicated that in February 1917, the German Admiralty sent no fewer than thirty-six U-boats to sea; in March the number rose to between forty and fifty-seven and the following month forty-seven to fifty-eight. Nonetheless, these relatively few vessels "were responsible for a veritable slaughter in the shipping lanes." But the Admiralty had reached a decision, probably wise in the event, that the Home Fleet destroyer flotillas must remain where they were to screen the heavy ships in their periodic sweeps to keep Germany's formidable surface fleet out of the North Sea. British resolve never weakened in this matter, despite the conclusion of naval authorities that recent U-boat assaults on Allied hospital ships were deliberately undertaken "in order to make us escort them with destroyers."[14]

Much of the anxiety in British naval circles, mounting steadily toward despair, could be traced, as officials readily acknowledged, to the very limited weaponry at hand to fight the U-boat. Most of the antisubmarine war of 1915–18 was crude in the extreme. If U-boat captains were constrained by the sharply limited sight lines of their tiny periscopes and were forced to risk surface sailing during daylight hours to find their prey, their enemies possessed only crude underwater detection equipment—hydrophones—prone to mislead, together with a few depth charges too often set to ignite either above or too far below a slowly maneuvering submarine.

But Sims soon grasped the logic of convoys as the solution to defeating the U-boat. A—if not the—key to success against the menace was to be found in clustering ships together in convoy. Convoys, in fact, had been in use since the earliest days of the war, albeit on a limited basis. Not only had they carried Anzac troops to the Middle East, using escorts of light cruisers to fend off German commerce raiders such as *Emden*, but protection of the Grand Fleet from U-boat attacks during its periodic sweeps of the North Sea depended absolutely upon its screen of swift, fast-reacting escorts. In effect, Royal Navy destroyers were doing a very effective job of convoying the capital ships.[15] Why could not British merchant ships, sailing collectively as its battleships were doing, be escorted in the same way? Once he grasped this point, Sims threw his considerable and ever-growing weight on the side of the convoy enthusiasts, making his argument with a force and frequency that the British dared not ignore. After all, the American admiral held in his hands the number of destroyers that could make the system work.

Through careful thinking and analysis during his first weeks in London, Sims thus stumbled upon the basic element of antisubmarine warfare: the secret of success lay not in U-boats sunk but in their suppression, not in their destruction but in their containment. If U-boats could be kept away from ships, they could not sink them. Conversely, convoys could act as a fatal lure. When a U-boat did discover a convoy, it would be forced to confront a number of alert, well-armed escorts as it maneuvered for either surface or underwater attack. Sims understood that *sole* reliance upon the kind of antisubmarine patrolling in effect in 1917 was a largely useless hit-or-miss affair. Patrol craft had to either detect, that is, stumble upon, a U-boat or react to a submarine attack.[16]

Precisely because the submarine was a brand-new instrument of war with sharply limited range and no technological sophistication beyond an ability to dive and remain underwater for a time, the German admirals and captains of 1915–18 were unable to develop effective strategies for it. They never solved the problem of successfully attacking convoys. In particular, the wolf-pack concept, necessarily grounded in high unit production, long-range wireless communications, advanced torpedoes, and onboard plotting devices, lay beyond the imagination and capabilities of the first-generation U-boat sailors. Had they grasped the technique and had German shipyards managed to produce the requisite number of boats, the Kriegsmarine might have won the victory that eluded them. Of equal if not greater importance was the fact that in 1917–18, Germany did not possess the entire coastal strip of western Europe from North Cape to the Spanish border, with its numerous harbors and ports from which U-boats in 1940–43 would find immediate egress to the North Atlantic. Because their bases were confined to just a handful of

Channel and North Sea harbors, German submarines in World War I were forced to transit coastal waters and operate in high-seas zones that took days to reach. Working largely alone until the final stages of the war (the German Admiralty would gather 8 submarines together in May 1918 for concentrated attacks against convoys; their indifferent success discouraged any further such efforts), the U-boats ultimately proved unable to disrupt the great maritime supply lines that funneled massive numbers of American troops and massive tons of war matériel from grain to typewriters to British and French ports. It is now generally accepted that Germany lost 178 submarines during the conflict, about half their overall force, which was a strikingly smaller percentage than in World War II. Most of the boats that perished had withdrawn from the open ocean once the convoy system came into being and were hunting for individual merchantmen in or near the relatively shallow coastal waters of France and Britain, where they could be more easily detected and destroyed by Allied air and naval units.[17]

Suppression if not defeat of the U-boat menace would be achieved not only through the convoy system, but also by the continuation of aggressive patrolling. The tactic required a significant infusion of antisubmarine war craft into the maritime war zones off southwestern England, the Channel, the Bay of Biscay, and the Mediterranean. Only the United States Navy possessed sufficient resources to decisively tip the balance in the U-boat war.

Even as he worked the convoy issue with colleagues in the deeply divided British Admiralty, Sims, joined enthusiastically by Ambassador Walter Hines Page, began bombarding the White House and Navy Department with cables insisting that the fleet release a substantial portion of its destroyer force for duty in European waters. Sims shrewdly played on his president's vanity. In a cable to Washington just a week after Wilson had signed the declaration of war, the admiral urged that "the maximum number" of antisubmarine vessels, including small patrol craft, be made available to the Allies "at once," not only as a solid gesture of support but also to exert "some strategic leverage" on the conduct of the war before an American Expeditionary Force arrived in sufficient numbers on the western front. Support and repair ships should be sent along, together with sufficient construction and staff people to develop substantial base facilities for the navy at Queenstown (now Cobh) and Berehaven (Bantry Bay). Implicit in his message was development of similar facilities in the port towns of western France as the American naval presence inexorably grew. Finally, Sims committed yet another act of personal heresy when he rather casually mentioned that no elements of the battle fleet were needed at this time and that little or no effort should be made to defend the East Coast from German U-boat attacks, as the focus of action would remain thousands of miles to the east.[18]

The message was not well received. Wilson shared with his navy subordinates a keen commitment to Mahanian principles, grounded in an obsession with maintaining fleet integrity in anticipation of major offensive actions. Dribbling away fleet resources in attempts to prop up a wartime associate could prove feckless. Moreover, the president soon developed a skepticism about the Royal Navy that closely reflected that of David Lloyd George. Drawing on the conclusions of a single American journalist and author (ironically named Winston Churchill) that the lords of the Admiralty were "unequal" to the tasks before them, Wilson wrote Daniels on July 2, urging an insistence upon offensive "plans of our own." Two days later, Wilson wrote Sims directly, expressing both surprise and dismay that the Admiralty seemed unable to assert Britain's naval preponderance effectively. "In the presence of the present submarine emergency they are helpless to the point of panic." The president was not being wholly unreasonable. Just several weeks before, Jellicoe, oscillating between the measured optimism he had expressed to Sims and outright despair, told an inter-Allied meeting that if those Channel ports from which German U-boats sailed were not captured through a land offensive in Flanders, Britain could not carry on past 1918 due to massive shipping losses. Queried more closely the next day, the seemingly hapless admiral told his startled audience, "There is no use discussing plans for next spring—we cannot go on." In his letter to Sims, Wilson sought to charge the war at sea with audacity, even in the face of "great losses."[19]

Jellicoe's infuriating waffling notwithstanding, Wilson's impatience with his British associates was misplaced. As a number of scholars have recently emphasized, His Majesty's Government and the Admiralty in particular had harbored deep concerns, stretching back to the Napoleonic era, about enemy occupation of the northern coasts of France and the Low Countries that directly threatened the United Kingdom. Britain's sea dogs and generals would have liked nothing better than to bounce the Germans out of the Belgian ports from which the U-boats deployed and invasion fleets might be gathered. But from the outset, the remorseless, ever-growing demands of the western front for more and more manpower and matériel forced strategists and soldiers to consider the Belgian coast a "peripheral" area of interest. The presence of powerful enemy naval concentrations in the nearby Helgoland Bight together with the quiet but unmistakable fears of the French ally that London might use any pretext to pull its army home put paid to any idea of a massive amphibious assault on Ostend, Zeebrugge, and Bruges, no matter how attractive the idea continued to be.[20]

As his first days and weeks in London passed, Sims discovered a sympathetic audience in both Whitehall and Downing Street that was absent in Washington. Despite Jellicoe's ostentatious despair, elements within and beyond the Admiralty had been moving for some time to address the Submarine Menace. They were driven in large measure by the continuing loss of tankers bringing the precious fuel oil from the New World that drove a growing portion of the Grand Fleet. At one point, Beatty had to order his massive armada to steam at only three-fifths speed during its North Sea sweeps to conserve fuel.

The Admiralty had timidly embraced the convoy idea as early as December 1916 when it authorized "protected sailings" of vessels carrying critical war materials between Norway and the Orkney and Shetland Islands. A handful of armed trawlers and converted fishing vessels were employed as escorts. The following February, after German submarines began "slaughtering" colliers bringing precious coal from Welsh pits to French homes and factories, the Admiralty instituted "controlled sailings . . . rough and tentative convoys" across the Channel. By the end of March, the Admiralty had six weeks' evidence of their success, and, according to the official British naval history, it had to grudgingly conclude that "the reduction of losses in a trade which had hitherto been particularly afflicted was decidedly impressive."[21]

But a spirited and not uninformed opposition remained. Not only were Britain's destroyer flotillas incapable of providing escort, strained as they were past the breaking point by patrol-duty and screening responsibilities, but Jellicoe's own people were convinced that unless naval escorts composed a "very large" percentage of the overall convoy, the system itself would constitute "an additional danger" in the war at sea. This conclusion had especially gripped the mind of Admiral Duff, director of antisubmarine operations.

The pleas of the French along with his prime minister's strongly voiced concerns and Sims's forceful arguments in favor of the convoy system helped Jellicoe change his mind. On April 30 he called Sims to the Admiralty. "When I arrived he said that the projected study of the convoy system had been made. . . . It had been decided to send one experimental convoy from Gibraltar. The Admiralty, he added, had not yet definitely decided that the convoy system should be adopted, but there was every intent of giving it a thorough and fair trial." Thus, with "dire warnings of disaster" from Oliver and the Admiralty staff ringing in its collective ear, the "first ocean convoy" of the Great War set sail.[22]

Results were spectacular. On May 20, every ship arrived in England without incident. Moreover, initially skeptical merchant captains and engineering officers realized with amazed delight that they could, indeed, steam and maneuver in columned numbers safely and with discipline both day and night. Just four days later, the Royal Navy organized the first convoy from the New World that sailed from Hampton Roads, with the cruiser HMS *Roxborough* the leading escort. That convoy, too, got through without incident, and the Admiralty immediately "instituted regular convoys out of Hampton Roads every four days beginning in mid-June. By July, the convoy system had been extended" to ships sailing from New York and several Canadian ports, chiefly Halifax, Nova Scotia.[23]

The conversion of the British Admiralty to convoying was a critical step in the U-boat war, but American acceptance and participation were vital if a two-million-man army was to cross the Atlantic to throw a decisive weight into the Allied cause. Despite open reservations about British abilities and intentions, the White House and Navy Department proved game to try the system. The Allies, in turn, had their own reservations about American abilities. How big an army the Yanks could throw into the western front was always a question, given America's limited sealift capabilities. In May, France dispatched Marshal Joseph Joffre to Washington to probe American intent and capabilities. This hero of the Marne who in 1914 had blunted the initial German offensive at the gates of Paris, but was perceived as having faltered at Verdun, was himself pessimistic about the new partner. He told Secretary of War Newton D. Baker that a force of "400,000 would be our limit, and that one French port would be sufficient to receive it."[24] However, Joffre did repeat Montague's earlier argument, urging the importance of sending a token military force to Europe immediately as a signal of American intent.

The first US commitment had already reached European waters. Just hours after agreement had been reached with the Anglo-French delegation in Washington to send a division of destroyers to the war zone, an obscure lieutenant commander named Joseph Taussig who commanded the half-dozen ships of Destroyer Division 8, US Atlantic Fleet, from the bridge of *Wadsworth* was telephoned at home in northern Virginia by a junior officer aboard his command ship. Like her sisters, the two-year-old, eleven-hundred-ton *Wadsworth* was lithe (315 feet), fast (thirty knots with all four funnels belching thick black oily smoke that would choke a horse), and well armed (four four-inch guns—one forward of the small bridge structure, one on each side of the gallery deck house, and one aft together with four triple-tube twenty-one-inch torpedo tubes). The navy's tough training regimen, however, had revealed flaws in armament layout. "The gallery guns possess three advantages . . . a good platform for loading crew on most bearings, they are dry for use in nearly all weather, and they have the questionable advantage of extreme depression which might be of use in firing at a submarine close aboard." But the guns "cannot be fired forward of ten degrees on the bow because of the proximity of the bridge and . . . at least one gun is restricted in its fire aft by a nearby boat."[25] Each destroyer carried slightly more than one hundred men; in wartime fifty more would somehow have to be accommodated.

Now, Lieutenant (jg) Falge told his skipper, "I have bad news for you. We have just received orders to leave at daylight for New York to fit out for long and distant service. I think we are going abroad." Taussig was thunderstruck. But he promptly issued orders to the vessels under his command to rendezvous near the Cape Charles Lightship at 0800 the next morning. *Wadsworth* left her anchorage two and a half hours earlier, stranding ashore fifteen crewmen who were not due back from liberty for some time.

It was a strange moment for the destroyer sailors that Sims had trained so assiduously. One of them remembered that "we were at war but a dim, distant war on the other side of the ocean. . . . The possibility of seeing action looked small." Most men looked forward to months and years of patrolling along the East Coast, looking for phantom German surface raiders, while "the battlewagons would have all the fun, helping the British bottle up the Kaiser's fleet."[26]

Steaming at twenty-six to twenty-eight knots, leaving broad wakes of foam and black dust astern, the five (not six) destroyers of Division 8—*Wadsworth, McDougal, Wainwright, Connyngham*, and *Porter*—reached New York Harbor just before six on a quiet Saturday night and moored at the Brooklyn Navy Yard shortly after. "Of course nobody paid any attention to us. So, just as I supposed, the great emergency requiring us to sail at daylight was no emergency at all, and it would have been much better had I been given some discretion in the matter and allowed to remain in Hampton Roads until my libertymen returned. But it is the way we have in the Navy. Somebody somewhere is generally prone to 'fly off the handle.'"[27]

Taussig would have reason to invoke his philosophic temper over the next several days. Little more than twelve hours after he reached New York, the energetic commander had arranged to have his five ships docked for engine repairs, for the crews to go on Sunday liberty in New York City, and for his wife to come up from Virginia for a few days. Then, calling on the shipyard commandant, he was informed that orders had come from Washington for the five destroyers, plus sister ship *Davis*, to sail promptly for Boston. Only an energetic telephone call to Washington allowed him to remain in New York overnight to fetch the liberty parties. He telegraphed his wife to head to Boston instead.

"There certainly is a lack of communications somewhere," he wrote in his personal diary. "But what can we expect? Our Navy Department is absolutely unorganized so far as its duty in connection with carrying on a war is concerned. Evidently things are very much upset at headquarters. Perhaps someday we will have a real General Staff, but until that day comes we must continue to expect to be buffeted around in all manner of ways."[28]

At eight on the morning of April 23, 1917, Taussig's little fleet sailed out of the Brooklyn Navy Yard for Boston. Charles Blackford, a young but experienced crew member aboard *McDougal*, recalled that "no one saw us off but indifferent yard workers." All the excitement that day would occur at a nearby pier where the giant new battleship *New Mexico*, festooned with flags, was being readied for commissioning. Yet Blackford and his mates would soon conclude that their "little craft that slipped past in the morning mists" would not only be "the fighters of this war," but largely the next as well, while battleships declined to the status of "museum pieces."[29]

Taussig spent six days in Boston fuming while his ships took on supplies (including heavy clothing). Washington was not silent, merely ambiguous. At one point early on, an impatient Taussig telephoned his chief of naval operations direct. "The conversation was very unsatisfactory from my point of view." Benson refused to name a sailing date, but insisted that "we must sail immediately on receipt of orders" and "be ready for any contingency." The Navy Department would take care of all problems. With twenty-two years' service, Taussig "knew better than that." He did learn that when Division 8 finally did sail, it was to report to British authorities in the "English Channel." Taussig at last took matters into his own hands and announced he would sail for England on the twenty-fifth. The department promptly responded that the twenty-fourth would be better, sending him sealed orders to be opened once at sea. Shortly before five in the afternoon on the designated day, the division departed at last for the war zone, leaving those few wives and family members fortunate to live in Boston or to have reached it in time waving sad good-byes from the dock.[30]

Once at sea under clear evening skies, Taussig felt both "blue" and angry.

There is no telling when I will see my family again or what is in store for us. Then it still sticks that the Department did not treat us right. Instead of nagging us and not giving us any information, I feel sure that the proper procedure in this case would have been for me to be ordered to Washington and get the situation explained to me confidentially. I feel that the Department kicked us out rather discourteously instead of saying to us: "You fellows are up against a tough proposition. The Department knows that you will do your best and wishes you success. Good-bye and good luck." If we had been treated that way I would be in a much better frame of mind tonight.

The following noon, several hundred miles at sea, his six little ships in column, Taussig opened his orders and learned he was going to Queenstown, Ireland, where base facilities would be made available by the Royal Navy under whose command he should place himself. There were no instructions or information on enemy submarines, "or how they were operating. We were certainly on our own resources."[31]

The destroyer crews were first "stunned," then ecstatic, as they learned of the orders via flashing light from *Wadsworth*. Recalling the Irish "colleens" at home, the prospect of girls became the chief topic of thought and conversation. Aboard *McDougal*, "The crew went about singing 'My Wild Irish Rose,' 'Mother Machree' and 'Tipperary.'"[32]

Division 8 made the passage to Queenstown in nine days through typical midspringtime seas, rough and windy. Taussig found that during most of the voyage, his small, narrow ships could best steam at only twelve knots, "and we have been rolling so much that the mess table has not been set up" since the day of departure from Boston. "We have been holding our plates in our laps." One can only imagine conditions in the cramped and crowded crew's quarters aft. Passage was beyond the fuel capacity of the destroyers, and Taussig's ships were the first ever in the United States Navy to be refueled under way.

Maumee was a three-year-old, fourteen-thousand-ton vessel deliberately designed as a "fuel ship." Young Chet Nimitz, who had designed the ship's diesel engines, had tinkered with the possibility of underway refueling while the oiler was undergoing overhaul. He and the ship's officers studied the deck plans of the navy's more recent destroyers, including the location of fuel-filling valves, chocks, bits, "and strong points for towing." Designing towing rigs and drafting plans for underway refueling, Nimitz and his colleagues distributed their work "to any destroyer that might need them." Taussig and his captains, ever alert and eager for new ideas, were thus prepared for the refueling exercise that would guarantee them passage all the way to Ireland. *Maumee* took station some three hundred miles south of Cape Farewell on the southern tip of Greenland and performed the job flawlessly. Heavy seas forced the refueling to be done ship by ship on the oiler's leeward side at just five knots. But Division 8 completed the task in less than a day and steamed on toward Ireland, though persistent leaks in *Wainwright*'s condenser forced the division to stop several times in midocean.

A planned rendezvous with one British destroyer failed to materialize. On May 3, another found the American ships and, through calming seas, led them into Queenstown the following morning at fifteen knots.[33]

Taussig had wondered if anyone in Britain knew that an American destroyer force was on its way. He would soon find out. His division entered harbor under a brilliant sun that shone "on the green hills rising above the town." Across sparkling waters, the Americans saw that ships in the harbor flew the Stars and Stripes; the gesture was matched by "public buildings and private houses" throughout the town, while "along the shore, thousands of people cheered and waved." Several days later, Taussig noted that the people and authorities continued to "make considerable fuss over our arrival." British naval authorities—including Jellicoe himself—cordially greeted the Yanks in person or by letter. The following week, Sims wrote Daniels directly of the "excellent impression given by our officers and the ships and crews under their command." The hosts were surprised by the self-contained qualities of their guests' ships. Unlike British destroyers, American ships required little yard time, even after a strenuous transocean voyage. "The vessels themselves caused a great deal of complimentary comment," Sims added, "and, contrary to expectations were found to be well equipped for their prospective duty, with the single exception of 'depth charges.'"

Sims later wrote of the enormous emotional impact generated by his navy's arrival in the war zone. At home there was pride when word came that Taussig's destroyers had reached Queenstown. A far greater sense of relief was generated in Britain among a public most of whom—the London upper crust notwithstanding—were well aware of living amid a "dreadful tragedy" made manifest on clear days along the Sussex and Kentish coasts by the sound of distant gunfire erupting on the western front just beyond the Channel. A motion-picture photographer had come aboard each of Taussig's ships as soon as they arrived, and rumor had it that his film was actually flown to London for showing in the movie palaces the following day or two. Whatever "spiritual" value the rabidly Anglophilic Sims may have ascribed to Taussig's arrival, no Briton could escape realization that the first contingent of American warships "represented . . . the material assistance which our limitless resources and our almost inexhaustible supply of men would bring to a cause which was really in desperate straits."[34]

The traditional role of all navies to uphold and extend social courtesies and pleasantries was punctiliously followed by both sides. Movie cameramen recorded the American officers' every public move. In a famous exchange during their first meeting at dinner, host Sir Lewis Bayly, commander of British forces in Ireland, supposedly asked Taussig how soon he and his ships would be ready for sea. Taussig—a veteran of Sims's rigorous Atlantic destroyer flotilla—allegedly replied, "We are ready now, sir, except, of course for refueling!"[35] The young American commander would prove as good as his word.

He also proved a born diplomat at a time when the British desperately needed help. Springtime was coming to Northwest Europe and its adjacent Atlantic waters with steadily improving weather and ever more hours of sunlight for the U-boats to do their work. The American lieutenant commander and his British overseer quickly established a smooth working relationship. "This principle of cooperation" remained steadfast as the American destroyer presence at Queenstown grew. The force soon became "an American Unit" commanded by Sims in London but always subordinate to British direction. It was, Taussig noted, a pattern quite similar to that which already obtained on the western front, where British forces under Marshal Douglas Haig and, by 1918, American forces under John Pershing "operated under orders from Marshal Foch in conjunction with the French Army." Taussig later wrote that the degree of efficient cooperation between the two national navies at Queenstown far surpassed his fondest imaginings and "has seldom, if ever, been equaled in its smoothness and effectiveness."[36] The happy scene was marred by a single blemish. The destroyer crews eagerly awaited shore leave and the chance of an encounter with Ireland's famed colleens. Alas, the coxswain who took Taussig ashore on his initial visit returned "glum." "If I saw one, I saw a hundred," he reported, "and not a one had any teeth. Their hair looked like rope and they had no shape. You can have 'em," he concluded.[37]

On June 4, less than a month after the first American destroyers reached Ireland, a half-dozen armed yachts left the Brooklyn Navy Yard and steamed slowly down the harbor. Manned by regular navy officers, their crews, in the words of their future commanding officer in France, included men "from more different walks of life than probably ever assembled on a man of war." One yacht crewman expressed the matter with greater pungency. With a mixture of contempt and affection, he characterized his mates as "green a lot of landlubbers that ever stumbled down a gangplank for the first time. Only two were experienced competent seamen. The rest varied from a farm hand to designer of theatrical costumes, from city gangster to newspaper artist. . . . They looked for nothing else than getting sick."[38]

For more than a month, work was pushed to the utmost to prepare the yachts for foreign service. Furnishings and decorations of peaceful days were removed and stored in Brooklyn warehouses. White sides and glittering brightwork were hidden under coats of battle gray. Fore and aft, three-inch guns were mounted, and guns of smaller caliber were located on the upper decks. Cutlasses and rifles lined bulkheads of paneled oak or mahogany. Everywhere about the ships, improvised quarters, in former smoking rooms, libraries, and sun parlors, housed crews expanded by wartime necessity to four or five times the original quota required to operate the yachts in time of peace.

The small warships tarried for five days at Tompkinsville and then on June 9 set out to sea on a leisurely journey to Brest via Bermuda and the Azores. They were the USS *Kanawha*, *Noma*, *Harvard*, *Vedette Christabel*, and *Sultana*. Fittingly, and probably deliberately, they arrived at the French port on July 4 and promptly became the "U.S. Patrol Squadrons Operating in European Waters." Together with sister ships *Corsair* and *Aphrodite*, which had arrived a few days earlier, they were the first American naval vessels to operate in French waters.

The armed yachtsmen found immediate employment. Shortly before entering harbor, *Noma* sighted a periscope. Hours later, SS *Orleans* was torpedoed, possibly by the same submarine that *Noma* had sighted. *Sultana* brought the merchant ship's thirty-seven crewmen and thirteen armed guardsmen into Brest. Ten days after arrival, squadron commander Captain W. B. Fletcher and his staff established quarters ashore "and began the first active cooperation with the French Navy against the enemy submarines." Within hours, the yachts commenced "strenuous patrol activities" out of Brest. As a result of their "constant," "continuous," and "thorough" activities, U-boat attacks along the coast sensibly diminished. Five other armed yachts reached Brest by early autumn, the last three coming through heavy storms with "badly leaking decks." The newcomers displayed such "unusually fantastic schemes of camouflage" that they were immediately known as "the Easter Egg Fleet," since "every conceivable color" had "been incorporated in a riotous speckled pattern on their sides."[39]

As the armed yachts and destroyers made their first contributions to the American war effort, the army under command of General John J. "Black Jack" Pershing prepared its own "First Expeditionary Division" as an initial token of American resolve to fight on the western front. The division's organization, muster, domestic transport, and shipment across the Atlantic via convoy became the template of the American experience in World War I, as two million men followed "the First" to France in the eighteen months before the Armistice.

The division comprised roughly fourteen thousand troops in two infantry brigades, a field artillery brigade, a regiment of engineers, separate machine-gun and field-signal battalions, and supporting supply, medical, commissary, ammunition, ordnance repair, and sanitation forces. It was cobbled together from battle-hardened units in the Southwest, mainly Texas and Arizona, that had fought border wars with Mexican bandits in recent years together with a few enthusiastic recruits who had enlisted just before or after the nation's entry into the war. On June 3, the troops began moving toward their port of embarkation, Hoboken, New Jersey. The division history noted that "every effort was made to keep the movement secret," but people along the route, already whipped up into war excitement, if not frenzy, "guessed the destination and cheered as they passed." The soldiers picked up the mood. "The men were in a state of high enthusiasm and were proud of the distinction that came to their regiments by being selected in recognition of their efficiency. . . . In their imagination, adventure and great deeds lay before them and the present was relatively unimportant. Partings were not sad for them because all expected to return," and they spent their energies consoling those left behind who did not entertain such sanguine convictions.[40]

As the troop trains approached Hoboken on June 8 and 9, they were stopped to wait for night. Then under cover of darkness, officers and sergeants disembarked the men and marched them through empty back streets to the city piers, where ten hastily converted troopships awaited. By daylight on the tenth, they were all on board, and the vessels cast off and dropped down to an anchorage in lower New York Bay to await their naval escort.

At the moment, the navy possessed just two transports of its own: *Henderson* was in the final stages of construction; *Hancock* was old, slow, and leaky. Britain "had ships ready for use," but only a handful had yet crossed the Atlantic. No fewer than seventeen German passenger and cargo vessels had been seized in Atlantic ports immediately upon the declaration of war. Chief among these prizes was the enormous and still fairly new liner *Vaterland*, which was slightly larger than the late *Titanic*. But German crews had done a hasty job of sabotage, forcing American shipyards to take the German vessels in hand for rehabilitation and reconversion to wartime use. The work went quickly, but in the interim the hard-pressed navy was forced to obtain needed vessels from over a half-dozen steamship companies.[41]

Late in May, Daniels and Benson transferred Admiral Albert Gleaves from his post as head of the Atlantic Fleet destroyer force to "Commander, Convoy Operations in the Atlantic," soon to become the "Cruiser and Transport Service." Gleaves was delighted with the move, since his command was by now being systematically denuded of vessels for service in European waters. At least one of Mayo's staff officers, however, was outraged that his boss had been left completely out of the decision; Gleaves was a capable officer. His departure "deprived the fleet of the destroyers and auxiliary craft" of the leadership that "would be essential if it were to be actively employed *as a whole* against the enemy." Traveling to Washington for orders or directions, Gleaves was told by Josephus Daniels: "Admiral, you are going to the most important, the most difficult, and the most hazardous duty assigned to the Navy. Good bye." Gleaves then returned to Norfolk and sailed his flagship, the armored cruiser *Seattle*, to New York to gather what resources he could find for his navy's first adventure in modern convoying.[42]

He discovered a host of problems that had to be solved within days before the troops arrived to embark. The requisitioned transports had all been mail steamers or fruit carriers, with limited passenger carrying capabilities. None of the vessels had been built with watertight integrity as a prime factor; should a vessel be torpedoed, the existing arrangement of compartments and bulkheads would make mass escape difficult, if not impossible. Given time constraints, however, little could be done in the way of fundamental structural alterations. Instead, in less than two weeks, guns were placed at the bows and sterns of each transport and crews drafted from the navy to man them, lookout stations and internal communications systems were established, and berthing accommodations were hastily fitted in each transport, along with mess facilities and food-storage areas. "Sanitation of the ships was improved as far as possible." Life preservers were procured in a quantity 10 percent higher than the number of embarked troops and crew, and "sufficient life rafts were provided so that if lifeboats on one side could not be launched because of the listing of the ship or other reasons, all hands could still be accommodated."[43]

The escort posed its own problems. It was a decidedly mixed bag of age and capabilities, reflecting the transitional state of American naval operations as emphasis shifted from fleet action to antisubmarine warfare. In all, Gleaves could muster one armored cruiser (*Seattle*), a scout cruiser (*Birmingham*), two otherwise undesignated cruisers (*Charleston, St. Louis*), a former German auxiliary cruiser (*DeKalb*) that had been seized on the outbreak of war, two converted yachts (*Corsair, Aphrodite*), armed colliers *Cyclops* and *Kanawha*, together with *Hancock* acting as a cruiser transport and thirteen destroyers. Among the destroyers were the new *Allen* and *Shaw* (the latter having just arrived after a hasty summons from the West Coast). Thus, despite its heterogeneous nature, the screen represented a formidable force.[44]

On June 7, just a week after his arrival in New York, Gleaves issued his first set of orders. The convoy would sail in four separate groups, the fastest (fifteen knots), followed by the second capable of making fourteen knots sustained, the third thirteen knots, "and the fourth group, 11 knots."[45] Each group escort was led by either an armored or a first-class cruiser. Gleaves and Benson immediately grasped the fact that these largely useless components of the battle fleet could find sudden and highly effective employment as convoy escorts. Not only were they fast and well armed enough to keep a U-boat or two or three under the waves, but the admittedly scant number of six- and ten-inch guns that many carried could nonetheless keep all but the boldest enemy heavy units at bay, should Admiral Franz von Hipper with his German battle cruisers somehow break out into the Atlantic to raid the convoy routes. Of equal importance, the cruisers had the coal-bunkerage capacities to make the entire transocean voyage without refueling.

The thirteen destroyers at Gleaves's disposal were another matter. They ranged from *Wilkes*, *Allen*, and *Shaw*, commissioned the year before, to the "flivvers" *Lamson*, *Flusser*, and *Preston*, tiny 740-ton coal-burning ships that had been in commission for eight to ten years—a lifetime given the rapid pace of destroyer development.[46] Even *Wilkes*, *Shaw*, and *Allen* would need to refuel once. Gleaves thus ordered *Maumee* to maintain station and refuel the destroyer screen. He also placed fuel bunkers aboard the armed collier *Kanawha* as added insurance. The admiral later noted with pardonable pride that "oiling at sea was one of the maneuvers" that he had developed during his time as commander of the Atlantic Fleet destroyer force. On May 28 *Maumee* had refueled the second division of destroyers dispatched to Queenstown "at the rate of 35,000 gallons per hour in moderate seas, and with the wind blowing at a half gale."[47]

Unfortunately, the seven "flivvers" could not make it to European waters with just one refueling. Gleaves ordered them to stay with the convoy as far eastward as possible after topping up their bunkers, so "as to permit them to proceed to St. Johns, Newfoundland, without again refueling." The several "one tonners" of the screen could and would take the convoy all the way to Europe and report to Queenstown for further duty. In a later, undated, order, Gleaves informed the convoy that an indeterminate number of "U.S. Destroyers from England will be met" at a certain unnamed position to reinforce the screen as the convoy passed through the U-boat killing grounds east of longitude 17'W. Finally, the "coal burning destroyers" would escort the convoy only to such "distance as will permit destroyer to return to U.S. without refueling."[48]

The escort also included *Corsair*, *Kanawha*, and *Aphrodite*. These three steam yachts (*Corsair* had been J. P. Morgan's personal vessel) had been acquired just weeks before the American declaration of war as part of the 1916 program to identify and, when necessary, requisition civilian shipping for wartime antisubmarine use. Prior to formal commissioning in late April and mid-May, they were fitted out with three-inch .50-caliber guns and depth charges. With generous cruising ranges, Gleaves assumed all three would successfully complete the entire trip across. Should that not be possible, they would be directed to Fayal, in the Azores, to refuel "and thence to destination." They would remain in European waters upon completion of their convoy duties. *Aphrodite* would become a station ship in England; *Corsair* and *Kanawha* would see extended and honorable service off France.[49]

Sailing date was initially set for June 9, but various logistic and technical problems delayed departure for five days. The restless soldiers sitting aboard their troopships in sight of the then modest spires of Manhattan were kept busy with endless drills (including abandon-ship exercises) and physical training. At last, on the morning of the fourteenth, the transports and escorts of the first group made their way down the bay to the Ambrose Channel Lightship, where they made rendezvous and set off toward the battlefields of Europe. Groups 2 and 3 followed within hours; Group 4 departed three days later. In countless towns, villages, and cities across the country, "there was much anxiety." Enemy submarines were out there somewhere on the broad Atlantic; when and where would they strike? Aboard the troopships, "daily rumors" spread among the fourteen thousand men of the First Division that "submarines were near." As the hastily mustered gun crews aboard the transports "practiced at imaginary targets . . . the soldiers enjoyed speculating" on their skills. Troop morale, already high, was further enhanced by repeated drills and by the realization that the navy was determined to keep its charges as safe as humanly possible. And as an additional bonus, the North Atlantic this June proved benign.[50]

However, Gleaves and his group commanders were kept on edge by a series of incidents. *Terry* of Group 1 never got out of New York Harbor, fouling its propellers in the torpedo net in the narrows. The Brooklyn Navy Yard made hasty repairs, and the destroyer subsequently sailed three days later with Group 4. *Corsair* proved unable to maintain speed with the first group due to an "inexperienced" engine-room crew. Within hours, Gleaves had it drop back to escort the slightly slower Group 2, while bringing destroyer *Fanning* up to take its place. Two days out, *Roe*, a sister 740-ton "flivver" to *Fanning* and *Terry*, developed what was described as "serious trouble"; Gleaves ordered it to lie to, make temporary repairs, and return to New York. It would reach European waters soon after, escorting a later convoy across the Atlantic. Shortly after *Roe's* forced departure, *Lamson*, *Preston*, and *Flusser* turned back as their coal supplies inexorably dwindled.[51]

Nerves tightened as the four groups, minus six of their original escorts, steamed toward the submarine zone. "One night on board the *Seattle* . . . one of the ship's powerful searchlights was suddenly flaunted across the sky." The beam was quickly doused but had been clearly, if briefly, visible for miles. A sailor had inadvertently turned it on; "no evidence of intent or of disaffection could be found." But, true to his name, *Seattle's* captain, D. W. Blamer, was determined to make an example of the unfortunate young man; potentially fatal careless-ness could not be ignored or dismissed in wartime, and the unknown seaman was "severely punished by court-martial as a warning." On June 22, four days out of St. Nazaire, at longitude 25'50"W, Group 1 believed itself to be under submarine attack. Lookouts on *Seattle* saw "in the extremely phosphorescent water . . . the wake of a submarine crossing fifty yards ahead" of the bow from starboard to port. "A few seconds later, *DeKalb* and *Havanna* sighted torpedoes and opened fire" with their few deck guns as the alleged torpedoes whizzed harmlessly past both ships. The convoy columns promptly swung smartly to starboard and port and increased to full speed. The incident passed; *Seattle's* crew subsequently heard unfounded rumors that French intelligence had learned that U-boats from a secret base in the Azores had planned to intercept the con-voy.[52] No such base existed.

But had an attack in fact taken place? Longitude 25'W was roughly 250 miles beyond the U-boat's habitual hunting grounds east of longitude 17'W, where international shipping began to funnel into ports in the British Isles and northwestern France. A small cluster of ships would have been extreme-ly difficult to find in the broad ocean reaches. Moreover, it was night and the water phosphorous. Throughout the war, as Sims noted, American sailors hastily drafted from farms and city streets across the country—together with their landlubberly soldier cousins—were often spooked by sea conditions into believing there were enemy submarines where in fact none operated. In Group 3, *Kanawha* claimed to have sighted a U-boat, and the ship went to general quarters, but no one else in the convoy saw anything and the crew of the armed steam yacht soon stood down.

However, the second convoy group, now reinforced by *Davis* from Queenstown together with half-dozen British destroyers from Southampton, reported a far more plausible incident late in the morning of June 26, at longitude 6'W, roughly 100 miles off the French coast. Two U-boats were sighted and "successfully evad-ed," while the American destroyer *Cummings* rushed at one of the submarines, churning the seas with its screws, its four "pipes" belching black smoke that filled the sky. It must have been a frightening sight to the alarmed U-boat crew on deck who promptly dove below as their submarine did the same. The tenacious destroyer followed down the submarine's bubbly wake and dropped a depth charge whose explosion produced "several pieces of lumber and oil" along with some further "debris." But, as would so often be the case in the coming seventeen months of war, no one could determine if the U-boat had been sunk.[53]

As Group 2 successfully fought off the two U-boats, Group 1 reached St. Nazaire to the inexpressible relief of soldier and sailor alike. The last moments at sea proved to be the most nerve-racking as Group 1 waited offshore through the night for French pilot boats to take it into harbor. The convoy had just sailed through debris-filled waters in the Bay of Biscay, testament not only to the presence of enemy submarines but also to their effectiveness. Several U-boats were reported still operating in the immediate area, yet to Gleaves's astonishment and relief, none attacked, thereby forfeiting an incredible opportunity to sink not only transports and warships but American morale as well. As the convoy at last reached harbor, "cheers broke forth and enthusiasm rose with the realization that the voyage was approaching a safe end." For Gleaves and his sailors, arrival in France (all four groups reached St. Nazaire by July 2) was victory in itself. The "entire country, which felt we were stepping into the unknown," now knew that their "efficient" navy could safely convoy the "hundreds of thousands" of troops "to come."[54]

As Gleaves sailed home to oversee the entire enterprise, he pondered the many lessons that the success of America's first convoy revealed, not the least of which was the value of the armored cruisers as escorts. Following the success of *Seattle* as both a war and command ship, all of these strange vessels were hastily collected at Norfolk and New York. The story of one encapsulated much of the navy's experience in the early days of the war. *South Dakota* was at Bremerton, Washington, when Wilson issued his declaration. Peacetime uncertainties had reduced its normal 830-man crew to a skeleton. Moving with an alacrity that would have stunned Taussig had he known of it, 800 sailors from the Naval Militia of the Pacific Northwest were promptly drafted into the national naval volunteer force and put aboard the thirteen-thousand-ton four stacker. *South Dakota* was soon ordered through the Panama Canal and into the South Atlantic to search for the armed German merchant raider *Seeadler*. In November, following fruitless searches, the thirteen-year-old cruiser with its four eight-inch and fourteen six-inch guns was ordered to convoy duty and subsequently made eight round-trips across the Atlantic from Halifax, New York, and Hampton Roads.

As was true of so many ships and their men, sea duty proved rewarding but frustrating. According to a later press release, "At no time during the war" did *South Dakota*'s crew ever "get ashore in Europe. As soon as they delivered their convoy to destroyers off the European coast, they headed back for America."[55]

Coming ashore in France, soldiers and sailors alike found a population numbed, stunned, and deeply corrupted by war. Like other French Atlantic ports, St. Nazaire was overcrowded, its facilities overwhelmed. Troops had to disembark in small waves. Some had not stretched their legs on land for twenty days. The various elements of the First Division were quickly marched to Camp 1, about three miles from town, where barracks had been hastily constructed by German prisoners of war. The work was shoddy, the buildings "inadequate. None of the comforts and conveniences that later divisions found at St. Nazaire or experienced in the modern camps in the homeland existed for this pioneer band of American soldiers."

What was available to soldiers and sailors alike was vice, at once ready and lurid. The soldiers of the First Division were mostly a hard-bitten lot, toughened and coarsened by years of frontier duty. The farm and college boys, the city clerks and small-town apprentices who followed, were heartbreakingly naive. Only the very top levels of increasingly rigid industrial class society had traveled much. Farm and village America from which so many recruits—army and navy—came remained as it had always been: desperately insular and unsophisticated, where lives spun out simply without motion pictures (still largely confined to cities and Middletowns), commercial radio, or other forms of mass communications and entertainment. Boys who counted a trip to Chicago from Cedar Rapids or Muncie as a lifetime experience were sent off to faraway military and naval centers for hasty training, then "ferried three thousand miles across the Atlantic," in sweaty, bewildered anxiety. America's homesick, profoundly dislocated lads were ripe for plucking.

Lawrence Stallings, who was there, remembered it all. "Private John Doe" (and Seaman Bill Smith as well) "stepped upon French soil and went with his buddies to the nearest bar where he had his first taste of alcohol, other than the bite of sherry in a Christmas syllabub, or the port wine his father poured down the hole in the center of the holiday fruitcake. After four two-ounce shots of *Rhum Negrito* topped off with two fizzes made with a concoction of the French labeled *Niger Gin*, a steerer took him and his friends to one of the six major league brothels on the waterfront, where the girls worked forty to forty-five tricks each twenty-four hours," until, worn out, they were relegated to one of the many "minor leagues," where their burnout advanced steadily.

Initially, both military and naval authorities assumed a hands-off policy toward the conduct of their personnel. "The liberty restrictions for the Navy were simple: keep out of any disturbances, keep out of restricted areas, and obey the shore patrol." As one officer told his libertymen, he cared not a whit if they spent the night with a woman; his job was to keep them out of trouble. After roughly four months, it became clear that French women and their "steerers" *were* the trouble, as venereal disease rates in both services skyrocketed. To the French, the Americans were constantly making "a great uproar in the 'Red light' district" of St. Nazaire—and later Brest and the other French ports of debarkation—that was quieted only by the "truncheons" of the military police. To the Americans, it was innocence defiled. By midautumn the costs of vice had become so pronounced that both the US Army and the US Navy forbade their people from openly consorting with French women on pain of nonjudiciary punishment or worse.[56]

But they always had huge, ungovernable Paris, where military writ ran nowhere insofar as vice was concerned. Just several hours away by train from the coastal ports, Paris welcomed "thousands" of bluejackets in 1917–18, anxious for all and any sorts of fun they could find. This would be particularly true of those destroyer and armed-yacht sailors usually based in Ireland or England, where life ashore was astringent and whose ships came to France just once or twice, escorting the troop convoys all the way through the submarine zone. One contemporary source stated that no fewer than seventy-five thousand girls and women sold themselves on the streets of the City of Light during World War 1. Many had come from elsewhere, "husbandless," their spouses either at war or dead. They were left to fend for themselves as best they could in a vast city made heedless and brutal by war. Their gaiety was forced and anxious. Professor Still notes that "more than 2,500 hotels were open . . . most of them houses of assignation." Those prostitutes who worked the streets solicited openly, boldly confronting individuals and groups of men, taking their arms and making their propositions.[57] Military and naval authorities could only wonder, in the words of a wartime song, how you were going to keep them down on the farm—or in barracks or on ships—after they'd seen Paree.

A handful of sailors resisted temptation, finding interest, if not adventure, in other parts of western France or disgust at its wartime degradation. Young seaman Searcy B. Dysart found himself "among people with a strange language, different kind of money and strange customs." Gazing at several cathedrals in "very old" Rouen one day, he concluded that "they must have been real pretty when they were new." Chief Petty Officer Leroy Collins found Paris a marvel of tourist attractions from Napoleon's Tomb to "3 different Cathedrals." Bordeaux, however, "is a rotten town in fact so rotten it stinks."[58]

The initial contingent of the American Expeditionary Force, like the millions who came after, began their training on French soil. Exasperated captains and majors of the transportation corps engaged in "a turmoil of disputes" with officials of the French National Railway to get the First Division and the thousands of Yanks who soon followed into more permanent and satisfactory training facilities on the Marne, closer to the battlefields.[59] But thanks to the US and the British merchant marines, the Yanks were about to come over in an ever-greater flood.

An effective expanding convoy system would require some months to fully implement. In the meantime, it was imperative to maintain pressure on the U-boats in their operational zones while bringing American destroyermen up to the highest standards of antisubmarine warfare. Taussig may have made naval history of a sort by telling Admiral Bayly upon arrival that his six-ship command was ready for sea at any time. But Bayly knew better. The first task was installation of proper equipment. *Wadsworth* and its sisters promptly went into Haulbowline dockyard to off-load excessive supplies and to be hastily fitted with depth charges and "fighting lights" for emergency identification (which neither Taussig nor his officers and men had ever heard about). As the American crews began rigorous, if hasty, training by their British hosts in the Royal Navy radio and signals systems, Bayly and Commander E. R. G. R. Evans, the official liaison officer with the Yanks, used the several dinners and social occasions before Taussig and his commanders set sail on their first patrols to provide the enthusiastic novices with some idea of what to expect once at sea. To their credit, Taussig and his people did not allow confidence to shade into arrogance. They listened to what they were told.

Evans was a remarkable officer; second in command of Scott's ill-fated Antarctic expedition in 1911–12, he was in the process of becoming the youngest captain in the Royal Navy due to heroic exploits against a German destroyer force in the Channel a few weeks before. He had amassed a wealth of information on antisubmarine warfare that he gladly shared with his mesmerized American listeners. Bayly added his own thoughts that came out as a list of cautionary dos and don'ts. One day as the American captains were leaving Admiralty House, Bayly confided that his superiors in Whitehall were "dreadfully afraid" of insulting their new allies; Bayly would have none of it. His job was to be "perfectly frank" and to keep his cousins informed whether they were doing well or ill.[60]

Bayly preached that above all else, the Americans must understand that the moment they cleared harbor, they were in mortal danger of submarine attacks and must act accordingly. "Constant vigilance" was the price of survival. "Look out for yourselves—for a lucky shot, a chance shot may end your career." Bayly planned to pair each American destroyer with a British partner on six-day search-and-destroy patrols in the Irish Sea and adjacent Atlantic waters out to 20'W latitude, after which they would put into Berehaven in Bantry Bay—an incessantly windswept "place . . . gloomy and hopeless . . . made dismal by low clouds and rain"—for two days of rest and then out again individually for another six days and two back in port at Queenstown. "Once a month," Bayly added severely, "or say after five hundred hours of operation, you will be permitted to have a period of five days in which to overhaul your boilers and rest." While this was the schedule followed by the handful of available British destroyers, it soon proved too much for any ship or crew on patrol to adequately fulfill, particularly once convoy escort was added to their burden.

At sea, Bayly continued, destroyer crews must beware of stationary periscopes; they might be decoys with bombs attached. Destroyers encountering survivors of sunken ships should beware of rescue; only after the entire immediate area had been thoroughly searched was it "permissible to pick them up." Torpedoed vessels that remained afloat should be approached with special caution. U-boats that had formerly sailed away as rapidly as possible were now remaining in the area, hoping to loot the damaged victims if conditions favored. So, "if you see a ship struck, or come upon one having been struck, be sure to go after the submarine. The rescue work must wait," for the three chief duties in antisubmarine warfare were to destroy enemy U-boats, to convoy and protect shipping, and only then "to save lives if you can. . . . To lose an opportunity to sink a submarine means he lives to sink other peaceful vessels and destroy more lives."[61]

There was more: Destroyers were not built to tow large transports or cargo ships and should never tow a distressed sister ship unless within a convoy. Searchlights should never be used; they disclosed positions. Therefore, night rescues should be done as best as possible without illumination. "On moonlight nights keep a cover on the searchlight as the moon's rays may brighten the surface of the lens, revealing a ship's position." And, of course, no matches should be lit on open decks after dark. A destroyer's speed must depend on wind and sea, but no destroyer should steam at less than thirteen knots. In convoy, "be sure to change course at break joint with the convoyed ship—that is, if the convoying vessel ahead of her turns to port the vessel convoyed should turn to starboard." On independent patrol, each destroyer was responsible for one to three zones that had been marked out in squares of thirty to at most fifty miles. Each zone encompassing the most heavily traveled shipping routes rated a warship. A destroyer should never simply proceed from one end of the assigned area to the other and back again; a U-boat skipper would quickly pick up the pattern. There should be frequent and irregular course changes, and captains should exploit fog, smoke, haze, or squalls to gain the greatest possible advantage in U-boat hunting. To further obscure positions and intentions, radio signals should be short in port as well as at sea; once written orders had been hand-delivered at Queenstown or Berehaven, a destroyer skipper "did not need to request permission to depart, but could leave at his discretion."[62]

Their heads reeling from this and much other advice, the six skippers took their destroyers to sea on Tuesday afternoon, May 8, 1917. Clearing the swept channel five miles beyond Daunt Lightship, "we stood out for our various areas," and promptly ran into an entire flock of phantom U-boats. *McDougal* was the first to open fire on a buoy that the British minesweepers had planted to mark their field of activity. As its bemused sister *Porter* stood by, the destroyer blazed away with its forward four-inch gun, and the captain took out his stopwatch, later observing that his command "broke all records for '*misses per gun per minute*.'" Shortly thereafter, it was *Wadsworth's* turn. A lookout reported a periscope. "Down we charged on it, full speed," only to discover a boat hook floating with the hook downward.[63]

As the vessels steamed on, keen watches were maintained on fo'c'sles, and bridges, in crow's nests, and on the roofs of the afterdeck houses. "If during those first four days of patrol duty there was anything afloat within range of visibility that was not seen and reported, I should like to know what it was." Taussig and his bridge officers sent the crew to general quarters "on an average of at least half a dozen times daily, and the number of times the forecastle gun was manned cannot now be estimated." On the first night out, *Wadsworth's* officer of the deck dropped a depth charge on what he thought might be "the luminous wake of a submerged submarine." Nothing came of the incident. Captain Evans, along for the ride as observer, was not overly impressed with his hosts' keenness; having fought the U-boats for more than two years, he was plainly concerned that Taussig and the other American skippers might be wearing out their crews. But Taussig had some good points to make in defense. Not only had Bayly and others ashore painted the U-boat war in perhaps overly lurid colors, but out at sea, once alone in their respective patrol areas, the Yanks would find the waters "strewn" with wreckage from recently torpedoed ships. "We could steam through miles and miles of this stuff, barrels, boxes, crates, lumber," and other materials. "Now and then there would be a big patch of oil spreading out a mile or more" on the calm or choppy gray waters, "marking the place where some tanker had gone down. Open boats, usually empty, and now and then grewsome [sic] dead horses would float by." SOS signals from a distant ship were often received together with word that a patrolling vessel in the vicinity had picked up survivors.[64]

Along with its sister ships, *Wadsworth* encountered a number of freighters passing through on the way to a French or British port. Taussig escorted each ship to the limits of his zone, "breaking joints" by passing across the freighter's bow every time it changed its zigzag course. Having reached the zone limit, either *Wadsworth* contacted the destroyer, sloop, or trawler in the adjacent area, passing on escort responsibilities, or if, as was often the case, there was no Allied vessel available, the freighter was waved on with expressions of good luck to take its chances steaming alone for the last portion of its voyage. Exceptions were made for especially valuable ships that might be escorted up to a hundred miles beyond a destroyer's zone of responsibility until another warship appeared to maintain the escort.[65]

On its first patrol, *Wadsworth* was out only four days while the other five vessels were assigned patrols of six and eight days in order to establish a pattern in which no more than a third of the patrolling force was in port at one time. But even less than a hundred hours at sea wore down the American crews; eight days were clearly too much. While this first antisubmarine war hardly matched the intensity and drama of the second a quarter century later, it did demand ceaseless vigilance and consistently excellent seamanship and seakeeping that, along with the stress of seemingly endless submarine sightings, emotionally drained officers and crew alike. "I was very tired," Taussig later admitted. "It seemed to me then that unless we relaxed our vigilance . . . or unless our personnel was increased, the schedule would be too hard to continue indefinitely." Evans emphatically agreed and upon his return to Queenstown "evidently told Admiral Bayly so." Bayly promptly reduced the patrol time to five days out, three days in, which relieved stress markedly.[66]

Taussig had already grasped the essence of the U-boat war. In a diary entry following the first cruise he expressed confidence:

> At present the submarines are avoiding the patrol vessels and are going after un-
> escorted merchant ships where there is very little danger to them in the attack. If
> this is so the best defense will be to have so many patrol vessels that all valuable
> ships can be escorted as soon as they get in the danger area. . . . If enough patrol

vessels become available to keep the submarines down or make it extremely dangerous for them to attack merchant vessels, then their operations become a failure from their point of view, and in order to get at the merchant ships they must first destroy the patrol vessels. Perhaps the conditions will require this action on their part before very long.[67]

Omens were certainly favorable, for more and more American warships were filling the harbors at Queenstown and Berehaven (the latter already choked with torpedoed ships that had somehow limped in or been towed in). Bringing *Wadsworth* into Queenstown after his second patrol, Taussig discovered another division of US destroyers in harbor; like his own, they were all "thousand tonners," the most modern vessels the navy possessed. Ten days later, a third division steamed in, this time comprising 750-ton "flivvers," older ships from 1910 to 1912, but still eminently capable of antisubmarine work. By the end of July, thirty-seven US destroyers supported by two depot ships were based in Queenstown.[68]

The Yanks divided their time between patrolling and escorting the convoys of American reinforcements for France that they met far out at sea "or the ordinary convoys of merchantmen coming to the British Isles." The experiences of *Jenkins* were typical. The 887-ton, 293-foot flivver with its 107-man crew arrived at Queenstown with the third group of destroyers on June 1, 1917. Just ten days later, while escorting a single merchantman, it collided lightly with the 250-foot British minelayer sent to relieve it. "Only a few rivets were popped and water flooded a few spaces." There were no casualties, and after hasty repairs at Queenstown, DD-42 was back on patrol. On July 17, a U-boat was sighted dead ahead, and *Jenkins* crammed on speed as the German "pulled the plug" and went under. *Jenkins* dropped several depth charges over the submarine's presumed position with no result.

The destroyer witnessed some action two months later. The British Q ship *Cullist* had flushed a U-boat and damaged it. The German "made a run for it," unwittingly heading straight for *Jenkins* and its sister *Ericsson*. The light of a late-afternoon day on the eastern Atlantic was fading. "The boys from the *Ericsson* got off two shots" that unfortunately missed. Then the ship's skipper decided to ram the clearly damaged submarine, but this, too, missed. In growing darkness, the U-boat got away. By midautumn, *Jenkins* was fully caught up in the convoy war, steaming to meet one cluster of twenty ships that had arrived at "rendezvous 'B'" five hours ahead of time, protecting broken-down vessels as they made hasty repairs, assisting torpedoed vessels, and picking up survivors.

Jenkins's sisters shared the burdens and excitements. Early on the morning of September 8, *McDougal* (DD-54) was escorting a convoy "just south of [the] Lizard [Peninsula on the Cornish coast]" when lookouts sighted a U-boat through the darkness shadowing the ships. The captain promptly rang up flank speed and circled the spot where the sub had last been seen, ordering a close pattern of the few depth charges he possessed to be dropped. Shortly, "a large amount of oil appeared on the surface," which led captain and crew to conclude that they had achieved "a likely kill." They apparently had not, though heavy damage to German nerves cannot be discounted. *Downes* (DD-45) came across in November, and operated on convoy escort duty inbound to British ports, across the Channel, and outbound to rendezvous with the ocean escorts. It also spent time patrolling against U-boats off the Irish coast, "making numerous attacks with no sure results." And finally, there was the inevitable, and inevitably melancholy, aid rendered to "distressed ships" and their crews. In July, *McDougal* plucked twenty-four survivors of a British merchantman from the sea. One afternoon several weeks later, *Conyngham* learned that the British vessel *Karina* had been torpedoed a short distance away. The destroyer "sped to her assistance," lifting thirty-nine sailors and passengers from the cold waters off the Irish coast. By November fifty-two American destroyers were operating from not only Queenstown but also Brest and Gibraltar.[69]

The demands on the navy proved never ending. Even as its destroyer force was building up at Queenstown, British authorities requested help in the Mediterranean. Despite lingering presidential concerns over the shape of the naval war, the gunboat *Sacramento* was promptly sent from New York to Gibraltar, followed shortly thereafter by the small cruiser *Birmingham*. As the American contribution slowly grew, it was incorporated into an international force of British, French, Japanese, and Italian vessels. Gibraltar was far from the main theater of naval operations, yet it was the center of the critical transportation, supply, and communications routes linking the western front with the Middle East and India. The handful of German and Austro-Hungarian submarines operating out of the Adriatic was effective in sinking unescorted merchant vessels.

In August the Admiralty placed further pressure on the naval forces at "the Rock" when it decided to run convoys between England and Port Said, Egypt, every ten days. The Convoy Section at Whitehall would be responsible for them, not the British commander in chief, Mediterranean, who was having his hands full meeting current escort commitments to convoys running between Gibraltar and Oran as well as Malta and Egypt.oweve However, there was a distinct catch to the plan. The England-to-Egypt convoys were to be "synchronized" with the Gibraltar convoys when reaching the "danger zones" on both the Atlantic and the Mediterranean sides of Gibraltar, thus requiring a substantial increase in escorts that the British, with their straitened circumstances, could not meet. According to the semiofficial British history of the naval war, while French and even Japanese destroyers appeared, "it was largely owing to the American reinforcements at Gibraltar that the local command was able to meet the calls being made upon it." Allied naval circles hoped that once an effective convoy system was introduced, losses could be brought "under control just as rapidly as . . . in the Atlantic." That, in fact, never quite happened. For the roughly five thousand American sailors who manned "a variegated assortment of scout cruisers, gunboats, coastguard cutters, yachts, and five destroyers of antique type," life at the Rock and in the Med was always "hard-pressed."

The antiquated destroyers were none other than the division of primitive 420-ton "destroyer torpedo boats" built near the turn of the century that had spent subsequent years patrolling East Asian waters from their base at Cavite, near Manila, after an epic voyage from Norfolk. Now they were summoned back westward. On August 1, the venerable *Bainbridge* led its four sisters out of Manila Bay and steamed for Suez, retracing the earlier route: Borneo, Singapore, Sri Lanka (requiring a prolonged stay for repairs), and Mumbai. The little fleet reached the southern terminus of the Suez Canal on September 23. Following a week in Port Said (no doubt no steamier than Manila), the tiny destroyers braced for submarine action. Escorting several ships from Malta to Naples, *Bainbridge*'s lookouts saw a surfaced U-boat stalking one of the merchant vessels. Literally pouring on the coal, its few guns manned, *Bainbridge* raced toward the sub, only to see it submerge. With no depth charges yet aboard, the primitive little destroyer had no choice but to break off action. The convoy reached Naples safely, and the destroyer division, after some badly needed rest, at last reached Gibraltar on October 20.[70]

By the end of the summer, the Allies and their American associates were putting the final touches on a complex and sophisticated convoy system just as the first recruits of a new two-million-man American Army—an "Expeditionary Force"—were coming out of the training camps. American forces were gathering at Gibraltar, and the rapidly expanding destroyer force at Queenstown was being augmented by an armed-yacht contingent at Brest that also periodically hosted some of the Queenstown destroyers escorting vessels all the way to France. A handful of other American sailors whose stage was the sky, not the sea, had also reached French soil by this time, determined to make their own unique contributions to the war.

The ever-accelerating American buildup in European waters (and skies) placed an enormous administrative burden on Sims. As late as August, the admiral worked with just two staff assistants, supplemented by whatever other officers whom he could purloin from elsewhere. Sims dunned his superiors in Washington for more help. A half-dozen officers arrived, and by October, with more appearing, Sims had a chief of staff, Nathan Twining; an assistant chief, W. R. Sexton; and a naval aide, John Vincent Babcock, who together with the admiral formed a kind of executive council with overall supervisory authority over various operational sections that came into existence during the last quarter of the year and on into 1918. The enormity and variety of the American effort are reflected in the breadth of the sections that included convoy routing, antisubmarine warfare, direction of ships in the cross-Channel coal trade, intelligence and counterespionage, publicity, correspondence and communication, medical care, disbursements, and aviation. By summer 1918, Sims's headquarters staff and sections oversaw the activities of 370 ships "of all classes," roughly seventy-five thousand officers and men, and hundreds of aircraft distributed over forty-five bases from Scotland to Corfu. While Sims personally signed a set of general instructions to all base and force commanders, detailed supervision of such a sprawling enterprise from a single location was clearly beyond the capabilities of any individual, executive committee, or even operational section. In a letter home, "Sims admitted to his wife that he signed routine orders 'without looking at them.'" Admiral Albert Niblack, who commanded US naval forces operating from Gibraltar, told a postwar congressional committee that he received "about fifteen cablegrams a day" from London that provided a broad range of information, including ships' sailings, transfer of officers, word of incoming supplies, and dispatch of materials together with "all kinds of information" on submarine warfare that came from Sims's operational branch. Under questioning, Niblack added that Gibraltar passed its own operational information on to London and reacted to news and information received in a timely operational manner. "We never closed."[71]

The American naval command system in Europe was thus forced to decentralize. In ways it proved a benefit, reinforcing the navy's peacetime emphasis on individual initiative. But in other ways, it produced chaos when headstrong officers with agendas of their own got off the reservation and began making command decisions without proper consultation with either Washington or London. This proved particularly the case with the navy's fledgling and ambitious aviators.

Aloft

A HUNDRED YEARS AGO, countless minds and hearts on both sides of the Atlantic were thrilled by the fact that man could actually leave the ground and soar into the near heavens on artificial wings of canvas held up by struts and wires and propelled by the newfangled internal combustion engine. No industrial technology had advanced with greater speed. In 1909, just six years after Orville Wright had staggered ten feet into the air and flown for barely two hundred feet over the sands at Kitty Hawk, Louis Blériot "performed what was then considered the perilous feat" of crossing the twenty-mile English Channel in a "heavier-than-air machine." Five years later, as Europe raced toward general war that none could as yet really foresee, fourteen pilots prepared to participate in an air race from London to Paris and return. A writer for the *International Herald Tribune* noted on July 9 that crossing the Channel by air was now "a mere incident in a day's work. Aviators have flown from London to Paris and vice versa so frequently that the feat has become a mere commonplace."

Bold engineers like American Glenn Curtiss dreamed of spanning an entire ocean in great seaplanes, and even before a treaty terminating the Great War of 1914–18 could be signed, three American seaplanes did just that, crossing the Atlantic from Newfoundland to the Azores with one continuing on to Lisbon and Plymouth. "Scarcely had that feat been accomplished" when British aviators Alcock and Brown made the first nonstop flight across the Atlantic from Newfoundland to an Irish peat bog, where they successfully set down after only sixteen hours of flight.[1]

During its first decade and a half, aviation in general developed within a complex, often helter-skelter context, but the origins of US naval aviation were

particularly complicated. The navy's acceptance of the "aeroplane" was grudging at best, despite its promising deployment at Veracruz and the subsequent
activities of a handful of daring aviators. In 1915, the department did create a
handful of enlisted support rates and billets and found funds to modestly expand
a raw training station at Pensacola on a remote corner of the Florida Panhandle.
Congress also looked askance upon naval aviation until the prospect of national
intervention in Europe's massive bloodshed became too real to ignore. The new
Aerial Age that had emerged in the skies over the western front demanded a
response, and that came in the form of a "National Advisory Committee for
Aeronautics." A year later, the House appropriated three and a half million
dollars specifically to naval aviation (a million and a half more than Secretary
Daniels and CNO Benson requested). Both a Naval Flying Corps and a Naval
Reserve Flying Corps were established to formalize recruitment, training, and
support activities, which continued to be concentrated at Pensacola. But a true
flying corps never materialized in the brief time before American entry. On
the day that Wilson signed the declaration, the navy's aircraft inventory totaled
54: 45 seaplanes, 6 "Flying Boats," 3 "land planes," and 1 airship. These various
machines—which were in the process of being standardized for efficiency of
production and operation even as they were being steadily improved—were
flown by 34 officer-pilots who in turn were supported by 14 other officers and
239 enlisted men. So as with other elements of the US military and naval establishments, a modest nucleus had been set in place for a forced-draft wartime
expansion. Secretary Daniels had now grasped the potential of airpower at sea
and was keen for his navy to operate in as many dimensions as possible.[2]

Germany's declaration of unrestricted submarine warfare galvanized the nation's growing aviation community, whose members vividly recalled the recent
shock when Hans Rose and his U-boat made their unexpected appearance in
Narragansett Bay. Some enthusiasts acquainted with the shifting tides of the war
also knew of the widely held belief in Allied circles that submarines might be
detected and destroyed more readily from the air than from the sea's surface. In
his epic if brief flight over the Channel in 1909, Blériot claimed to have seen
"a line of British submarines under water." By late 1915, British and French bi-
plane pilots were claiming submarine kills in the shallow waters off northwestern Europe, where detection was maximized and escape more difficult. Two
years later, according to one later account, Royal Naval Air Service planes "of
all types" sighted 168 U-boats and bombed 105, sinking 6, and possibly more
listed as destroyed by accident or by surface vessels. Unhappily, as was so often
the case in the antisubmarine operations of 1915–18, wartime claims were not

substantiated by postwar assessments. According to J. David Perkins's authoritative count in 1999, the only U-boat destroyed directly from the air in 1917 was UB-32, sent to a shallow grave by bombs from seaplane 8695.[3] Nonetheless, the ability to spot and attack submerged U-boats from above seemed so obvious and compelling in 1917 that the National Advisory Committee for Aeronautics immediately called for the establishment of no fewer than eight coastal patrol stations from Maine to Florida immediately upon American entry into the war. The private Aero Club of America (ACA) swiftly echoed and amplified the committee's recommendations by calling for voluntary aviation patrols.

Wilson's declaration of war prompted the Navy Department to establish an ambitious training programs for prospective flyers. It appropriated a number of privately owned airfields and aviation schools and added those of the Naval Militia at Squantum and Bay Shore on the Massachusetts coast. New base construction and programs were initiated on both coasts. Training itself was standardized. New classes of cadet pilots were formed every ninety days for an eighteen-month course (later reduced under the steadily expanding demands of wartime). Initially, both heavier- and lighter-than-air novices were to be educated together, but it was soon discovered that this approach was "impractical." While the vast majority of "pursuit"- and seaplane pilots continued to train at Pensacola and the newly acquired facilities, lighter-than-air aspirants were assigned to the "balloon and dirigible school" at Goodyear Corporation's facility in Akron, Ohio. Shortly thereafter, the department also negotiated a contract with the "Curtiss Exhibition Company," which had led the way in developing efficient heavier-than-air craft for domestic and foreign markets over the past decade. The company agreed to train an ever-greater number of airmen at its school at Newport News, Virginia. Aircraft production and design standardization also got under way. On May 23, a previously established Joint Technical Board on Aircraft recommended that the navy procure 300 training aircraft ("school machines"), 200 "service" and 100 large seaplanes, together with 100 "speed scouts."

These bustling activities were directed from a newly formed Office of Aviation (Operations) in Washington, whose director, Lieutenant Earle F. Johnson, "supervised training . . . had cognizance over the enrollment of candidates for pilot training," and "directed the movement of personnel by coordinating" their assignments with the director of the Naval Reserve Flying Corps, Lieutenant Commander John Towers. An important aspect of the navy's wartime programs from the outset, the training office by November 1918 had become "one of the largest sections of the Aviation Division," located in the Bureau of Navigation.[4]

But it took months for the navy to establish an efficient pipeline of men and machines that began with training and manufacturing and ended with flyers climbing into various French, British, and Italian (and in the last months a relative handful of American) aircraft on Allied airfields. In the interim, a disparate group of volunteers partially filled the void. Two weeks after the United States entered the war, Secretary Daniels dispatched a message to Sims, requesting "immediate and full information on British naval aviation," including "description of aircraft types employed and tactics that had proved most successful." Britain had devoted "enormous" resources to aviation, not only as a weapon in the war against the U-boat but also to protect the Isles from aerial attack and to "provide eyes for the fleet." By early 1918, the Admiralty was deploying an impressive range of weapons systems in the air: dirigibles, kite balloons, land planes, seaplanes, "and the world's most advanced flying boats"—craft that had been designed by Commander J. C. Porter on the basis of earlier aircraft built for him by Glenn Curtiss. Despite that American connection, the British response to Daniels's request was unsatisfactory. The exclusion of data regarding seaplanes and seaplane tenders was especially frustrating. The French Ministry of Marine, on the other hand, had already requested help from American aviators to implement their own antisubmarine campaign. As Washington understood it, the ministry offered to train the American novices at French facilities on or near the Atlantic Coast, with the stipulation that the trainees become proficient in overwater flight. Daniels and Benson wasted no time. They promptly ordered formation of the First Aeronautic Detachment of the United States Navy—popularly known as the "FAD"—which soon set sail for Europe. Leading the detachment was "aggressive and energetic" Lieutenant Kenneth Whiting, one of the more remarkable flying sailors of the time, who had served in both the Atlantic Fleet and the Asiatic Squadron and on both surface ships and the first generation of American submarines. A hard-drinking "daredevil," Whiting had allegedly once had himself fired out of a torpedo tube to test its feasibility as an escape mechanism.[5]

Joe Cline was a typical FAD recruit. Having served four years in the Illinois Naval Militia, Cline enlisted in the regular navy on April 3 as a "Landsman for Quartermaster (Aviation)." Promptly sent to Pensacola for flight training, he found himself thrown in with several hundred other young men. As "student aviators," they enjoyed no cadet status; "in fact," Cline recalled, "there was no ground school or flight instruction provisions for such a large group." The handful of regular naval aviators had no idea what to do with these enlisted men who "were utterly green," if "inexpressibly eager." So the students did some drilling and were shunted into a few indoctrination classes (for which Cline had little need after four years in the militia) when suddenly a request came down from Washington for 100 volunteers for "duty in a foreign country." The landsmen for quartermasters would be trained as pilots; the landsmen for machinist's mates would be trained in "maintenance and overhaul." Using this group as a nucleus, Whiting cobbled together his detachment comprising 6 officers and 122 enlisted volunteers. "One thing brought us together," Cline remembered. "Mechanics, carpenters, college students, taxi drivers, farmers— we all wanted to fly." Whiting was able to seed the group with only a few important aviation pioneers before the detachment sailed to France in late May 1917 in separate groups aboard the navy colliers *Jupiter* and *Neptune*. Both ships were slow, seas were occasionally rough (destroyer *Perkins* sideswiped *Jupiter* at one point), and the detachment's two elements did not reach St. Nazaire until June 5 and 8, respectively.

Then began a period of frequent, frustrating dislocation for Cline and the hundreds of aviators that eventually came after, as their naval superiors at home and in London "continually shift[ed] plans and priorities." Such confusion would continue well into the final summer of the war and makes it extremely difficult for the historian to trace beyond individual careers just where, how, and how many of the flyers finally found action. David Ingalls, another early arrival in France, summed up so much of US naval aviation in the Great War when he "bemoaned the fact that training never seemed to end." Constant reassignments to new aircraft and fighting fronts were the norm: "from flying boat patrol training to land-based combat instruction to seaplane escort duty" and cross-line bombing raids, then back to escort duty, followed by training in British—and Italian—bomber aircraft, "and finally" for some "assignment to a British combat squadron" just to the rear of the western front trenches. With no prewar aviation doctrine and few resources in either men or matériel, "it took many months to get" America's naval aviation program "headed on a winning course."

"After we arrived in France," Cline later wrote, "nobody knew what to do with us," although French women and children greeted the Americans like heroes. Whiting's orders were vague, but he clearly was to place the detachment under overall French control, much in the manner that Taussig and Bayly worked out their arrangements at Queenstown. After several days traveling around the Brest area, finding locations and building suitable temporary quarters (including occupation of barracks that had once quartered Napoleon's troops), and making mandatory calls on local officials, Whiting went off to Paris, where he found his French hosts somewhat flummoxed. "Operating virtually independently of command oversight," Whiting began discussions only to discover that a "serious misunderstanding" existed. Preliminary discussions with French embassy people back in Washington had led Whiting—and his superiors—to believe that "untrained student pilots and mechanics would be welcomed and could be instructed quickly in France." The French made clear their delight at seeing the Americans, but the detachment with 65 prospective pilots and 38 "untrained mechanics" together with "various other personnel" was—well—rather "unbalanced," n'est-ce pas? "Every plane and pilot," the hosts continued, required more than ten additional support personnel, "including a cadre of observers proficient in dropping bombs, firing machine guns and discharging other important duties." And there was the matter of chauffeurs, "fabric workers, joiners, motor boat coxswains and engineers." Perhaps it would be best if at least 14 of the prospective American sailor-pilots could be trained as observers instead. The sides could at least agree on one thing: the American flyers would be trained and employed in antisubmarine warfare. Following prolonged and intense, but friendly, negotiations with both the War and the Maritime Ministries, Whiting and his hosts reached agreement. The detachment would be split up. Twenty-five prospective mechanics would travel to St. Raphaël on the Mediterranean coast for training, while the prospective pilots, observer, gunners, and bombardiers would take the same "shortened course" at Tours given to French aviation cadets. Following completion of their training, the "pilot ensigns" would be assigned to the seaplane school at Lac Hourtin, near Bordeaux. There the 25 now well-trained mechanics from St. Raphaël would join up, forming the nucleus of a US naval aviation presence in Europe.

Whiting, still operating on his own, acceded to French suggestions that his people would eventually operate three seaplane bases on French soil. "A station at Le Croisic near the mouth of the Loire River would protect the approaches to St. Nazaire and offered a convenient site from which to attack U-boats operating around Belle Isle and Ile d'Yeu. A second base at St Trojan near the Gironde River would guard the route to Bordeaux. These two ports seemed likely debarkation points for the anticipated stream of American troop and supply convoys." The third proposed base slightly torqued the American sailor-flyers' mission. Dunkirk on the Channel was far from transatlantic convoy routes. But it could provide immediate air escort to the Channel convoys and was close to the front in Flanders. It was thus particularly positioned to mount air raids against the major German naval bases at Bruges, Ostend, and Zeebrugge on the Belgian coast, from which the majority of U-boats deployed. In fact, a British bomber group had been operating in this fashion since 1916.[6]

Whiting's prospective pilots found the shortened course at Tours short, indeed, when at last they arrived by truck on the rainy night of June 20. None of the boys had had any ground-school instruction, "and few of us had any ideas about the theory of flight." Flying outfits consisting of a heavy coat and a leather "crash helmet," and a pair of goggles were passed among the 8 to 10 students who constituted each instructional group. The French instructors spoke no English, the American youngsters no French. The instructional aircraft was a "warped wing" Caudron G-3 with two cockpits, one behind the other, powered by 90-horsepower Anzani or Le Rhone engines. Instruction was primitive. Sitting in the rear cockpit behind the novice, the instructor would push forward on the student's head if the nose was too high; if the nose was too low, he would pull the student's head back. A tap on the right shoulder meant the left wing was too low; on the left shoulder, the right wing was too low. "A flight lasted about twenty minutes," and after each one the instructor "would pull out a pasteboard card with a line drawn down the center," with one side written in English, the other in French. Often screaming and yelling, instructors gave their pupils "hell" in French, all the while pointing to the board and leaving each student to figure out from the English-language side what his faults had been. One instructor in particular would rave at his pupils. Assigned to teach them dead-stick landings from two thousand meters, Lieutenant or Captain Benaush would throw his "hat" away at any pretext. Worse errors would result in a dumping of hat and cane. It was said that if he threw away his pipe also, the student was a dead man.

Cline estimated that roughly two-thirds of his 50-man group at Tours soloed in "less than five hours of dual instruction." After that, each of the fledgling pilots undertook an eighty-mile cross-country hop to a British air station near Vendôme. Upon return, they were expected to execute a dead-stick landing from four thousand feet on a "small field we called the salad patch." Their final test involved soaring to eight thousand feet and maintaining that altitude for an hour.[7] Then it was on to preliminary seaplane training on a small lake near Bordeaux, where the pilots lived in tents and ate outside under the trees at big planked tables. Cline soloed in his first seaplane ("this little boat") "after three hops with an instructor for about fifteen minutes each." Finally, those who had survived were sent to St. Raphaël for final training in a variety of large seaplanes. Cline and his fellow aviators at last completed training in October 1917. Meantime, those who had "washed out" were sent, along with most of the machinists' mates who had not chosen to become aviation mechanics, to various aerial gunnery and other aviation schools "all over Europe" to be trained as aerial observers. Once their training was complete, the pilots experienced the same fate. "We were really a split-up outfit," Cline remembered, "that became attached to every man's army and every man's navy. . . . We flew with the French, the British and the Italians. Some of us even flew with the United States Marines, but most of us never fired an American machine gun or dropped an American bomb, or even saw an American-made plane until we got back home."[8]

Whiting was able to secure one more commitment from his hosts during his initial visit to Paris. Once it was constructed, the Yanks would be permitted to operate their own aviation school at Moutchic, roughly thirty miles from Bordeaux and just four from the Bay of Biscay. The first students would not appear before October and would train at Lac Hourtin, three and a half miles away, until facilities were finished. In the meantime, Cline and a number of other FAD members who found themselves at temporary loose ends were put to hard work at Moutchic, "setting up hangars" and "building barracks . . . on sandy ground recently cleared of dense pines."[9] By this time, 29 members of another prominent volunteer outfit, the First Yale Unit, were crossing the Atlantic in pairs and threes and fours on various transports.

As David M. Kennedy has noted, American enthusiasm for war was strongest among "the educated classes," whose youth were "thought best fitted for command." Many of these youngsters, especially those in the Ivy League schools, had been to Europe as lads and schoolchildren. They knew the Continent and loved its countries and cultures. Late in 1916, a "preparedness frenzy" swept the eastern colleges, even as hundreds of young Americans rushed to Europe to "drive ambulances, serve with the Red Cross," or volunteer with the French Foreign Legion and its rapidly forming aviation branch that became the Lafayette Escadrille. "Still others traveled to Canada to join the British Army or Royal Flying Corps." Even before Wilson had decided upon war, a mass meeting at Princeton "had to be convoked" by the university's determinedly pacifist president "to restrain undergraduates from flocking to the recruiting stations." Tellingly, John Grier Tibben was forced to accept a gift of two "'flying machines' so that students might form an all-Princeton 'aviation corps.'"[10] Yale students were already aloft.

Like a host of fellow idealists in and beyond the Ivy League, F. Trubee Davison had spent some time—in his case the summer vacation of 1915—driving American Field Service ambulances on the western front. Returning to New Haven in the fall, this rangy son of a prominent Wall Street financier began regaling classmates on the wonders of wartime aviation, which was making enormous strides under the impact of ceaseless battles in the skies above France and Flanders. One who knew Davison at the time remembered a handsome, somewhat rugged-looking youngster, "endowed with the gift of leadership . . . and the summer in France had brought him into direct contact with the war. It was no longer hearsay. He knew what he was talking about. Most of us can remember how eagerly we listened, in those days, to any one who had come from overseas, whose personal impressions served to vivify the censored columns of the daily press." Davison soon collected a group of youthful enthusiasts, eager to fly and make their mark against the Hun. Among them were Artemus Gates, Robert Lovett, David Ingalls, Allan Ames, and Kenneth MacLeish, who summarized the feelings of many whose ardor seems now firmly of another time and place. "War is terrible," MacLeish admitted to his parents. "But there are two or three things that are worse. The brutality of Germany with respect to Belgium, the statement by Germany that international law and humanity are mere scraps of paper compared to her needs, the wanton murder of helpless American women and children, the open insults to the honor of the United States—they're all worse than war!" Life was worth sacrificing, he continued, for the sake of humanity and "the assurance of the laws of Christianity."[11]

Unfortunately, there were few planes and even fewer places to learn to fly them. Both the army and the navy were "woefully behind" in developing suitable programs. Lacking both aircraft and instructors, Davison's dream of forming a coastal patrol unit appeared stillborn. The young man was not to be deterred. With his twenty-nine-member "Yale Unit No. 1" in place, he contacted the ACA, which put him in contact with Rodman Wanamaker, the prominent department-store owner, philanthropist, and aviation enthusiast who had recently opened a flying school at Port Washington, on Long Island's north shore. Wanamaker generously offered the Yale youngsters a Curtiss flying boat and an instructor to go with it. "Still attending school full time, the Yalies not only learned how to fly but how to clean and maintain aircraft, and at Port Washington and later New London, took part in training exercises with battleships, destroyers, and coastal patrol ships." The boys, many of whom were football players, enhanced their reputations as Big Men on Campus. The editors of the November 14, 1916, issue of the *Yale Daily News*

(price: three cents) . . . praised Davison and his squad, noting that "because little is known about naval aeronautics in this country, their work is the work of the pioneer. Instead of being dismayed that neither the Army or [*sic*] the Navy could supply them with textbooks or information to guide them in their work, they set to work to experiment and find out for themselves. . . . [I]n the near future they will probably be in a position to make valuable contributions regarding scouting at sea, map-making and photographing from the air, locating submarines and mines of different color at different depths, under various weather conditions.

Winter weather closed their training, but Germany's mounting hostility made it clear that the navy would need pilots such as these as fast as possible. As it re-formed in early 1917, the group adopted the name "Aerial Coast Patrol #1," and in March the navy urged the unit to join its Reserve Flying Corps. On the twenty-fourth, the boys were sworn in and journeyed as a group to Palm Beach, Florida, for a final four months' training, under Navy Medal of Honor winner Lieutenant Edward McDonnell assisted by two civilian aviators, "a small crew of petty officers and mechanics and an assortment of civilian aides and staff." The group never received formal ground training, listening instead to occasional lectures and concentrating on "hands on instruction" from the staff. Flying one of Glenn Curtiss's prewar F-boats that sped along at sixty-five to seventy miles per hour and could reach forty-five hundred feet, the youngsters "never . . . thought about how much or how little we were working. The more we did," David Ingalls recalled, "the more we flew, and that was the mark we were shooting at." Following further training at Huntington, New York, near Long Island Sound, the group scattered far and wide. Tragically, Davison was not with them, crashing on the eve of graduation.

Davison's sad fate reflected the tumultuous times. The Yalies had suffered "several narrow escapes from disaster" during their training, due as much or more to the crudities of their aircraft as their own inadequacies. The Burgess Dunn plane "was a very hard machine to turn" in turbulent weather. The slightest "bump" would straighten the aircraft out of its turn. Going aloft one windy day, John Vorys and a companion came a cropper as they tried to land their unstable craft. On final approach, the plane suddenly augured in from roughly seventy-five feet "about one foot from the beach." The men were shaken but unhurt.

Neither were support personnel immune to the idiosyncrasies of the aircraft they serviced. On another occasion, seaman mechanic Wells offered to start the R-3 being piloted by Allan Ames. The motor backfired, and Wells was struck first by one end of the propeller in the arm, and then the other sliced into his head, crushing his skull. The youngster died in the hospital that night.

Trubee Davison obviously took these incidents and others deeply to heart. By the time that a three-man naval aviation board arrived at Huntington to clear the unit's members for flight duty, Davison had worked himself to exhaustion and was clearly ill. He fainted the day before the qualification flights, and several of his mates urged him to postpone going aloft. Davison would have none of it; he was the unit leader, and it was his duty to lead. He did confess an apprehension about handling the flying boat he was to pilot for qualification. While he himself had been an instructor for some time, he had flown on different aircraft—the Burgess and N-9s and "R"s. Now he openly admitted a "lack of confidence" in handling an aircraft whose qualities were unknown to him. He would become one of the early victims of a pioneer aircraft industry still seeking vainly for the elusive basic design that would permit the safe mass training and qualification of aviators.

July 28, 1917, dawned bright and clear over Long Island Sound. Davison led two other fliers aloft, Robert Lovett and Artemus Gates (both destined for distinguished government careers in the defense field). The flight test stipulated climbing to six thousand feet, followed by a descent to three thousand, "then shutting off the motor and landing within three hundred feet" of a target vessel, in this case the yacht *Shuttle*. Davison performed admirably until the final moment, when he misjudged his glide, stretching it too far on a turn. The aircraft promptly sideslipped and fell into the sea. The impact separated the nose structure from the compression strut, and the force of surging water into the wreck drove Davison back under the engine mounted directly behind the cockpit. His legs caught in the tubular braces, struts, and wires of the broken aircraft, which managed to remain afloat with Davison's head above water. As the wreck slowly began to sink, daring crewmen aboard the yacht and members of the unit who were there as observers managed to cut Davison loose. He was first rushed to a local hospital and then transferred by train to New York City. But his back was broken; several vertebrae were crushed. Crippled for life, the gallant youngster refused to surrender and within a year was assisting the navy in evaluating new aerial weaponry; his career, of course, was finished.

"Eventually all but six" of the Yale Unit served in Europe, and they were widely considered the nucleus of US naval airpower in the war. The head of the aviation desk at US Naval Headquarters near the end of the conflict recalled that "whenever we had a member of the Yale Unit, everything was all right. Whenever the French and English asked us to send a couple of our crack men to reinforce a squadron, I would say 'Let's get some of the Yale gang.' We never made a mistake when we did this."[12]

In his Paris negotiations, Whiting had clearly pushed far out in front of the immediate interests of his service and his government. The situation he created was intolerable for a variety of reasons. First and foremost, the United States was an associate, not a formal ally, in the war against the Central Powers. Wilson was determined to keep it that way to obtain maximum leverage for American (read: his) interests at the peace table. US ground, sea, and air resources could not be employed piecemeal to meet the shifting needs and whims of the Allied High Command. Pershing was successfully resisting such efforts, and it would not do for the navy and its component elements, especially its fledgling air force with limited resources in men and weapons, to cave in at the outset to Anglo-French imperatives that might lock in the much larger force forming at home. Second, Whiting's agreements with the French did not extend to the formation of naval air bases in Ireland and along the English Channel coast. Indeed, "Despite the breadth and magnitude of Whiting's conversations" in Paris, "Admiral Sims remained completely unaware of his work." Sims had no idea that a First Aeronautic Detachment had reached France "or that its commander seemed to be committing the United States to an expansive program of bases and, by implication, determining Navy strategy and tactics for combatting the submarine menace." Sims was further embarrassed by his British colleagues, who belatedly realized their error in not exploiting nascent America's naval aviation capabilities. "Sims first learned of Whiting's activities at a meeting with the Board of Admiralty, which pointedly inquired why America was secretly concentrating a large air force in France when, from the Royal Navy's perspective, the most vital area was the English shipping routes." A chagrined Sims agreed that protecting British coasts and approaches was where antisubmarine activities of all kinds needed to be concentrated.[13]

Clearly, Whiting had to be bridled and the locus of decision making placed in London, where overall American and Allied naval policies were being centralized and coordinated. Fortunately, a potential solution was already at hand. Official Washington realized early on that a common approach to the air war on the western front involving both the army and the navy was essential for efficient prosecution. A joint mission was hastily cobbled together, and on June 17, just nine weeks after formal American entry, Army Major R. C. Bolling, with Commander George C. Westervelt, the senior navy representative, sailed for Europe, charged with studying "air development among the Allies and recommending a policy and program for the American air services."[14] Meanwhile, the Navy Department dispatched a senior officer, Captain Richard Jackson, to the Paris embassy to ride herd on the venturesome Whiting.

But Whiting proved irrepressible and Jackson a posturing fool, relatively easy to work around. In late July and early August 1917, Whiting dispatched four "lengthy memos" to Secretary Daniels that together not only covered most of the naval aviation activities in France but also established the template for the entire subsequent American naval aviation effort in Europe. Whiting insisted that pontoon-equipped seaplanes rather than flying boats or land-based aircraft were the best antisubmarine weapon in the American aviation arsenal. They, along with a few lighter-than-air ships, should be deployed, as the French suggested, from a dozen bases bordering the Bay of Biscay and southern English Channel. Whiting urged Daniels to approve four large bases supporting twenty-four seaplanes apiece and eight smaller stations deploying eighteen seaplanes. At Dunkirk alone, an unspecified number of "fighting scouts, along with patrol/bomber aircraft," would be based for direct attacks against the German U-boat bases in Belgium. Geoffrey L. Rossano, the leading authority on US naval aviation in World War I, characterizes Whiting's report to Daniels of July 20, 1917, as "possibly the single most important document in the development of the overseas aviation program." Whiting's "lengthy cable" of August 4 describing in detail the number of critical roles that naval aircraft could perform in the antisubmarine war was of equal importance. "Shortages of personnel and material" were all that kept the United States from playing an immediate major role aloft. Following "lengthy review," the Navy Department approved Whiting's recommendations, "and by the end of the summer work had begun at several sites including Moutchic, Dunkirk and Le Croisic."[15]

Upon their return at the beginning of September, members of the Bolling mission at once ratified and amplified Whiting's recommendations. In their own unanimous report to the secretaries of war and the navy, they recommended, inter alia, "that air measures against submarines take precedence over all other air measures, that the United States establish and operate as many coastal patrol stations in Europe as possible" (thus opening the door to construction of naval air stations at appropriate locations along the British and Irish coasts as well as in France), "and that European aircraft be obtained for use at those stations until the more satisfactory types manufactured in the United States became available."[16]

The deficiency in American-built aircraft, and the pilots, observers, and mechanics to man and maintain them, was already in the process of being rectified in factories, classrooms, and airfields on both sides of the Canadian–American border. While the navy's pioneer aviators in Europe like Joe Cline and members of the Yale Unit seldom saw, much less flew, American planes, the Curtiss H series of flying boats became the centerpiece of the navy's antisubmarine war from aloft during the final months of the war.

Glenn Curtiss has been credited as the father of American naval aviation, and there is much evidence to support the claim. Beginning his career, like the Wright brothers, as a bicycle manufacturer, he quickly became bewitched by the possibilities of the motorcycle and then aviation. Curtiss put his first sea- or "hydroplane" aloft in 1910, and that year and through the next he began training the navy's first flyers, not at Pensacola, which had not yet been established, but at North Island, in San Diego Bay. Eager to sell his crude aircraft to the navy, he enthusiastically supported his pupil Eugene Ely's flights off and onto the decks of navy cruisers. Determined to keep pace with developments in Europe, Curtiss went to England and the Continent a number of times both before and during the world war. Curtiss's chief contact was Royal Navy commandeer J. C. Porter, who designed a number of ever-improved flying boats—then built by Curtiss—between 1914 and 1916. By the time of American entry, the Curtiss manufacturing company was poised to produce wheeled aircraft for the army and flying boats for the navy. Hobbled by long-standing patent wars with the Wright family, Curtiss happily acquiesced in government pressure to resolve the matter, thus freeing him up to manufacture as many planes of as many kinds as he could.[17]

The navy soon concluded, however, that placing the fulfillment of all their needs in one private commercial basket was not in the best interests of the war effort. Eight weeks after American entry, "the Navy found it feasible to construct and put into operation its own aircraft factory." Several compelling factors drove the decision. First, Curtiss and the handful of other private commercial aircraft builders would be flooded with orders with which they could not "cope." Second, the Navy Department wanted partial control over not only the manufacture but also the design of aircraft, presumably to incorporate aviation lessons being learned both in the States and on European battlefields. Finally, by manufacturing at least some wartime aircraft, the navy could assess and hopefully control costs. Not specified but clearly considered by department officials was the need to dictate the pace, direction, and employment of naval aviation in the postwar world.

Once decided on its course, the department moved with commendable speed. Site surveys were begun, based upon size and costs of the proposed factory. By July 27, Secretary Daniels approved a location on the Delaware River, and Congress provided the million dollars for construction. Ground for the Naval Aviation Factory (NAF) was broken on August 6, and a manager, Commander F. G. Coburn, was appointed three weeks later. Coburn estimated he could get the factory up and running within one hundred days. He exceeded his schedule. The first mechanic was hired on October 1, and by the end of 1917 the factory was in full operation. Roughly a quarter of the workforce was female, with women guaranteed equal pay for equal work.

Navy designers promptly revised Curtiss Company aircraft plans "to fit the production methods employed by the Factory." By October, the form for the first of fifty flying boats was laid, and mass production of what became the navy version of the H–16 began. The aircraft was impressive even for a later age; for 1917 it was an amazing achievement, given that only fourteen years had passed since Kitty Hawk. The upper wing spanned ninety-six feet, and the hull was forty-six feet long, accommodating four to five men, including a pilot, one or two observers who could handle machine guns and drop small crude bombs on a U-boat, a "mechanician," and a radio operator. "On March 27, 1918, just 228 days after ground was broken and only 151 days after receipt of the original plans, the first NAF-built H–16 made its initial flight." Several days later, the disassembled aircraft and a sister were shipped to Killingholme, England, for war service. The first ordered batch of fifty planes was completed by July 7. How effective these aircraft would be remained to be determined.[18]

Manufacturing was one of two elements in the production of a naval air force. The second was training not only of pilots but also of the ground-support force to be sent abroad to reassemble the aircraft as they came in from the States and to repair and maintain them under combat conditions. One immediate solution to the dearth of naval aviators was to accept the offers of foreign governments to provide basic training. On July 9, 1917, twenty-four future naval aviators reported to the University of Toronto for flight training under the direction of the Canadian Royal Flying Corps. One of them, J. Sterling Halstead, who became US Navy pilot number 160, remembered the boys being told at the outset "to take notes on everything so that we could bring back to the U.S. Navy complete information on the subjects taught, the equipment and the methods used." Standing on the station platform awaiting orders and transportation, the young Americans were fascinated by the "aeroplanes" that constantly passed by overhead, "motors roaring and wings flashing in the sunlit air as they banked and turned." A few of their Royal Flying Corps hosts took them aloft on "joy hops" that seemed to be over before they began. By the time the twenty-four students had completed flight training in October, they had endured weeks of drill and absorbed a multitude of lessons from combat-hardened Canadian and British flyers on all aspects of flying. In ground school, the eager Yanks mastered the theory of flight, knowledge of rigging and aircraft engines, bombing, aerial photography, and enough information of a meteorological and astronomical nature to gain proficiency in aerial navigation. They were "strongly schooled" in the use of both the Lewis and the Vickers machine guns and "the workings of various aerial gunsights then in use." Battlefield landscape mock-ups were used to hone skills in artillery spotting and overall observation, together with the use of "wireless" to report findings to the troops and headquarters below.

Then it was on to "flying camp" at Deseronto, some seventy miles from Toronto, where a number of the boys managed to crash their planes without seriously injuring themselves, surviving unanticipated landings on hangar roofs, faulty landings, flat tailspins, and inhospitable landing terrain. When at last they went aloft solo, many were gripped by a kind of "monotony of tension." One recalled sitting "up there for two hours waiting for the tail to fall off." Halstead added that "there were many things we knew could happen, but they never did." Halstead's own successful solo flight was not without folly and danger. He drew a relatively new JN-4 "Jenny," which proved to be a lovely little aircraft, easy to fly. As the afternoon wore on, Halstead noodled along at several thousand feet, mesmerized by shifting patterns of light and geography on the ground below. "Watching the night come on was so engrossing that I overlooked the significance of what I was seeing. Suddenly the light in the west vanished and darkness crowded in." Knowing he was just a few miles north and east of the camp, Halstead turned in that direction, only to have his "new and stiff" engine suddenly seize up. Gliding along in the night sky, knowing his plane would suddenly plummet any instant, Halstead did the only right thing. Pushing the Jenny's nose down, he went into a steep dive from about a thousand feet. As the dark outlines of treetops quickly materialized below, the engine "miraculously" kicked over again. The air pressure building up on the propeller from the dive "had cranked the engine." The shaken youngster found the field easily, for a "motor lorry" stood nearby, its headlights illuminating the landing zone. Halstead brought the plane down without incident. He had earned his wings.[19]

The Toronto contingent split up immediately upon returning home. While a few went on to fly the skies of western Europe, roughly a score of these highly trained youngsters became the nucleus (along with a number of Pensacola-trained regulars and professors of the new discipline of aeronautical engineering) of a forced-draft, rapid expansion of naval aviation training set forth by the Navy Department on July 13, 1917. Ground schools were established at, among other locations, the University of Washington in Seattle; the Dunwoody Institute in Minneapolis; Gerstner Field on the shore of Lake Charles, Louisiana; the naval base at Hampton Roads; a brand-new facility on what had been rough farmland on North Island in San Diego Bay; and, most important, the

Massachusetts Institute of Technology (MIT), which became "the main ground school for the Naval Reserve Flying Corps."

Preliminary flight schools, which very quickly concentrated on training pilots to master the multitude of seaplanes and flying boats coming out of the Curtiss and Naval Aviation Factories, were established at Bay Shore, Long Island; Key West and Miami, Florida; and Lake Belsena, Italy. Only Pensacola had the facilities, the trained teachers, and, perhaps most important, the tradition (short though it was) to successfully carry out advanced flight training. As the need for naval aviators dramatically expanded, however, many pilot candidates were hastily shipped overseas to complete their flight training for specific missions, in particular aircraft at a score of schools across the British Isles and western and southern Europe, among which were Moutchic, Lake Belsena, and the Royal Flying Corps' School of Special Flying at Gosport, England. No single arm of the US naval service expanded as rapidly as aviation. From the 34 pilots and 54 aircraft available on April 6, 1917, naval aviation grew by November 11, 1918, to 1,656 certified pilots (of whom 1,237 were overseas), 891 ground support officers at home and in Europe, and 21,951 enlisted aviation ratings.[20] Aircraft totaled over 2,000.

Training of mechanics and repair personnel had lagged a bit. The first group of 50 enlisted men dedicated to servicing American aircraft did not arrive at the Naval Aviation Factory until January 1918, but thereafter training and subsequent transfer abroad went swiftly and smoothly, though as time went on, untrained sailors were sent to both England and France for on-the-job training.[21]

All that was missing as the autumn of 1917 waned was a comprehensive plan bringing America's ever-growing naval airpower in Europe under central control for both administrative and decision-making purposes. Sims was convinced that his headquarters was the only appropriate place. As US naval presence had grown steadily at Queenstown, Brest, and Gibraltar, "the staff controlling the whole had necessarily to be located in London," with decentralized administration exercised by subordinates at each separate base. From the outset, Sims had been the American point man in Europe for all naval matters. Jellicoe ordered his subordinates to "place all their sources of information and their communications" at his disposal. "They literally opened their doors and made us part of their organization. I sat in daily consultation with British naval chiefs, and our officers had access to all essential British information just as freely as did the British naval officers themselves." First Lord of the Admiralty Sir Eric Geddes spoke in the same vein to Parliament. "We have," he said, "the advantage of constant consultation with Admiral Sims who attends our daily staff conferences.

We have American officers working in various sections of the British Admiralty on exactly the same footing as British Officers." Anglo-American naval cooperation, Geddes concluded, was "as nearly complete as possible." Sims was understandably proud of what he accomplished, and he concluded that "with all this information, the most complete and detailed in the world, constantly placed at our disposal," and an unprecedented "spirit of confidence and friendship always prevailing, . . . it would have defeated the whole purpose of our participation in the war had the American high command taken up its headquarters anywhere except London."[22] As early as midsummer, Sims was writing Benson, complaining that the burgeoning naval aviation program lacked administrative coherence and operational focus. Several members of the Bolling mission were advising him, but both Jackson and Whiting in Paris were simply off the reservation.[23]

By now, Benson dared not ignore or override his chief London representative. The man was proving invaluable as a conduit to both Allied Powers. Sims, in turn, "already had his eye on exactly the man he wanted" to run the naval air show. Commander Hutchinson (Hutch) I. Cone was an old friend with a service-wide reputation for getting things done. Cone was currently chafing in the backwater of the Panama Canal Zone, and at the end of May he wrote his old friend, "For God's sakes get me over there with you in some capacity as soon as possible." Orders were soon cut, sending Cone to London, where, with Sims's enthusiastic encouragement, he promptly began a "thorough overhaul" of all US naval aviation efforts from Ireland to Italy. Following personal meetings with Sims, Whiting, and others and a review of pertinent correspondence and documents, the energetic, newly promoted captain set off on a rapid tour of potential base sites in Ireland and England and then went to Paris, where he relieved both Jackson and Whiting in late October, assuming the title of commander, US Naval Aviation Forces in Foreign Service. Soon, however, he saw the wisdom of bringing his headquarters to London under Sims's immediate direction. By the end of 1917, he was ensconced at Grosvenor Gardens, where several recent and far-reaching decisions among the Americans and their Allies would provide him with the authority he needed to dramatically expand and rationalize the American naval war in the air.[24]

"Drab Efficiency"
The Making of the Convoy System

NEVER BEFORE HAD maritime America, naval or commercial, confronted such a task as lay before it in the summer of 1917. No American army of any size had ever crossed the Atlantic to fight; no American army of the size now contemplated for dispatch to the western front had ever before been raised and trained. "Previous to 1916," a contemporary report stated, "the idea of a United States overseas expeditionary force numbered by millions would have been generally regarded as a remote if not impossible contingency. Consequently no extensive peace-time preparations had been made for such an undertaking. The task of providing a transport fleet was, therefore a pioneer work."[1]

Just ten weeks after the first British-escorted convoy had sailed from Hampton Roads and two months after Gleaves had taken the first American-escorted convoy across the Atlantic, a sophisticated system was rapidly crystallizing across the world ocean. Even as Gleaves set forth, the first of four British "experimental convoys"—each comprising fifteen or so vessels, all centered around precious "oilers"—set out from Hampton Roads. All four reached port safely. The equal success of "experimental convoys" on the route between Gibraltar and the United Kingdom demonstrated that convoys possessed "intrinsically great powers of evasion," supplying "a fairly conclusive answer" to those within British naval and governmental circles who had doubted the success of the convoy system. In short, "the passage of these convoys through the danger area" with but a single torpedoing ("an isolated incident") showed that "if the system could be developed and extended, it would alter the whole aspect of submarine warfare."[2]

Following Gleaves's return with the first westward convoy (escorted roughly six hundred miles into the Atlantic by Queenstown destroyers), army and navy officials quickly got down to work. Gleaves was summoned to Washington and conferences with Daniels and Benson. "I strongly urged that the operation of the transports be taken over entirely by the Navy," Gleaves later wrote, "and that they be fully manned by Naval officers and crews. Shortly after, the War and Navy Departments jointly recommended this plan."

Service cooperation was paramount if an efficient convoy system was to be quickly put in place. Gleaves and his people liaised closely with Hoboken port director Major General D. C. Shanks and with Major General Grote Hutchison at Norfolk. In Washington, War and Navy Department officials drafted a formal charter setting forth lines and areas of responsibility that the president signed as a confidential order. "The dividing line of authority in the transport service was made at the docks; the Army superintended the docks in the ports of embarkation and debarkation, providing and loading passengers and cargo." From the moment lines were cast off or anchors raised in Gravesend Bay or Hampton Roads to the moment the anchors went down or the lines went over in Liverpool, St. Nazaire, and, later, Brest, the navy was to have sole responsibility for transporting the American Expeditionary Force.

"Providing a transport fleet was pioneer work. Ships had to be obtained, officers and crews enrolled and trained. It was necessary to have docks, storehouses, lighters, and tugs, coaling equipment, repair facilities, and all the varied machinery for operating and maintaining a large transportation service. An efficient administrative organization had to be developed and red tape had to be cut." This prodigious task accomplished not only in US ports but also in Britain and France was done in record time. Finally, the first convoy had yielded a trove of experience that Gleaves quickly pounced on as the basis of a doctrine. He summoned the captains of both the transports and the warships to "frequent conferences" whose "frank discussions cleared the air." A set of confidential orders, "special and general," were hammered out, "which taken together" created a "flexible . . . thorough and practical" organization.[3]

From the outset, the overriding need was for ships, and here the Americans lagged substantially. A Shipping Board was in place, but according to its chairman, Edward N. Hurley, after decades of neglecting commercial shipbuilding, "our . . . experience was scant; our shipyards were entirely inadequate." Congress moved swiftly to enact legislation transforming the Shipping Board "from a body established to restore the American Merchant Marine to its old glory . . . into a military agency to bridge the ocean with ships and to maintain the line of communication between America and Europe. Conceived as an instrumentality of peace, the Board became an instrumentality of war. Unlike other military agencies—the Army and Navy—it began with nothing—no ships, no officers, no crews, no organizations. . . . Our resources, however, were almost incalculable and incomparable." A newly formed Emergency Fleet Corporation (EFC), begun with six employees "in three small rented rooms," expanded over half a year to "more than a thousand people in sixteen offices across the country who assumed supervisory responsibility for one thousand one hundred eighteen vessels of various types building in one hundred sixteen yards whose laboring force had expanded seven fold from a modest base of fifty thousand. The Corporation began disbursing money to the yards at the rate of over a billion dollars annually."[4]

Initially, the shipyards concentrated on either the 431 vessels that the government had requisitioned from the private sector or the commandeered German ships stranded in East Coast ports. Among the ships requisitioned by the EFC from the private sector were fifty-eight cargo vessels displacing eighty-eight hundred deadweight tons. All bore some variations of the word *West* (*Westboro*, *West Cusseta*, *Westerner*, *Western Ally*, and so on), and all but three that were being completed at the Merchant Shipbuilding Company in Chester, Pennsylvania, were being finished in various shipyards in Seattle or Portland, Oregon, after which they sailed through the Panama Canal to East Coast ports for convoy duty across the Atlantic. The desperately searching EFC also "found a valuable source of shipping on the Great Lakes." By November 1918, sixty-four cargo vessels working the lakes had been commandeered, "refitted . . . for ocean service and brought. . . down to the sea-board." In some instances, the ships were so large they could not pass through the Welland Canal connecting Lakes Erie and Ontario, and so their hulls "were cut squarely amidships, the parts were sealed by watertight bulkheads, and the sections were taken through the canal, then refitted in east coast yards."[5]

The German vessels stranded in New York and other seaboard ports were some of the best, largest, and most modern passenger ships in the world, ideal for ferrying a huge army across to France. Unfortunately, after three years of internment, the physical integrity of these ships had deteriorated markedly. Worse, before being removed and sent home in 1914, their crews had managed to sabotage the engineering spaces of nearly every vessel. According to a 1918 report issued by Navy Secretary Daniels, the chief damage was to the massive cylinders. Broken cast-iron parts in the main engines, boiler damage due to "dry-firing," and the deliberate sawing in half of piston and connecting rods together with boiler stays were of serious but secondary nature. Following a hasty survey, the Shipping Board that had assumed ownership of the ships determined that the navy should concentrate on the repair of the damaged cylinders. A senior assistant in the Bureau of Steam Engineering then made the highly controversial decision to "make all repairs where possible by electric welding" rather than mechanical patching. Engine builders and marine insurance companies mounted a vigorous opposition; electric welding had been in use for some time, but never on the scale proposed for repairing the ex-German liners. The navy countered that time was of the essence. Getting these ships seaworthy outweighed every other consideration. In winning the day, it transformed a new technical procedure into routine, while the great liners took to the seas in time to transport a sizable section of the American Expeditionary Force to France.[6]

The EFC also turned its attention to actual shipbuilding, commissioning and financing costly new government-owned yards to get the job done as quickly as possible. According to one authoritative source, the outbreak of war in 1914 had begun a veritable maritime industrial revolution in the small commercial cities along Puget Sound. Seattle, Tacoma, and lesser towns set to work meeting the "worldwide demand for both wooden and steel vessels, sail, steam, motor and auxiliary. . . . Many new shipyards were established and existing ones expanded." After April 1917, Puget Sound yards devoted themselves to helping to construct the "bridge of ships" that would take American armies to France and supply them lavishly. Inevitably, peace would bring widespread closures, impoverishment, and consequent labor strife.[7]

Although the new government ships would comprise five categories, including wooden ships, composite wood and steel vessels, concrete ships, and standard hulls of prewar design, the most striking innovation, based on the prewar construction of bridges and offices, was the fabricated steel ship designed by the celebrated naval architect Theodore Ferris. "The Germans were sinking vessels so fast that it became apparent we must adopt extraordinary methods" to get hulls into the water and out to sea swiftly; fabrication was the key. To obtain the kind of ships required, Ferris had to overcome the peculiarities of vessel design that included "queerly curved" hulls and pieces. Fortunately, he and his colleagues could draw on successful prewar work at the Chester Shipbuilding Company.

> Ferris produced the design of the fabricated ship which the Fleet Corporation built. Here was a design with practically rectangular midship cross-section, a deck that was flat, a bottom that was flat, a ship with sides so straight that there was scarcely any sheer, and a stern that was square. Straight lines and flat surfaces were

called for wherever it was practicable to apply them. Old ship-builders, accustomed to the odd traditional shapes of which vessels were built, simply gasped. I have no doubt that Mr. Ferris' personal reputation as a great naval architect had much to do with the acceptance of the fabricated design. At all events, without his aid, yards in which fabricated ships were built hardly could have taken shapes rolled and punched in steel mills hundreds of miles away and assembled them into vessels which have not been surpassed in sea-worthiness and general utility. By saving a single rivet in the plate of a single ship similar rivets for similar plates were saved in dozens of identical ships assembled in the same yard. A plate so shaped that it was necessary to trim an angle meant a corresponding saving of labor in scores of similar plates. Thus, literally thousands of operations became unnecessary. The saving in labor and material was incalculable. That system could be applied only in yards devoted to the assembling of dozens of ships exactly alike in every respect. The principle of assembling a mechanism from interchangeable parts, a principle which had given us cheap good watches, locomotives and automobiles, was applied with brilliant success to the construction of ships.

Taken as a whole these fabricated ships were a brilliant success—a vindication of a new principle in ship construction and a monument to the ingenuity and skill of American engineers. The principle of assembling standardized parts not only simplified construction but repairs as well. When the *Liberty Glo* struck a mine, December 5, 1919, she probably would have been abandoned as so much junk had she been an ordinary ship; for she had parted, and the forward section was lost. The after section was salvaged and berthed in Rotterdam. All the necessary material was sent abroad from this country to repair her, and she afterwards reëntered the service.[8]

The need for speedy construction, however, placed severe limits on the kind of merchantmen built. The government order for eleven hundred ships overwhelmed the capacity of East, West, and Gulf Coast yards, also busily constructing destroyers and other "small boys." The next available facilities were smaller yards on the Great Lakes. But the locks on the canals leading to the Atlantic were 270 long, 45 feet wide, "with a 14 foot controlling depth. This determined the dimensions of the famous 'Lakers'" that would have to haul much of the country's war matériel overseas. As a consequence, "more than one-half of the ships ordered by the Emergency Fleet Corporation were very small for ocean-crossing vessels of their time." Both steel- and wooden-hulled vessels proved to be "uneconomic miniature ships" whose three to four thousand deadweight tonnage limited carrying capacity to that of the British compound-engined freighters of the 1870s that had driven cargo-carrying sailing ships off the world ocean.[9] And as with the forced-draft destroyer construction program that provided only a handful of ships prior to the Armistice, so the Fleet Corporation oversaw the creation of a large merchant marine that did not fully materialize until 1919 and 1920.

Troop ships were in a category of their own. The US Navy's Cruiser and Transport Force ultimately mustered some forty-five commissioned vessels to carry the American Expeditionary Force to France. Two of the ships had gone across on Gleaves's first convoy, "leaky" old *Hancock* and the brand-new *Henderson*. The rest were former merchant passenger liners, seventeen of German origin. Fortunately, Britain "had the ships ready for use and 48.25 per cent of the American Army was transported" to European ports "in British steamers; 2.5 per cent were carried in French ships, and 3 per cent in Italian. The remaining 46.25 per cent were carried in United States ships, and all but 2.5 per cent of these sailed in United States naval transports"—a portion of the four-hundred-plus ships either commandeered from private firms or enemy passenger vessels seized in American ports at the beginning of the war. According to a respectable British source writing soon after war's end, "Of the rather more than 2,000,000 American troops sent to France before the Armistice, 911,047 were transported in American Naval transports; 41,534 in other American ships; and 1,075,333 in British ships or vessels chartered and manned by us."[10]

Whatever the specific makeup of any convoy, the system as a whole not only provided effective defense against the U-boat menace, but also incorporated the most recent advances in transportation and communication—steamships, railroads, telegraphs, and telephones—upon which the world's first truly global economy had been recently built. Each convoy was organized along the lines of America's "great aggregation" of transcontinental railroads. Just as the Southern Pacific, Santa Fe, New York Central, and other roads employed a dozen or so "gateway" places—San Francisco, Pittsburgh, Chicago among them—to assemble freight cars from a thousand different places, so "shipping destined for the belligerent nations was similarly assembled in the years 1917 and 1918 at six or eight great ocean 'gateway'" ports and formed into convoys for "through routing" to the British Isles, France, and the Mediterranean. Dakar on the West Coast of Africa became the center of convoy makeup for ships steaming up from Cape Horn and across from Brazilian, Argentine, and other eastern South American ports. "Vessels which came to Britain and France by way of Suez and the Mediterranean ports found their great stopping place at Gibraltar—a headquarters of traffic which in the huge amount of freight which it 'created' became almost the Pittsburgh of this mammoth transportation system." From Gibraltar, convoy lanes extended north, east, and south to England, France, Italy, Salonika, Palestine, Bizerte, and Algiers.[11]

The four gateway North American ports were Sydney on Canada's Cape Breton Island, Halifax, New York, and Hampton Roads. "The grain-laden merchantmen from the St. Lawrence Valley rendezvoused at Sydney and Halifax. Vessels from Portland, Boston, Philadelphia, and other Atlantic points found their assembly headquarters at New York, whose convoy directors initially dispatched a convoy apiece every sixteen days to either Liverpool or Southampton. Ships from Baltimore, Norfolk, the Gulf of Mexico and the west coast of South America proceeded to the great convoy centre which had been established at Hampton Roads." The latter port was even busier than New York, with convoys sailing every eight days to British east and west coast ports.[12]

By August 11, 261 vessels had left American harbors for England and France; only 1 had been attacked and sunk by a U-boat. America was still in the process of gathering and training its vast citizen army, so troop transports were a minority in most early convoys. The great majority of vessels were freight and stores ships, crammed with every conceivable kind of matériel the Doughboys—and American naval construction crews—would need, from pencils, typewriters, food of all sorts, blankets, and tents to small arms, cannons and millions of rounds of ammunition to trucks ("lorries"), graders, disassembled aircraft, and even railroad locomotives.

Nonetheless, by the end of 1917, nearly two hundred thousand men, their equipment, and their supplies had been carried by American vessels and a slightly larger number of British transports to European ports with operations just beginning to reach flood tide. As the American Expeditionary Force steadily gathered strength in the last months of the year and on into 1918, convoys from the New World were divided into two distinct classes. Those composed of the freighters and storeships carrying foodstuffs to help sustain the armies and the civilian populations of Britain and France together with equipment for the western front sailed a northern route through the Western Approaches to offload in English ports, with a greater or lesser portion of their cargo subsequently transshipped across the Channel to France by other convoys. Most of the troop transports ferrying the two-million-plus-man army from New York and Hampton Roads made directly for the French Atlantic ports of Brest, St. Nazaire, La Pallice, and Bordeaux along a more southerly route through the Western Approaches, though a relatively few Doughboys reached France via British ports and the English Channel.[13]

Headquarters for the global sealift system, the "central nervous system of a complicated but perfectly working organism which reached the remotest corners of the world," was the convoy room at the British Admiralty in London, headed by Vice Admiral Sir Alexander Duff. Whether in South America, Australia, "or in the most inaccessible parts of India or China," Royal Navy and British government representatives were in every port, however small and flyblown, from which merchantmen sailed, liaising with the local shippers and receiving news and instructions from headquarters. The convoy room regulated sailing dates, routes, rendezvous points, arrival times, and, above all, rerouting of convoys to avoid known U-boat positions. Duff's chief American deputy was Captain Byron Long, whose task it was to coordinate the movements of US convoys with the "much more numerous" Allied convoys.[14]

The convoy room was dominated by a huge chart covering an entire wall and accessed by ladders "not unlike those which are used in shoe stores." The chart contained

a comprehensive view of the North and South American coasts, the Atlantic Ocean, the British Isles, and a considerable part of Europe and Africa. The ports which it especially emphasized were Sydney (Cape Breton), Halifax, New York, Hampton Roads, Gibraltar, and on the west Coast of Africa, Sierra Leone and Dakar. Thin threads were stretched from each one of these seven points to certain positions in the ocean just outside the British Isles, and on these threads were little paper boats, each one of which represented a convoy. When a particular convoy started from New York, one of these paper boats was placed at that point; as it made its way across the ocean, the boat was moved from day to day in accordance with the convoy's progress. At any moment, therefore, a mere glance at this chart, with its multitude of paper boats, gave the spectator the precise location of all the commerce which was then *en route* to the scene of war.

Corresponding "little circles . . . marked off in the waters surrounding the British Isles" showed the location of suspected German U-boats, each one of which had been "shadowed" since leaving port and its course continually updated.[15]

The entire operation depended absolutely on the new medium of wireless communication. "The war stimulated the development of three types of transmitters: the arc, the alternator, and the low power vacuum tube." The first two were designed specifically to boost power for long-range communications. And by 1918, the US Navy had "receiving apparatuses as good as, and in most cases better than, that [*sic*] used by any other nation and vastly superior to any equipment in commercial use." The convoy system benefited immeasurably from these developments as well as the radio direction finder. At the time of American entry, the navy had installed active RDFs on its battleships and big armored cruisers, and work was under way at the Navy Research Radio Laboratory on developing smaller coils for the destroyers' SE 995 direction finders. In May, the lab reported that the addition of a single vertical wire to the antenna system would give "positive direction to the transmitting target." Modifications were swiftly made to the RDFs aboard Stateside destroyers (many of which were about to deploy overseas), and upgraded SE 995s "were shipped to Brest for installation" in destroyers already operating in European waters. This explains, in part, at least, why all the early Queenstown destroyers escorted their incoming charges to France at least once. Destroyer skippers quickly developed plans to exploit the new system, not only to locate U-boats and effectively concentrate hunter-killer groups against them, but also for the critical work of assembling and escorting convoys in thick weather. Contemporary accounts of the convoy war from the perspectives of both the bridge and the conference rooms ashore seldom mention the vital role played by radio direction finding in detecting and shepherding large flocks of ungainly ships to their destination in the foulest weather. The public was (and a century later often still is) left with the impression that consistently excellent escort work was due exclusively to the talents, even genius, of young British and American destroyer captains. While many undoubtedly developed a real gift for convoying, ever more efficient detection technology ensured that convoy work was far safer and more routine than it might otherwise have been.[16]

Not only did midocean convoys maintain (brief) contact with the Admiralty, providing status reports (including submarine attacks and sightings) and requesting emergency assistance, RDF effectively tracked the U-boats themselves by and through their frequent radio signals home. British and French naval intelligence had by 1917 reached a high state of sophistication especially in the field of radio interception and analysis. William Reginald (Blinker) Hall had been appointed director of British naval intelligence in November 1914. A keen observer of communications techniques, he immediately grasped the importance of RDF and seeded the English coastlines with stations whose information was transmitted in a steady flow to the famous "Room 40" in an unobtrusive building next to the Admiralty in London. From there it went to the Convoy Room and thence into American as well as British hands. As early as the end of April 1917, the Admiralty stated that its information "with regard to submarines entering and leaving their bases, and their approximate where-abouts while operating . . . is fairly exact."[17]

RDF was particularly critical in the antisubmarine war, for German U-boat captains were, in Sims's words, "particularly careless in the use of wireless." The "Germanic passion for conversation" was irrepressible. "Possibly . . . the solitary submarine felt lonely. At any rate, as soon as it reached the Channel or the North Sea, it started an almost uninterrupted flow of talk" with both its bases on the Belgian or German coasts and other U-boats. The Germans also possessed RFD, and they knew that submarine messages were being plotted and analyzed. Nonetheless, "the fear of discovery did not act as a curb upon a naturally loquacious nature." As another naval specialist later wrote, "Whenever the German vessels opened up with their radio, which they did with Teutonic regularity nearly every evening at the same hour, they would with a Teutonic lack of imagination disclose their position." From the unending message traffic, French and British analysts could plot not only *what* the submarine was doing and *where* it was, but also *who* it was.

Early capture of German naval codebooks made the analysts' job infinitely easier. Probably their greatest single achievement was the interception of the notorious Zimmerman Telegram. When the United States entered the war in part because of that German blunder, French as well as British intelligence officials shared "a great deal of information" not only with Sims but also with the Navy Department in Washington.

In the great Convoy Room above a bustling city, so far from the storms, the rolling icy waters, and the fog and mists of the North Atlantic, "the prospective tragedies of the seas were thus unfolding before our eyes." A convoy from New York, steaming toward its rendezvous, was heading directly for an area known to contain a half-dozen U-boats. Fortunately, a simple wireless message to the convoy to change course and steam fifty miles southward was sufficient. The U-boat commanders never knew how close they had come to triumph; they knew only frustration.[18]

Convoying, however effective, was a far from perfect system; it generated its own problems and tensions, and its effect in reducing casualties, particularly among the early troop transports, was due to German restraint rather than Allied policy. Kaiser Wilhelm steadfastly refused to declare war on the United States, even after the first American troops reached France and, later, began killing German boys. A month after the American declaration, von Holtzendorff instructed his U-boat captains not to attack American ships, and "as late as the fall, Germany hesitated to deploy U-boats in American waters to avoid antagonizing the United States further." Within the convoy system, sharp tensions existed between British and American authorities over a number of issues, all of which revolved around the chronically insufficient number of ocean convoy escorts. While the U.S. Navy tipped the balance in the U-boat war decisively toward the entente powers, the British did provide 70 percent of the destroyer escorts for all convoys, the United States roughly 27 percent. In the Western Approaches, however, margins were much less dramatic. By September 1917, some sixty-six destroyers had been ordered to the three "western commands"—Buncrana, Plymouth, and Queenstown—responsible for this area so critical to the Allied war effort. According to Britain's official history of the war at sea, Britain provided thirty vessels, variously detached from the Grand Fleet, Gibraltar, and the Channel ports of Dover and Portsmouth. "The United States provided the remaining thirty-six by their prompt and energetic answer to our appeals for help." It was this "reinforcement," the official history concludes, "which must be looked upon as the final contribution which made the new allocation of forces possible."[19] At the same time, both London and Washington readily agreed that their design and limited capabilities (fuel, seakeeping, limited armaments) rendered America's subchasers inadequate as convoy escorts, though excellent as coastal patrol craft. Nonetheless, throughout the war, the British provided the vast majority of these vessels as well. Sims tried unsuccessfully to concentrate control of all global shipping, including troop transports, in the British Admiralty, where his American section enjoyed close relations with the Royal Navy. Daniels, Benson, and their subordinates in the Navy Department, however, would have none of it, continuing to organize the gathering and sailing of all troop transports from the New World, including those headed for British ports.

Convoying proved an insatiable consumer of naval resources. Fortunately, Germany's U-boats were constrained by limited size and thus fuel and torpedo capacity. They could operate for a sufficient time only in the North and Irish Seas, in the Atlantic on the Western Approaches to Britain and France, and in the Bay of Biscay. With the kaiser adamantly refusing to undertake a comprehensive U-boat war against the American coast until it was too late, the US Navy assumed a fairly relaxed posture that the Admiralty in London had long striven to change. As early as May 1915, well before *Deutschland* and Hans Rose appeared in American waters, Admiralty intelligence had insisted that Berlin maintained a U-boat patrol capable of laying minefields off most US harbors and Chesapeake Bay. Not until late in March 1918, however, did the US Navy develop a comprehensive plan for protecting shipping in domestic waters. Sims might have been sensibly afraid of what the U-boats could do off European coasts, but he had little fear of an offensive in American waters. He cabled the Navy Department at the end of April that the long-range German cruiser U-boats were not only cumbersome and slow but also fragile and incapable of deep dives to safety. "If cruiser submarines are sent to the North Atlantic seaboard," he continued, "no great damage to shipping is to be anticipated. Nearly all shipping eastbound is in convoy and it is unlikely that any appreciable number of convoys will be sighted, and if sighted will probably not be attacked. The shipping westbound is independent, but is scattered over such a wide area that the success of the cruiser submarine would not be large, and war warnings would soon indicate areas to be avoided." But once committed to war the Navy Department moved swiftly to establish an effective antisubmarine regime. Coastal convoy lanes and routes were established, active U-boat hunting was undertaken by aircraft and submarines based in the Caribbean and along the Atlantic Coast from Key West to Boston and finally Nova Scotia, nets were set in and defensive minefields laid off the major East Coast ports, and "limited escort offshore" by subchasers and "9 destroyers" was begun, as were antisubmarine communications networks. By June, the Admiralty was insisting to Sims and his people that it was "practically certain" that one U-boat, "probably U-151," was off the Atlantic coast. By this time, the navy was alert. "The first definite information of the activity of the German raider off the American coast was received by radio on May 19 at 12:14 p.m." when "Atlantic City radio intercepted an SOS from the American steamship Nayanza, 6,213 gross tons, advising that she was being gunned" and gave her position. While somewhat shot up, the vessel did not sink.

The kaiser and his admirals, however, still hesitated to initiate a full-scale U-boat "blockade" of the United States. That reluctant decision finally came in July with the dispatch of three of the long-range "cruiser" submarines (nearly all Germany possessed) to American waters along with several smaller submarines of markedly limited range and thus time on station. The task of this little flotilla was to disrupt the American war effort by any means available, torpedoes, mines, or gunfire. On the twenty-sixth, the Admiralty told Sims that based on a "reliable authority," the harbor works, "cranes etc. at Wilmington [North Carolina? Delaware?] were considered by the Germans as favorable objects of bombardment." The greatest fear on both sides of the ocean, however, revolved around possible U-boat attacks on the transatlantic and Caribbean undersea communications cables through which passed by the spring of 1918 roughly fifty-five thousand messages a day between Washington and western Europe. In

all, a half-dozen U-boats made the passage to American waters, and the ubiquitous U–151 apparently did cut several cables in the course of its major mission
of minelaying but failed to materially disrupt the flow of messages due to quick
response and repair by American vessels. Nonetheless, the half-dozen U-boats
recorded more than twenty sinkings, including armored cruiser *San Diego*, leading the navy to further strengthen its antisubmarine patrols.

In the end, the US Navy expressed deep and pardonable pride in defeating
a U-boat campaign against its shores of some morally questionable dimensions.
An early postwar analysis of losses concluded, "It is apparent that the submarine
intended to take no chances, and where the vessel appeared large enough to
probably be armed the torpedo was resorted to, whereas the small helpless craft
(sailing vessels, tugs, barges, motor boats) were openly attacked" by gunfire "and
ruthlessly destroyed. Of the vessels destroyed or injured by mines all were large
vessels." The navy's conclusions were stark, uncompromising, and suffused with
hatred and contempt. "The German campaign, by means of submarines on the
Atlantic coast of the United States, so far as concerned the major operations
of the war, was a failure. Every transport and cargo vessel bound for Europe
sailed as if no such campaign was in progress. All coast-wise shipping sailed as
per schedule, a little more care in routing vessels being observed. There was no
interruption to the coast patrol which, on the contrary, became rather more active," despite the fact that the subchasers and converted yachts that constituted
the overwhelming proportion of the patrol were notably outgunned by the U-
boats they hunted. In marked contrast to what would occur a quarter century
later, "there was no stampede on the Atlantic coast; no excitement; everything
went on in the usual calm way, and, above all, this enemy expedition did not
succeed in retaining" any vessels that had been designed for duty in European
waters."[20] But resources were never increased at the expense of the transatlantic
convoys, which by the summer of 1918 were pouring men and supplies into
France at a prodigious rate.

The system never deviated from its basic structure. Gleaves's cruiser and
transportation service escorted each cluster of ships out of New York or Hampton Roads into the Atlantic for several hundred miles before the escort screen
of older destroyers and armed yachts peeled off and headed back to port for a
brief rest before either going out on patrol or protecting yet another convoy.
Thereafter, save for an armored cruiser or two for protection against maraud-
ing German battle cruisers that never appeared, most convoys were minimal-
ly escorted until they approached the U-boat hunting grounds that began at
roughly longitude 20°W, where British or American destroyers (or both) from

Devonport, Queenstown, and later Brest as well picked them up and accompanied them into British or French ports.

Both the US and the Royal Navies appreciated the Yankee destroyers' superiority for convoy work. The American ships "bore only a general resemblance" to their British counterparts. Hull shape, gunnery and torpedo arrangements, number of stacks, and so on gave the American vessels "quite a contrasting profile." But it was their ability to stay at sea, to steam long distances without refueling, that gave them the edge. In keeping with their navy's practical two-ocean mission (especially once the Panama Canal was opened just days before Europe fell into war), American destroyers were built "with the widest possible cruising radius." They were "expected" to steam "to the West Indies, to operate from the Atlantic to the Pacific, and in general to feel at home anywhere in the great stretch of waters that surround our country." The Royal Navy's destroyers, on the other hand, while more heavily gunned and marginally faster, were built to operate in the far more restricted home waters of the British Isles, where refueling and reprovisioning were ready to hand.[21]

Convoy life assumed a steady routine, a particular pattern. As slowly moving clusters of ships from New York or Hampton Roads approached European waters, anxieties on every vessel mounted. Would the destroyers from Ireland or France find the convoy and escort it to Liverpool or Brest? If not, what then? Terror began not in the trenches but on the sea. Sims wrote that "the boys all had exciting experiences with phantom submarines." Indeed, he continued, there was probably not "a single one" among the two million members of the American Expeditionary Force "who has not entertained his friends and relatives with accounts of torpedo streaks and schools of U-boats." The admiral's tone was jocular, if not dismissive. But fears were tangible and legitimate. There *were* U-boats out there, together with their hundreds of victims floating on great ocean swells, awaiting rescue.[22]

Similar anxieties gripped destroyer captains on their tiny, wind- and rain-swept bridges as they sought to make rendezvous. The paucity of destroyers relative to the convoys to be escorted was a never-ending problem throughout the final stages of the war, solved only by making these precious vessels do double duty. British and American destroyers escorted outbound convoys from French or British ports past the latitude 20° danger zone, generally parting company at or after dusk as the convoys sailed on to New World ports. The destroyers then "raced through the night" to find their designated incoming convoys.[23]

"'Getting your convoy' was a searching test of destroyer seamanship."[24] Reporter Ralph Paine, who rode the destroyers for a time, noted that poor weather might scatter a division, requiring a time-consuming reassemblage. Often the radio brought news from a troop or cargo convoy that it was a day or so behind schedule. "This meant many more miles to run in search of the great steamers which were steadily ploughing toward the danger-zone." Captains betrayed no signs of worry, but their manner often "was not quite so blithe" and their "eyes were tired." No escort ever failed to find its convoy, but "the dread of missing the ships at the rendezvous or losing them during the night" never left the minds of escort commanders. Usually navigating by dead reckoning (too frequent radio communication was forbidden for obvious reasons), the destroyers invariably found their convoy, often at dawn, "spectral shapes, lofty, majestic, moving in column, and so far preserved from attack. Trained, obedient to the word, the destroyers took their stations ahead and on the flanks, very small and nimble besides their unwieldy charges, swinging against the sky-line or disappearing to all but the funnels between the lifting seas."

On his way to European waters, Paine found himself aboard one of the early passenger liners "cracking on at nineteen knots" through the U-boat zone in 1917. Navy gun crews stood by their weapons; smoke boxes to foil a U-boat's angle of attack were ready to be thrown overboard. Anxious passengers were "girdled" in life preservers, alternatively thrilled and appalled to be risking their lives. Among them was a US senator on his way to London. Where was the Navy? he kept asking. "Where were those destroyers which the captain of the ship assured them would be sent out to take care of them?" Throughout an anxious night, the man and a number of fellow passengers fretted as they walked the decks. Then, as morning slowly broke, two and then three specks appeared on the horizon. Growing ever larger, the three destroyers "raced out of the eastward" to circle the big ship's bow. The crews were dressed in dungarees, sweaters, and oilskins as they went about their work, seemingly oblivious to the huge ship nearby, save for the heavy seas it generated. Paine guessed that the destroyermen were probably "cursing" the nearby leviathan "because its speed made life miserable" for the small ships, "bucking and pounding and twisting in the rough water."

In fact, many a destroyer sailor was "thrilled" to be doing such important work. Gone now for Charles Blackford, his mates aboard *McDougal*, and the other destroyer sailors were the endless weeks of "senseless patrols." Aboard the escorts, officers and lookouts raised their binoculars toward the decks of the great troop transports, "packed with dense masses of brown, at a distance like blotches of paint smeared fore and aft and along the rails." The life-belted troops stood for hours on end, gazing at the destroyers as they dipped and rolled on the flanks of the convoy. Whatever cheers the doughboys might have raised were blown with the wind, but to the men on the escorts, the sight of these thousands heading toward the battlefields of France to fight the Hun was always an awesome sight. "At last we were doing something logical: forming a screen about a group of ships rather than acting as a guide in reverse to submarines. We felt our responsibility. The lookouts kept alert, scanning the horizon for any indication of a submarine." For those aboard the liners and transports, the destroyers meant nothing less than deliverance. "They loved the Navy. It was magnificent. The country had never appreciated its noble bluejackets. The senator laid aside his lifebelt, invaded the smoking-room, and swore he would vote for any naval appropriation desired."[25]

To the hundreds and thousands of doughboys packed aboard large and not so large troop transports, the Atlantic voyage was a never-to-be forgotten adventure as part of a larger anxiety. Leonard C. Kenyon "crossed the pond" in May 1918 as part of a convoy of nine "good sized boats," initially escorted by one of the navy's armored cruisers. All of the vessels save the cruiser and Kenyon's transport, which served as a flagship, were painted in blue, pink, and green dazzle camouflage.[26] Within hours of putting to sea, the convoy swelled to fourteen transports carrying more than thirty-three thousand men, as well as a Belgian relief ship. Sailing through calm seas, the cluster of ships periodically split into groups of two so the navy gunnery teams could engage in target practice. Kenyon was "hungry all the time." But all other comforts were available. Fresh water was no problem. Entertainment came in the form of frequent "movies" and band concerts. One evening at dinner, "'Marconi' the $200 a week Hippodrome man played his concertina," followed by a number of enlisted men "singing, playing and reciting."

Then the deaths began. "Wilhelm, a man in our Supply Company died of appendicitis." Within five days, twenty-five men were stricken with either scarlet fever or pneumonia or both; several perished. As the weather deteriorated at midocean, men became violently seasick and took to their bunks, where they were "hitting the side of the bed and then the wall." A week after leaving New York, the convoy reached the war zone. A few destroyers appeared and then inexplicably disappeared. "We wear life belts and canteens at all times. Sleep in clothes and rise at 4. Stand at 'abandon ship' for an hour both at dawn & at dusk." Within hours, "11 destroyers" joined the convoy, while the armored cruiser "disappeared, presumably back to the States." A dozen days after leaving New York, the convoy, ship by ship, entered the narrow channel at Brest, "big hills of rock in the bay . . . houses very interesting . . . fields very green," and the air "exceedingly clear." The following day, May 24, "three large steamers full of troops followed us in . . . making the total landed at Brest this week at about 50,000 or more." Kenyon was clearly a man of his time and place in which white supremacy and class privilege were as natural as the air he breathed. As the troops slowly trundled off their vessels, he casually applied the *n* word to the enlisted stevedores "from the states" unloading the ships "by aid of cranes & nets."[27]

Most of the two million who crossed the Atlantic had never seen a large body of water, to say nothing of an ocean. Each had been issued a card to carry on his person as a reminder not to talk loosely and to respect censorship. One soldier penned a satirical response that revealed the underlying anxieties of these millions of landlubbers suddenly in the midst of hostile seas.

Censorship

We're sailing away to God knows where,
To a promised land that's "over there";
The plains of France or Italy's Alps
May furnish our quota of German scalps.
Unknown to us is the end of our trip,
We sail on the good bark "Censorship."

How do we bunk and what of our chow?
And how is the army anyhow?
Any low spirits among the bunch?
Say, how many fellows have "lost their lunch"?
Ask not; some spy might get a tip—
It's all deleted by censorship.

Perchance we've sighted a submarine.
Perchance again none has been seen,
A hydroplane or German barks,
Or maybe only a school of sharks.
The sheers of the censor merrily clip;
You don't get much through the censor-ship.

Do we have "In cadence, exercise"?
Do rumors, as usual, prove to be lies?
Drills and inspections from morn till "taps"?

Anyone caught in a game of craps?
To you the answer I'd gladly slip
But we sail on the tight boat "Censor-ship."

You ask if we have Red Cross nurses or no?
Do "Tea hounds" flirt with mermaids also?
And to quicken our spirits in case they lag
"Say, Pard, what're chances to borrow a fag?"
All of this dope I have on my lip,
And it's stopped right there by censorship.

But we'll see the end of this war, we hope,
With its fear of the treacherous periscope,
When safe will be the bounding main,
As we come sailing home again.
With wonderful tales crammed in our grip,—
And we won't sail back on the "Censorship."[28]

Initial impressions and later recollections of what happened at sea were both often wrong. Yeoman Johnny Arthur Didway, aboard the transport *Henderson* on her second convoy, remembered the guns of another "transport," *Charleston* (actually an armored cruiser) blowing the "covering tower" (that is, conning tower), off a U-boat, provoking a wholesale abandonment. According to Didway, the submarine was towed to port, where "they blew it up." Such an incident never occurred. On *Henderson*'s third convoy, Didway claimed to have been part of a great sea-air battle some seven miles off St. Nazaire involving no fewer than seven German submarines. Four U-boats were sunk. That battle never happened in the way, intensity, and outcome portrayed. The U-boat hunters themselves were frequently prone to exaggeration. Oftentimes a bit of oil mixed in with the exploding waters together with a puff or two of smoke was enough to convince sailors of a kill; occasionally, aircraft would site a U-boat through clear waters sitting on the bottom following a depth-charge attack, leading its antagonists to believe they had gotten it.[29] Regrettably, they never did. The kaiser's U-boats and their crew were tougher than that.

The crux of America's war at sea in 1917–18 was, as a destroyer captain told Ralph Paine, "a question of tonnage and a safe road across the Atlantic. Otherwise there was nothing doing for the Stars and Stripes, no matter how many armies were raised and trained. And it was up to the destroyers to get them into

France. Nothing else to it." Even the most veteran destroyer skipper on convoy escort "never quite got used to" the crushing responsibility as he did his tedious, dangerous job time and again, month after month.[30]

As the convoys came across the Atlantic in ever-greater sizes and numbers and the destroyers' major role shifted from patrol to escort work, command duties changed and expanded. Skippers who had been responsible for policing one to three patrol zones on their own now found themselves, as escort commanders, responsible for entire clusters of ships. The monotony and boredom of life at sea became laced with ever-greater dangers and challenges that led to often numbing exhaustion. Convoy work was a never-ending process, particularly on stormy nighttime seas with no lights permitted, or in rain and fog. Some merchantmen invariably straggled, their engine-room people unaccustomed to steaming at the "absolutely uniform number of revolutions" required to maintain station. Still other vessels ordered to steam at near maximum speed lost power when forced to bank fires to clean boilers. Destroyers often signaled merchantmen to "close up," receiving the inevitable reply, "We are doing our utmost."

And most of them were, for life at sea aboard the merchantmen was as rough and even brutal as it was for their escorts. Horace Taylor came from a family of mariners who traced their lineage back to the Isle of Wight; after years at sea, his father established a nautical academy in California that young Horace helped run before setting out on several journeys to the Far East. In November 1917, Taylor found himself in "cold, god-foreseaken" New York City, where he joined the SS *Clara*, "a 'captured' Austrian tramp of pretty large size." The ship and a growing number of others sat for days in the freezing East River before at last getting under way in convoy. Once at sea, "Everything is wet. Sea is breaking all over the ship. Don't know if we are traveling North or South." Machinery soon broke down, the helm stuck for several hours, forcing *Clara* to maneuver on its engines. "Why in Hell didn't I stay in Manila—or at Honolulu," Taylor wrote in his diary. There was much worse to come.

Several days out and "Ye Gods, our room is full of water. Sea water all over the place splashing around has ruined all our clothes. Even the bunk is wet." The storm blew itself out some days short of Halifax and bedding and clothes dried. On December 6, *Clara* swung to anchor in Halifax Harbour fifteen minutes late when "all of a sudden there was a hell of an explosion" that left the wheelhouse and wireless room "ruined," jarred the compass out of its bowl, "smashed" the barometer, and "broke" the thermometer. As stunned crewmen lay about knocked flat or frantically clutched rails and stanchions, all believed that a German bombardment was under way. "Every mother's son of us" was "ready to shake hands with his Satanic Majesty." In fact, a French vessel, *Mont-Blanc*, laden with a cargo of picric acid, TNT, guncotton, and benzol had collided with the Belgian relief ship *Imo*, whose bow breached the hold carrying the benzol. The French crew promptly abandoned ship as *Mont-Blanc* drifted, smoking, toward the downtown piers and fetched up against Number 6. Moments later, as a crowd gathered to watch firefighters try to extinguish whatever blaze was on board, fires reached either the TNT or the guncotton. *Mont-Blanc* exploded with a horrific roar. The blast, exceeded only by the later atomic bombings in Japan, instantly killed more than fifteen hundred people, injured hundreds more, and leveled large areas of the city. "Every ship in the harbor is more or less damaged." A "big cloud of smoke" raced toward *Clara*, briefly smothering the ship. For days thereafter, the forest across the river remained afire, while Halifax Harbour "is a solid mass of oil, horse flesh and wreckage of all kinds" and the city itself "continues to burn. The horizon is all red from the reflection."[31]

When the shaken crew, ship, and convoy made their way out of the ruined port some days later, they promptly ran into the hurricane-force winds and mountainous seas that characterized the Newfoundland banks in winter. Taylor and his mates routinely stood four-hour watches on open-bridge wings with temperatures ten degrees below zero. "Ye Gods! What a night," Taylor wrote in his diary at one point. "Eighteen hours of Hell. No relief on the bridge for 12 hours. Twelve hours of the worst punishment I ever went through. Everything adrift. I saw the Bos'n smashed to pieces before my eyes. A big sea rolled him along the deck and smashed him against the Engine Room bulkhead." The next day: "Everything wet and cold and damp. It will be just good luck if this wagon ever reaches France. Great fun to wake up and find a foot of sea water in your room and not a light in the ship. Not even a candle or a dry match."[32]

Joe Taussig and his mates spared little time for concern about the bruised bodies and minds of their charges. Their only job was to get the ships through, which proved tough enough in its own right. Many destroyermen came to actively dislike their counterparts in the transport service, whom they quickly concluded had "joined the Navy to keep out of the Army. We had heard them boasting about shirking work and sleeping while on lookout. They were always complaining, although living in luxury compared to us." Dislike often turned to dockside insults and threats, though apparently to no outright brawling. During the later stages of the war, the transport sailors proved so obnoxious at Queenstown, "their liberty parties reel[ing] about town, insulting girls and women, picking fights and giving us all a bad reputation," that a delegation of destroyer sailors asked Bayly and his people for relief. "Presently a regulation came out that sailors on transport ships were to wear white hats ashore," while all other American sailors stationed abroad would wear the traditional navy-blue flat hats. "The public soon discovered the difference, which made it pleasanter" for the destroyermen.[33]

As the winter of 1917–18 came on to the North Atlantic, escort work "meant living almost continually in wet clothing, the vessel rolling thirty to forty degrees six times a minute for days on end, bucking head seas that would raise the whole forepart of the vessel free of the water as far aft as the foremast." Eating anything like a nourishing meal was impossible, real sleep was unattainable, and seasickness struck even the saltiest of sailors. New forced-ventilation systems proved useless, and a crewman coming off the bracing winds on deck "had to hold his breath as he went down the ladder" to be struck by stale air fouled by "unwashed bodies, vomit, and dampness." Spray sucked below by the ventilators mixed with "dripping oilskins and sweating metal off the overhead [ceiling] and sides" of a compartment. "Bits of food and vomit swished from side to side on the deck against the after bulkhead." Twenty-four or thirty-six hours out of Queenstown or Brest, men lost any sense of time and began "to doubt if there really was a place without motion, vibration, creak of working metal, slosh of water and wind, spray and cold. The ship seemed a Flying Dutchman that had forgotten the last port and would never reach the next."[34]

Taussig usually positioned *Wadsworth* at the rear of a convoy and if a ship fell behind too much would send his destroyer between the laggard and the rear of the convoy, which usually prompted a puff of smoke from the freighter's stack and a burst of speed. Until merchant captains gained confidence through experience, convoys often scattered "widely" after dark, with "timid" skippers concerned to avoid collisions, especially since each vessel was running in a darken-ship mode. Thus, the escorts spent many a tedious morning rounding up their charges and getting them back in order, only to have to repeat the process the following day. "Communications were a particularly difficult problem at first. Some of the ships carried only one radio operator, and no signalmen who understood the semaphore system." Language was also a barrier. So the escort captains took their destroyers close alongside the dilatory or out-of-position merchantman and delivered messages by word of mouth through a hailer. "This was not always easy when the wind was howling and a big sea was running." Foreign skippers—French, Italian, Scandinavian—would often profess not to hear; Taussig suspected they really failed to understand. One escort commander, goaded beyond endurance by a recalcitrant Italian merchant captain who failed to respond to "the international flag hoist, semaphore, radio and megaphone," took his ship alongside and shouted: "'You blank, blank, blankety blank, when I hoist the flag X you head south blank, blank quick, savvy?' and without a moment's hesitation came the answer: 'All right, Sir!'"

More than occasionally, a merchantman would fall out of the convoy with a broken engineering plant, requiring a tow by another freighter or a tug if nearby. Stormy weather brought the threat of shifting cargoes, "leaving us to wonder whether or not" the stricken vessel "would turn turtle." There were times when the crew of a cargo ship "would *think*" their vessel torpedoed and would race for the lifeboats, occasionally even lowering them to the water, before one of the escorts appeared to calm things down and get the crew back aboard. Because time was of the essence in getting troops and cargoes to England and destroyers were chronically overscheduled, convoys would often split up if the Irish Sea appeared empty of U-boats. Vessels were left to steam the last hundred or so miles to Liverpool or even Channel ports independently, which frequently provoked the anguish of merchant skippers, who let the escorts know of their unhappiness, especially if, as often happened, murk and fog obscured important landmarks ashore, making navigation extremely difficult.

As time went on, however, "the whole conduct of the merchant convoys improved," and a climate of professionalism developed. The growing number of destroyers as escorts together with the assignment of "commodores" as overall commanders of the merchant ships brought "a decided advancement in station keeping, signaling, etc. Especially was this evident in certain inbound convoys" to Liverpool or Brest, "which had been carefully drilled" on the trip across the Atlantic. "On one occasion," Taussig recalled, he had been given command of an eight-destroyer escort for a thirty-two-ship convoy. Deeming the escort too weak, the Admiralty in London sent eight British destroyers to join up, and Taussig ordered them to act as an outer screen. When one discovered a submarine and charged to attack, "the convoy and escort a total of 48 ships" turned away simultaneously "without the least bit of confusion."

America's destroyer sailors, in conjunction with their British opposites, were also developing new tactics as more and more ships came on line. Bolder U-boat commanders disdained the inshore killing of single ships; if the Allies clustered their merchantmen in convoys, the Germans would come after them. "This gave the escorting destroyers the much-desired opportunity for transforming their *role* from the defensive to the offensive, by undertaking a vigorous counterattack." Earlier on, the number of depth charges a single destroyer could carry was restricted by availability. But as more and more American factories produced more and more charges, the destroyers increased their carrying capacity from a mere handful up to thirty per vessel and beyond, allowing each ship to engage in "barrage" tactics, "the laying of a large number of depth charges in rapid succession while the destroyer was proceeding at good speed." The tactic did not lead, as many hoped, to a major expansion of U-boat kills, but it maintained the pressure of suppression on enemy submarines.[35]

Still, despite all best efforts, disasters occasionally happened. Convoys inbound from the New World funneling into the ever-narrower Western Approaches or the Straits of Gibraltar often met flocks of outbound ships. In an age before radar and long-range aircraft surveillance, when wireless schedules and waves were easily disrupted by the elements and wartime restrictions on the use of radio were strict, unsuspecting convoys or their destroyer escorts could blunder into each other in the dark of night when fog or murk obscured running lights. Suddenly, strange vessels appeared where moments before there had been empty seas.

Bill Halsey, skipper of destroyer *Benham*, was on his bridge one "inky black and drizzling" night in March 1918 when the ship suddenly "passed between two steamers on opposite courses about 500 yards apart." Neither vessel showed any lights. "It sure is a hell of a sensation! You see nothing until they are right on top of you, and then only a black hump with no possibility of telling which way they are heading." Halsey had no choice but to keep his tiny warship on course, "and pray you will go between them," which *Benham* did. Collision was an ever-present possibility and the greatest calamity in the "ship infested waters" of the Western Approaches, "Hun subs and mines nothwistanding."[36]

Conditions were no better farther south. Near dawn one morning off Gibraltar, a subchaser sailor standing at the rail beside the engine-room hatch glimpsed "a huge gray shape" cutting through the fog and "roaring past." "For the next fifteen minutes bedlam reigned" as a half-dozen Royal Navy destroyers charged "helter-skelter," in and out among forty-two cargo ships. Inexplicably, there was not a single collision. Both sides blamed the other, but the British had the last word, expressing dismay at the seamanship and navigation of a convoy "arriving ten minutes ahead of time at a rendezvous set three days before." Other convoys were not so fortunate, as ships sideswiped each other in the dark with screams of torn metal. Lifeboats and other deck gear splintered or were torn off, while sirens abruptly keened their terror. Some vessels were T-boned; others avoided collisions by frantic turns of the helm. Bewildered escorts from both groups were caught in the middle, their captains often helpless to do anything in the chaos. In one encounter in the Western Approaches, *McDougal* found giant ships bearing "down on us from both directions, sheering away just in time," until one merchantman smashed into the destroyer's stern, tearing away some twenty-five feet, as "cleanly cut as if a great opener had gone through." As the big vessel "simply vanished" into the night, *McDougal's* tiny, narrow bridge became "crowded with officers, quartermasters, and lookouts," while the captain frantically issued "ahead and astern orders to the quartermaster at the engine-room telegraph as ships popped out of the mist on one side or another." As its engines shut down, the wounded warship began to wallow in steep wave troughs until it was taken in tow and brought to Liverpool for prolonged repairs.[37] That such catastrophes were few and far between was attested to by the relatively few losses of ships in convoy. In most instances, superb seamanship and cool heads prevailed.

All agreed that destroyer life and antisubmarine warfare were a young man's game. Terror was never far away. "Fish, particularly porpoises, sent my heart into my boots time after time during those patrols" in the dark winter and early spring nights of 1917–18. In the phosphorescent waters off the British Isles and France, a porpoise "has a strong resemblance to a torpedo." Suddenly, a wake is seen heading at high speed straight for the ship. There is no time to maneuver, only to suck in one's breath. When the wake reaches the ship's side, men brace for the explosion that never comes. Instead, the porpoise suddenly appears on the other side, swimming blithely on, oblivious to the panic it has created.[38]

When a vessel completed its week or so at sea and steamed past the Daunt Lightship and into Queenstown Harbor or past the fort and into Brest under often leaden skies that dripped rain, the weary destroyer skipper could expect the usual signal from Admiralty House on the hill inviting him to a relaxing dinner or tea with Bayly and his charming young niece or, if in France, dinner with colleagues in a plush restaurant with a reasonably good wartime kitchen. For the Queenstown skippers, there were also excellent dinners and stimulating company on tennis courts and golf courses at the Royal Yacht Club in nearby Cork. Halsey remembered alsH""the break" from sea duty as always "gay." Stressed-out young captains renamed the Yacht Club the "Royal Uncork Yacht Club" and devised a special decoration, the "FIR," or "fell in the river," for their many colleagues who failed to navigate the road back to the ship unscathed.[39]

But between these pleasantries was a workload of formidable proportions. Instead of writing brief patrol reports as before and overseeing what minor repairs were needed, a captain, if escort commander, would have to write a lengthy, detailed report on the fate of his latest convoy and then turn to mastering materials on the next convoy to be shepherded, its number of ships, cargoes, destination, course, speed, anticipated U-boat strength along the route, and so on, together with any peculiarities that might arise within or about the convoy.[40]

In-port life was worse for those destroyer crews who called Queenstown home. The little town offered few attractions beyond a few bars, and while nearby Cork was available, young Charles Blackford and his shipmates discovered that "the better hotels would not accept enlisted men, and the poorer ones were unlivable by American standards." Nonetheless, Cork soon came to be the place to go on liberty. Paine insisted, probably with some measure of truth, that the bluejackets were "mostly wholesome youngsters, very boyish in appearance," who came from "good homes, from people who are proud of them and their service." Inevitably, however, the lads came into conflict with the locals, especially the Irish rebels or Sinn Feiners whose love for Germany was not only open but ardent. As Sims noted also, as with a later war, the Americans in their attractive uniforms had more money than the local youth "and could entertain the girls more lavishly at the [silent] movies and ice cream stands"— and presumably elsewhere as well. "Gradually, trouble began between the men of Cork and our sailors," though no one could discern its exact cause. "At first, only a few drunks were beaten and robbed," Blackford remembered. Then the American sailors with Irish girls were set upon by small mobs. "A group of gobs on their way to Blarney Castle were stoned while going through town." The sailors fought back promptly and with undoubted relish. "Occasionally," one would be returned from Cork to Queenstown "in a condition that demanded pressing medical attention." Matters came to a head one day when an infuriated Sinn Feiner set upon his former girlfriend on the arm of a sailor as the couple "promenaded" down Cork's main thoroughfare. As the "hooligan" sought to tear the girl away, the sailor struck him hard, knocking him to the pavement and fracturing his skull. Soon the young Irishman died, and the navy was forced to place Cork off-limits to enlisted men.[41]

Paine believed that most of the young sailors disdained the "frowzy bars where unlike England liquor was not rationed as a wartime measure." He hinted that this may have been due as much to the presence of a small army of shore patrolmen strolling the streets "swinging short heavy sticks with a loop at one end and displaying no sympathy" for rowdiness. Despite the growing restrictions, a number of youngsters did find Irish girls to date, court, and even marry, though confinement to Queenstown kept prospects low. Wartime provided unprecedented opportunities for rapid advancement to petty-officer ranks and even the dream of becoming an officer one day, so "ambition and the feeling that it is a privilege to be playing the big game are the factors that check discontent." The opportunity to stay out of the trenches also doubtless played a role. Soon, Americans residing in London raised twenty thousand dollars for an enlisted men's clubhouse in Queenstown. Run by the men themselves, the wooden single-story barracks-like building contained a stage for the men to mount their own entertainment, "a large moving-picture theater, library, a dormitory with comfortable beds where a man could get a real night's sleep ashore, and a restaurant that served unlimited amounts of hot-dogs, steak, sandwiches, coffee and pie."[42]

Many men, however, found this enforced wholesomeness not to their liking and searched elsewhere for something to do. "Movies and a skating rink" provided some diversions; many sailors "eventually found a hangout," lazily romancing shopgirls in their workplaces—candy stores, groceries, and the like. Occasionally, "in-port routine would be broken by a sudden call to go to sea." Recall flags were raised afloat and ashore, whistles screamed, and the Shore Patrol "began combing the bars and hangouts." Security remained tight. A century ago, the American "gob" ashore wore a flat navy-blue hat with his ship's name embroidered on a ribbon around the hat. Shore patrolmen would burst into an establishment crying, "Show your hats, sailors, show your hats!" They never named a ship, but when they saw it on a hat, "they would tap the owner and say 'back to your ship, sailor, back to your ship.'"[43]

Like the western front—and unlike World War II—there were no USO shows; no glamorous entertainers from Broadway or Hollywood stopped by. Whether morale at Queenstown could have been sustained much beyond the twelve to sixteen months' exposure to wartime conditions is hard to say.

As the number of antisubmarine ships in both navies grew throughout the last half of 1917, patterns of patrol and escort out in the Atlantic and in the Irish Sea never varied. The work was "monotonous and dreary"; frustrations were high and available weaponry limited both in number and in effectiveness. "For days, the men lived in a world of fog and mist; rain . . . seemed to be almost the normal state of nature," and the destroyers engaged in battle with "oil slicks, wakes, tide rips, streaks of suds, and suspicious disturbances in the water."[44]

Escort resources were always at a premium. Some fast transports were forced to sail the Atlantic on their own until they reached the submarine zone east of longitude 20°. Early on Sunday afternoon, November 3, 1917, the SS *St. Paul*, a rather elegant two-funnel fifteen-thousand-ton, 550-foot passenger vessel completed in 1895, departed New York for Liverpool. The twenty-two-knot ship had just been assigned to naval service by the War Shipping Board and was unescorted as she steamed into the Atlantic. Among the forty-seven first-class passengers ("and apparently not many 2nd class") were Admiral Albert P. Niblack, on his way to Gibraltar to command all US naval forces in the Mediterranean; the lord chief justice of England; British journalist Lord Northcliffe; and a young US Marine aviator, Captain Alfred A. Cunningham, on his way to Paris to help prepare for the substantial influx of naval and Marine Corps aviators that was expected in the coming months. Rumor had it that the ship also carried fifty million dollars in gold bullion in its hold.

The crossing was made in bad weather, the ship "cold and uncomfortable." As *St. Paul* approached the U-boat zone off southwestern England, nerves tightened. For caution's sake, Cunningham decided to sleep in his clothes. He fretted at the slow pace. "We only made 348 miles the past 24 hours, which is pretty slow going. The Captain says he hopes to get to Liverpool Monday and that we will reach the 'zone' tomorrow night. I took off my uniform this morning and am now wearing 'cits,'" having heard that "the boches either sink boats with officers in uniform or capture the officers and I have no desire to needlessly spend the balance of this war in a German prison camp. . . . I consider myself well 'camouflaged.'" The ship eventually reached longitude 20°W early Saturday morning. Niblack assembled all officers in the dining room and gave them lookout assignments to augment those of the crew. Cunningham found the long hours of endless sea scanning among the "most strenuous" he had ever passed.

> I stayed on watch until 10 a.m., went back on at 2 p.m. and stayed until after evening twilight. This looking for submarines is the most nerve straining duty I ever did. You must see them first, and, as their periscope is very small, the odds are against you. You feel that the slightest negligence on your part might lose the ship and all on board. I freely strained my eyesight while on watch today. I am confident that I saw the periscope of a submarine today, but, as it did not reappear, I might have been mistaken. The ten minutes after I saw it were anxious ones.

Strain was eased appreciably by the sudden appearance of destroyers *Conyngham* and *Jacob Jones*, "camouflaged to the limit," their hulls "mottled all over with the most crazy colors and designs." Everyone was delighted to see them, not because of "the slight additional protection they give as to the fact that if we are sunk, they will pick us up from the lifeboats." Everyone aboard *St. Paul* knew that merchant ships were strictly forbidden from stopping to pick up survivors. "Without the destroyers we would have to drift around the North Atlantic in an open boat" for several days in winter weather, not a happy prospect. On her last voyage, *St. Paul* had rushed past a dozen lifeboats "full of people" who were fortunately found two days later by a destroyer. "We passed some wreckage this afternoon, but could not make out what it was. What with watch keeping, worrying about being torpedoed, and seeing the destroyers, the tough Marine aviation pioneer had "had a most strenuous day and am all worn out."

The following day proved even worse as the ship entered St. George's Channel and moved up the Irish Sea toward Liverpool, "the zone thickly infested with German submarines." Long hours of watch keeping on the bridge yielded views of other merchantmen being escorted by destroyers and an SOS call "from some poor ship south of us saying they were being chased by a submarine. . . . The Germans are certainly keeping things busy around here," Cunningham wrote uneasily in his diary that night, "and I understand are sowing mines everywhere. If we get through tonight, we are fairly safe. However this St. George's Channel is supposed to be alive with subs." Fortunately, the night was "misty and foggy." Following "another night of expecting to be torpedoed any minute," *St. Paul* came abreast of the Liverpool Lightship and took a pilot aboard. Writing the following day from a comfortable suite at the Savoy in London, Cunningham remembered bidding "our good friends the destroyers good-bye and they headed for sea" to escort another ship or convoy through perilous waters.[45]

As the destroyer sailors "stuck to" their jobs "doggedly," the shape and pace of the antisubmarine campaign began to change and with it the whole complexion of the war at sea. The first discernible change came in the early autumn of 1917. Wreckage suddenly became "less plentiful," distress signals "less frequent and imploring." Departures from Queenstown became "quiet, almost commonplace, so smoothly" had the growing American destroyer fleet "fitted in to the daily routine of war." Approaching the open seas, some sailors donned life preservers, but more to keep out the cold of an impending winter than with any serious thought of being torpedoed. Gun crews "found what shelter they could and the lookouts climbed to the tiny baskets at the mastheads where they crouched behind the canvas screens to keep an eye lifted for Fritz." Captains who had been "spruce" and "precise to the last button" of their uniforms ashore now climbed into "sheepskin jackets, sea-boots and knitted helmets," while forsaking their tiny staterooms below to "snatch sleep" fully clothed "on a transom" in the chart house just steps below the bridge.[46]

The enemy, too, began to draw conclusions from the erratic statistics. When word of the convoys reached German naval circles soon after the system began, it "immediately produced concern." As early as May 20, the German Embassy in Switzerland correctly reported the loss of only one Allied merchantman out of the first sixty-nine-ship wheat convoy from America. The kaiser's ambassador added that the "English" were so buoyed by this achievement that some in Whitehall "now believed that the U-boat could no longer interdict traffic from the United States." Further reportage from abroad began to undermine Berlin's confidence in the submarine war. In June, Army Chief of Staff Paul von Hindenburg warned Chancellor Bethmann-Hollweg against publicizing an autumn deadline for victory. The U-boats would still probably prevail, but establishing a firm date for their triumph would further erode faltering public morale if it did not materialize. Bethmann's reply reflected a growing sense of reality in some German circles. The survival of Austria-Hungary to year's end was problematic, Britain would not fall anytime soon, German victories in the East could not counterbalance corresponding failures in the West, and, most disturbing, France would not fall now that American aid was forthcoming. Walther Rathenau, a former economic minister and prominent industrialist, added somberly that with the United States in the war, Britain and her new associate could surely build enough ships to offset Germany's U-boat war, no matter how skillfully it was prosecuted.[47] As is so often the case in times of military or political conflict, the view from the other side of the hill, though unknown or dismissed, is often much worse.

September's events later convinced the author of Britain's official history of the war at sea that "the flood-tide of German success seemed for the first time to be slowing down towards a period of slack water, possibly even towards an ebb." Up to this point, all of the many Anglo-American efforts seemed to have made little difference. The organization of the convoy system across the Atlantic and to Scandinavia together with the "beef" and coal trades across the Channel to Holland and France had not made an appreciable dent in the level of U-boat sinkings. Nor had reorganization of the coastal route in the Channel, the laying of "immense" minefields in the Helgoland Bight (employing new and far more effective "horned mines"), or the ever-growing number of destroyers, patrol boats, airplanes, and even submarines that were fitted with advanced acoustical and visual devices. Further measures, too, had been taken. Merchant ships and some destroyers had recently been fitted with "kite balloons" to expand surveillance and "smoke boxes" to make a screen between potential victims and their undersea assailants. Every American freighter and transport was provided with a naval armed guard manning three- or five-inch guns on bow and stern. Funnel smoke was reduced. Nothing seemed to work.[48]

Then, during the last three weeks of the month, the cumulative effect of these efforts began to take hold. Shipping losses declined significantly. From an average of 438,000 tons a month for April, May, and June, they dropped to 330,000 tons in August and 196,000 tons in September. U-boat losses spiked commensurately. From eight in May, four in June, six in July, and five in August, they jumped to eleven in September. October mercantile losses were slightly worse, "276,000 tons—80,000 ton more than in the previous month," but still less than in any month since Germany had commenced unrestricted submarine warfare. Moreover, the rise in lost merchant shipping tonnage was due in large measure to "very heavy losses in the Mediterranean where the local convoy system had hardly begun, and in inshore waters" where the U-boats began to concentrate, looking for individual victims from dispersed convoys or the coastal trade.[49]

Clearly, a dramatic turn had been reached, and the cause was not difficult to determine. The principal zone of U-boat operations had been the Western Approaches in the broad areas around the Scillys and Land's End, "crowded with defenseless shipping." With the convoy routes perfected and running straight through this region, U-boat captains found that the area had been abruptly "evacuated." Targets suddenly disappeared. A formerly successful U-boat campaign was abruptly thrown "completely out of gear." However, most convoys were composed of vessels steaming to various ports, forcing the clusters to break up hours from Liverpool, Southampton, St. Nazaire, or Brest, leaving countless cargo vessels (though not the precious troop transports) to steam alone. U-boat commanders obediently followed their prey, moving into the English Channel and Bay of Biscay to find unescorted vessels that either had just left a convoy or were looking to join one. But operations in these relatively constricted and shallow waters increased the submarines' vulnerability while reducing their effectiveness. Submarine chasing in coastal waters was a far easier game for the Allied and American navies and air forces. Moreover, precluded from surfacing to sink single hapless victims quickly and cheaply with a lone deck gun, U-boat commanders were forced to rely on their limited arsenal of torpedoes to ensure a kill. "Now it was numbers of torpedoes carried which determined the endurance of a U-boat," and with limited numbers of torpedoes came limited ranges. The process was gradual, not abrupt, and Allied optimism was somewhat premature. Shipping losses rose slightly in the last months of 1917 before diving irrevocably the following spring. According to naval authority

Antony Preston, 3 ships totaling 2,950 tons were sunk by German U-boats in 1914; the following year, 640 ships totaling nearly 1.2 million tons were sent to the bottom by German submarines. In 1916, the figure was 1,301 ships aggregating more than 2 million tons. During the darkest year, 1917, no fewer than 3,170 Allied, American, and neutral merchantmen went down, a total of just under 6 million tons. In 1918, the figure was drastically reduced to 1,280 ships of slightly more than 2.5 million tons. The official British naval history closely tracks these figures.[50]

No single individual could claim credit for this favorable trend, but William Sowden Sims in London had become as close to an indispensable man as could be found anywhere in the western camp, although for long months senior political and naval circles in Washington were loath to admit it. Sims never ceased pressuring his superiors in Washington to get more and more units of the American fleet into the war against the Central Powers. Such incessant prodding had an opposite effect. Benson, in particular, was adamant that Mahanian principles grounded in the idea of a concentrated battle line must be maintained. On July 4, Wilson himself cabled Sims directly that Germany's U-boat war had completely flummoxed the Royal Navy. Implicitly sending another declaration of independence across the Atlantic, Wilson wrote: "From the beginning of the war I have been greatly surprised at the failure of the British Admiralty to use Great Britain's great naval superiority in an effective way. In the presence of the present submarine emergency they are helpless to the point of panic." Every American proposal, the president added, had been "rejected for some reason of prudence."[51]

Two days earlier, Secretary Daniels summarized US strategy in what historian Jerry W. Jones has labeled a dogmatic memo to Secretary of State Robert Lansing. The United States would not jeopardize the integrity of its battle fleet through "disintegration" (though it was willing to send the entire fleet to European waters), and "the offensive must always be the dominant note in any general plan or strategy." Behind the Daniels memo was talk in White House and senior naval circles of a massive amphibious assault or assaults against the German-held Channel ports. In reply, Sims sought to set his superiors straight. The admiral had just accompanied Jellicoe on a visit to the Grand Fleet at Scapa Flow. Through its periodic sweeps of the North Sea, Sims reported, the heavy units of the Royal Navy were keeping German surface forces bottled up in port, allowing the Admiralty to devote more and more resources to the antisubmarine war. Several days later, Sims cabled "Opnav" in Washington that the Admiralty had requested "the four strongest coal burning battleships" in the American arsenal together with a half-dozen destroyers be sent to Scapa Flow, along with an indeterminate number of submarines that "could be very usefully employed in [an] anti-submarine" capacity. Five predreadnought British battleships were being placed out of commission to free up their crews for assignment to the Grand Fleet's light-cruiser and destroyer forces. Sims added, "Our oil burning battleships could not be supplied" from the relatively small British petroleum reserves, while "more than four" coal burners "would unduly increase [the] burden" on the Royal Navy's stock of coal "and would necessitate additional screening vessels not now available." Whatever Daniels's and Benson's inclinations may have been, the president remained unmoved; he suspected Sims of suffering a severe case of clientitis—that inclination of those sent abroad to assume the attitude of their hosts. Moreover, there lurked in the president's mind, and those of many subordinates, a suspicion that their British colleagues were holding back, husbanding naval resources so as to maintain the supremacy of the Royal Navy in the postwar world. Such sentiments quickly reached British ears (not via Sims), stimulating long-standing counterfears that the American cousins, aspiring to postwar global naval supremacy of their own, wanted to withhold the bulk of American sea power in order that Britain might fatally bleed its merchant marine as well as naval [strength].[52]

The president's impatience with the course of the war at sea often got the better of him. In an early August visit to the fleet flagship *Pennsylvania*, he burst out that the Anglo-American navies were "hunting hornets all over the farm and letting the nest alone." He added dramatically that he was "willing to sacrifice half the navy" to crush the German submarine bases in Belgium and the homeland. Sims's biographer is scathing: "In failing to grasp the drab efficiency of the convoy," Elting Morison wrote, the president and all those who shared his prejudices "committed the very error of dispersing their energies 'all over the farm' in attempts to find" other solutions to the U-boat problem when the solution was already there in front of them.[53]

Nonetheless, some in the British Admiralty had already grasped Wilson's frustrations and those of his senior subordinates, including the chief of naval operations. A Captain Gaunt wrote that Benson never really complained exactly "but points out that all we do is ask for things as they come along, but there is no settled policy that he can put forward and say we are working along those lines." Jellicoe promptly sent a policy report to Wilson containing a mission statement that set forth the four goals of the Royal Navy, including "protection" of communications to armies in the field and of British trade, disruption of the enemy's trade, and homeland defense and security.[54] The president was not mollified, but when he learned that Sims was criticizing Benson and *his* staff, he realized that matters were spinning out of control. Following a late August White House meeting with his chief naval advisers (in which he reiterated his partiality for a major amphibious assault on German ports), Wilson ordered Admiral Mayo of the Atlantic Fleet to England on a fact-finding mission.

The result was an Inter-Allied Naval Conference held on September 4–5 with Eric Geddes, Britain's first sea lord, in the chair. The meeting managed to clear much of the air, resolving a number of outstanding differences. As the conference opened, Jellicoe laid before it two alternate plans for future naval operations against Germany. The first argued for "the Allies" to jointly "undertake a stupendous blocking operation against all the German harbours in the North Sea and the Baltic," employing every old battleship and cruiser in the British and French inventories as blocking ships. This acknowledgment of if not deference to American sensibilities was quickly shot down. Jellicoe's own subordinates as well as the Japanese delegates convinced Mayo that a bold fleet action against the Channel ports harboring a portion of the German U-boat fleet was impossible due to heavy enemy defenses. The Gallipoli fiasco could not have been far from anyone's mind, and the Japanese openly reminded Allied colleagues of their own difficulties in successfully blockading Port Arthur in 1904–5. The Grand Fleet was indeed doing its job in bottling up the German *Hochseeflotte*, thus allowing ever-stronger pursuit of antisubmarine activities.

Jellicoe's second plan envisaged "an immense mine field" to be laid across the North Sea between the Shetland Islands and neutral Norway, thus blocking the most ready U-boat access to the Irish Sea and the near Atlantic. The idea of a "multilayered underwater 'vertical wall of mines'" had been suggested the year before by Rear Admiral Reginald Bacon, then in charge of the generally ineffectual Dover Barrage, composed of nets, mines, and "drifter patrols" by trawlers. The conference endorsed the plan but emphasized that while it had great merit, it was premature in light of available resources. At least one hundred thousand mines would be required, far more than Britain and the United States possessed. When Jellicoe formally resumed his plea on September 22, naval authorities in Washington agreed to expedite the production of mines to create a vast field in the upper North Sea as soon as possible. "The Conference then reviewed the existing methods of operating against submarines without expressing any serious criticism of what was then being done, and without making any novel suggestion." Jellicoe introduced the worrying problem of imminent enemy deployment of its big "cruiser submarines" that could range far out in the Atlantic to decimate the ranks of those many merchantmen still traveling alone or even in lightly escorted convoys. Perhaps something could be done by way of establishing a radio station in the Azores. Here Sims intervened decisively. "Was not the future of every form of antisubmarine warfare bound up with the extension and development of the convoy system; in fact, was not this system the one and only method of placing the Uboats on the chessboard of submarine warfare in a position of strategical and tactical checkmate?" Recent statistics were on the American admiral's side, and the conference adopted his views.[55]

While Mayo returned home still doubtful that the British had an effective plan to win the naval war beyond requesting more and more American resources, the conference in fact "served to show the Entente Powers how much they would have to depend upon American assistance for improving the position at sea." The new reality energized both the Admiralty and the Navy Department. Relations were "significantly improved"; Jellicoe and Benson agreed to initiate direct correspondence, while Sims and Benson buried the hatchet in a series of heartfelt messages, practically clearing the way for Sims to act as American spokesman in Allied naval matters, especially with respect to convoying. By the end of September, the Navy Department informed the Admiralty that four more cruisers would be added immediately to the transatlantic convoys, with several more to follow once an ongoing reorganization of cruiser forces was complete. "In addition to these reinforcements, they would at once send a patrolling force of submarines and a monitor to the Azores, to check the depredations of the German submarine cruisers on the outer trade routes," while lending wholehearted cooperation in the establishment of a radio station and intelligence center at Ponta Delgado.[56]

The prodigious efforts involved in convoy operations paid off handsomely. From the beginning, American and the few French transports took their cargoes of troops to France—Brest, Le Havre, La Pallice, and Bordeaux. Soldiers carried over in British and Italian vessels were first landed at Southampton and were then sent across the Channel in overnight convoys composed of a small number of permanently based, modestly sized US transports and in British cross-Channel steamers. The rapidly growing number of supply ships went mostly to Liverpool, their cargoes destined for fast transshipment to France. This arrangement quickly generated a new source of conflict between the British and American naval high commands over the best use of American destroyers. In Washington, members of Benson's staff believed that "the impelling reason of the British" for adopting convoy "was protection to food and war supplies in transit. Our basic reason was protection of our own military forces in crossing seas." As early as July 1917, with the American buildup scarcely under way, Daniels cabled Sims that protection of the transports carrying the AEF was the "paramount duty" of the Queenstown force. Convoying of supply ships to the United Kingdom was of secondary importance. Benson added his opposition to transferring any of his precious destroyers to the British Home Fleet for escort duties. Sims replied that it would be a "radical mistake" for the United States to ship troops in such numbers to France as to interfere with the supply lines that were sustaining much of the entire Allied war effort. The Queenstown destroyer force continued to operate with preservation of merchant shipping to and from British ports chiefly in mind.[57]

The issue remained unresolved until mid-October, when the transport *Antilles* was sunk in Quiberon Bay, outside Brest. It was returning from France empty of troops but with 234 people aboard. The sinking was swift, losses were relatively severe (67), and the lesson seemed obvious: German submarines were shifting their operational grounds, finding their best opportunities off the coast of France. Two weeks later, the lesson was reinforced when a U-boat torpedoed the transport *Finland* "only a few hours after leaving port." *Finland* was also on a return voyage, and among her passengers were the traumatized survivors from *Antilles* who not surprisingly rushed for the lifeboats, "taking with them some of the lowest elements" of the crew. The captain and "the better elements" drove the panicked crowd back from the boats, and *Finland* was able to stagger back to Brest. Both *Antilles* and *Finland* were manned by civilian crews, and the US Navy quickly scraped together enough sailors so that thenceforth all troop transports were manned by regular service personnel.[58]

Clearly, the escort force at Brest had to be strengthened as the Yanks funneled more and more troops into the port. Still, little was done until Daniels and Benson received support of the sister service. On December 2, Pershing cabled the War Department that the United States Army must have enough troops on the western front to help forestall or beat back a widely anticipated German offensive in the coming spring. As the War Department, in response, accelerated the shipment of troops across the Atlantic, Pershing appealed directly to Benson. "Nothing," he wrote on January 8 of the New Year, "could possibly be more important than the rapid movements of our transports under protection." The navy's destroyer flotillas should be removed from any service with Britain's Home Fleet, "or elsewhere" (that is, Queenstown), to ensure maximum protection of the troopships coming into Brest. Though Pershing did not say it, and indeed may not have been aware of the trend, the recent movement of the bulk of German U-boats from the Western Approaches to the coastal regions of Britain and France was also a major factor in changing naval opinion. Benson responded promptly to Pershing's initiatives by creating a new entity, the Naval Overseas Transportation Service—or NOTS—to expedite the ferry of troops overseas.[59]

Benson also insisted that Brest be transformed from its use as a base for the few destroyers, older torpedo boats, and converted yachts on antisubmarine patrol and escort duties in the Bay of Biscay to "the primary base" for his modern destroyer flotillas.[60] This presented a conundrum, since the harbor was relatively small and there were no permanent base facilities, which meant that for some time, the importance of cargo ships would be at least equal to that of the transports. With characteristic vigor, American construction teams set to work building a substantial infrastructure in the town—administration buildings, mess halls, barracks, and so on—though the new base commander, Rear Admiral Henry Wilson, flew his flag not ashore but aboard destroyer tender *Prometheus*. By August 1918, "the number of vessels operating out of Brest exceeded the numbers at Queenstown: twenty-four destroyers, two tenders, and three tugs at Queenstown; thirty-three destroyers, sixteen yachts, nine minesweepers, five tugs, and four repairs ships at Brest." As American troops in France increased to more than 2,000,000 men, a member of Sims's staff later wrote, maintaining an uninterrupted supply line grew ever more difficult. "Stoppages," however temporary, were inconceivable, for they would compel an immediate halt in Allied military operations.[61]

While many convoys were largely under British protection and many of its vessels under British registry, a substantial number continued to be shepherded by the US Cruiser and Transport Force, which at its apex numbered twenty-four cruisers (many of them small and practically obsolete) and forty-two transports manned by 3,000 officers and 42,000 men. Three American transports were torpedoed and sunk during 1917–18. In addition to *Antilles*, they included *President Lincoln* and *Covington*, while *Finland's* survival of a torpedo hit was matched by *Mount Vernon*. All five were on return trips from Europe and thus not only empty of troops but also weakly escorted, or, in the case of the *President Lincoln*, sailing alone at the margin of the U-boat zone. Tragic as was the loss of life and ships, it was in marked contrast to the situation existing at the apex of the U-boat campaign, when "in six weeks, in the spring and early summer of 1917, thirty armed merchantmen were torpedoed and sunk off Queensland, and in no case was a periscope or a conning tower seen."[62]

The loss of the transport *Tuscania* in February 1918 gave an indication of the dreadful fate that would have awaited the AEF had a U-boat campaign directed specifically against the transatlantic troop ferry succeeded. Commissioned in 1914, the stylish-looking British two stacker began transport duties in 1916 between Halifax and Liverpool. Shifting to Hoboken, she set sail on her final voyage near the end of January 1918, with 2,000 American soldiers and a crew of 384 aboard. Joining Convoy HX-20 at Halifax, she crossed the Atlantic, heading for Le Havre. On February 5, "a bright crisp winter day" off the west coast of Scotland, the convoy was spotted by UB-77. In a daring maneuver, the German submarine got close enough to the convoyed vessel to fire two torpedoes. The second scored a direct hit on *Tuscania*, which promptly listed and slowly began to sink. As hundreds of surprised doughboys, including members of the Sixth Battalion, Twentieth Engineers, rushed up from belowdecks to their abandon-ship stations, urging each other to keep calm, the shattered ship stubbornly held its own for a time. On a nearby vessel, popular journalist Irvin S. Cobb and several hundred others watched *Tuscania* struggling desperately to survive. By seven that evening, some 1,000 men had gotten off by lifeboat, by raft, or onto the decks of escorting British destroyers. Another 1,350, however, remained aboard. The destroyers, together with trawlers and small craft from nearby fishing villages, worked feverishly to remove these men from the foundering ship, even as at least some of the warships continued to hunt the U-boat. The behavior of the British escort suggests that the commander rather lost his head in the crisis. Survivors recalled seeing at least one of the destroyers weaving in and out of the straggly line of waterlogged lifeboats and rafts, dropping depth charges despite the presence of men in the chilly waters. "The noise of the depth bombs, the bursting of the distress and illumination rockets, together with the reports from the destroyer's deck gun created the impression that a naval battle was in progress." Indeed it was, but the hunt hindered the search for survivors, which was kept up until early morning, at which time all those picked up were brought into nearby Irish ports. It was then discovered that 230 passengers and crew remained unaccounted for, 201 of whom were doughboys.

Ironically, those who ultimately perished were among the first off, their waterlogged lifeboats and rafts drifting uncontrollably at the mercy of wind and waves "quite a distance before the rescue work had fairly commenced." As the chaotic scenes unfolded behind them, these wretched souls, ignored and "with no guidance," were ultimately dashed to pieces on the nearby cliffs of Scotland after which the cruel sea slowly gave them up to discovery. Across the Atlantic, press and public were outraged; this was the first—and would be the last—troop transport sunk while carrying the AEF to France, but no one could be certain until the following November that another such tragedy might not occur. In 1920, a monument to the martyred soldiers was erected at the top of one of the cliffs.[63]

Destroyer sailors paid a price for their growing success. Britain lost a number of these vessels in Atlantic and Channel operations. Early on the afternoon of October 15, 1917, it was the Americans' turn. *Cassin*—among the first destroyers to reach Queenstown under Joe Taussig—was patrolling independently off the south coast of Ireland at roughly fifteen knots through "considerable wind and sea." Twenty miles south of Mine Head, the lookout aloft spotted a German submarine running awash four to five miles off the port bow, and the destroyer, its crew racing to general quarters, promptly gave chase. Three minutes later the U-boat submerged, while *Cassin's* cramped little bridge filled with the commanding officer, W. N. Vernou, and his executive and engineering officers in addition to the usual watch-standing personnel. Vernou concluded that the submarine would change its southeast course. Shortly thereafter, *Cassin's* bridge people sighted a torpedo three to four hundred yards away coming fast just below the surface. Realizing that it would hit dead amidships in one of the engine or fire rooms, Vernou immediately ordered double emergency full speed and the rudder hard over. For a moment, it appeared that the torpedo would pass astern, but then the weapon porpoised, turned sharp left, and slammed into the destroyer aft above the waterline, igniting two great explosions among the depth charges equivalent to 850 pounds of TNT. The explosive strength could have been fatally higher had not Gunner's Mate First Class Osmond K. Ingram, a sixteen-year veteran who was manning the after four-inch gun mount seen what was about to happen, raced the few paces to the depth charges, and begun disarming them. He never completed his task, being blown to bits as he worked. But his action undoubtedly kept tragedy from becoming catastrophe. His absence went unnoticed, until the crew was mustered at quarters after containing the damage. Ingram's act of incredible courage was commemorated by christening a new destroyer in his name, the first time any American warship had been named for an enlisted man.

Inspection showed that about thirty-five feet of the stern was either blown off or completely wrecked, as were the after crew's quarters and storeroom. Incredibly, some twenty-odd sailors escaped with only minor injuries as a bulkhead held, keeping the Atlantic from flooding the rest of the hull. Fireman First Class F. W. Kruse was blown out of his port-side bunk just a few feet forward of the torpedo's point of impact, stumbling forward as far as number 4 stack, where he was discovered in a state of total unconsciousness but obviously seeking his battle station in number 2 fire room. The after engine and fire rooms (and an adjacent magazine) remained intact so that the engines could still be worked. But the rudder had been blown off and the stern warped to starboard. With a wrecked starboard turbine, the hapless destroyer fell into a sea trough and became "absolutely unmanageable" for a time. Judicious use of the port engines brought the ship back to a reasonably steady state, permitting alternating straight courses followed by slow turns. After a half hour "when we were in approximately the same position as when torpedoed," *Cassin's* crew saw a submarine conning tower roughly fifteen hundred yards off the port beam. Number 2 four-inch gun opened fire, and the submarine disappeared after several near misses.

Throughout a long afternoon, evening, and night, the wounded vessel was guarded by an American sister ship, three British sloops, two trawlers, and a tug. In the morning, almost twenty-one hours after the torpedoing, the British sloop *Snowdrop* arrived to tow *Cassin* into Queenstown for repairs that would consume the next ten months. Not until the following July was the ship deemed fit for duty.[64]

Three weeks later, the small armed yacht *Alcedo*, weighing 987 tons, with ninety-four men on board left Quiberon Bay in the afternoon as part of a small convoy bound for Brest. Twelve hours later, in the midst of the 12:00 to 4:00 a.m. midwatch, a crewman aboard the yacht sighted a U-boat and at just the moment that general quarters sounded, UC-71 fired a single torpedo at close range from its surface position. *Alcedo* never had a chance. The captain attempted a quick course change, but the helm answered "sluggishly." *Alcedo* was hit port-side well forward and promptly began to sink. Eight minutes later she slipped beneath the waves with twenty of her crew either dead of wounds or drowning. Survivors, including the captain, took to two lifeboats, both of which were picked up and taken ashore after a grueling night.[65]

Eleven days after that, USS *Chauncey* (DD-3) died 110 miles west of Gibraltar while escorting British merchantmen in from the Atlantic. She was one of the gallant little 420-ton first-generation destroyers that had spent most of their lives in Asiatic waters before coming back west with *Bainbridge*. On the dark night of November 9, *Chauncey* collided with the freighter *Rose* and went down within minutes, taking her captain and twenty crewmen into the depths with her. On December 6, the Navy suffered its second and last destroyer loss of the war. *Jacob Jones* was returning independently from Brest to Queenstown, having been part of a convoy escort from latitude 20°W to the French port. Recently, the ship and her sister *Conyngham* had rescued nearly five hundred souls from the torpedoed British armed merchant cruiser *Orama*, acting as convoy escort.

This day, the other five ships returning to Ireland with *Jacob Jones* had steamed on ahead out of visual range. A light mist spread over the waters that late afternoon near the Isles of Scilly off the southwest coast of England; seas were "smooth" as the destroyer steamed in a zigzag pattern at thirteen knots. Captain David W. Bagley was in the chart house just below the bridge when he heard someone call out, "Torpedo!" *Jacob Jones* was about to bear out Bayly's somber dictum that any ship faced doom once beyond harbor. Like a knife in the water, a torpedo that had been fired from three thousand yards away raced toward the destroyer as the officer of the deck, Lieutenant (jg) Stanton F. Kalk ordered flank speed and helm hard over. Once again a torpedo broached, alternately porpoising and diving before striking the destroyer's after fuel tank between the auxiliary room and the after crew's compartment, three feet below the waterline. A horrific explosion ensued, though neither oil nor ammunition in the nearby magazine ignited. The mortally stricken vessel quickly settled by the stern, which prevented anyone from setting to "safe" mode the depth charges in their stern chutes. Oiler D. R. Carter attempted to close the watertight door between the auxiliary and engine rooms, but water pressure overwhelmed him as the sea rushed through the ship, drowning many of those who had survived the explosion.

Bagley immediately tried to send a distress signal, only to discover that the masthead with its antennae had collapsed and all electrical power had been lost. He then ordered a few rounds from the fo'c'sle four-inch gun fired manually to attract attention, but there was no response. The destroyer began settling fast, and a fever of disciplined activity began among the surviving crew, who launched boats and rafts before abandoning ship. The chief electrician and a third-class quartermaster "remained on board to the last, greatly endangering their lives thereby to cut adrift splinter mats and life-preservers. . . . Weighted confidential publications were thrown over the side. There was no time to destroy other confidential matter," which went to the bottom in any case.

As *Jacob Jones* began to go under, Bagley ran along the deck, ordering the last few men aboard into the water. Eight minutes after the torpedoing, the destroyer twisted slowly through a 180-degree arc and sank by the stern, igniting the depth charges, which shattered several nearby boats. A number of those who had survived were killed; those who were not, including Bagley, Kalk, and Executive Officer Norman Scott, were numbed and dazed. As the men struggled into rafts and what boats remained, they were cheered on by the chief boatswain's mate and a handful of others. Gasping and shaking with cold and exertion, the men saw a slowly moving submarine on the horizon that came to within eight hundred to a thousand yards of the struggling group, where it plucked two sailors from the water as prisoners. What Bagley and his people could not know was that the U-boat was commanded by none other than Hans Rose, who, since his dramatic appearance in Narragansett Bay and adjacent waters in 1916, had earned a further reputation in Allied circles by his propensity to constantly call home over his wireless and to wage submarine warfare in an almost uniquely humane manner. "Sometimes when he torpedoed a ship, Rose would wait around until all the lifeboats were filled; he would then throw out a towline, give his victims food, and keep all survivors together until the rescuing destroyer appeared on the horizon, when he would let go and submerge." Rose now sent a brief message to Queenstown, informing Anglo-American authorities of the loss of *Jacob Jones* and giving the position of the survivors before scuttling away.

Bagley quickly gathered the rafts together and designated Gunnery Officer J. K. Richards to command. After distributing as many emergency and medical supplies as he could to each raft, Bagley and Scott set off for the Scillys to get help, using the crippled motor dory rowed by four crewmen. The night was clear but windy; the December waters of the North Atlantic were bone-chilling. As the shaken and shivering survivors huddled in their rafts, Lieutenant Kalk, himself a victim of the depth-charge explosions, nonetheless swam from raft to raft through the frigid water to ensure that the weight of each was more or less evenly distributed. "Game to the last," Kalk exhausted himself and perished on one of the rafts, allegedly in the midst of a vision of the Statue of Liberty. During the night, Boatswain's Mate Charlesworth removed some of his own clothing and passed it to more thinly clad shipmates.

Bagley and his companions steered by the stars as they rowed doggedly through the night and on through the morning hours. Shortly after noon the dory was spotted by a small British patrol vessel roughly six miles south of the Scillys. Coming ashore, Bagley discovered that the rafts, though split apart, had been separately found. The most fortunate had been discovered by a British steamer the night before, the rest early that morning following "a most trying experience" that can only be imagined. Two officers and sixty-two or sixty-four crewmen (accounts vary) out of a total complement of scarcely over a hundred lost their lives when the *Jacob Jones* went down.[66]

The Yanks got a measure of revenge when *Fanning*, a 787-ton "flivver" commissioned in January 1912, recorded the one incontestable American kill of a German U-boat. *Fanning* had reached European waters as part of the escort of the first convoy sent to France the previous June. On the early afternoon of

November 17, 1917, the small destroyer quietly cleared Queenstown Harbor as part of a division led by Commander Frank Berrien in sister ship *Nicholson*. The mission was to escort a western-bound convoy ("O Q20") of empty vessels from French and British ports heading for North America as far as longitude 20°W and then pick up an incoming convoy whose freighters and transports were packed with supplies and troops for the western front. Quickly finding their charges, Berrien's small warships mingled in the convoy, carrying messages, giving instructions, and doing all the routine matters necessary to bring civilian ships into stipulated formation. By four o'clock, the convoy had been shepherded into position. As *Fanning* was racing to its post on the rear flank, Coxswain David Loomis, on bridge watch, saw a tiny periscope "of the 'finger' variety ... glistening in the smooth water." Lieutenant Gustav Amberger's U-58 had been waiting outside Queenstown for several weeks, hoping to ambush a convoy. Here was his chance.

Nearly filling U-58's periscope was the big British merchant ship *Welshman*, an irresistible target that Amberger was determined to sink. But swinging his periscope around in a precautionary search, Amberger discovered *Fanning* charging down on him. The German skipper promptly withdrew his attack and dove deeper. In order to achieve a proper attack angle, *Fanning* had to make a wide turn to get into position, no mean feat since Loomis had spotted the small periscope just briefly. But the destroyer's officer of the deck, Lieutenant Walter Henry, demonstrated superb seamanship, bringing his ship exactly over the spot where U-58 had been seen. He dropped a single "ash can" that exploded so hard that *Fanning*'s main generator was temporarily knocked out of service.

Nothing happened. No oil patches or bubbles appeared. For five, ten, fifteen minutes while *Nicholson* joined her sister, "everything was quiet as the grave." Down below, however, there was chaos. *Fanning*'s depth charge had wrecked U-58's motors and jammed its diving rudders so that the submarine could either take its chances by sinking to the bottom, hoping not to be crushed by water pressure in the process, or surface to fight it out or surrender. After some hesitation and frantic but useless efforts at repair, Amberger realized he had no choice and blew all tanks to get to the surface. Sailors on the slowly circling destroyers saw the stern of a U-boat, "tilted at thirty degrees," suddenly appear, followed immediately by the conning tower and then the entire boat. Stunned officers and crew could detect no damage to the sub, whose number was now clearly visible. They immediately opened fire with their four-inch guns, while *Nicholson* dropped another depth charge close aboard, prompting Amberger's "well-fed form" to pop out of the conning tower, hands raised, crying out a guttural "Kamerad! Kamerad!" The Americans ceased firing as more crewmen erupted out of hatches, arms raised. The destroyers moved in to take U-58 in tow to Queensland. Realizing what was afoot, Amberger sent several crewmen below to open the sea cocks, and U-58 began to sink while the rest of its crew dove into the chilly waters and toward the waiting Americans. To *Fanning's* crew, most of the Germans seemed exhausted, and so rescue operations were promptly initiated and man after man was hauled aboard. One of the Germans was too weary to adjust the lifelines around his shoulder and "appeared to be drowning." "Like a flash," two *Fanning* crewmen "jumped overboard, swam to the floundering man, and adjusted the line around him as solicitously as if he had been a shipmate." Unfortunately, Franz Glinder was "too far gone" and expired on the destroyer's deck. By this time, the scuttled U-boat was halfway to the bottom of the Irish Sea. *Fanning* promptly returned to Queenstown with its prisoners to a hero's welcome from Bayly and everyone else.[67]

At that moment, any kind of victory produced an almost hysterical response among the Allied peoples, for the wars on the western front and in Italy had reached a desperate stage. The Flanders Offensive was in its final exhausted gasp, while the Austrians were pounding the Italian army to pieces at Caporetto. The U-boat menace, while sensibly declining, nonetheless remained high; shipping losses still pointed to possible disaster in the coming year. With the Allied war effort flagging even as American resources began to be sensibly felt, it was clearly time to organize a coherent effort to reverse existing trends both ashore and at sea.

The success of the brief September naval conference suggested to British authorities that bringing the American associates into a broader meeting to work out overall military, naval, and diplomatic strategies might yield fruitful results. The year 1918 looked to be a time of even greater crisis; every resource available to the Anglo-French Allies had to be mobilized. Even before Mayo had left London in September, the British War Cabinet suggested convening an even broader meeting to "enhance cooperation" between Washington and the Allied Powers. Wilson's initial reaction was negative. The president continued to believe that the best way to obtain his peace aims was to retain diplomatic autonomy, which required distance and aloofness. But influential adviser Colonel House won him over with the argument that if the Central Powers won the war, there would be no chance for a generous peace.[68]

Late in October, Wilson appointed House head of the delegation to an Allied council meeting, sending Benson along as chief naval representative. "It had been recognized for some time that though the presence of American dreadnoughts in the North Sea would be of material help to the British Grand Fleet, they would need supplies and accordingly the discussion of their coming to Europe had been postponed until . . . the shortage of shipping had become less acute." For three years, Britain's Grand Fleet had successfully guarded the North Sea while maintaining a material and moral superiority over Germany's *Hochseeflotte*. Jutland, however, had sensibly shaken the Royal Navy's morale. To many an admiral and tar, the margin of superiority seemed always narrow. By the time House and Benson left for Europe, the Submarine Menace was deemed sufficiently in hand that so that a squadron of dreadnoughts could strengthen the Grand Fleet, and Sims cabled Washington to that effect.

Reaching London several weeks before the *Fanning* incident, Benson was soon won over to the British perspective. Not only must the flood of antisubmarine vessels to the war zones continue, four of the older coal-burning dreadnought battleships—perhaps more—should be sent as well. In the event, a total of six American battlewagons would be sent to Scapa Flow; no fewer than four or five were always present. Benson surrendered his Mahanian principles to the new and enticing realities of world politics. In a long memorandum, he argued that the Grand Fleet truly needed bolstering. Moreover, the battleship force was the only element in the US naval arsenal that had so far seen no action. But the paramount consideration in Benson's mind now was that powerful American naval reinforcements would demonstrate to the British and everyone else the vital importance of the United States Navy in postwar global affairs. "There should be no possibility of an impression, at home or abroad, among the hostile, allied, or neutral, that we are performing an auxiliary or secondary part in the military prosecution of the war."[69]

Benson's new commitment extended beyond offering up his fleet's battleship and destroyer forces. He also agreed to a further substantial strengthening of Sims's London headquarters to include a planning section to develop strategy in close conjunction with its British counterpart. Sims promptly assigned three of his top-notch officers, Captains Frank Schofield, Dudley Knox, and Harry Yarnell to the section, together with occasional inputs from Marine Colonel R. H. Dunlap and a Mr. "L. McNamee, U.S.N." Captain Nathan Twining supervised the enterprise.

Although admitting "comparative ignorance . . . of the technical side of aviation," the four together with Sims's already well-entrenched aviation assistant Hutchison Cone quickly overcame Benson's long-standing aversion to naval air, convincing the CNO that his flyers also could play a major role in the antisubmarine war. Perhaps the most important decision Benson made with respect to naval aviation was his endorsement of a substantial air station at Killingholme, on the Lincolnshire coast, and the accumulation of sufficient personnel, "specialty lighters," and large flying boats to mount a major long-distance bombing campaign against U-boat facilities across the North Sea in Belgium and Germany.

With Benson's support at last ensured, Cone immediately set to work broadening naval aviation's presence and activities in the U-boat war. With Sims's endorsement if not enthusiasm, he created his own administrative, intelligence, and planning sections within the London headquarters to manage a steady growth of air stations and aviation schools on both sides of the Channel, including "sections for Public Works, Supplies," and a "Repair Base." He placed surgeon H. H. Lane in overall charge of medical affairs and then established an Executive Committee with himself in charge to coordinate these diverse and steadily growing activities. Finally, in recognition of Whiting's undoubted contributions to naval air, Cone appointed him base commander at Killingholme. Following a quick visit to France, Benson also enthusiastically supported an ambitious "Northern Bombing Campaign" that would be staged in part by US Navy and Marine Corps flyers operating from Dunkirk and other nearby French coastal airfields against the same enemy bases in the Bruges-Ostend-Zeebrugge area.[70]

Benson's trip to France was part of the extended House Mission that at Paris agreed to the establishment of a Supreme Allied Council to oversee the entire war effort. Among the subordinate agencies was an Inter-Allied Naval Council. Formerly, and still legally, an "Associated Power," the United States and its navy were now fully integrated into the Allied cause and all that would flow from therefrom.

Sending the Hunters

WELL BEFORE WILSON'S declaration of war, farsighted officials in the Navy Department realized that antisubmarine warfare might overwhelm the fleet's resources. The United States would have to find fresh platforms if it was to help win the U-boat war; its destroyer flotillas were simply not enough. They quickly turned to two weapon systems, one already in place, the other a promising solution.

From the outset, America's submariners had closely followed the fortunes of the war at sea. They knew that in a frantic search for any kind of effective antisubmarine platform, the British in 1916 had begun assigning their own hydrophone-equipped boats as hunter-killers in the North Sea and Channel. Within a few months, antisubmarine warfare had become "the primary mission for British submarines," and a new class, the "R" boats, was built for this specific purpose. Surely, there was a role for Yankee subs as well.[1]

Captains and crews alike were undeterred by the almost fatally limited capabilities of their boats. At the top of the line were eleven "L" class, of which seven were in commission. Displacing roughly 450 tons surfaced, the 165–68-foot submarines were driven through the water by two 450-horsepower diesel engines, permitting a surface speed of fourteen knots. But while surfaced the L boats were capable of steaming two-thirds of the way across the Atlantic to England at eleven knots, their submerged endurance on their single 800-horsepower electric motor was but twenty-five miles at eight to twelve knots. All in all, the speed of the L boats, according to one authoritative contemporary source, was "three or four knots less than that often made by the Huns."

Each vessel mounted four eighteen-inch torpedo tubes in the bow and a three-inch .23-caliber deck gun forward of the small, low conning tower. All the available boats "had been freely criticized with respect to engines and periscopes." The engineering plants were chronically unreliable, particularly in heavy seas. "Further they annoyed the crews by excessive smoking and the failure of mufflers and muffler valves, with inadequate provision for ventilation." Periscope lenses were of poor optical quality and of low power. Worse, they were unhoused, which meant that heavy seas were "likely to expose the top of the bridge and even the conning tower." Such vessels were obviously barely capable for the missions they were about to perform.[2]

But Submarine Command Atlantic was infected with an almost fatal optimism and in the summer of 1917 firmed up plans to dispatch seven L boats together with four older Ks and one E class to the war zone in two divisions. All that was required were blessings from on high, and in the aftermath of the naval conference at London in September, permission was granted. The four K boats would base at Ponta Delgada in the Azores, and the seven Ls together with E-1 would deploy from Bantry Bay on the south coast of Ireland, though in the event the latter boat remained in the Azores. "Marginal fuel capacity and the unreliability of their rudimentary two-cycle diesel engines" dashed initial hopes that the submarines could make it across on their own. Instead, the K boats departed Philadelphia and New York in October, rendezvousing off the Massachusetts coast with the submarine tender *Bushnell* and the ancient protected cruiser *Chicago*, each of which proceeded to take two boats apiece in tow. The little fleet first struggled up to Halifax and then the 1,700 miles out to the Azores. Towing the unique hulls proved strenuous and complex; at several points, the boats cast off and attempted to steam on their own. But repeated engine failures frustrated the efforts. The subsequent year at Ponta Delgada proved uneventful because repeated mechanical problems kept the boats "out of service for much of that period."[3]

Bushnell promptly returned to Newport, Rhode Island, and early that December the tender joined by two oceangoing tugs prepared to take the L boats plus E-1 in tow to the Azores on their way to Bantry Bay. The enterprise nearly ended in disaster. Months later amid the shiny silverware and bright napery of a London restaurant near Cleopatra's Needle, one of the submarine skippers recalled a fearful trip as the room began to fill with "girls in pretty shimmering dresses" and "young army officers with wound stripes and clumsy limps." Days at New London had been spent wrestling cans of condensed milk, meat, butter, and chocolate down the narrow hatches of tiny vessels, cramming every space with supplies, while the engineers fretted and fussed about their machinery. One raw, damp, and misty morning the ships got under way well before light.

Out on the "immense stretch of the greyish, winter-stricken sea," the tender and tugs pulled their tows slowly along, decks awash. For two days the weather was wonderful, "a touch of Indian summer on December's ocean." Then, toward nightfall of the second day, the hurricane struck, "a perfect terror," the young skipper remembered. As the seas rose and the wind shrieked, it became apparent that the formation could not remain together. Tows were hastily cast off, and it was every ship for itself. "One by one the submarines disappeared into that fury of wind and driving water." At least one "snatched" a last signal from *Bushnell* before the tender was "swallowed up in the storm." At dawn, "the ocean was a dirty brown-grey and knots and wisps of cloud were tearing by close over the water. Every once in a while a great hollow-bellied wave would come rolling out of the hullabaloo and break thundering" over a tiny, laboring hull. Essential bridge lookouts were lashed in place, drenched within three minutes and occasionally nearly suffocated as tons of water came pounding down. Discomfort was increased by clothing; bathing suits might have been more appropriate (Nazi submariners a quarter century later did often strip to trunks both above and belowdecks in the semitropical warmth of the Caribbean and central Atlantic). But because of time and place, the sailors aboard the L boats were clad in warm but bulky foul-weather gear. The boats rolled far more than the seventy-degree inclines their instruments could measure. The young captain recalled that there were times when he thought his boat would just make a complete revolution. Below, the air quickly became foul, for no one dared open a hatch. In the narrow compartments crammed with machinery, gear, and supplies, the incessant and violent pitching, lurching, and rolling transformed a routine six-foot movement into an "expedition." Fortunately for all, everyone had developed good sea legs by this time; motion sickness was not a problem to be added to all the others.

For forty-eight hours officers and men endured their dark, cramped hell as the wind began ripping off deck plates, adding quiet fears—and worse—of sinking through sudden hull failure. Submergence was not an option because it would use up the ship's electricity and the oil to generate it. Cooking was impossible, but somehow the men got fed cold food and all hung on, while above decks "the disk of the sea was just one great ragged mass of foam all being hurled through space by a wind screaming by with the voice and force of a million express trains." Soon there was a new terror as ice began to form on the superstructure, "and we had to get out a crew to chop it off" with little to hang onto and waves inexorably crashing aboard. Somehow, the job got done.

One tug and a submarine with its compass smashed ran back through the storm to Boston; the rest of the tiny flotilla endured until the weather at last moderated and the skies cleared. For three days, interiors were bailed out and cleaned up; then another storm hit, though not as bad as the first. *Bushnell* and its charges at last straggled one by one into Bermuda and then headed for the Azores, where they re-formed and set out for Queenstown on January 19.

Once again the tiny flotilla was beset by foul weather. A gale struck the first evening out, "which partially scattered the Division." For several days, *Bushnell* and its charges suffered through another ordeal of heaving to, running at slow speed, losing towing hawsers, and getting slowly under way again. At one point, heavy seas caught Lieutenant Cunneen of L-11 off guard, throwing him on his back across the bridge rail. The badly bruised skipper, fearing severe internal injuries, went below, where he clung upright to a rod above his head for thirty-six hours because lying down caused unbearable pain. Finally, the seas abated sufficiently to transfer him to *Bushnell* for medical attention along with his chief machinist's mate, who had suffered chlorine poisoning, and a seaman with an injured finger. Several sailors were swept off bridges and decks by smashing seas. One, Gunner's Mate First Class R. A. Leese of L-1, was seen floating stunned and motionless next to the boat. Captain Van de Carr promptly swung his submarine around but after the turn Leese was seen to disappear beneath the waves. "He wore rubber boots and heavy clothing. After circling the spot for one hour" in moderate seas, Van de Carr "gave the order to proceed." His boat reached Bantry Bay on the twenty-fourth. The rest of the flotilla staggered into Queenstown a day later and spent the next week under repair, directed by the indispensable *Bushnell*. By the end of the month, all had reached Berehaven in Bantry Bay, where the L boats were promptly assigned an "A" designation to differentiate them from a class of British submarines.[4]

From the outset, it was obvious that American submarines, no matter how intrepid their crews, were far too small a resource to make any significant contribution to the war. Nor were the Yankee destroyers of sufficient number to tip the balance decisively in the war against the U-boats. That menace clearly required a flock of antisubmarine vessels to contain. As the country entered the war, a solution of sorts was coming into being in the form of several hundred surprisingly stout and durable, easily produced 110-foot motor launches carrying a handful of depth charges and small guns. They were called subchasers, and while they could never claim a U-boat kill (although one historian asserts, without documentary evidence, that an unidentified SC destroyed a German sub in November 1917), their very ubiquity was just what was required to subdue the enemy.[5]

The marriage of transportation with the internal combustion engine in the nineteenth and early twentieth centuries produced, among other inventions, the automobile, the airplane, and the motorcycle. Steam-driven launches and yachts had become prominent in western maritime circles after 1870.

The first small boat powered by a gasoline internal combustion engine was tested by Gottlieb Daimler on Germany's Necker River in 1886. Several years later, Englishman William Lanchester transformed an earlier combination of screw propeller and steam engine by attaching a more powerful gasoline engine to the propeller to create a true motorboat. Thereafter, motorboat technology advanced dramatically, especially in the United States, where naval architect John L. Hacker began experimenting with radical new hull designs that could produce in the smallest motorboats speeds comparable to those found in turbine propulsion for larger ships. Another Englishman, shipbuilder Arthur Yarrow, took the inevitable next step toward transforming motorboats into small warships. In 1905, Yarrow constructed a fifteen-foot torpedo-carrying motorboat employing Italian engines. Another British builder, the soon-to-be-famous John Thorneycroft, promptly improved the Yarrow design with a forty-foot vessel. The Italians themselves entered the lists in 1906, "and the French built a steel-hulled, eight-ton boat the following year."

The Royal Navy was the first to employ motor launches in antisubmarine warfare. By 1917, several hundred 80-foot "ML" class vessels, designed and built in American yards for coastal defense, were on station in the Channel and Irish Sea. In the previous year, the appearance of *Deutschland* and U-53 at Baltimore and in Narragansett Bay, respectively, generated such public alarm that it galvanized an energetic young assistant secretary of the navy named Franklin D. Roosevelt—himself an enthusiastic yachtsman—to approach his superiors with a plan not only to requisition as many privately owned vessels as possible but also to hurriedly build "subchasing" motor launches for the United States Navy.

With his usual dash and spirit, FDR, as he would come to be known to later generations, turned naturally to wealthy and prominent friends in the Eastern Seaboard society to obtain as many vessels as possible. Not surprisingly, these patriotic gentlemen agreed to surrender their oceangoing toys—for a price. Most suspected that their ostentatiously spic-and-span vessels upon which many a lavish party had been thrown would see hard service on North Atlantic and European waters. They would not be mistaken.[6]

As for the mass-produced subchasers, four decisions were quickly reached. To facilitate rapid construction, several hundred would be built to a common design; construction would be decentralized, distributed among more than a dozen boatyards on all three coasts and in the Great Lakes; the vessels would be built of wood since all of the steel available to the navy was dedicated to the construction of fleet vessels; and, finally, the new subchasers would be large and seaworthy enough to deploy and operate effectively against U-boats not only in American coastal waters but overseas as well should the need arise.

Put in overall charge of the enterprise, Roosevelt turned to naval architect Albert Loring Swasey, "one of the best yacht designers in the United States," who came up with "a powerful creature": eighty-five tons, 110 feet long, 16 feet wide, with triple screws powered by three six-cylinder, 220-horsepower gasoline-driven engines. The wooden-hull form was that of a whaleboat, with steel bulkheads, "a swinging sheerline like that of a modern destroyer," flared bow, and flat stern, "a design unsurpassed for sea work since the time of the Vikings."

Initial armament included two 3-inch .23-caliber guns and two machine guns. Soon, the after three-inch battery was replaced by a depth-charge projector called a "Y-gun" that proved to be a most effective weapon. "Asdic"—a precursor of sonar that employed electronic pulses to detect more or less precisely the hull of a U-boat as it twisted and dodged beneath the waves—came into being only near the end of the war and was not widely available. American chasers, yachts, and destroyers had to make do with cumbersome underwater hydrophones designed to detect U-boat engine and propeller noises. These could be readily defeated by a U-boat "sitting on the bottom" with its machinery shut down or releasing misleading noises. It was also a rare hydrophone man indeed who could always separate U-boat machinery from the multitude of surrounding noises in the water.

Those who assumed that Swasey would provide his tiny ships with great speed were dumbfounded to learn that the chasers were designed to cruise at roughly seventeen to eighteen knots. The architect grasped the fact that antisubmarine warfare would require a multitude of instruments and weapons, requiring a relatively large crew (two officers and twenty-four enlisted men) to handle them and sufficient cruising range (one thousand miles) to stay at sea for some days at a time—particularly if engaged in prolonged chases with the enemy. The U-boat's top surface speed was little better than fifteen knots; underwater it was restricted to eight or nine at best. To Swasey, "extreme speed was not worth the price in the sacrifice of seaworthiness, cruising range and comfort." Indeed, comfort in the chasers included racks for enlisted men and bunks for officers.[7]

Swasey's design proved popular with French purchasers, who snatched up 20 of the first 100 Chasers and eventually another 80 more. Moreover, initial construction had to compete to some extent with the nation's broader naval building program, which, until shortly after Wilson's declaration of war, was oriented toward capital ships; thereafter, the chaser program had to compete with other resources, shipyard workers, and, upon unit completion, crewmen. As a consequence, the first of the little wooden vessels did not appear on navy rolls until July 1917. Thereafter, new units—mostly built in New York–area yards—followed slowly to the end of the year, as ships' crews mustered, got to know the intricacies of their small and crowded craft, and began to sort out contacts with their mates. Events would show that too many subchasers were built—441 in all, 303 of which served on active duty, mostly in European and East Coast waters. The surfeit allowed the navy to assign at least a few vessels to collateral duties. SC-309 and 310, built on the West Coast at Bremerton, were assigned police and coast-guard duties in Alaska.[8]

One prominent source has argued that pressing personnel problems on every level forced naval officials to man the chasers "with exceedingly in-experienced officers and men." This was certainly true of the enlisted ranks who with but very few exceptions were stocked with landlubbers who had never been to sea before starting a trip across the Atlantic. Officers, however, were of a different breed. Many of these reservists came to active duty from wealthy or comfortable East Coast backgrounds where, as youngsters and then young adults, they had sailed or motorboated the coastal Atlantic waters from Maine to Florida. What all crews lacked, however, was "any knowledge of naval tactics."[9]

As soon as available, the new vessels were herded into six-ship squadrons and their officers sent to service schools at Newport and Hampton Roads or east-ern colleges and universities, including MIT, to be immersed in brisk, rudimen-tary training programs in the new and uncertain art of antisubmarine warfare. Plans were laid to dispatch more than a hundred subchasers for antisubmarine duty in British, French, and Mediterranean waters. Eventually, 134 were sent across for duty. But in December 1917, a particularly cold and blizzard-filled winter fastened itself on American ports and harbors all up and down the At-lantic Seaboard, making every kind of maritime work from coastal patrol to the mustering of convoys to on-the-job antisubmarine training at sea a hazardous and exhausting business.

For officers and men, the ordeal of their service started the first day they went to sea, and "the sheer physical endurance and will power" required to man the tricky little vessels became clear. Swasey's design, superb as it was, contained one major flaw. "Unless the sea was dead calm, the subchasers rolled wildly." Ensign George Dole wrote his father that SC-93 was "wet as a duck" and rolled so badly that all gear below- as well as above decks had to be tightly lashed. "But the boat is on top of everything, and what water does come on deck, and we get considerable green water, does not stay there long. She shakes it off and is ready for another before the next one comes, which pleases me muchly."[10]

Before most chaser crews could get any real sea duty, Brooklyn's Marine Basin and Long Island Sound became caked with ice; Block Island Sound was totally covered. On one typical day, the temperature plummeted to fourteen below Fahrenheit. Aboard SC-93, "all the exposed metal work, bolts, steel plates, port fittings, etc." in the cramped, narrow officers' quarters forward were covered with a quarter inch of frost. The pilot-house windows coated up so quickly that they had to be kept open at all times when at sea, exposing the bridge crew to the elements.[11] Alexander Moffat, coming aboard to command SC-77, found the crew had literally not been fed for several days, forcing the men to scavenge among sympathetic crews on surrounding ships. One petty officer told him that the chaser's initial captain had probably been "deranged." Looking around his new command, Moffat was inclined to agree. The chronically cold and hungry sailors were sullen, though not yet mutinous, and Moffat suggests that the crews of the other five boats in the squadron were in little better shape. Unlike George Dole, many officers hastily thrown into the rapidly emerging chaser fleet proved unable to translate their previous sailing and motorboating skills to wartime navy life; navigation in particular flummoxed them. Nonetheless, in their haste to get the promising new weapons out to the war zone, navy officials decreed that training must go on, and one evening they abruptly ordered one of the first contingents at the Brooklyn Marine Basin to hustle up to New London through ice and fog for classroom and at-sea training.[12]

Barely escaping the basin and blundering its way toward New London through ice-strewn waters in the middle of the night, Alexander Moffat's squadron nearly ran aground on the northern tip of Long Island, near Montauk Point. With their hastily dropped anchors lost in deep, fast-running, ice-choked water, they drifted safely away with the slowly moving pack ice out into Block Island Sound. Moffat recalled that "as we were being set clear of any hazards to navigation, there was nothing further to do. I set the watch and spent the remainder of the night with as many of the crew as could jam into the quarters aft trying to get warm from the galley stove. By keeping the hatches shut, we managed to raise the temperature in this part of the ship to fifteen degrees Fahrenheit." With morning came clear skies and a brisk northwest wind. Recorded temperatures promptly dropped to fifteen below, but with the development of windchill estimates still twenty-plus years in the future, Moffat and his men could not guess that an accurate windchill reading might have been thirty-five degrees below zero. "We were almost in the middle of Block Island Sound, frozen in solid," Moffat continued. "Fisher's Island was a lavender streak on the horizon to the north; Block Island barely discernible to the East." Some of the crew built a bonfire on the ice and took pictures, while Moffat walked a half mile to the lead chaser to contact the squadron's badly confused navigator. Soon, shifting winds opened up leads, and Moffat took over navigating the six launches toward New London, where tugs had broken ice to get them into their piers.[13]

Just how far navy officialdom was aware of the early-winter ordeals in the Atlantic suffered by both the submarines in transit to European waters via the Azores and the battleship force that would depart for Scapa Flow via the Grand Banks in late November is unclear. Certainly, the brutal winter conditions should have given pause to those planners who were about to dispatch the first squadrons of subchasers to foreign seas. As historian Todd A. Woofenden has written, "To cross the Atlantic in a 110-foot motorboat was an audacious undertaking." As with the submarines, the chasers "were too small and had too little fuel for long runs." Their maximum fuel capacity was just twenty-four hundred gallons of gasoline, "sufficient for a 650 mile range under three engines at 15 knots" or a thousand-mile range running two engines that would produce twelve knots.

But the navy was emboldened by the truly remarkable seakeeping qualities of these tiny craft. Just before winter struck, Sherman Hoyt, a famous yachtsman of the day and wartime assistant superintendent of naval construction, went out on a trial run on one of the new chasers, whose young captain, albeit a regular navy man, was obviously unacquainted with the complexities of small boating. Setting out into the race off New London in a full autumnal gale, "blowing against several knots of tidal current," the skipper ordered his small vessel "deep into the wild seas" and then took the helm himself "and to Hoyt's astonishment proceeded to make every steering mistake in the book." Shaken by the ordeal he had submitted his men, his ship, and himself to, the captain told Hoyt as they neared the dock that obviously the chasers could stand up to any pounding the Atlantic might provide, "since nobody could manhandle a ship as badly as he had just done."

The transatlantic course the Navy Department chose for the Europe-bound chasers replicated that of the submarines, a relatively southern route from the East Coast (in this case New London) to Bermuda, then on to the Azores, the Mediterranean, or French or British ports.[14] By the time the first groups of subchasers set out, changes in command had weeded out most, though not all, of the flagrantly incompetent officers. Crew morale improved markedly as commanders saw to it that their sailors and petty officers were at least reasonably well fed aboard the small craft, and they appealed more or less successfully to their young charges' sense of pride in self and ship. Captains and engine-room chiefs found a handful of "jewels" of "alert, intelligent," competent men among the twenty-four aboard each chaser. Training cruises through the icy seas and occasional blizzards off New England in the early winter of 1918 seemed tough enough to guarantee safe passage to the war zones thousands of miles eastward.

Many of the newcomers, including Moffat, who was transferred to command SC-143, found their new boats appallingly short of essential materials, and they promptly set their new crews to work "robbing the fleet" of critically needed equipment. The men set to with such gusto that they also appropriated "all kind of equipment that was neither necessary nor called for." Ray Millholland, chief engineer on another chaser, sent his men on liberty with instructions to "liberate" badly needed gear. "About ten o'clock that night my engine drivers came straggling aboard, with not strictly a sober man in the party" but with their peacoat pockets filled with "three automobile tool kits, six Ford spark coilers, a round dozen spark plugs, and a miscellany of pliers, files, and chisels."[15]

Finally, on a "bitterly cold day" in January 1918, the first chasers left New London for Bermuda on the initial leg of their journey to the war zones, "bucking the drifting ice of the Thames River, and fearful of smashing our paper-shell bows and wrecking our propellers." By dusk they were off Block Island, twenty little motorboats escorted by a single armored cruiser. Darkness fell on a "bleak and tempestuous sea"; the force commander ordered all running lights doused, and the tiny fleet "barged along in the inky blackness, absolutely blind." Then a threatening storm struck full blast. Down in the engine room of Millholland's chaser, "one could hear, above the din of laboring engines the hungry roar of the frothing seas breaking against our bows, and the eerie shrieking of the wind through the wireless rigging. With hatches battened down and a wretchedly inadequate ventilator-fan futilely attempting to clear the compartment of smoke, the air soon became a viscous, gagging fog of oil vapors." Everyone became seasick almost at once in the rolling, pitching, lurching room. "There was no relief, except to hang a bucket around our necks and go on tending the engines." One man suddenly slipped on the oily deck plates, "sprawling" over a "poorly guarded revolving shaft coupling." The chief engineer instantly shut down the port engine, and the man was "pulled from the thrust-block well," bloody and unconscious, but at least alive.

"The storm seemed to know our destination, for it blew just as enthusiastically on the fourth day as it had done that first night. . . . With all those green crews and untried ships," Millholland had expected the raging seas to "swamp at least half of them." At one point, a chaser did disappear, and the captain of the armored cruiser became frantic. When the missing vessel turned up in Bermuda some six hours ahead of the fleet, it transpired that the commanding officer had been an old-time sailor who, knowing his winds and waves, simply pulled out of formation onto a new course to avoid the worst of the tempest.[16]

Several weeks later, another contingent left New London. Based on the experience of the first, the navy decided that the chasers should be taken in tow, and the armed yachts *Yacona* and *Wadena* and the tugs *Mariner*, *Lykens*, and *Mohican* (French) were given the duty. As with the first group, roughly a third of the chasers in the second contingent were destined for service in the Mediterranean, where, despite their best efforts, the handful of American, British, French, and Japanese destroyers, yachts, and trawlers operating out of Gibraltar and on the newly formed net-and-mine barrier across the Adriatic at the Straits of Otranto had been unable to suppress the twenty- to thirty-odd Austrian and German submarines operating out of Pola and Cattaro. To the officers in Sims's London headquarters, subchasers, those "vicious-looking little war vessels," could in their scores presumably provide the perfect solution. According to one of his intelligence officers, Sims quickly grasped the situation and ordered that the first chaser contingents assigned to foreign duty be sent to the Mediterranean, though the admiral apparently did not designate their precise mission or its location.[17]

For some chasers, like Moffat's SC-143, departure was a chaotic mixture of frantic last-minute searches for vital equipment not yet received and collisions in an ice-choked harbor that required last-minute repairs. Other chasers sailed without incident. On the third day out, the inevitable storm struck the flotilla. Some skippers, now confident of boat and crew, found the experience exhilarating. Dole boldly sailed his SC-90 under its own power all the way to Bermuda, writing about stormy seas that "sure looked majestic and grand. It was a beautiful sight and the boat did all that could be asked of it. The engines were right on the job in pinches," and living conditions were, on the whole, "fairly comfortable." Winds hurled across the wild seascape at velocities up to eighty-five to ninety miles an hour. Waves consistently reached twenty to twenty-five feet, though one awed sailor swore they were two hundred feet tall. At one point, the cloudy sky briefly tore apart, revealing a sun that seemed "majestic" to the besieged sailors below.

Moffat's SC-143 had an altogether different experience, the kind that led another chaser skipper to state that when his small craft "was doing her usual dance, the sun looked 'like a maltese cat flying across a horizon of scrambled eggs.'" The steady daylong rise in winds to gale force and driving spray had forced Moffat to maintain the helm in a hard-over position for some hours to keep the bow roughly into the seas. Near dark, a particularly vicious comber "struck the pilot house so solidly" that the little structure literally groaned in protest as it was shoved slightly aside. The forward- and port-side windows were smashed in, and only their thick foul-weather gear saved the two men on watch from being sliced and diced by flying glass. The helmsman promptly reported that the steering gear had frozen and could not be moved. Moffat concluded correctly that maintaining the helm's hard-over position for so long had bent the vertical shaft between the steering gear and rack and pinion below sufficiently to lock the mechanism in place, accentuating the starboard cant of the wheelhouse. "Fortunately," the hatch in the pilot-house deck that "gave access to the officer's quarters below had a high coaming which prevented the inches of water and broken glass" from sloshing over, and the hatch was promptly closed. Moffat also knew that the rudder stock on which the steering quadrant was mounted was above deck, and with heavy seas coming aboard, he had his men lash boat boom tackles taken from the mast to the tiller, allowing it to be swung by hand; the cable to the locked-up steering gear was cut with a hacksaw, and rudder control was regained.

But the chaser was badly damaged, and by his own admission, Moffat began to lose his nerve. One of the manhole covers had been swept away, flooding the lazaret stowage area aft all the way to the main deck. Most of the food stores were ruined. The deck ventilators had all been "swept clean," leaving openings that had to be imperfectly stuffed with signal flags. The twelve-foot lifeboat lashed amidships was still in its chocks but split into end-to-end kindling by the steadily pounding seas. Moffat had lifelines rigged from the wheelhouse to the stern, and the entire twenty-seven man crew, save for the helmsman and the engineers in their tiny spaces below, were lashed to the lee side, "most of them in a torpor of misery, drenched and weary, too seasick to feel hunger or thirst, too numbed to know fear."

Moffat felt it, though. Fear for his ship and for himself "lay like a quivering lump in my belly. Never had I seen anything like these racing seas, backs streaked with foam, tumbling crests that folded like breakers on a beach. From time to time a fiercer squall transformed a whole crest bodily to the back of the sea to leeward." The little motor launch "staggered up the crest of each wave to be cuffed viciously and buried in a smother of white water" that hurled the craft broadside into the following trough, threatening an imminent capsizing that never quite came. Instead, the steep waters fetched the chaser up "with a shattering jolt" that each time caused Moffat to wonder how "any structure built of wood" could last in this insane theater of noise, wind, and water that "lifted, battered and dropped" his tiny command "in an endless succession of dizzying falls while the decks shouldered off tons of churning water."

Just before the radio was incapacitated by flooding waters, intercepted messages indicated that the entire flotilla had been literally blown to the four winds, with a number of vessels disabled. The tug *Mariner* and its tow SC-177 were the only ones in sight. Soon *Mariner* began to founder, as its seams opened up, the pumps failed, and incoming water snuffed out the boiler fires. At the first sign of crisis, the tug cast off its tow. While horrified sailors aboard SC-143 looked on, the tug began to go down by the bow. Moffat's totally incompetent executive officer (the only other commissioned man aboard) found the moment to stagger out of his bunk, filthy and disheveled by crippling seasickness, to demand that he relieve his commanding officer. Moffat, who had been trying to get rid of the man for weeks before sailing, all but had him arrested and returned to his tiny cabin by one of the few crewmen still functioning. That man then reported that in addition to the flooded lazaret, "every seam in the hull is spewing water," and the galley was full of water to the stovetop and to the lower racks in the enlisted men's quarters. The engines, however, were standing up.

As *Mariner*'s plight steadily increased, yacht *Wadena* suddenly appeared out of the gloom and in an act of incredible seamanship threw over lines to the tug, manned a life raft, and, in three trips to the sinking vessel, rescued all hands. "Five minutes later," Moffat later wrote, "the *Mariner* wearily lay down. Four seas passed over her—then she was no more." *Wadena*, however, did not dally to check the plight of SC-143 but promptly steamed off on a route that Moffat hoped would lead to Bermuda. The young skipper managed to obtain the rapidly disappearing ship's base course, and as seas finally moderated and winds died, he, his crew, and his battered little motorboat at last spied Gibb's

Hill Lighthouse and staggered into Hamilton's snug harbor for food, sleep, and repairs. In the following days the rest of the flotilla, most of the chasers under resumed tow, came in over the reefs to the narrow but well-protected anchorage, where they tarried for some weeks, drilling and training in nearby waters, tended to as necessary by the mother ship, *Leonidas*, that had come down from the States even before the first chasers had arrived.[18]

In early April 1918, following an extensive period of rest and refit, a total of thirty-five chasers, accompanied by *Leonidas*, the old armored cruiser *Salem*, and several armed yachts left Bermuda for the Azores through calming skies and gentling seas. The fleet would not be alone, for it was to escort a convoy of "cliff-sided" transports "loaded with colored troops, labor battalions bound for Brest." As dawn broke on the first morning out of Bermuda, the men of the "splinter fleet" (as the chaser sailors proudly designated themselves in contradistinction to the "iron navy") proved as susceptible to folly as a the rawest destroyer crews at Queenstown. A nervous lookout spied "a suspicious looking light" on the eastern horizon. It must be the masthead light of an oncoming ship, which according to standing instructions needed to be identified, if not stopped and searched. The officer of the deck aboard Ray Millholland's chaser ordered a shot across the bow, which was duly delivered. The convoy promptly went crackers. "Sirens *blooor* hoarsely; electric gongs clang a nervous call to battle stations." Aboard *Leonidas*, a sleepy, pajama-clad force commander awakened from a sound sleep "looks in the direction indicated by the alert Officer of the Deck" and sees "dead in the east, the Morning Star" winking "roguishly" back. Disgusted, the man dressed down the bridge crew and returned to his cot.[19]

At-sea refueling was readily accomplished from a dedicated tanker. Following another prolonged stay in the Azores, where the original chaser squadrons were joined by reinforcements, two squadrons set off for an undisclosed Mediterranean base via Gibraltar and Malta, while Moffat's group of six chasers escorted the cargo ship *Julia Luckenbach* to Belle Isle, off the French coast. The *Luckenbach* assignment required a novel means of refueling at sea, for the cargo vessel had no means of direct refueling. Eventually, much against his will, its captain was induced to carry 160 fifty-gallon drums of gasoline on deck, which were periodically released into generally calm seas to be picked up by this needy chaser or that. Deposited on deck, each drum's contents were then emptied into the fuel compartments by hose. Completing their assignment, the chasers were finally ordered on to Brest after some confusion and barely made the journey through waters known to be submarine infested before fuel was exhausted.[20]

Some subchaser contingents remained at Ponta Delgada, patrolling Azores waters for largely nonexistent U-boats, while the majority of later squadrons staging through moved on either to the Mediterranean, via Gibraltar and Malta, to "Base 25" on the island of Corfu near the mouth of the Adriatic or to existing bases on the English and Irish coasts.

In May, Moffat's contingent, just arrived at Brest, received orders to transfer to Plymouth; other chasers were already on their way to Queenstown or Berehaven. In September 1918, thirty-six additional chasers arrived at Queenstown.[21] It had taken slightly more than a year, but the United States Navy's antisubmarine fleet was at last in European waters in force.

Josephus Daniels (NH 2336)

Rear Admiral William
Sowden Sims (NH 2846)

(*Right*) Chief of Naval
Operations William Benson
(NH 59803)

(*Below*) Destroyer *Wadsworth* off
Queenstown, 1918, in dazzle
camouflage (NH 702)

Destroyer USS *McDougal* (NH 854)

USS *Leviathan* (NH 71; ID 1326)

USS *Fanning* captures U-58, the only confirmed American U-boat kill of the war (NH 54063)

The 450-ton destroyer *Chauncey* lost in a collision off Gibraltar (NH 55093)

Jacob Jones, the only US destroyer lost to enemy action (NH 52123)

Submarine K-6 at the Azores, December 1917 (NH 52393)

An informal painting of US Battleship Division Six entering Scapa Flow in early December 1917. If the American ships look stylized after their transatlantic ordeal, the British response is historically accurate. (NH 2685)

Admiral Hugh Rodman, commander, Battleship Division Six that became Battleship Division Nine of the British Home Fleet between December 1917 and November 1918 (NH 48940)

Battleship *Florida* in Scotland's Firth of Forth off Edinburgh with the Great Railway Bridge in the background (NH 58841-KN)

Three subchasers at New York City returned from overseas: SC–217 on the Otranto Barrage and 224 and 351 with Unit 2, Plymouth, England (T. Woofenden Collection)

Subchaser 126 under way (T. Woofenden Collection)

Battle formation of submarine chasers (T. Woofenden Collection)

Subchaser 113 crew (T. Woofenden Collection)

Lieutenant "Juggy" Nelson at Base 25, Corfu, greeting British officials
(T. Woofenden Collection)

US Navy minelayers steaming in two parallel columns of four during
the laying of the North Sea Barrage in the summer and fall of 1918
(NH 41736)

Curtiss H-16 flying boat on the ramp at Naval Air Station, Queenstown, Ireland, 1918 (NH 2596)

H-16 flying boat at Anacostia Naval Air Station, Washington, DC, October 1919 (NH 89696)

Destroyer *Jarvis* in the dockyard at Brest following its collision with sister ship *Benham* in the Bay of Biscay, 1918 (NH 52189)

Battleship Boys

IN NOVEMBER 1917, Benson prepared to fulfill the pledge that he had made at London. On the thirteenth, Daniels informed the CNO that following consultations with Mayo, four dreadnought battleships, *New York*, *Florida*, *Delaware*, and *Wyoming*, "the best coal burners in the fleet," would "form [a] division to be dispatched to England. These ships after docking should be ready to sail about 25 November." Kentucky-born Rear Admiral Hugh Rodman would be placed in command.[1]

At some point, a decision was made to include a fifth modern coal burner, *Texas*. Following its presailing overhaul, however, the twenty-seven-thousand-ton, 573-foot vessel carrying ten fourteen-inch guns ran aground off Block Island while heading for Port Jefferson, New York. The big craft, "full of ammunition," was beset "from the bow all the way aft beyond the cranes which was well beyond amidships." For a week the battleship lay stranded while air compressors blew out excess water. The machines hauling on "the huge cables we had astern" got *Texas* off. The vessel's "inner skin" was not pierced, but hull damage proved serious enough to demand another dry-docking at the New York Navy Yard, "while our friends in the rest of the division proceeded to Europe." The commanding officer escaped court-martial. While *Texas* completed repairs, sailed back to the Chesapeake for further training, and at last sailed alone for the Orkneys at the end of January 1918, Captain Blue, "a protégé of Josephus Daniels," resumed his former post as chief of the Bureau of Navigation. To add to that irony, he retired from active duty in July 1919 with the rank of rear admiral. As one observer concluded, "You can run aground and get promoted to flag rank."[2] *Texas*'s passage across the Atlantic, while characteristically rough, proved relatively benign. Not so that of the other four battlewagons. Theirs was an ordeal that no one who experienced it could ever forget.

Francis Hunter, who had joined the "Naval Reserve Force" as an ensign in March 1917, was originally assigned as an assistant in establishing a subchaser training center at Bay Ridge in New York Harbor. After three months, however, he was ordered to Annapolis for reserve officers' training during "a summer hot as Hades." Along with 150 other candidates, he sweated and sweltered through seventeen-hour days. His reward: duty aboard the battleship *New York*. Arriving in Norfolk, the young man found the twelve-hundred-man crew on edge, for no one knew if the big ship "would even go over." Following two months cruising in home waters, however, the battleship was ordered "suddenly and secretly" to the Brooklyn Navy Yard for frantic preparations. "On the hazy drizzling afternoon" of November 22, 1917, "enshrouded in a veil of mist, we steamed under the great East River spans to the sea," destination Norfolk and rendezvous with the three other coal-burning dreadnoughts that would constitute Battleship Division 9. Two days later, "four great anchors" came out of the bottom mud of Lynnhaven Roads, "eight huge funnels furiously belched black, as sixteen propellers took up a droning throb that for days to come we knew would be incessant." Steaming out into the Atlantic, "the line of . . . monsters laid their course northeast."[3]

Although not absolutely top-of-the-line vessels like the recent fourteen-inch-gun oil burners *Arizona*, *Pennsylvania*, and *New Mexico*, *New York* and its three cousins were formidable ships for their time. Commissioned in 1909 and 1910, respectively, *Delaware* and *Florida* were 520-foot vessels displacing well over twenty thousand tons. Both steamed at twenty-one knots maximum and carried a main armament of ten twelve-inch naval guns. *Wyoming* and *New York*, both commissioned in 1912, were improved classes whose 554- and 565-foot hulls displaced twenty-six and twenty-seven thousand tons, respectively. While achieving no increase in speed, *Wyoming* mounted a main battery of twelve twelve-inch guns, while *New York* carried ten fourteen-inch guns.[4]

For five days, sea and sky remained benign as the great ships and their single destroyer escort plowed steadily toward the Old World.[5] In those far-off days a century ago, there were no space satellites, no sophisticated measuring devices to warn vessels of the location, intensity, or course of storms at sea, and so no way to maneuver away from advancing bad weather. The only signs of an impending tempest besides darkening skies and roiling seascapes were onboard barometers measuring atmospheric pressure. As the formation reached a point roughly one hundred miles east of the Grand Banks of Newfoundland on the morning of the twenty-ninth, "a different tale began to unfold." The midnight-to-four watch started "under a big yellow moon." Two hours later, it was surrounded by "a nasty ring . . . growing more and more intense." By three, a stiff breeze had blown up, and scud began to fly from wave tops. Bridge crews saw their barometers begin a precipitate drop that eventually reached 29.00. At midmorning under dark skies, the battleships and their destroyer found themselves plunging through heavy seas, with "spray, rain and hail" flying past the decks. By dinnertime relieving deck watches struggled precariously to their posts on hands and knees through ninety-mile-an-hour gusts. "Green spray prevented more than fifteen feet of vision from a protected spot; while in the open, eyes were valueless." Hunter found his gun crew on the veranda deck, huddled before the hatchway to the five-inch mount, terrified that in reaching for the hatch they might be swept away. He sent the men below "by forming a human chain"; obviously, manning the gun under such conditions was useless. "A foot of water swept constantly over the deck, carrying all before it."

Now a prime weakness of US battleship design began to be felt. Staying with custom from the Age of Fighting Sail, America's dreadnoughts compromised the integrity of their hulls by placing most of their secondary battery in gun decks built just below the main deck and perhaps twenty feet at most above the waterline under full battle-load conditions. In foul weather these decks with their five-inch guns were enclosed by protective steel shutters that proved wholly inadequate against the tempest that raged off the Grand Banks at Thanksgiving 1917.

As seas and winds continued to rise, smashing into hulls with ever-greater force and making conversation on open bridges and other spaces impossible, many shutters sprang, letting in tons of seawater with every roll. Elsewhere, the relentless waters sought out every aperture and opening, no matter how small. Twenty- and twenty-seven-thousand-ton battlewagons began to take on water throughout their 500- to 550-foot lengths. Belowdecks, full turkey dinners were determinedly served to officers in the wardrooms, and the rising crisis was unclear. But all too soon, ships began to pitch as well as roll, and water, forced into "every conceivable opening, rushed below in a most alarming manner."

All through a sleepless night, the "frightful" weather increased. Above decks, pounding seas snapped stanchions and battered lifeboats to kindling, while shrieking winds snapped off radio antennas. In *New York*'s wardroom, "The music cabinet and phonograph capsized with a crash, followed shortly by the clattering smash of all drawers of silverware and table gear as they dropped bodily on the deck." While officers and crewmen fought to secure gear, "the huge ice-chest went over with a shock that would have gone clear through an ordinary deck." The lower decks, filled with saltwater, had become awash in a vile slime of "meat, grease, milk, vegetables," and fruit. In the large enlisted mess room, tables and chairs "slashed from side to side, carrying all before them." More and more sailors became violently seasick, adding to the unpleasantness. By early morning, water in Hunter's cabin was ankle deep, and all ventilation ceased everywhere below, as electricity was diverted to all pumps that worked to capacity. Still the waters rose. Sailors in *New York*'s forward storerooms reported six inches of water on decks; four hours later they reported eight feet. The air grew foul, as the hundred-mile-an-hour gale drove the force "like a toy across the Grand Banks." The lone destroyer, *Manley*, drifted off to struggle into Queenstown days later. *Delaware* disappeared in the wild murk, while *New York*, *Florida*, and *Wyoming* struggled more or less successfully to retain formation, though navigation and searchlights were nearly useless due to flooding of electrical boxes. At one point, *New York* "strayed from course" due to a malfunctioning gyrocompass. *Wyoming* managed to flash over course corrections by signal lamp.

As the second night came on, the big ships slowed to eight knots, then four, vainly seeking respite of some sort from the implacable elements. Great hulls took fifty-degree rolls even as they pitched steadily. Exhausted officers stripped off foul clothing and boots, collapsing into bunks still above the rising waters for blessed hours of uneasy rest. Through the next morning the ships grimly breasted howling wind and crashing seas until, aboard *New York*, alarming word came down from the bridge just after noon that the pumps were failing to hold their own and the ship was slowly going down by the head. All hands were ordered to turn to and form bucket brigades. For the next "five long hours," officers and enlisted men alike "bailed for their lives." Slowly, the brigades managed to vent more water than came in. "Then finally, toward evening, the fury of the hurricane abated just enough to satisfy the pumps." Crewmen strained beyond endurance dropped where they were. The enlisted quarters above the engine and fire rooms and adjacent to the galleys were filled not only with slimy, nauseating waste of various kinds but also with fumes and heat sufficient "to make a veritable inferno. The thermometer registered 115 degrees in that vile air which men were forced to live in."

At six in the evening, aboard *New York*, Captain Charles F. Hughes at last pronounced the crisis over. Cleanup and stock taking began. The bow had suffered some damage "inside and out," though not enough, it transpired, to require a dockyard. "Our forward cabins had been drenched and storerooms soaked.

Twelve thousand pounds of sugar, five hundred gallons of paint, and five hundred gas masks were ruined, together with a storeroom full of clothing." The next day, the three battleships, with *Delaware* hopefully somewhere nearby, came into the "glorious blue of the Gulf Stream" and resumed their arc-like course toward Scapa Flow, passing just south of Iceland. To the intense pleasure of all, the fleet was bang on course, despite few opportunities to take either sun or star sights. Steaming alone, *Delaware* was actually the first to meet the British cruiser *Constance* early in the morning of December 6 at the rendezvous point off the northwest coast of Scotland. Twenty-four hours later the other three battleships appeared, and at noon on the seventh the still storm-beaten ships, their upper works filled with smashed gear of various sorts, sailed into Scapa Flow through a golden day toward a historic union with the Royal Navy, whose men, tars and admirals alike, greeted the Yankee cousins with bands, cheers, and salutes.

The Americans, in turn, were stunned by the grandeur of the world's greatest fleet. This did not prevent Hugh Rodman, now commander of the Sixth Battle Squadron of the Grand Fleet, from making a not so subtle point to his British hosts and superiors. His obligatory call on the fleet commander via trawler through Scapa Flow's traditionally rough water completed, he allegedly told Beatty that his navy didn't believe much in paperwork, so "whenever you have anything to bring to my attention, come and see me." Slightly nonplussed, Beatty allegedly replied, "I'll just do that, Admiral."[6]

Rodman later wrote with pride how quickly his officers and men integrated with the Royal Navy, achieving proficiency if not mastery of British signals, radio codes, maneuvering orders, fire-control methods, battle instructions, and seakeeping in strict formation. Much of the undoubted ease with which the Americans slid into British practices was due to Rodman's own willingness to subsume his command to that of the hosts. "Rodman understood that two independent commands within one force simply would not work." As the admiral himself later expressed it, "I realized that the British fleet had had three years of actual warfare and knew the game from the ground floor up; that while we might know it theoretically, there would be a great deal to learn practically." Yet "within twenty-four hours after our arrival, we were using the British code intelligently and with confidence, and within three days we took part in a major fleet operation in the North Sea and had no difficulty in conforming to their tactical maneuvers as directed by their code of signals."[7]

In fact, while the Yanks did attain competence with impressive speed, not all went well. The British found American signaling and radio equipment to be "primitive." But the real problem was gunnery. Just ten days after arriving at Scapa Flow, Rodman's Sixth Battle Squadron accompanied Beatty's flagship and other elements of the Grand Fleet to Rosyth, "Britain's newest dockyard" and home to its battle cruiser fleet just a few miles up the Firth of Forth from Edinburgh. Everyone spent the Christmas holidays in the city, and liberty was granted lavishly to the battleship crews, the first and, with one exception, last time that the men would enjoy true shore leave in their eleven-month sojourn abroad. The crew of *New York* endeared themselves to the Scots—and to their colleagues in the Grand Fleet—by staging a largely impromptu Christmas party for the town's "waifs and strays." On the way back to the Orkneys, the Americans engaged in their first serious gunnery practice in Pentland Firth. The results left officers and men alike "in shock and disappointment," while the British cousins doubted the very "proficiency of the American squadron." Beatty wrote King George V that, in historian Jerry W. Jones's summary, the cousins' "spread of broadsides" was "excessive" and their rates of fire "less than satisfactory." *Delaware* and *New York* had performed acceptably, Jellicoe wrote; *Florida* and *Wyoming* had not. *New York*'s gunnery officer insisted his men had "really shot well," and Mayo's Atlantic Fleet gunnery officer later maintained that whatever deficiencies the Sixth Battle Squadron had displayed were due to "stage fright."[8]

According to his memoirs, Rodman spent long hours assiduously courting Beatty, his staff, and, on several occasions, King George V, a naval enthusiast who enjoyed visiting his fleet. The Kentuckian spun many a "yarn" over coffee and cigarettes aboard both British and American flagships while using the social occasions to swap experiences and gain further knowledge and insights of British practices for his officers and crews. Rodman's junior officers continued the mutual courtship with numerous rounds of tennis with which Beatty and his teenage and subteenage sons were wholly smitten. Across a hundred years, the Americans' fawning attention to their British hosts is little short of embarrassing. On the other hand, the commander in chief of the Grand Fleet and his people could only have been impressed by the undoubted professional competence of his guests in action. Initial deficiencies in communications and gunnery were subsumed, at least in part, by the Yanks' undoubted flair for good seamanship. Passing in and out of the narrow, rocky entrance to Scapa Flow and operating in the winter waters of the North Sea under often stormy skies required skills of the highest order, and this the Yanks possessed from the outset.[9]

Beatty took the American cousins to sea soon and often with the intent not only of incorporating them into the British battle line but also to train them as independent convoy escorts on the critical Scandinavian run that lay within easy range of enemy naval bases on the German and Belgian coasts. By February 1918, just two months after the American fleet's arrival, Sims wrote Benson "to say that Rodman's handling of the situation seems to me to have been admirable. He is certainly persona grata with everybody and is spoken of in the highest terms not only by the British but by all of our people who come in contact with him."[10]

Just nine months after Woodrow Wilson's unprepared country had gone to war, the Yanks had achieved impressive, if not miraculous, results. Europe's Great Powers had been more or less preparing for a massive conflict for at least two decades, though few if any dared acknowledge the fact. The Americans had been determinedly isolationist, with a small professional military and a growing maritime fighting force focused on doing battle in Mahanian terms but nothing else. British authorities had been well aware that "Mr. Daniel's party came into office" in January 1913, "pledged to the reduction of expenditures on naval and military defenses." If "the first gunshot in Europe" twenty months later put paid to that idea, the Americans remained determined to do nothing to invite participation. Shortly after the Armistice, Mayo, the Atlantic Fleet commander, admitted that "prior to our entry into the war, the United States Navy was anything but a well-rounded fighting machine." "Conditions" had caused the service "to grow more in one direction than another.[11]

But in less than a year of war, the US Navy had begun an impressive mastery of modern combat at sea. From his London command post, Sims had successfully pressed for major strategic changes in Allied antisubmarine warfare centered around the concept of the convoy. To make that concept successful, his navy contributed a substantial percentage of the ocean and inshore escort resources to ensure the safe passage of an unprecedentedly large, and as it turned out reasonably efficient, fighting army to the battlefields of France; it had developed new warship types—the subchaser, armed yachts, and the dedicated antisubmarine destroyer—that contributed significantly to the tenacious harassment of the kaiser's U-boat fleet. At the same time, Washington had dispatched a significant battle force to assist the Royal Navy in suppressing Germany's mighty High Seas Fleet. Finally, the United States was fielding the first elements of a naval aviation force whose fliers were dedicated to the antisubmarine war, but who would find themselves called upon in coming emergencies to fill a vital volunteer role in the air above the western front. Nineteen eighteen would prove to be the year in which the United States, led by its navy, would at last ascend unquestionably into the limited ranks of the world's greatest powers.

Keeping the Seas

Bloody stalemate. Ruthless "set-piece" warfare out of trenches stretching from Ypres and Vimy Ridge near the English Channel through the Somme and Verdun to the Swiss border (and, for a time, to Gallipoli) in which millions of men died, "struggling in the slime," flinging themselves futilely against barbed wire and entrenched fortifications, mowed down by heavy artillery and machine-gun fire, while at sea great fleets fought inconclusively as U-boats threatened to become the ultimate weapon. This is the vision of the western front in the First World War that we all carry with us, "etched" into the collective culture of Europe and the United States.[1]

It is accurate if one concentrates on the awful thirty-nine months that elapsed between the German Army's failed attempt to reach the Channel in November 1914 and the spring of 1918. But in March of the latter year, buoyed by the infusion of a half-million *soldaten* from an eastern front now shut down as a result of revolution in Russia, Erich von Ludendorff unleashed the German armies in a series of slashing offensives out of Belgium and into northern France, ultimately threatening Paris itself.

As the lines of the British and French armies collapsed in the face of the "Michael Offensive," then restabilized, bent, and sagged but never again broke, salvation lay in the hands of the American Expeditionary Force, whose presence—despite Pershing's initial determination to fight independently—ultimately stiffened the Anglo-French ranks. As the growing military might of the United States fed into the defense against the advancing Germans, all depended on the war at sea. If the kaiser's U-boats (possibly supported by his battle cruisers) could reverse Germany's recent ill fortune and disrupt a significant portion of the transatlantic convoy system bringing America's half-trained soldiers and their precious supplies to the western front, German arms might yet prevail, despite growing privations and despair at home. If, however—as happened—the convoy system remained intact and well-equipped doughboys appeared in ever-swelling numbers on the western front, Germany's armies, strategically blind and impoverished by an overstrained transport network, were doomed.

Throughout the last eleven months of the war, Sims's Planning Staff in the London headquarters produced a blizzard of memoranda—seventy-one in all. Knox, Schofield, Yarnell, and Dunlap, with Twining coordinating the work, were restrained by only a single stipulation: "Neither the Planning Staff nor any member thereof is to engage in any administrative work whatever." Policy planning and recommendation were to be their sole preoccupation and responsibility. During the first three weeks of 1918 alone, the four men produced detailed information and firm recommendations on such diverse subjects as "The North Sea Mine Barrage," "Submarine Hunting by Sound," "Employment of Auxiliary Cruisers," "Closing the Skagerrak," and "Assignment of Destroyers to the Grand Fleet." The effort climaxed on January 21 with a twenty-one-page memorandum titled "Estimate of the German Naval Situation." To read these papers is to understand the course of the war in general, and at sea in particular, during its last eleven months.[2]

In American eyes, the Submarine Menace remained acute almost to the end. In Memorandum No. 9 at the end of January, Knox and his colleagues wrote, "The attainment of the subsurface command of the sea is of immediate and paramount importance to the Allied forces. Victory or defeat depend upon the solution of this problem." America and its associates had already lost more than twelve million tons of shipping, and as Lawrence Sondhaus has discovered, that shipping, despite widespread assumptions to the contrary, had not been replaced on a one-to-one ratio, nor could American yards take up the slack, preoccupied as many of the largest were with fulfilling Wilson's "Navy Second to None" pledge. "The effect" of this chronic "shortage of shipping," the Planning Staff concluded, "is apparent on the whole allied land front from the North Sea to Mesopotamia." At the end of March, the Planning Staff returned to the issue. "The shipping situation is becoming more and more critical. Unless a check is placed on the enemy's submarines, it may become necessary to cease the transport of United States troops and stores to France, in order to meet the urgent requirements of the Allies as regards food" for their civil populations "and resources" for their war effort.[3]

Despite the gloom, the convoys came across the Atlantic in ever-greater sizes and numbers. The US Navy's forty-five troopships made 302 individual round-trips, carrying 683,000 men. Only 16 voyages were made in January. By May, the number had doubled and stayed in the mid-30s from then until October, when 43 trips were made. US vessels other than navy transports made an additional 111 individual voyages, carrying 33,000 soldiers to England or France. The number of troops transported in British ships during the final eleven months of the war was even more impressive: in a total of 387 individual voyages (within convoys), more than 1,152,000 doughboys sailed "over there." Only 9 voyages were made in January, 4 in February. Thereafter, the numbers grew dramatically. By May, 75 voyages were made by British troop transports engaged in the round-trip Atlantic ferry. By July, British transports had completed 89 voyages. Supplementing the US Navy and British transports were a handful of American Army together with other foreign transports. The entire enterprise was supported by hundreds of freighters bearing cargoes of any and all types of matériel. In all, a total of 18,653 ships in round-trip voyages were escorted through the Western Approaches and adjacent waters. They carried not only goods and supplies to the AEF but also great quantities for the civilian populations of England and especially France.[4]

Nonetheless, destroyer boys had as little respect for the merchant seamen who manned the cargo ships as they did for the transport sailors. On one occasion, *McDougal* dropped several depth charges on a submarine that induced the engine-room gang on a nearby freighter to abandon ship in belief they had been torpedoed. Their panic led to a general charge to the lifeboats that included officers and men topside. The steamer was left "with her engines running, steaming blindly in the convoy. Later, the shamefaced captain and his officers returned to their abandoned, slowly turning, vessel and got it back on course, then picked up the crew from various rescue ships."[5]

When the first American naval contingents arrived in 1917, wartime Brest contained "but a few elements of the French Fleet." Reserve Ensign Joseph Husband recalled shortly after the Armistice that "the streets of the gray town were deserted. Gone were the seamen that for centuries had given it its glory; gone too were the young men fighting and dying on the northern lines of France." Then, "within the brief span of a year," Brest was transformed. "Great transports" swung at their moorings beyond the breakwater, while within, "wasp-like destroyers" rode at their anchoring buoys in ever-greater numbers. "Khaki-clad soldiers by the hundred thousand were to look upon the gray town and pass on to their duty in the north." A new command, "United States

Naval Forces in France," ably presided over by Vice Admiral Henry B. Wilson, came into being, incorporating "constant organization and amplification" to administer the vast buildup of American forces on the western front.[6]

The buildup at Brest began slowly, grew inexorably. The 25,000 men landed in January 1918 increased to 62,000 in April. "In May, the full flood began," as nearly 120,000 Yanks came ashore and moved to the training cantonments and then the front. By September, more than 143,000 were streaming off the transports into the lighters that took them ashore. In all, nearly 900,000 American troops landed at Brest alone in the last ten months of the war.

The arrival of each of the 122 convoys was an "inspiring sight" as they appeared through the dawn, riding single file across blue or gray seas under a sky often soft with clouds. "On the eastern horizon a white lighthouse lifted sharply from the thin line of the coast. The great troop ships, famous liners of other days, rose and fell heavily on the low swells, their high sides striped and blocked in a strange" camouflage "of blue, gray, white and black." The decks were "brown with a solid mass of soldiers, straining their eyes to get a first glimpse of France," from which many would never return. The destroyers, "lean, lithe sea-whippets" whose bows dipped and rose rhythmically, kept a keen watch for telltale signs of U-boats, while overhead "two great yellow French dirigibles" and "four grey hydroplanes, soaring in wide circles," strengthened the antisubmarine force.

Sounds of an army band came over the water as the convoy at last passed into the channel. "On the south, great brown rocks lifted from the sea and on either side of the entrance to the harbor, the black cliffs of Finistere, like twin Gibraltars, marked the approach." Coming up channel, soldiers and sailors glancing leftward saw a "gray and ancient city" rising "sharply from the historic fortress at the water's edge." As the destroyers moved on into the inner harbor, the transports dropped anchor outside the breakwater and began discharging their human cargo, headed for the fearsome jaws of war.[7]

Antisubmarine warfare along the French coast and adjacent waters replicated that elsewhere, with long days of struggle against an enemy force "secret, elusive, and mysterious. There were thrusts in the dark from an unseen enemy; there were engagements fought and won between ships invisible to each other. Never could there be a moment of relaxation; never did an empty ocean, blue under a summer sky or gleaming in the moonlight, assure the absence of the enemy."[8]

Escort work became increasingly dangerous in 1918, as the number and size of transatlantic convoys inexorably grew. In March, the 1,000-ton destroyer

Manley, which had staggered across the Atlantic in the storm-lashed wake of Rodman's battleships, was escorting a convoy off Queenstown when it accidentally brushed a British cruiser and its depth charges detonated. The destroyer's stern was "practically destroyed." Worse soon followed, as fragments from the explosion pierced two fifty-gallon gasoline drums and two tanks containing one hundred gallons of alcohol. "The leaking fluids caught fire as they ran along the deck and enveloped the ship in flames which were not extinguished until late that night." In all, *Manley's* executive officer and thirty-three enlisted men were killed. Despite the gallant efforts of a British ship to rig a tow, *Manley* remained adrift until two British tugs managed to take it in. "She reached Queenstown at dusk the following day with more than 70 feet of her hull awash or completely under water." Sent to Liverpool for repairs, the destroyer never touched the seas during the remainder of the war.[9]

The following month, three of the navy's oldest destroyers, *Stewart*, *Whipple*, and *Truxton*, tiny 420-ton sisters to *Bainbridge* and *Chauncey*, were escorting a convoy into Brest at night under cloud-covered skies when off Quiberon Bay, a nearby ammunition ship, *Florence H*, "suddenly burst into great gouts of flame." Survivors later said that an explosion in the number 2 hold "had lifted the deck and blown out the ship's starboard side." As the three destroyers dashed in to see what assistance they could render, the "water round the burning ship was . . . littered with blazing powder-cases and wreckage, so tightly packed that they floated away to leeward like huge rafts." The water was also covered with "flaming oil-fuel," while ammunition "exploded in all directions." The escorting yachts with their wooden decks dared not venture toward the stricken vessel, which "had split open amidships and was vomiting tongues of flame" into the night sky "like a volcano." But despite the explosive dangers contained in depth-charge racks on their sterns, the destroyers never hesitated. Their crews could hear men crying out in the water. The only way to rescue them was to "plough through" the debris blazing on all sides. Lieutenant Commander H. S. Haislip took *Stewart* into the fiery seas, "clearing a way for her consorts to close in behind." Sailors threw lines overboard whenever a survivor was found, while others "jumped overboard" to rescue those too weak or near drowning to save themselves. "Boats were lowered, and pushed their way through the burning flotsam to get at men beyond. All the time, the flames from the *Florence H.* lit up the sea until it was almost as bright as day." When the shattered hull finally slipped beneath the waves, it took forty-five officers and men with it. But thirty-two others had been saved. Jesse Whitfield Covington, cook third class, and Frank M. Upton, quartermaster, of *Stewart* won Congressional Medals of Honor that night.[10]

Just thirty days before the end of the war, destroyer *Shaw* suffered horrendous damage. A brand-new 1,100-ton ship built in California and hastily brought around to New York and then to the war zone the year before, the destroyer was shepherding the Cunard liner *Aquitania* packed with eight thousand soldiers and crew across the Channel to France. *Shaw* had completed one leg of a routine zigzag when its helm suddenly jammed just as the bows were "aimed straight at" the "great wall side" of the liner. With no room to maneuver and determined that his tiny but sharp-bowed ship would not smash through the liner's thin steel skin and sink or badly damage it, Commander William Glassford determined to sacrifice his destroyer. Ordering "all back full," Glassford ensured that *Aquitania* would be the one to strike. For long, terrifying seconds, crewmen aboard the "little" destroyer awaited their fate as the huge liner loomed ever closer at near right angles. Twin plumes of bow wave "played round the forefoot" of the great ship. Beyond the stem, *Shaw*'s awed crewmen glimpsed "huge wall sides, with their rows of" lighted portholes "towering to the sky like . . . some great building." Masts and smoke-belching funnels together with "a few excited faces peering over the bow" completed the scene just before the great vessel, nearly fifty times the size of the destroyer, struck amidships near *Shaw*'s bridge with "the speed of a suburban railway train."

Tortured metal screamed amid the "crashing, shuddering impact" as the tiny destroyer was flung nearly on its beam ends. Scarcely affected by the crash, *Aquitania* rushed on, cutting *Shaw* in two, slicing off ninety feet of the bow, instantly killing two officers and ten enlisted men. The forward boiler room was torn open, the bridge wrecked as both masts toppled onto the deck. In falling, the mainmast somehow fouled the starboard propeller. Seconds thereafter, sparks set fire to the fuel oil in the forward tanks, and *Shaw* "burst into flame." As two sister destroyers raced up to rescue men on the bow that had drifted some ninety feet away, flames reached ammunition boxes, which began to explode. With remarkable composure, the crew extinguished the flames and got the engines and steering gear back in operation. A skeleton crew of twenty-one remained on board to somehow get the wreck into Portland Harbor, forty miles away, under its own power. "A photograph of the damage shows a great heap of shapeless, crumpled steel extending as far as the forward funnel, with, on top of it, the circular bridge structure canted over to port at an angle of nearly eighty degrees." The destroyer's war was over. Under repair for months, it finally sailed to the States with a new bow at the end of May 1919.[11]

Such experiences stressed men to the breaking point and beyond. When *McDougal* staggered into Liverpool for repairs following its fearsome convoy collision in February 1918, the crew engaged in at least one street brawl with British tars, and loose tongues almost led to other fights. On one occasion, a drunken swabbie looked up at a picture of the monarch above a Liverpool bar and shouted, "To hell with King George!" "To hell with President Wilson!" came a voice from behind. Swinging around to have it out with the man, the sailor saw a "husky Anzac who outpointed him on every dimension." Thinking quickly, the Yank held out his hand and cried, "That's what I say! I'm a Republican."[12]

Although the authoritative *Dictionary of American Naval Fighting Ships* lists but one other destroyer (*Stockton*) involved in a nonfatal wartime collision, naval journalist Ralph Paine, returning home sometime late in 1918, encountered a former destroyer captain whose "nerves had cracked" from what he claimed had been a near-fatal collision the previous autumn. He was an older man, mid-forties, and a "mustang," someone "commissioned from the ranks after serving for years as a warrant officer." He confessed to Paine that he simply could not stand the pace of destroyer life in wartime. "He had made a fine record for himself and his ship through more than a half-year of it," before his unnamed vessel was "cut down in a collision last fall." He told Paine that one should "expect little things like that. Running without lights, fog, thick weather, nervous merchant skippers,—the wonder is that we keep clear as much as we do. This boat of mine was almost cut in two. She sank until her deck was awash and there she hung,—almost under but still floating." The devoted crew got the ship back to port, "and she came out again, after a few weeks as good as new." It was different for the captain. "Uncomplaining, quietly heroic, he was so broken and unstrung that he was able to sleep no more than two hours in the twenty-four. All night long he read and smoked, walked the deck, or lay in his bunk, and thought himself lucky when he drowsed off for a little while during the day." The man knew that regaining his physical health and mental equilibrium—"mending his nerves"—would be a "long haul." He would live outdoors, fish and hunt, "and try to forget the war."[13]

Just who this man was or might have been is impossible to determine. The closest approximation would have been Lieutenant Commander Robert Lawrence Berry of *Manley*. But the dates and conditions of *Manley's* ordeal as Paine described it are wrong, and the biographical facts are totally in error. Berry had graduated the Naval Academy in 1900, age sixteen, which would have put him in his early thirties at the end of World War I. On the other hand, Paine did not tell many tall tales, realizing that the stories he did write were sufficiently compelling not to require embellishment. But in this case, he may have done so in order to protect a vulnerable individual while emphasizing the extraordinary strains of destroyer life. Alternatively, he may have woven together the stories of several destroyer officers, none of them commanders, to make his point.

Patrol duties changed little during the final eleven months of the war; frequent tedium continued to reign. Along the French coast, life aboard the armed yachts was at first more comfortable than aboard the destroyers. Deck spaces were wide, "and numerous tiled bathrooms" reminded the crew of the ship's former status. But routine escort duties placed these vessels in greater harm's way than it did the faster, more maneuverable destroyers. "Coastal convoys feared mines more than" U-boats and rocks, shoals, and weather more than anything else. An enlisted sailor confided to his diary that "we have long since learned that our most dangerous enemy is not the submarine. First it is the fog. Secondly, rocks and perhaps mines." Still, the U-boats were ever present, lurking in the numerous shipping channels from Brest to St. Nazaire to the Gironde, sowing mines and occasionally torpedoing ships. The Americans responded promptly, sending a squadron of converted minesweepers in July 1917 that became fully operational in September. Thereafter, the cat-and-mouse game in mining and sweeping continued until Armistice Day.[14]

A typical merchant convoy began with a lively, multilingual presailing conference between the convoy's French pilot, the captains of whatever Allied or American destroyer might be available, and the armed-yacht skippers. Often convoys lifted their anchors and "stole out" of harbor after dark, "moving like shadows, showing no lights," even in the brightest moonlight and with "uncommonly tranquil" seas. Once in the Bay of Biscay, straggling became a problem, and "the guardian yacht . . . would signal to close up" as a French destroyer dashed about, shooing the miscreant back into line. Soon, messages began "piling up" in the yacht's chart room bespeaking nearby crises: "From: SS _____ 'SOS. Am being torpedoed thirty miles west of _____. . . . Am being shelled. Shot just missed by 500 yards. . . . Am still being shelled. Hope to see you soon.'" A destroyer or yacht swiftly turned away from the convoy to race toward the disaster area, messaging the beleaguered victim to maintain course. "We are heading for you. . . . Hold on. Help is coming." Then, from the merchant ship, "Escaped. Thank you." And from the yacht, "Well done."

Many days, morning fog rolled across the water, obscuring ships, coastline, and the bay that was the convoy's destination. Anchor chains came down, as it was dangerous to proceed so close to rocky shores in the murk. Yankee yachting captains, however, were known for their boldness. At day's end, the fog often lifted sufficiently for a yacht's skipper to catch a glimpse of light to guide him in. French pilots were often hesitant, but the youngsters standing on the yachts' bridges signaled the convoy to follow. With "dash and resolution," the yacht's captain would "boldly, adroitly" lead the vessels in his charge safely into the crowded roadstead of an old fishing port and then prepare to take another convoy back north.[15]

No armed yacht worked harder or longer along the French coast than *Corsair*, J. P. Morgan's former trim, rakish three-hundred-foot steam ship. Arriving in the war zone late in June 1917, the vessel, armed with four three-inch guns and depth charges, immediately began convoy escort work. Its nineteen-knot speed was ideal for the many missions it undertook in the next seventeen months. It performed its first rescue in mid-October, taking off survivors from the torpedoed *Antilles*, then searching fruitlessly for the aggressor U-boat. Ten months later, the cargo vessel USS *Californian* struck a mine and began to sink as *Corsair* stood by to pick up the crew. Finally, in September 1918, *Corsair* raced to the spot several hundred miles off the French coast where the sixteen-year-old Norwegian freighter *Dagfin* had broken down and was drifting uncontrollably in heavy seas. This time, the yacht towed the big ship all the way into port.[16]

Corsair never sank or even severely damaged a U-boat, but its sister *Christabel* did. On a late May afternoon in 1918, *Christabel* was nursing along the British merchantman *Danae*, which had fallen behind its La Pallice–to–Brest convoy. Weather clear and seas smooth, no U-boat should have approached an enemy warship. But UC-56 was foolish enough to do so, and a lookout aboard the yacht spotted the submarine's wake some six hundred yards on the port quarter. As *Christabel* spun and raced toward the spot, the wake suddenly disappeared, but "a few blotches of oil" on the surface indicated where the sub either was or just had been. *Christabel's* crew dropped a single depth charge, and then it and *Danae* went on their way "for nearly four hours, when suddenly a periscope appeared about two hundred yards away, on the starboard side." The Americans concluded that the enemy had been stalking them all along, awaiting a favorable moment to let fly a torpedo or two. Again, *Christabel* raced toward the U-boat, which was clearly "making frantic efforts to submerge." Reaching the spot where "disturbed" water indicated the submarine's probable position, *Christabel's* men dropped another charge set for seventy feet, while the radioman sent out calls for assistance. The detonation of the depth charge produced the usual mushroom of water, but immediately thereafter a secondary explosion came up through the water column, a "horrible and muffled sound coming from the deep, more powerful and terrible than any" that an exploding depth charge could produce. Several men were knocked sprawling on the yacht's deck, and the ship's officers concluded that *Christabel* itself had either been torpedoed or at least damaged by its own charge. "Great masses of heavy black oil" bubbled to the surface, together with "completely splintered wood" and other wreckage. The yacht and its charge soon rejoined the convoy, convinced that they had gotten a sub. They all but did, for several days later a "battered" UC-56 "crept painfully into the harbor at Santander, Spain, "injured beyond repair" and, in any case, interned by the Spaniards for the duration of the war. As Sims later noted, "For all practical purposes," *Christabel* could claim a U-boat kill.[17]

Down in the Mediterranean, *Lydonia* performed an eerily similar act. The armed yacht had been built in 1912 in the Pusey and Jones yard in Wilmington, Delaware, for William A. Lydon, who loaned it to the navy in August 1917. Formally commissioned two months later and promptly sent on "distant service," *Lydonia* was a far more modest vessel than Morgan's masterpiece of marine architecture. Displacing a mere 497 tons, the 181-foot, 12-knot vessel carried the usual four three-inch guns and depth charges. The yacht reported to Niblack's command at Gibraltar sometime very early in January 1918 to commence escort duties between "the Rock" and North African ports, chiefly Oran and Bizerte.

In February, *Lydonia* made two attacks on U-boats without success. Luck was to change less than three months later. Late on the afternoon of May 8 in rough seas, the yacht was helping to escort a Bizerte-to-Gibraltar convoy, together with the British destroyer *Basilisk*, when UB-70 fatally torpedoed a British merchantman. The two escorts promptly raced to the scene of the submerged attack and for fifteen minutes mounted a "thoroughly coordinated" depth-charge attack where the sub was thought to be. The heavy seas and need to rescue survivors from the sinking merchantman precluded a thorough investigation, but German records later showed UB-70 departed home for a deployment in the Adriatic Sea never to be heard of again. Its estimated position at the time it disappeared strongly suggested that it was sunk by the two escorts following the torpedoing of the merchantman, and so it has been recorded. Just a week later, and again as evening approached, gunboat *Wheeling* and the yachts *Surveyor* and *Venitia* were escorting another convoy from Bizerte when a British freighter was struck. "At that time, the submarine gave no further evidence of its existence." Nonetheless, the convoy commander ordered *Venitia* to remain on the scene and attempt to locate the U-boat if for no other reason than to keep it down while the convoy went on its way. Soon, however, the yacht struck pay dirt in the form of the submarine's wake. Dropping the usual pattern of depth charges, the crew had no idea if and how badly they had hit the U-boat.

They soon found out that Sims believed they had all but destroyed it. "Three days afterward, a badly injured U-boat put in at Cartagena, Spain, and was interned for the rest of the war. Thus," Sims later wrote with scarcely contained glee, "another submarine as good as sunk." Unfortunately, the postwar record indicated that the only German U-boat to be interned at Cartagena during the war was U-39, attacked on May 18 by French escort ships, bombed by French aircraft and forced into the Spanish port that same day.[18]

For those destroyer crews assigned to continuing patrol duties in the Western Approaches and adjacent British waters, frustration and occasional heartbreak remained the norm. To the very last weeks and days of the war, cargo ships and freighters steaming alone or in some instances even in convoy went down with their crews and what passengers there might be, leaving a handful of survivors stunned and freezing, bobbing on a vast empty sea until rescue came—or did not.

January 1918, a typical Atlantic patrol. For "three interminable and tedious days and nights," torrents of rain had fallen "straight as plummets from a sky flat as a vast ceiling." Rainwater greasy with oil sluiced along the narrow decks and spilled over the sides of laboring, rolling destroyers. Just as the rain had begun, a "weak and fragmentary" radio signal had staggered over the airways from a ship calling for immediate help and then "had ceased abruptly like a lamp blown out by a gust of wind." There was no time to get a precise fix on the sender. Several destroyers steamed off in the general direction, and during the afternoon watch a lookout in the crow's nest on one of the ships reported a floating object off the starboard bow. Soon other reports reached the small, cramped bridge, indicating that the ship was making its way into a vast debris field of floating containers, rotting fruit and vegetables, bits of wood, fragments of coal, and life preservers. The skipper ordered his lookouts to try to find some identification, but there was none. "Mile after mile went the destroyer down the rain lashed sea, mile after mile of wreckage opened before her." Suddenly, someone called out that there was a lifeboat ahead showing a flag. The captain raised his binoculars; yes, there was a small, gray boat with a shirt tied to a mast or an oar. Could there be any survivors? As the destroyer slowed and came alongside, crew members debated. Of course, no one was alive; the boat was awash. But someone had raised a flag, hadn't they? No! "Those poor guys are goners long ago." Peering down as the destroyer came alongside, the bridge people could see that the lifeboat was held up by its floating tanks. "A red flannel shirt hung soggily against an upright pole, and coloured the shaft with the drippings of its dye." The interior of the boat was just a deep puddle, and floating in it were the fully clothed bodies of two men, side by side. A third man wearing a kind of seaman's jacket sat at the stern on a seat just under water, "with his feet in the water and his body toppled over on the gunwale. . . . The wet cloth of his trousers clung lightly to his thin legs and revealed the taut muscles of his thighs." Sailors on the destroyer's deck threw out boat hooks and brought the tiny vessel in. "A sailor cried out that all were dead. 'Any name on the boat, Hardy?'" asked the officer standing by. "'No, sir.' 'Very well, cast off.'" The captain ordered the pathetic little craft sunk by gunfire and got his ship on its way.[19]

The American submarine crews who joined the war against the U-boats early in 1918 found Bantry Bay a "spacious" body of water set against a "wild and rugged coast where it was easy to slip seaward and where there was depth of water for maneuvers beneath the surface." Home port was the town of Berehaven on the Beara Peninsula's southern shore. The submariners quickly realized, as had the destroyer crews earlier, that they had a lot to learn from their British hosts, who had, among other things, "systematized the optimum procedures for the approach and attack of surface targets and computing the lead angle in launching torpedoes." British skippers had also developed a crude "attack trainer that imaged model ships through a periscope during simulated engagements."[20]

As with the destroyer divisions, Bayly assigned a topflight officer to lead the British training efforts. Martin Eric Naismith had been one of a half-dozen British submarine commanders to win the Victoria Cross for penetrating the treacherous waters of the Dardanelles to operate successfully against Turkish shipping in the Sea of Marmora. Naismith prescribed a course of incessant exercises at sea both in and beyond Bantry Bay, including "crash dives" and mock "periscope to periscope" attacks and defenses against U-boats. Fears that a U-boat itself might penetrate the bay and interfere with the exercises were never far from anyone's mind, and, of course, there was no real defense against friendly destroyers and patrol boats that had orders to shoot or depth-charge at will any submarine encountered. The Americans soon learned that wartime conditions did not permit the leisurely practice of keeping the periscope up for most of an attack approach. They would instead have to acquire "sporadic target data during brief, hard-to-detect 'looks.'" This change of pattern required a shift in responsibilities. Executive officers took charge of maintaining a boat's depth and speed to allow the captain to concentrate solely on managing the entire attack.[21]

The ubiquitous Ralph Paine rode along on one of the exercises. The unidentified American sub was to find, stalk, and kill an "enemy" U-boat impersonated by a British submarine. Well aware that Naismith was aboard the British vessel as an observer, the unidentified American sub captain ordered a hasty but well-executed crash dive. "With almost no sound or sense of motion and at a gentle slant the submarine sank to twenty-six feet and hung there poised to get her bearings for a torpedo attack." "Sensitive as a toy balloon," the undersea craft had to be kept balanced by the "skillful juggling" of valves, pumps, and horizontal rudders manned by several enlisted men sitting on stools in front of large depth-gauge dials. "The whirring sound of these controls was all that disturbed the tense silence" once the captain had successfully "trimmed" his boat. Soon the submarine's hydrophones picked up the other vessel, and with torpedo tubes already manned, the sub fired a quick shot and then surfaced to await confirmation that it had indeed killed the target. "Soon the British boat emerged a half-mile away and signaled that she had been theoretically destroyed."

Paine discovered the grimness that underlay life aboard these tiny, crude undersea boats. The ever-present dangers of operating in a war zone, which included possible destruction by a friendly destroyer or trawler as much or more as by an enemy U-boat, were trumped by the "chill, unremitting discomfort" of life within the hull. Even the short tours of sea duty stretched the stamina and stability of each crewman to the limit. No one was ever "comfortably warmed until they reached port again" and the mother ship's cozy bunks and hot food. At sea, the men constantly shivered "in a space so cramped that physical exercise to stir the blood" was "impossible." Dedicated sleeping or living spaces were nonexistent. Bunks and a crude table for meals had been rigged for the three or four officers aboard—captain, exec, engineer, and navigator—in the only open space available. "The men slept on the [deck], in nooks and corners among the intricate and numerous machines which filled the boat, or suspended hammocks in impossible places and slept like bats dangling from the roof of a shed." Cooking, "after a fashion," was done on an electric stove, and the inevitable navy coffeepot was kept going as a morale booster. No one complained; this was the all-volunteer submarine service, and if a man could not hack it, he was soon gone. All of these boats had struggled across the Atlantic against smashing waves, howling winds, rain, and snow. Nothing affected them now save frustration, which remained a constant companion.[22]

While British, French, and Italian submariners could confirm destruction of eighteen German U-boats throughout the war, the Americans in little more than half a year of operations "failed to make a kill." In fact, that claim might well be in error, but it remains the verdict of history. As submarine historian

Edward C. Whitman observes, the melancholy record "was not from lack of try-ing." Lewis Bayly, who remained in overall command of operations off the coast of Ireland, designated the seven US "AL" boats as Berehaven Division 5 and assigned them regular patrol "billets" in the same gridded operations areas to the south and east that were being patrolled by British and American destroyers. On March 6, 1918, the first two subs went out. The basic patrol tactic was to cruise at periscope depth during as much of the day as possible, searching the assigned area for German submarines transiting on the surface, and then to come up at night to recharge batteries. On the average, three of the seven US submarines deployed on eight-day patrols, while the others filled their in-port time with refitting, gaining the latest intelligence information, and working on various tactics, including proper trimming of the boat. By this time, Allied and Ameri-can naval intelligence had meshed almost to perfection, and the submariners at Berehaven, along with their colleagues in the antisubmarine war elsewhere, "had a vast amount" of information at their disposal. "They knew almost every time a boat left a German base, and often who was the commanding officer."[23]

On at least one occasion, an American naval observer took command of a British submarine in the North Sea for several days when the captain, executive officer, and more than half the crew were struck by the influenza, or "Spanish flu," that was beginning to ravage the Western world. Unfortunately, or perhaps fortunately, no enemy of any kind was sighted on this patrol, nor were the Americans much luckier in their own boats. The record shows that between March and November 1918, US submarines reported thirteen sightings of ene-my U-boats. Eleven torpedoes were fired, resulting in four unsuccessful attacks. As Dwight Messimer has observed, this was not at all a bad record insofar as the Allied submarine war against the U-boats was concerned. The eighteen enemy losses during the entire war came at enormous effort. "During 1917 and 1918, British submariners in all theaters had a contact to sinking ratio of thirty to one." Had their American colleagues been presented with the same opportuni-ties, they might well have claimed a kill or two.

Messimer pinpoints the problem at the heart of the anti-U-boat campaign waged by Allied and American submariners: surfaced U-boats not only pre-sented often narrow targets but were also immeasurably faster and more nimble than the submerged boats that stalked them. It was almost mandatory that for a submerged boat to sink a surfaced enemy submarine, the target had to be nearly broadside to the attacker and completely unaware of its presence. The attacking captain had to maintain his boat in perfect trim, with torpedoes set perfectly, which then had to run absolutely true.[24]

Lack of success was undoubtedly due in some measure to the patrol areas assigned. The AL boats usually operated in the open seas to the south and west of Ireland. By early 1918, however, the implementation of the convoy system had driven most German U-boat captains to seek their prey in the shallow coastal waters around the British Isles and western France. But even when Bayly expanded operations areas to include St. George's Channel and the Western Approaches to the channel, the Americans found their luck unchanged. Their best chance came early on. On May 22, AL-1 under command of Lieutenant (jg) G. A. Rood was running close to the Isles of Scilly when, near noon, he spotted a surfaced U-boat "in light condition." Rood immediately took his submarine down and began stalking the enemy by means of his underwater "listening tubes." It is unclear whether Rood lost the German and found another or whether, two and three-quarter hours later, he surfaced to find the original target. What he did see at five thousand yards' distance was a U-boat, "dead ahead." AL-1 possessed the finest periscope in the American flotilla, so Rood submerged again, coming up at intervals, showing the most feathery of periscope wakes until he got within six hundred yards of the unsuspecting enemy. He flooded all torpedo tubes. "The Hun was exposing a full broadside and evidently scented no danger." A quietly exultant Rood fired two torpedoes, one aimed at the U-boat's bow, the other at its conning tower. As the second torpedo sped away, Rood brought down the periscope with the words "Save a dinner for Captain Smaltz." Regrettably, there was to be no dinner for the enemy commander. The young skipper failed to maintain the sudden change of trim on his boat. When the torpedoes were fired, AL-1's bow rose, ruining his aim.

As the torpedoes raced toward the U-boat, its on-deck crew spotted their peril and, disdaining quick submergence, raced for their deck gun. "Dense black smoke shot out" of the vessel's port exhaust, while its captain backed down hard on the starboard motor, swinging his ship's stern toward the source of the two torpedoes, which winged past seconds later, "probably" passing within just a few yards of the U-boat's bow. Fleeing hastily, the U-boat unleashed a barrage from its gun toward the source of the attack. AL-1 fired several torpedoes at the rapidly disappearing enemy, but it was too little, too late.[25] Rood had committed a rookie mistake, perhaps understandable under the circumstances, but still regrettable. What was even more surprising was that the enemy let himself be nearly taken so soon after another attack in roughly the same area.

The AL-11 skippered by Lieutenant (jg) A. C. Bennett was running barely surfaced when in midafternoon on May 11 a U-boat was sighted off to port, distance six thousand yards. Bennett changed course to intercept, moving ahead at best speed on both motors. According to the boat's war diary, Bennett "ran at 20 feet, dipping under between observations." Flooding "all tubes for attack," the young skipper again estimated the enemy's course (60°) and speed (ten knots). Closing to between nine hundred and a thousand yards, Bennett let loose with two torpedoes "at intervals of five seconds, periscope angle 15°. One torpedo was seen to broach. The other torpedo began a straight hot run but warhead exploded at distance of 500 yards from this boat and 200 yards short of enemy's track." With the premature explosion, the enemy promptly pulled the plug and went under. Bennett believed he had made a perfect approach, and the boat's log strongly suggests that rotten luck rather than error kept him from a kill.[26]

Despite all efforts to avoid friendly fire, it was a constant threat both off the American coast and in European waters. Just prior to departure for his patrol "billet," each submarine captain was given a memorandum detailing outgoing and incoming convoys, their course and speed, their call signs and orders, "and a list of day and night recognition signals." The chief objective, of course, was avoidance, especially at night, when both submarines and convoys would be running without lights. But should they blunder into one another, it was hoped that contact could be swiftly and safely made.

For much the most part, the system worked well, but it was not flawless, as Lieutenant J. C. Van de Carr of AL-10 discovered on probably his second patrol in late March. At five o'clock in the evening, running a northerly course, he spied in the distance what he thought was a U-boat. Visibility was poor, and as Van de Carr approached the vessel he realized it was a British destroyer. "Confident that he had not been seen, he gave the order for a quick dive and went down to 100 feet." Unfortunately, in his haste, he allowed the boat to take on a bit too much water. To overcome negative buoyancy, he gave the order to "blow out a few hundred pounds" from the tanks and run the bilge pump "for a few seconds." Moments later, the submarine was rocked by a "rumble," "crash," and "shock" that "suggested an earthquake at sea." The boat went dark for a time, as the "stunned" crew worked to get the emergency lighting system on line. Convinced that he had a U-boat beneath him, the British destroyer captain kept up the attack, and Van de Carr and his people concluded that it might persist for many hours. Van de Carr made the rather desperate decision for a rapid ascent to the surface by blowing the main ballast tanks and setting the rudder accordingly. Despite the rapid ascent, "some seconds" had to elapse before the sub could surface sufficiently and signal so as to avoid being rammed or cut to pieces by gunfire. To cut down the emergency time, Van de Carr ordered an officer and signalman into the conning tower with him "so that the instant" the boat emerged, "they could throw back the hatch and jumping out on the bridge give the day signal" (a smoke bomb on a colored parachute) and blinker across another agreed signal. In this instance, the Americans had luck on their side. The destroyer was a thousand yards away and, not surprisingly in the gathering gloom, had not even seen A-11. Once matters were settled, the destroyer captain, Jack Simpson, promptly pledged to give an astonished Van de Carr a "sumptuous" meal once ashore. It turned out that Simpson and his destroyer were American, not British, and that the two men had been roommates at Annapolis years before. They had not seen each other since.[27]

"The AL-4 and the AL-2 were the two lucky American submarines; for each had a record of making five contacts with the enemy, and combined they got on the track of the Huns only one less time than all the rest of our submarine navy put together."[28] Fortune certainly concentrated on the two boats, but it was as often ill as good. On patrol in late May, AL-2 first tracked a vessel that from a distance appeared to be a U-boat running awash, but after a prolonged stalk turned out to be a British trawler. That night, "running on the surface in the path of the moon," the sub blundered first into two trawlers, then three more. Frantic signaling resulted only in several efforts by the spirited trawlers to sink the intruder by ramming or gunfire. "The Yankee submarine was saved only because the last mentioned trawler was so near that she could not depress her gun sufficiently to hit the target and sent the shell screaming over the submarine's bow." Two months later, AL-2 "was fired on twice by American destroyers, the only damage being the wear and tear on the officers' nerves and the loss of the cook's front teeth," when in the fear and excitement of being shot at by four-inch guns, he removed the pins from smoke grenades with his teeth rather than pliers.[29]

Friends and enemies weren't the only threats that American submariners faced in this, their first, war. Inexperience, too, proved nearly fatal to them and their boats. The most dramatic incident occurred on May 18, when AL-4 was roughly thirty miles off Small's Lighthouse on England's west coast. The boat had been running a routine morning patrol thirty to thirty-five feet below the surface for several hours. The captain was getting some sleep after having been on watch through most of the night; the executive officer had been down for two days with the flu. Lieutenant Garnet Hulings, who had been on watch and thus was chiefly responsible for having just missed ramming a U-boat the month before as it frantically dove, had temporary command again.

"The sea being smooth, the depth was easily controlled," but Huling noted that when they periodically stopped to listen through their hydrophones for a possible enemy sub, AL-4 would settle a bit, "indicating a slight imbalance and negative buoyancy." The boat obviously needed an adjustment to trim. Huling ordered 300 pounds released from the tank and placed himself behind the sailor controlling the adjusting pump valve to make sure correct procedure was followed. It wasn't. The young man moved the wrong valve, though for quite some time, Huling saw no change in the adjusting tank gauge. As the boat began to settle alarmingly, Huling issued a series of orders designed to speed it up and regain control. As depth gauges "whizzed past" the hundred-foot mark, Huling ordered all ahead full, "hoping by the diving rudders to check the descent." In fact, the action sent the boat "down all the faster and before anything could be done to stop her she struck bottom at 294 feet. Heavy with 1,900 pounds of negative buoyancy, she had buried her nose in the soft mud," nearly one hundred feet below its estimated maximum safe operating level. Huling immediately shut down the engines and ordered all gear secured. Captain Lewis Hancock and the ill executive officer, Lieutenant K. R. R. Wallace, appeared immediately, and the three officers conferenced. Carefully, correctly, putting their best men on the diving stations, "they tried the safest measures first." Nothing worked; the excessive pressure of the seas outside defeated every effort to free the boat by its own means.

The sub began to leak, especially forward, around rivets, flanges, seams, and sea valves. "The hatches were also leaking slightly." The sailor manning the bow rudders now discovered that they could not be moved, buried as they were in the mud. The next step was to ramp up the engines to full and then reverse them. Nothing. "They tried going ahead with rudder hard right and then hard left—every eye glued on the gauges except those watching the gyro compass." A bit of movement, but not enough, and the expenditure of electrical power had become alarming. Less drastic stratagems were employed to no effect. The only reasonable chance of saving themselves now was to apply all possible pressure on the bow tank. The men's lives depended on whether it could stand the strain.

Before the order could be given, someone, it is unclear who, "hit upon a simple but effective means of changing the balance of the boat." Nearly the entire thirty-man crew (four officers, twenty-six enlisted men) were sent back to the shaft alley and crowded in there. By this time, "consternation" had appeared, but not yet outright fear or panic. With all in readiness, Hancock ordered maximum air pressure applied to the bow ballast, "pushing it higher and higher" until pressure was a full 50 pounds past the safe mark while "crowding speed on the motors." With the sub resting at an angle of two and a half degrees, Hancock and the handful of men at the gauges in the tiny control compartment amidships saw the bubble move and the bow with it. But at five degrees, the submarine still seemed "loathe to leave the bottom." As the angle reached six, however, the vessel suddenly wrenched free of the mud and started for the surface, ultimately reaching a fifty-degree angle as the men in the shaft alley aft were slammed around. When the boat reached one hundred feet, Hancock ordered the middle ballast kingstons open for blowing. The pressure in the tank was so great that it jerked the starboard valve open and broke one of the side blocks.

But structural damage was limited, and "as they reached the surface and opened the hatches, the AL-4 was a grateful and happy ship." The submarine and its crew had been tested "in every way. The middle and after main ballast tanks which had been designed to stand a pressure of 75 pounds, had been subjected to 127 pounds, without their leaking a drop into the battery tanks. And the forward trimming tank, built to resist a pressure of 90 pounds, had not suffered from" the 140 pounds ultimately applied. "Best of all," neither officers nor crewmen had exhibited the slightest signs of "panic or excitement." Hancock wrote in his war diary that "every man stood by his station in as calm and efficient way as if an ordinary drill were being conducted." Hancock's executive officer, Lieutenant Wallace, was so energized by the crisis that he pronounced himself cured and, indeed, suffered no relapse or need for further bedtime.[30]

One final striking incident in this strange undersea war occurred on July 10, when AL-2 was returning to Bantry Bay from yet another fruitless patrol, made even more frustrating by the attack of the two American destroyers in which the submarine's cook lost his teeth tearing pins off the smoke grenades used as signals. Nerves had just begun to calm by dinnertime. Seas were running heavy and visibility was poor when Radio Electrician Third Class P. Rayals on lookout spotted what might have been a submarine three miles away to the northeast near Fastnet Rock. With dark skies ahead and a bright horizon behind them, the men on AL-2's bridge felt distinctly uneasy, but Lieutenant Philip Ransom dutifully turned his sub toward the suspicious object. By the time he was relieved by Lieutenant Scott Umstead, the object seemed nearby. Umstead immediately called Captain Paul F. Foster to the bridge, but before Foster could reach the control room from the chart table where he had been working, the sub was shaken by a huge explosion. Racing up the ladder to the bridge, he was told by Umstead first that the ship might have been torpedoed and then that a torpedo had exploded not twenty feet away. Umstead had ordered hard left rudder, and, taking over, Foster completed the maneuver and then prepared to dive to ram the unseen enemy. It was a bold move, for if AL-2 had been hit, it could certainly dive, but doubtless never resurface. Nonetheless, Foster took the boat down to sixty feet to ram and just missed the presumed enemy, passing "so close that they could hear distinctly through their own hull" the U-boat's (if such it was) propellers running at full speed. Foster took up the underwater chase using his C-tube sound gear and oscillator underwater signaling set to remain in touch. Then a second submarine appeared dead ahead and, using its own oscillator, began communicating with the U-boat that Foster and his men had been stalking. Strangely, there was no response, and soon the second U-boat moved off to the south. With battery power declining, Foster chased for a time and then gave up, returning to the position where he and the first U-boat had clashed. For two hours, AL-2 "circled about, stopping frequently at 75 feet to listen more effectively." Nothing. "Then they imitated the call given by the enemy at a very high pitch—dash,dash,dash,dot—but their oscillator brought no response," and after surfacing and sending a contact message to Berehaven, Foster resumed the voyage to Bantry Bay. What had happened to the U-boat, and which one was it? Foster believed he had damaged the vessel, but several months later he was summoned to London to give a full account to Sims's highly interested intelligence people. After the war, it was revealed that UB-65 was lost on that day at that location. Possibly one of its own torpedoes launched against AL-2 turned back and destroyed it. Equally likely, the U-boat was done in when one of the often faulty magnetic pistols used as a primer for detonating torpedoes was set off prematurely by AL-2 passing overhead, exploding one of the U-boat's torpedoes "almost in the tube." Whatever the explanation, AL-2 could properly claim a kill through commendable courage and zeal, despite hesitance then and now to accept a more than plausible verdict.[31]

Strenuous efforts by every level of command notwithstanding, submarine duty in the Great War was unprecedentedly stressful. Not even the destroyer crews could claim to cope with the strains that confronted their brethren below. "As the men engaged for a longer period in this service, there developed troubles that were more lasting, such as rheumatism, nervous affections and indigestion," due largely to lack of exercise while confined in the cold and cramped hulls, "where the humidity was so great that moisture would annoy a man by dropping into his soup as he sat down to supper, or on his face as he turned in off watch." The tender *Bushnell* offered relief for those in port: clean bunks, good food, hot showers. But then it was off to eight days of war again, with all its demands and boredom amid fearsome confinement. Both in port and at sea, crews ate too much, and commanding officers deliberately curtailed intake, keeping their men always "slightly hungry."[32]

The relative comfort of tender life while in port proved insufficient to overcome the wear and fatigue of patrols at sea. For all the ersatz comforts that *Bushnell* offered, submarine crews simply exchanged one ship for another. Bayly, his people, and the submarine skippers determined that the solution was to get officers and men out of town for a time by means of liberal leave policies. The army had already realized that maximizing the contribution of the individual soldier required keeping them at the front for limited periods and "at frequent intervals" moving them back to those largely undamaged villages, towns, and cities—including Paris and London—"outside the atmosphere of war." At Bantry Bay, "one or two officers and half the crew" of each submarine were granted "a leave of absence" from the moment the men reached the tender's deck through the day prior to departure on the next patrol, thus providing everyone a full week of liberty every two months. There was sufficient time for officers and men to make trips to London or even Edinburgh. Such holidays "relieved the monotony of the patrols" as men swapped stories and memories.[33]

An early student of American submarine operations in World War I concluded that the conflict "proved the making of our Submarine Service." Public and service-wide distrust of "the silent service" evaporated as its officers and men proved their pluck and professionalism. Prior to 1918, "chief attention had been given to the improvement of the material"; after 1918, "it was directed to the training of the personnel." Despite "structural defects," America's submarines went to sea in wartime and often wintry waters "and kept at sea with great regularity. They responded to the demands made of them. Personnel had triumphed over material." Nowhere was this more pronounced than in the command structure. Officers and especially captains were now expected to know every aspect of their still primitive and tricky little craft and to employ that knowledge in fulfilling mission responsibilities. The AL boats at Bantry Bay carried out their missions with fidelity, courage, and intelligence. Above all, their very presence, along with British and French submarines, constituted yet another element confronting increasingly hard-pressed German U-boat captains and crews. AL-4, for example, "twice encountered U-boats" while on patrol and in both instances "chased them from the paths of friendly convoys."[34] The K boats and E-1 remaining at Ponta Delgada with questionable engine plants nonetheless deterred the German Admiralty from possibly contemplating use of the midocean Azores chain as a staging base for U-boat activities far out into the Atlantic. Nor could U-boat captains refuel at sea so long as the prospect existed of taking a torpedo at any moment from a hidden American sub that had struggled out of port.[35]

Finally, wartime submarine operations taught the Americans the invaluable lesson that if the nation was to complete and maintain a true two-ocean navy with global reach, its submarine arm required boats that could keep the seas with sufficient fuel for long-range independent operations while providing sufficient amenities for the crews to maintain efficiency. Before war's close, the first of the "S" boats—bigger, longer, beamier, and speedier—were on the builders' ways. Nearly a quarter century later in another, infinitely greater, naval war, they would serve for a brief time as frontline vessels, holding the line as best they could against another enemy in distant Far Eastern waters until relieved by far more modern boats.

Chasers

W<small>HEN</small> W<small>ILLIAM</small> S<small>IMS</small> reached England in April 1917, he found a public not only determined to put the U-boat menace out of mind, but also convinced that it could be readily solved. "There was not a London club in which the Admiralty was not denounced for its stupidity in not adopting" the "perfectly obvious plan" of annihilating the U-boats "in their nests," Sims recalled. To consume precious naval resources hunting enemy submarines in the vast Atlantic wastes while they sank ever more shipping was rank folly. "A swift and terrible blow" would resolve the Submarine Menace at a stroke. Just what that blow might be, however, remained undetermined a year later. The convoy system had sensibly lessened the U-boat's impact without eradicating it. In the final months of a war that no one at the time expected to end either soon or favorably, the Allies looked beneath the seas and to the skies for answers.[1]

It was inevitable that British and American naval authorities would consider the employment of mines. Eighteenth-century American David Bushnell is widely credited with devising the weapon. While studying physics at Yale, he discovered that gunpowder could be exploded underwater. During the American Revolution, he devised the first effective "sea mine," filling kegs with powder and then assembling a crude flintlock mechanism "adjusted so that a light shock would release the hammer and fire the powder."[2] This same principle, employing water pressure instead of direct contact to ignite an explosive, was, of course, the basis of the depth charge that was first heavily employed in 1915–18.

While the mine became an increasingly important part of naval warfare, particularly in restricted waters, its evolution was slow and unimaginative. As late as 1914, the only mines in existence were those that depended on a direct hit between weapon and vessel to be effective—hence the descriptive phrase *contact mine*. Nonetheless, in the months and years following the outbreak of war, the Royal Navy laid minefields off Helgoland and throughout the southern Channel to hinder, if not prevent, the exodus of both the High Seas Fleet and U-boats heading for their patrol stations in the Western Approaches and Irish Sea. The Admiralty went further, creating a barrier—or "barrage"—of trawlers, nets, and mines across the Straits of Dover, the main waterway of men and supplies to France as well as the shortest U-boat route to the open Atlantic. Regrettably, "nature favored the Germans." By 1918, the Royal Navy had planted thirty thousand mines in the Helgoland Bight alone, yet the U-boats moved in and out of their nearby bases, albeit with some trouble. Their passage was facilitated by the Germans' own minesweeping capabilities, together with the fact that the British minelayers could not long remain under threat from enemy light cruisers and destroyers.

Protective antisubmarine nets across the relatively still and narrow waters of a harbor entrance were one thing. The twenty-odd miles of perpetually rough, windy Channel waters were something else. Moreover, Channel tides came and went every six hours or so, creating "swift currents" that made it impossible to effectively anchor nets or, in the case of mines, attach them by heavy cables to a rocky, unstable bottom for any length of time. John Langdon Leighton, on Sims's London staff, later wrote that prior to the summer of 1918, U-boat skippers used the Dover Straits passageway with relative impunity and would return home to inform their colleagues just what to do. Later students enjoying the luxury of consulting German sources emphasized that passing through a World War I British minefield was no picnic. Most U-boats moved at depths of sixty feet or more, well below the anchored mines. But as the submarines passed by, they occasionally encountered the cables anchoring mines to the bottom. The steel ropes "scraped down the sides of the hull, setting up a terrific racket inside the boat. It was a nerve-wracking experience and no one got used to it. The danger was that the cable would snag on some obstruction on the U-boat," craning the mine down to strike the hull and explode. They needn't have worried. "In almost every case, the cable parted" under the power of the moving submarine. To increase the odds, U-boats began mounting serrated cable cutters on heavy metal extensions on their outer hulls and took advantage of the rapid tides to move quicker than a craning effect could take place.[3]

However compromised the notion of a "barrage" became by the failure of the mining component, the idea of an antisubmarine barrier remained (along with the name *barrage*), and here America's submarine chasers came into their own, both in the lower English Channel beyond the Dover Barrage and in the Mediterranean, where the Allies had earlier established a barrier across the Straits of Otranto in an attempt to confine German and Austrian U-boats to the Adriatic.

By early spring 1918, the navy had established major subchaser bases at New London and Charleston, South Carolina. From there, an ever-growing number of chasers were sent across the Atlantic via the Bermuda-Azores-Gibraltar or -Plymouth route to European waters. The Planning Division in London acknowledged the chasers as "sound hunting vessels" that "offered the most promising means for tactical offensive operations against enemy submarines." If the chasers "could develop to their full potential," a "solution to the submarine menace would be approached."[4]

A "lively" competition quickly broke out among the Allied navies as to where to base and how to use the boats. Naval commanders in England, Ireland, Gibraltar, Portugal, and Italy all clamored for the little craft whose listening devices together with adequate armament seemed to give them a powerful advantage. In one of their rare acknowledgments of friction with the British hosts, Sims's Planning Staff admitted they "combatted constantly" to avoid having to "split up the United States chasers into small detachments for use under British command" for patrol work "within small coastal districts." To Sims's people, the chasers' "evolution and success" depended on their amalgamation into "large units to operate offensively only, and under American command." Sims's order that a strong subchaser contingent be sent to the Mediterranean to assist in enforcing the barrage across the Strait of Otranto had apparently already taken effect. The question as to where the remainder of the chasers should be based was then referred to the Allied Naval War Council, formally established the previous November 29 and on which Sims represented the United States. Following a "general survey," the council determined that the chasers should be concentrated at Plymouth and Queenstown to patrol the relatively enclosed waters of the North Channel, Irish Sea, St. George's Channel, and English Channel.[5]

It soon became clear, however, that the tiny ships had their limits. Crews were untrained, especially in the use of depth charges that were poorly positioned on the decks, inviting devastating explosions in case of the most minor accidents. Service aboard the small, cramped vessels proved to be "very arduous," requiring frequent rest and exercise ashore to keep the men at peak performance. Repairs to machinery and hulls were often required. Finally, while Allied admiralties were beginning to appreciate the value of these hardy wooden-hulled vessels as active hunters, they also realized that the chasers were too small to be effective in heavy weather.[6]

By the end of June, two squadrons composed of thirty-six boats had gathered at Plymouth, designated "Base 27," under command of Captain Lyman A. Cotten. Destroyer *Parker*, whose captain, Commander Wilson Brown, would lead Task Force 11 in the earliest days of carrier warfare in World War II, was designated the squadron support ship. The assigned patrol area for the squadron included that portion of the English Channel from Start Point to Lizard Head off the towns of Plymouth, Davenport, and Falmouth. Here, U-boat activity was intense and targets plentiful, as cargo convoys, having been escorted through the Western Approaches, broke up, leaving individual freighters to sail on to their final destinations with greatly diminished or often no escorts. Sinkings occurred "on a considerable scale . . . causing great anxiety." Along with several British hunting units, Cotten's squadron "kept steadily at work for six weeks" until the middle of August, when a far more effective "movable barrage," instigated by Admiral Sir Roger Keyes in the Dover Straits to the north, caused the U-boats—and soon the Yankee warships that chased them—to shift operational grounds around to Land's End and up the Cornish coast, where colliers taking coal from Wales to France remained largely unprotected. Thirty subchasers were reassigned from Base 27 at Plymouth to Queenstown. Sims later insisted as a "historical fact" that "not a single merchant ship was sunk between Lizard Head and Start Point so long as" American subchasers "were assisting in the operations.[7]

In order to maximize their hydrophonic detection capabilities, the chasers hunted in packs or "units" of three, line abreast, with the unit leader in the center and a wing boat on either side. Eight hundred yards constituted the maximum standard distance between each boat. The chief obstacle to effective hunting in these early days of underwater warfare was, of course, the chaser's own engine noises, which distorted when they did not obliterate any other sounds emanating from below. Thus, the chasers were forced into two kinds of hunt, depending upon visibility and weather. "With low visibility and bad weather," Cotten instructed his crews, "use drifting hunt," that is, engines off, hulls moving at the whim of wind and tide, while hydrophones remained lowered, seeking out prey. "With high visibility and good weather use running hunt," that is, sailing under way with engines at full or medium throttle for a certain distance before stopping to lower hydrophones. These runs, Cotten ordered, "shall generally be not more than twice the listening range, unless proceeding to [a] designated" patrol "area."

The hydrophones consisted of either a "C tube" or a "K frame." The former was "a pipe structure in the shape of an inverted T, in effect an underwater stethoscope" that was pulled up against the hull when under way. When a C-tube-equipped chaser stopped for listening, the device was lowered a certain distance into the water column and then slowly rotated 360 degrees by a hand-wheel. The operator wore stethoscopic earpieces connected to the tube by other rubber tubes. When he detected subsurface noises, he continued to rotate the tube until the volume of sound was equal in both ears, allowing him to determine the sound relative to the ship's bow. The operator then called up the bearing by voice tube to the bridge, where the officer of the watch converted the sound from a relative to a magnetic bearing, and then alerted the other two units by phone—what later would be called "TBS," or "talk between ships." K frames, which theoretically could detect subsurface noises at a range of twenty miles, were triangular structures dropped overboard to windward and tethered in place "by means of cables . . . connected to a float." Two "active microphones" were then lowered from the frames into the water to detect sounds. Tracking devices aboard the chaser could ascertain direction, course, and speed, if in fact the noise detected was that of a U-boat. Reels of phosphor bronze trailing wires could also be dropped from the tubes to detect submarines hiding on the bottom.[8]

These crude means of detection proved extremely difficult to use. For the first time, man was probing the dense, often teeming water columns of the world ocean by sound. "Listening for a submarine," one contemporary admitted, was "a new development in Naval tactics," requiring a trained and discriminating ear on the part of the listener. Distinguishing the sounds of a submarine "beat" from surface noises was hard enough; accurately detecting a U-boat's sound signature from other underwater noises or even obstructions often proved impossible. In mid-September 1918, SC-254, operating out of Berehaven, detected what seemed to be engine sounds on its hydrophones and dropped a number of depth charges in Bantry Bay, only to discover that the supposed enemy was in fact an underwater rock formation. George Dole, commanding SC-93, wrote home from the Mediterranean that in the deep waters near the Straits of Otranto, it was "very difficult to tell when you have damaged a sub, in fact impossible to get any direct evidence," because there was so little even after a direct attack.[9] Many Austrian and German U-boats were able to slip through the barrier despite the dedication and vigilance of the subchaser crews.

Sims noted that the chasers' experiences were those of "the proverbial 'fisherman's luck.' Hours passed sometimes without even the encouragement of a 'nibble'; then suddenly one of the listeners would hear something which his experienced ear told him what might be the propeller and motors of a submarine."[10] Chaser crewman Ray Millholland remembered "an air of false laxity" pervading the tiny boats "drifting and listening for submarines . . . hour after hour and day after day with the engines stopped," except for the few hours out of twenty-four when the boats revved up to correct their positions due to the drifts of wind and tide.[11]

When a sound contact was infrequently made, Cotten's instructions stipulated that the chaser making the discovery immediately hoist a contact flag and make a report to the hunt commander "as soon as practicable." The two other vessels immediately went silent until the sound detected was recognized "within reasonable limits" as a submarine, which sent everyone on all three chasers to General Quarters. Geometry then came into play. The three chasers assumed formation of an equilateral triangle, with the unit leader at its apex. The leader gave the bearing and distance of the target and headed for it; the wing chasers adjusted their positions accordingly and steered a parallel course with the leader. When the lead chaser reached the last fix of the presumed U-boat, all vessels stopped and listened and then got under way again "*as soon as possible*." Cotten's instructions added that "the standard attack is in line abreast, distance between boats 100 yards. Each boat drops one depth charge 15 seconds before reaching the meeting point for sub and one at calculated meeting point." The leader then continued on course, while the wing boats turned away two compass points. All boats dropped a single charge after passing the meeting point with the target, fired their Y-guns thirty seconds after passing the meeting point, and then dropped a final depth charge forty-five seconds after passing the meeting point, thus providing a presumably lethal pattern of eighteen depth charges on or sufficiently near the presumed U-boat to sink or badly damage the craft. Cotten admonished all hands to watch the "vicinity of detonation carefully" for any signs of a submarine. If seen, each chaser should "maneuver promptly to press home attack." Each chaser was to turn back to the attack "by shortest route." When the last charge had been dropped, all three boats should head for the target's last presumed position, "stop and listen. After that," Cotten concluded, "be guided by circumstances."[12] Unfortunately, all came to naught. Despite detailed instructions (including an even more elaborate set of guidelines for the Mediterranean chasers drafted by E. C. S. Parker), endless cruising, promising contacts, careful evaluations, and spirited attacks, no American subchaser either in British or in Mediterranean waters ever sank a U-boat.[13]

Ironically, subchasing in the English Channel was defeated by its own methods. Largely ineffective in the deep waters on the approaches to French ports, the British Isles, and the Straits of Otranto, subchasing methods were assumed to work much better in the relatively shallow waters between England and France. In fact, the very volume of surface traffic in that perpetually crowded waterway largely negated hydrosound detection. According to M. S. Brown, who commanded one of the subchasers on patrol out of Portsmouth, the many convoys that passed to and fro generated persistent sounds that masked the engine noises of whatever U-boats might be present. Moreover, U-boats also possessed hydrophones with which they could hear enemy destroyers and subchasers "miles away." They were thus "practically immune" from surprise. In the few cases where a German submarine either surfaced close to an unusually quiet set of chasers or was caught by the sudden appearance of the sun that burned off the many fogs that afflicted the Channel, the U-boat simply "pulled the plug" and headed for the bottom before an equally surprised chaser could properly react. There, the submarine would "lie comfortably," awaiting the opportunity "to sneak off under cover of the next disturbance from a destroyer or a convoy."[14]

Life on all the boats was difficult. Their construction made them wet in even moderate seas, and living belowdecks was cramped and uncomfortable. As one character in the 1938 film *Submarine Patrol* remarks upon first coming aboard a fictional chaser, "This is magnificent! Like the inside of a mousetrap!" The waters of the upper English Channel proved so consistently turbulent that the subchaser crews were soon given eight days in port to four at sea, which reduced the number of hunting groups substantially. "After four days of being continuously tossed and thrown about," Brown later wrote, "I have come in with every muscle in my body as sore as a boil. No one pretended to sleep," he continued, "until the last night out, and by that time we would be so completely worn out that we managed to catch a few winks." Such discomforts stemmed from the nature of subchasing, which was purely a daylight game. In the absence of a nighttime contact, which seldom if ever occurred, the chasers "usually drifted between dusk and dawn, and in those choppy seas and tide rips a subchaser develops a motion all its own," which no one beyond the flotillas could begin to appreciate.[15]

The Mediterranean boats experienced their own set of difficulties. They had dribbled into Gibraltar throughout the early months of 1918 before passing on to Valetta Harbor, at Malta. The war here was not going well. Allied forces in Salonika were insufficient to mount a satisfactory offensive campaign to threaten the Austro-German southern flank. The entire eastern shore of the Adriatic thus lay in enemy hands. The comparatively few German and Austrian U-boats deploying out of Pola near the head of the Adriatic and from Cattaro (present-day

Kotor) farther down on the Croatian coast had a field day preying on Allied shipping throughout the central Mediterranean, disrupting supplies not only to Salonika but also to the Italian front as well as to armies in Palestine. The Allied plight had so encouraged pro-German elements in the Greek government that there was serious risk that the Allied army in Salonika would have to be withdrawn "and the entire Balkan peninsula given up to the Central Powers."[16]

To counter this threat, the Allies had established an imperfect antisubmarine barrage of mines, nets, and trawlers across the sixty-odd miles of deep water that constituted the Straits of Otranto between Italy and Greece. By early 1918, it had become a signal disappointment; Halpern calls it "completely illusionary. . . . The term 'barrage,' or even 'line' of drifting anti-submarine trawlers is a bit misleading," conjuring up as it does a continuous line of small craft with nets out "forming a serious barrier to submarines." In reality, only two-thirds of the fifty-three designated small craft were out in a typical month—July 1916—"and only ten had their nets in the sea." It was "no reflection upon the British," Sims later concluded diplomatically, "to say that barrage was unsatisfactory and inadequate, and that for the first few months, it formed a not particularly formidable obstruction." The British could afford only a handful of elderly destroyers to reinforce the trawler-and-net barrier; the Italians held their fleet in port, anticipating a massive surge of the Austrian surface fleet down the Adriatic. In May and again in June 1918, Austria's Admiral Miklós Horthy obliged, dispatching if not a surge, then at least a formidable force including battleships and cruisers against the barrier. Italian light forces sortied and badly battered the Austrians, torpedoing and sinking one of the Austrian battlewagons.[17] Misreading reality, Allied leaders concluded that the tide may have turned. If the U-boat "pests" could be "penned up" in the Adriatic, Sims wrote, "the whole Mediterranean Sea would become an unobstructed highway for the Allies."

Sims and his London staff thought they had a solution to the entire Balkan problem. In February 1918, they submitted their ideas to the Allied Naval War Council in Rome: seize the Sabbioncello Peninsula just above the city of Dubrovnik on the central Adriatic coast together with adjacent Curzola Island; then create an Allied naval base to block enemy U-boats from coming south from Pola and supply vessels from reaching Cattaro; next, lay a supporting mine barrage across to the Italian coast; and finally, attack Cattaro itself with Italian troops supported by American predreadnought *Virginia-* or *Connecticut*-class battleships. As more troops (including American soldiers and marines) became available, the Allies might strike inland to deal a mortal blow to Austrian forces in the Balkans. Italian authorities expressed some enthusiasm, but only if the enterprise was completely under their command. Washington was skeptical. Finally, as Professor Halpern emphasizes, the German spring offensive in Flanders and France put paid to the scheme.[18]

The Italians, in particular, had been clamoring for some time for American subchasers to reinforce the Otranto Barrage and took the matter all the way to the overall Allied Naval War Council. With a plethora of these vessels flooding Gibraltar and later Valetta, Sims quickly concurred and dispatched a trusted senior aide to the southern Adriatic to scout out a suitable base. Following careful inspection, Captain Richard Leigh determined that the Bay of Govino on the island of Corfu, off the Greek coastline, "would best meet our requirements." Renamed "American Bay," Govino became "Base 25." When the initial group of thirty-six subchasers finally arrived on June 4–5, 1918, via Gibraltar and Malta, officers and men alike realized that the small bay formed by Comeni Head and Fustipidima Point not only provided an adequate protected harbor for the chasers and mother ship *Leonidas* but also proved "far enough from settled regions to keep the Americans safely distant from malaria outbreaks" that "plagued the island." The thousand-odd men of the subchaser fleet and the crew of *Leonidas* immediately set to work converting "a barren and uncivilized cove" into a "modern naval base," with "shacks for Staff officers, repair shops, barracks, and a hospital." Within a few weeks, "the job was completed and the Forces were ready for operations."[19].

By August, the chasers were well settled in their crude base, and plans could at last be fashioned for strengthening the Otranto Barrier. Following conferences aboard the tender, the chaser skippers readily agreed to form ten chaser units of three boats each. "It was decided," one later wrote, "that a line, or barrage, of chasers was to be maintained across the Adriatic from Albania to the Italian coast, a distance of forty miles." Since the line was drawn not on a latitudinal parallel but between nearest points of land, the line lay approximately on an eighty-degree bearing. "The chasers were to hold this line." The Allied senior leadership recognized the limited utility of the subchasers in and of themselves. Each unit was "really supposed to operate with a 'killing vessel.' . . . The little craft would find a submarine; a more heavily armed ship would finish it off." British admiral Somerset Gough-Calthorpe hoped to obtain additional destroyers from home waters and even a squadron or so of American vessels from Queenstown. But demands were too great, and this new twist to antisubmarine warfare never materialized.[20]

Left largely to their own devices, subchaser skippers and the senior officers responsible for the barrier fashioned their own strategy. To avoid confusion and possible friendly fire, British destroyers would remain ten miles north of the barrier, while "other British crafts, such as trawlers, motor launches and kite balloon sloops," would patrol to the south. In practice, submarine patrols or chases occasionally lured excitable chaser captains much too close to British lines. "The line was to be held by twelve chasers for four days before being relieved. As there were ten units of chasers this gave a four on, four off, four on, eight off" schedule. Confidential charts, minefield and submarine-net emplacement maps, and information regarding recognition signals were given to each captain, "who already had his safe so full of such matter that there was little space outside the icebox and bilges for this last lot of official writing."[21]

The initial U-boat hunt, the first of thirty-four in all, took place between June 12 and 16, 1918, "with nine chasers in three units at intervals of three miles between vessels of a unit and a five mile interval between units." Then, and later, subchaser skippers and crews were keen but ignorant. By late August, the patrol lines stretched from the northern end of Corfu to Cape Neto, Italy, a distance of roughly 125 miles that could not be covered effectively throughout its entire length with available chasers. Sims asked for more vessels, but was careful to restrict his request to chasers already in commission, not new construction. As earlier with the destroyer request, the demands on the available chasers were simply too great, and Washington refused to authorize any transfers prior to the spring of 1919, when it was hoped the slack could be taken up not by the chasers, but by newer and bigger Ford-built "Eagle Boats."[22]

Life aboard the chasers in the summer of 1918 was rather grim. Alfred Loomis of SC–131 recalled that "the warmth of the summer latitudes" at Corfu "struck us like the blast from an open furnace door." Ray Millholland remembered "months, months, months of the same round of bully beef and hardtack until the very thought of the next meal was gagging." The crews continued to live aboard, where artificial ventilation was nonexistent. Sailors could condone cramped quarters and insufficient headroom, knowing they were vital to the safety of the ship, "but there has yet to arise a race of men who can live without fresh air or sleep peacefully in the fumes of gasoline engines." At dockside, it was possible to open portholes and fit them with scoops to catch the zephyrs that broke the oppressive, damp heat. But even this slight advantage was negated by the practice of clustering five or even six boats in a nest so that only the outboard boat could catch any light breeze. "The quarters aft were particularly insufferable," Loomis recalled, "because of the heat which billowed forth from the galley long after the fire had been extinguished following the evening meal." Officers and men alike took their mattresses on deck and slept reasonably well in the cool of the night.

At sea, conditions were much tougher. "Water and dampness" were everywhere. The constant rolling and pitching of the small wooden hulls were "nerve-wracking"; salt spray and spent exhaust gases "belching from the engine ports" added to the misery. In all but the gentlest weather, the engine room portholes, only two feet above the water, had to be kept "dogged down," that is, tightly shut, to keep gouts of water from coming aboard. Frequent following seas forced the men to clamp tight the heavy steel porthole protectors in the upper deckhouse as well. Rough seas often overwhelmed whatever watertight integrity the chasers possessed. Heavy seas crashing aboard "sometimes" swamped galley fires. Conditions in the fo'c'sle, where a dozen men ate, slept, and passed their off-watch hours, were, in Loomis's words, "unprintable." Not only the portholes but the hatch to the upper deck had to be kept tightly closed in a seaway. Fresh air could be obtained only through the deck ventilator, which of necessity had to be turned away from wind and spray. An artificial blower helped a bit but consumed too much precious on-board generated electricity to be much used. Steaming and battle efficiency inevitably suffered. "I have observed time and again that in smooth weather when the engine room ports and skylight could be left open to permit a free circulation of air for the machinist's mates on duty, the engines ran for hours without giving annoyance; and that on rough days with everything battened down tight, trouble followed trouble with disheartening regularity." At times, the engine room became so blue with smoke from oil poured on hot bearings that the men could not see the engines they were working on. Conditions were, ironically, worst in officers' country and the radio shack, where the distribution of portholes and vents combined with the sea's state provided the unpalatable alternative "of death by suffocation or by drowning. . . . Generally, we chose the moist variety. . . . But when in a particularly heavy seaway suffocation by fumes seemed preferable," officers and crew "took the gas," the worst of which was a compound of "burnt gasoline, oil and rubber." Several attempts at rigging crude ventilator and blower systems were inevitably confounded by the internal structure of the hull.[23]

Once a contact was made and the chase began, all hands went to and remained at battle stations. If the chase was prolonged, the cook was relieved to prepare battle rations, subject to immediate recall. Between chases, the regular watch system, and hour-long meals, there was little time left for sleep. The men spent what little off-duty time there was playing cards or scrubbing clothes. "Often on moonlight nights," a chaser officer recalled, "the phonograph was brought on deck and records tried out." On hot days when temperatures on decks could climb as high as 140 degrees and it became customary to lightly wet the decks below at sunset, a few men at a time were allowed to swim over the side, "but owing to the prevalence of sharks and the necessity of being ready for immediate action, the swimmers stayed within a few feet of the ship." While the men could sleep on deck under awnings when in port, "at sea they had to go below as sleeping on deck would interfere with immediate gun action, and this could not be allowed."[24]

D. J. Williams left New York City in mid-January 1918, making the usual trip across via Norfolk, Charleston, Bermuda, and Ponta Delgada (Azores), arriving at Gibraltar four months later, where he picked up SC-227, which would eventually serve as a wing boat in Unit F at Corfu. His brief diary reflects the stress, tedium, and occasional excitement of chaser duty in the Med. Shortly after Williams reported to the chaser, a U-boat was spotted off Gibraltar, and SC-227 was immediately ordered out on what was apparently an individual seek-and-destroy mission. The chaser made visual contact with a submarine near the coast of Spain and promptly attacked. Its two depth charges brought "a lot of fuel oil" to the surface, but the chaser was not credited with a kill because the U-boat managed to reach Spanish territorial waters. The chaser left Gibraltar on May 20 for Malta, making the thousand-mile trip in five days. Three days after arrival, the chaser was ordered to the Sicilian coast "to clear this place of subs as there was a large convoy of troop-ships passing." The chaser ran at full speed all night to reach its patrol area and then cruised for twelve hours until the convoy safely passed, "hell-bent for election." SC-227 returned to Malta for just twenty-four hours before being ordered out again on a mission to rescue survivors of a torpedoed merchantman. "Ran full speed for six hours," but reaching the site about a hundred miles off Malta, all the chaser found was debris, including seventy cases of lemons, which the crew took aboard and headed home.

Following a brief dry-docking, SC-227 headed for its new home at Corfu and at 4:00 a.m. on June 16, eight days after arrival, headed for its first patrol on the Otranto Barrage. Four days later, at 8:00 p.m., the three-boat unit got a clear bearing on what appeared to be a submarine. As the crew raced to General Quarters, the chaser revved up to full speed. Two hours of fruitless hunting later, the unit spotted two destroyers that failed to answer the recognition query. "Believing them to be enemy ships, we fired our 3" inch gun and put a shell through one of the strangers' engine rooms." The victim turned out to be a patrolling British destroyer, which wisely made the correct recognition signal and refrained from returning friendly fire. Williams and his mates heaved sighs of relief, knowing that the British badly outgunned them and could have shot them out of the water. After a five-day patrol, SC-227 returned to Corfu and for the next four months averaged five days on the barrage and three in port. Summer and early autumn seas in the central Mediterranean could be rough. During the first week in August, the chaser hit "five days and nights of nice, rough weather. One wave hit us and loosened our engine room deck house. Snapped our steering cable." Submarine contacts were few but, for that reason, exciting. Occasionally, the chaser would be called upon to assist and escort torpedoed ships limping back to port.

September was particularly stressful. Leaving Corfu on the eleventh, the chaser got a bearing "near Italy. Chased it and got over it and dropped three ash cans. Whatever it was," Williams concluded erroneously, "we got it." Returning to Corfu on the fifteenth, the chaser was out again on the twentieth, but minus a man. According to Williams, a crewman named Mike had come down with influenza. If it was, in fact, the Spanish flu, it was one of the earliest recorded cases in Europe, since the epidemic had just struck the American East Coast in a major way. Whatever this particular lad's illness was, informal diary entries and more formal reports from American warships all over the European theater of operations began recording incident after incident of men being struck down by the deadly virus. The Spanish flu would be an ever-present specter on the fighting fronts and behind the lines and in ports and bases for the remainder of the war.

Under way at the usual 4:00 a.m. departure time for another routine patrol on the barrage, SC-227 was assigned to the Italian coast. "We could not center sound on account of storm that came up. We had to run all night to keep from going on rocks." The October 4–9 patrol was "rough as hell" and frustrating, since an initially promising bearing proved to be yet another British destroyer.[25]

But in these final weeks of the war, the promise of real battle suddenly materialized. It began in secrecy. At the end of September, Hilary Chambers, executive officer aboard SC-215, was relaxing during the first day in port after a barrage patrol when word came to prepare to get under way. "Rumors began to fly thick and fast. . . . Every detail that might have a bearing on our movements was carefully noted." The nearby French fleet was getting up steam, and the men learned that there would be a doctor aboard the lead chaser and a pharmacist's mate on each. "Special gangs" of machinists arrived to go over every engine. At nine in the evening of September 29, a dozen chasers slipped out of Corfu and shaped course for . . . where? "Ordinarily," the antisubmarine nets would be closed at such an hour. Now they were open. The captain was tight-lipped. Following the Albanian coast north and west, the little fleet reached Bianca Strait and then shaped course due west. At 4:00 the following afternoon, it entered Brindisi Harbor. "Why we went there, what we had come for, or how long our stay might be was still a mystery." The outer harbor was full of Italian battleships and British destroyers "that did not seem to have been anchored for a long period." The inner harbor contained "immense masses of Allied shipping," among which were "the big Italian cruisers." When the chasers tied up to the quays in their usual nest pattern, no one was allowed ashore; the senior officers remained silent, and special guards were posted on the docks. Several hours later, the chaser skippers convened aboard the 95 boat and were told that the mission was a raid on the enemy port of Durazzo, across the Adriatic, about fifty miles south of Cattaro and not far north of Otranto Strait.

Allied forces in Macedonia had begun a successful offensive in September that knocked Bulgaria out of the war and promised to unravel the Central Powers' entire southern Balkan front. French general Fachet d'Esperey realized that German and Austrian forces might have to rely solely on Durazzo (present-day Durres) for supplies to stem the rising tide against them. D'Esperey asked the Allied navies "to neutralize the port as an enemy base." The Italians were not keen on the idea, but the French threatened to do the job alone if necessary, and plans were quickly put afoot for a raid. Halpern characterizes the elaborate three-echelon attack as attempting to kill a fly with a hammer.[26]

October 1 was spent sleeping, save for the engine-room people, who, working out of sight below, were able to overhaul their machinery. The rest of the crew emerged after sundown to overhaul "the entire battery." While sailors and junior officers toiled, the captains assembled on one of the British destroyers for detailed orders. They were told that Italian light cruisers together with British and Italian armored cruisers, all closely screened by British destroyers, would bombard Durazzo Harbor on October 2, while from 5:00 a.m. on, aircraft coming across the Adriatic from Italy would bombard the town itself for however long necessary. The task of the four chaser units, twelve boats in all, was to provide more distant antisubmarine coverage to the north, south, and west and between the bombarding units and Durazzo Harbor.

Some chaser skippers interpreted the coming battle in apocalyptic terms.[27] Millholland's captain, a man named McCloud, told his two chief petty officers in strictest confidence that "we are not expected to come out. We're a suicide fleet—slam right through the enemy's mine fields and smash their subs in their own harbor . . . and get out if we can." McCloud—or Millholland—was peddling hogwash.

At 2:00 a.m. on October 2, the raiding force left Brindisi and shaped course for Durazzo. Every chaser had its crew's mattresses rigged around bridge and chart house as splinter mats; the decks were sanded to prevent officers and men, especially gun crews, from possibly slipping in shipmates' bloodshed. Unfortunately, SC-244 fouled its propellers in wire debris leaving the dock and could not join up. Eight hours later, the force appeared off the enemy port. A "couple" of small torpedo boats promptly rushed out of the harbor but turned tail and fled when they spied the heavy smoke of the big Italian cruisers on the horizon. Smoothly, all elements of the fleet took their assigned positions. The big armored cruisers began steaming back and forth along their sectors, "sending salvo after salvo, which both sank the shipping in the harbor and destroyed the buildings in the town." The forts ashore began to fire in response, while the chasers watched the fight as they zigzagged along their patrol sectors. As the cruisers and destroyers came closer inshore, the northern forts opened up, and shells began falling near the chasers. The United States Navy had entered its first—and only—authentic surface battle of World War I. "We little chaser men were greatly thrilled and were proud as could be, for we thought at the time that the Austrians considered us of enough importance to send nine-inch shells at us," ignoring the fact that the enemy's real targets were the cruisers on the firing line beyond.

In the midst of the din and excitement, an enemy hospital ship was seen leaving the harbor and a U-boat was seen diving ahead. SC-215 promptly gave chase, abruptly breaking off action as a destroyer seized and boarded the hospital ship. Suddenly, SC-129 reported a submarine off the port bow, and then a third U-boat was detected. The chasers maneuvered as they were taught, weaving in and out as they depth-charged their prey while enemy shells screamed overhead. The 215 fired two shots from its three-inch gun at the "little hummock of white water moving rapidly," which was the barely submerged U-boat. The excited gunners' first shot inflicted superficial damage on the chaser's upper works, but a two-point shift allowed for a clear view of the enemy, and the second shot resulted in "a big column of water and compressed air" shooting six feet up from the surface. Knowing that the sub could not be badly damaged, the chaser pressed down the wake left by escaping air from the U-boat's damaged periscope, "and 128, maneuvering to the starboard side of the 215," one hundred feet away, got the enemy "right between us . . . and we let go fourteen bombs," that is, depth charges. A mass of debris erupted from the depths, but the chasers did not stop, for the 129 had detected a submarine sixteen hundred yards distant. That little chaser promptly set off on an intercept course and dropped charges too close aboard that crippled its engine. The U-boat, how-ever, foolishly raised both periscopes, which gave away its precise position, and the 129 limped over to drop numerous depth charges, which everyone believed destroyed the vessel.

Other chaser units saw no U-boats, but one performed heroic service. As shots from the forts fell around the chasers and Allied salvos went whipping overhead with a locomotive's roar, SC-130, stationed between the firing line and the shore, saw a squadron of destroyers intent on fulfilling their bombard-ment responsibilities about to blunder into an enemy minefield. Seeing a mine and sensing the implications, the chaser opened up with its three-inch gun into seas frothing and foaming from the passage of ships. An early shot exploded the mine, and, "never slackening her speed, the little chaser continued on her course toward this evident mine field to head off the destroyers and lay to be-tween the ships and the nearest mines." Alerted to the danger, the destroyers spun their helms and dashed off. Fortunately for all concerned, enemy fire that morning was wretched, and no Allied ship large or small was badly hit. Down in the cramped engineering spaces of his small chaser, however, Ray Millhol-land heard the shots from ship and shore racing overhead, rattling and shaking the machinery.

"It was a gay night at Brindisi on our return," Chambers remembered. Orders quickly came to return to Corfu, and within a month the Austrians had surrendered and the antisubmarine war in the Mediterranean was over. A number of senior chaser captains were subsequently decorated by the Italian and French navies for their exemplary behavior at Durazzo. Reflecting cur-rent opinion, subchaser historian Todd A. Woofenden plays down the glorious and heroic accounts of the subchaser crews. To a man, they believed they had destroyed two U-boats. There is no evidence that they did so. Durazzo itself proved, in hindsight, to be a paltry target. Halpern notes that the town was soon abandoned by the Austrians. Yet the chaser sailors had generally responded well to battle conditions as they saw and experienced them. Durazzo was what they had enlisted for, longed for, and they were not going to slight their actions. Sensational accounts of the battle in the American press amplified their sense of prideful accomplishment. The historian can leave it at that.

Barrages, Batteries, Bombers and Battleships

By 1918, THE cost-effectiveness of large antisubmarine barrages had become an absorbing issue within Allied naval circles. Despite disappointment over the failure of both the Dover and the Otranto Barrages, Jellicoe's suggestion raised at the Anglo-American Naval Conference in September 1917 of a massive mining barrier across the upper North Sea between the Orkneys and Norwegian coast to hamper U-boat attacks on the Scandinavian convoys as well as their access to the North Atlantic was still being considered at the highest levels. According to an early postwar US Navy report on the subject, at the time of American entry in April 1917, there were roughly five thousand mines in Allied arsenals "of a type which was comparatively unsuitable for anti-submarine operations." Moreover, the supply was inadequate, as the British wished to deploy at least seven thousand per month. Once America with its enormous productive potential joined the war, the British "and other allied Governments" provided "important military information," including experiences with mine warfare. The Navy Department's Bureau of Ordnance—BuOrd in US Navy parlance—promptly decided to produce at least one hundred thousand mines "at a rate of approximately 1,000 a day . . . of a type more suitable for anti-submarine operations than any then in existence."[1]

Nine days after America's entry, Rear Admiral Ralph Earle circulated a memorandum recommending the protection of merchant ships "by means of cellular construction" and "blisters" on the hull to absorb the explosive impact of torpedoes, together with the establishment of antisubmarine barrages in both the North Sea and the Adriatic. "The proposal to construct a barrage 250 miles long" across the North Sea "was so novel and unprecedented from every practical viewpoint that it was realized . . . that it would be difficult to obtain a prompt decision without preliminary propaganda within the" Navy Department. Sims's assistance was requested, his response discouraging. The British had tried barrages repeatedly in the Helgoland Bight and along the Flanders coast "with all possible means and found [them] unfeasible."[2]

Bolstered by presidential impatience with the British navy and its frustrating antisubmarine campaign, and further encouraged by the enthusiasm of Assistant Navy Secretary Franklin D. Roosevelt, the Bureau of Ordnance submitted a further memorandum on May 9 reflecting the kind of Yankee Can-Do that readily stimulated a combination of rage and contempt among the British cousins. The northern entrance to the North Sea was "very broad" and presented "immense difficulties" to any effective barrage. But it could be done for an estimated two hundred million dollars, "or perhaps twice that sum." Such effort would be worth every penny to confine the U-boats to the North Sea. Whitehall replied four days later: "From all experience Admiralty considers project of attempting to close exit to North Sea . . . by method suggested to be quite unpractical. Project has previously been considered and abandoned. The difficulty will be appreciated when total distance, depths, material, and patrols required and distance from base of operations are considered."[3]

The problem was not the nets so much as the mines. The Admiralty was right in rejecting nets that could be either pierced by submarines employing net cutters forward of their conning towers or weakened and swept away by stormy seas (or both). The number of contact mines that would be required for an effective field would be immense, four hundred thousand by some reckoning; the cost would be prohibitive and planting unacceptably slow. Throughout the late spring and early summer of 1917, the Bureau of Ordnance energetically addressed these vexing problems until through a combination of hard work and fortuitous circumstances (including the appearance of civilian inventor Ralph C. Browne), scientists came up with a solution that at once solved both the mine and the net problems, including the planting of an effective barrier across the North Sea. Browne had brought with him plans for a contraption he called a "submerged gun." Although wholly impractical, the system did rely on a new conception: an electrically charged wire that would convey a signal from contact with a steel hull to an explosive device. The Mark VI quickly emerged as the embodiment of the idea. It was a large "spherical" TNT-laden "cylinder" from which extended one or several charged antenna wires one hundred feet or more long. Any submarine merely brushing an antenna at any point along its length would produce "an electrical current, which instantaneously transmitted to the mine, would cause the mine to explode."[4]

In two memoranda to the chief of naval operations in late July, Earle summed up the weapon's transformative nature. The Mark VI resembled "ordinary types of naval defense mines" and was therefore "easily planted." Because of its anticipated efficiency, the "time and number of vessels required" to establish an effective barrier across the North Sea "will be reduced to a minimum." The TNT explosive aboard each mine possessed a "destructive radius of about 100 feet against a submarine." The wire antennas could be "of any desired length," the ends of which would be supported by a small buoy near the surface. Nets would no longer be needed, as the extended mine antennae would serve the same function, extending the destructive range of the mine from the zero feet of the contact mine to at least a hundred feet, perhaps more, given the length of wire and the size of charge of TNT contained within the mine casing. "In depths greater than 100 feet it is proposed to submerge the mine to a depth of 100 feet, since 100 feet is about its destructive range against submarines. At this depth the mine itself is entirely protected from wave action and only the light float or buoy is exposed to such action. Where conditions permit the antenna may take the form of a net, or the antennae of adjacent mines may be connected by horizontal wires forming an impassible barrier." Mines could actually be anchored to the sea floor in depths less than one hundred feet. "If a floating mine be desired, this mine may be suspended from a buoy in such manner as to be harmless to surface craft" but deadly to submarines.

Earle initially suggested that about 72,000 mines would be sufficient to establish an effective barrier across the upper North Sea and that the United States could produce the components for roughly 1,000 a day. Later, he urged that another 28,000 units be produced as "renewals" or reserves. Should a maximum of 125,000 mines be acquired, the estimated cost would be forty million dollars. Six weeks would be required to develop the final design of the Mark VI, assemble all materials, place orders, and start production. Thereafter, production could reach five thousand a week. The British would be asked to procure whatever anchors would be needed for the mines; weapon production itself would remain in the hands of the Americans. In the North Sea, Mark VI's would be sown in four lines placed one hundred feet apart, stretching the three hundred miles from the Norwegian coast to the Orkneys, resulting in the planting of one mine every twenty-five feet.

Earle added that "every effort" had been made to ensure secrecy. Pursuing a policy that would be repeated twenty-odd years later in the Manhattan Project, he added that various components of the Mark VI would be manufactured by different companies, "and no manufacturer need be informed as to the characteristics of the mine as a whole." In the end, five hundred contractors and subcontractors were involved in the manufacture of various parts that were then sent to a second location for "joining" and then shipped to Norfolk for transport to Scotland, where the mines would undergo final assembly, "complete for the first time, ready for planting." The firm chosen to produce the supersecret electrical firing gear within the cylinder itself "has taken such precautions that only three members of the company will know that the electrical apparatus used in the mine is intended for a mine." The admiral was confident that such secrecy could be maintained until the assembled mines were shipped off to Europe.[5]

The Mark VI was a brilliant response to the Submarine Menace of the time. Hitherto, U-boats could readily avoid stationary contact mines by sailing either above or below them. The Mark VI mine with its antennae placed at various lengths made such confident passages impossible, although further experiments and a "more mature study of the project" induced its authors to recommend the spacing of mines be increased to three hundred feet, to "reduce the danger of countermining."[6]

Jellicoe's subsequent endorsement of a North Sea barrage at the naval conference in London in September, though shot down by Sims in favor of an emphasis upon the convoy system, did indicate the new direction of British thinking, though elements in Whitehall and Scapa Flow remained skittish, fearing, among other things, that the Grand Fleet might become enmeshed in the proposed barrage with disastrous effect. Following the conference, the Admiralty Plans Division sent a memorandum to Benson, advocating a comprehensive barrage that would include both shallow and deep mines together with surface and aircraft patrols. In addition to the danger of passing through a heavy mine barrage, surfaced enemy submarine would be subject to attack of one kind or another "from shortly after leaving their bases until they cleared the Orkney-Shetland-line."[7] A high-level Anglo-American meeting at London on November 2 endorsed the North Sea Barrage. When the weather lifted the following spring, British as well as American minelayers would participate. Whether the barrage would work as effectively as Mark VI tests suggested remained to be determined as the United States and Royal Navies spent the final months of 1917 and the early months of 1918 in frantic preparation.

The mines had to be designed "to be very safe in handling," since manufacturers, assemblers, shippers, inspectors, and testers "were almost entirely without previous experience with mines and explosives." Remarkably, of the 85,000 mines shipped abroad before the close of the war, and the 57,000 planted in the North Sea Barrage, not a single one exploded on board ship, and those that exploded prematurely in the water at or after "drop" did not cause serious damage to any vessel. At the same time, "It was necessary . . . to create practically a complete new mine squadron," since the navy's two existing minelayers, *San Francisco* and *Baltimore*, possessed a combined capacity of only 350 mines. Vessels requisitioned from the civilian sector had to be of good size, yet sufficiently nimble to participate in tactical formations. They had to be in "serviceable condition as to engines, boilers, pumps, etc." Finally, they had to have "good cargo handling equipment adaptable for handling mines." Eventually, eight vessels generally found to be suitable for the task were taken in hand for conversion, while the navy hastily built a major plant for the assembly of mine components at St. Julien's Creek at Hampton Roads, near Norfolk. A "special transportation service" comprising twenty-four cargo ships was created to get the thousands of not yet completed devices across the Atlantic to Scotland's west coast, where they were then barged via the Caledonian Canal to final assembly facilities built by the British at Invergordon and Inverness.[8]

One early spring day in 1918, a young naval officer named D. Pratt Mannix joined his new command at the Erie Basin in South Brooklyn. Months earlier, Mannix had learned of "highly secret" plans to lay a vast minefield from Scotland to Norway; "it would be the greatest undertaking of its kind in history," and the ambitious Annapolis graduate sensed a real career opportunity. But there were terrible disappointments and dangers involved that the youngster would understand all too soon. The TNT packed into each Mark VI mine was so volatile that both the French and the British had refused to use it in their weapons systems. The minelayers involved in planting the North Sea Barrage would thus be filled with enough explosive to send everyone on board, and perhaps adjacent vessels as well, to Kingdom Come. No one could forget Halifax. It was little wonder that Mannix found only two other Annapolis men among his eighteen officers. "The others consisted of an ex-merchant skipper over fifty years old, two young college men who had never been to sea before, a millionaire looking for excitement, and a tall Dane from the Geodetic Survey who was an authority on tropical flora. The rest were Navy warrant officers and merchant service officers."

But it was the ship that appalled Mannix. *Jefferson* had just been renamed *Quinnebaug*, and notwithstanding official navy protestations to the contrary, a sorrier vessel, in his estimation, never existed. "She was an old ex-merchantman with canvas-covered decks like a ferry boat and all her internal fittings were of wood. . . . Ancient insides" had been torn up, transforming lounges and dining rooms into "long reaches of bare decks on which were laid complete systems of railway tracks with switches and turntables" to move the mines into position. Two big "barn doors" had been cut into the stern through which tracks ran "to end in a downward curve over the water." The navy had mounted a five-inch gun aft and a pair of three-inch guns on the forecastle. Mannix could not believe that the navy was asking him to take "this old discarded vessel," this "frail ship," across the Atlantic, there to "weather North Sea gales." The navy replied as military institutions have done for millennia: "no other ships were available."[9]

Had Mannix and his fellow minelayer captains known the conditions under which the Mark VI mines were produced, they might never have left port. But at least *Quinnebaug* and her sister minelayers did not have to haul any mines across the Atlantic themselves. Throughout the early spring of 1918, the twenty-four cargo ships brought thousands of mines without incident to Scotland, where they were finally assembled in dumps until needed by the minelayers.

Meanwhile, BuOrd and an Admiralty technical committee nattered endlessly over which service would be responsible for mining which areas, where and whether British or American mines were most effective, and responsibility for surface patrols to prevent the Germans from minesweeping. On New Year's Day 1918, Sims's headquarters issued a memorandum of procedures based on Admiralty proposals that had been accepted "in principle by the Navy Department." Since the Grand Fleet at Scapa Flow and other nearby anchorages would support the entire enterprise, its wishes and capabilities had to predominate, particularly since the forthcoming barrage, like those already in place in the Dover and Otranto Straits, would be composed of a mixture of mines and surface-patrol vessels. The Admiralty proposals were designed to "give greater freedom of movement and greater ease of support to surface vessels, while it imposes corresponding difficulties upon the operations of enemy surprise vessels." Sims's people were not wholly satisfied. The original line of the mining barrage had been designed to extend "from mainland to mainland," that is, from the Scottish to the Norwegian coast. The new Admiralty line "extends from island to island and has in it passages completely navigable to submarines," thus defeating the entire intent. Moreover, the barrage was not deep enough, and the failure of the barrage across the Dover Straits was due in large measure to the ineffectiveness of surface-patrol vessels to find and catch submarines.

Nonetheless, the Americans "tentatively" decided "to accept the new position of the barrage as outlined by the British Admiralty," while urging that "the barrage be completed in the vertical plane from coast to coast, except an opening in the surface barrage at the western end and in Norwegian territorial waters. Maximum placement of the minefields should be extended to a depth of 295 feet; surface mines to be fitted with 70 foot antennae and those below water with 100 foot antennae." Finally, the Americans suggested minor modifications to several of the three "areas" compromising the barrage.[10]

With Americans and British at loggerheads, Sims's planners and their Admiralty counterparts despaired of ever getting on with the project or being able to complete it properly. "Many minor changes in plan and material occurred from time to time. . . . [U]ncertainty and confusion" prevailed "throughout the operation." The crux of the British concern lay in effectively defending the antisubmarine surface-patrol vessels in Area C, closest to the Norwegian coast, from attacks by units of the enemy High Seas Fleet. It was clear to Admiralty analysts that such protection could not be guaranteed by the Grand Fleet from its distant anchorages at Scapa Flow or Rosyth. Germany's High Seas Fleet remained, to the end, the ultimate guarantor of its submarine war. Therefore, "its destruction is very desirable. It cannot be forced to fight, however; and in order to develop our maximum efforts against the submarine it is necessary to combine offensive [anti-U-boat] and defensive [defeating or neutralizing the High Seas Fleet] measures." In short, the Admiralty was insisting that final defeat of the High Seas Fleet had to be achieved before the Northern Barrage could be guaranteed of total success. "The Grand Fleet must be prepared to fight and defeat the enemy." But the bloody stalemate at Jutland had stolen some of the heart from Britain's sailors. The High Seas Fleet must be beaten "under our conditions of time and place."[11]

Admiralty concerns were never fully resolved. The best that could be done under the circumstances were frequent sweeps of the upper North Sea by the Grand Fleet (including the contingent of US battleships). In the end, the imperatives of antisubmarine warfare won out. The American memo of March 28 that emphasized the ongoing U-boat menace concluded with a section titled "Joint Appreciation of the British and American Planning Divisions" that a Northern Barrage closing off the top of the North Sea to U-boat passage offered the best hope of victory. British minelayers were already at sea getting the enterprise under way, and the following month the Yanks began their operations not in the North Sea but in the North Channel off the Irish coast, where *Baltimore*, operating alone, planted some 659 mines with what was at the time characterized as "extreme accuracy." The Americans came into the Northern Barrage with a full complement of minelayers in early July. The mission was prosecuted with such vigor and effect that within weeks, a "gradual closing of all areas" of the upper North Sea began to take hold. In reaction, increasingly desperate U-boat captains began to transit Norwegian territorial waters. Unrelenting diplomatic pressure from London and Washington induced the Norwegians "after much negotiation and delay" to announce on September 29—just six weeks before the Armistice—that they would mine their own waters, closing the last gap left to the U-boats.[12]

The final taste of home for the minelayer sailors had been bitter. As some went on a farewell leave, they discovered they had become pariahs among their fellows. At Hampton Roads, "Whenever one of them lighted a cigarette," sailors from the battleship squadron "ran away shouting that they could see the TNT under their finger tips." The ten ships led by *San Francisco* and *Baltimore* sailed to Scotland as a unit. The breakdown-prone *Quinnebaug* experienced its last incident in midocean when the "major air pump flew to pieces," necessitating a daylong tow interrupted by a submarine alarm that sent the flotilla scattering for a time. Mannix concluded that it must be a false alarm, because "no submarine captain could have failed to sink a twenty-year-old crippled ferryboat incapable of making more than a few knots." On-board repairs got *Quinnebaug* moving again, though a more plausible submarine alarm greeted the squadron as it approached Scottish shores. Soon the ships were anchored in the "blue waters of Invergordon harbor," a "nearly God-forsaken place" to some of Mannix's fellow mine sailors.[13]

At dusk on July 13, 1918, *Quinnebaug* and her sisters began their initial operation, a majority of the minesweeping squadron passing out through the submarine nets and meeting an escort of fourteen British destroyers from the Grand Fleet whose sole responsibility was to stand guard against U-boats. The squadron and its escorts headed for Muckle Skerry Light and then swung over toward Norway. A division of either American or British battleships together with Royal Navy light cruisers stood guard nearby against a sally by the German fleet. "Ten ships laden with high explosive, navigating in mine-swept channels, in submarine thoroughfares, and near mine-fields beyond sight of fixed marks" demanded a high degree of precision and quickness that were difficult to maintain given the fact that each vessel possessed its own power plant and thus its own idiosyncrasies. Commanding officers strove for an atmosphere of "careful habit" among their crews, "without making them jumpy or fearful." The goal was sustained attention bereft of overconfidence. "Unremitting pains were exercised to note and correct any irregularity or apparent slackness."[14]

Care could not prevent accident. Completing its first exercise, the squadron headed toward Cromarty Firth early on the morning of the sixteenth in a fog so thick that ships' captains and navigators could not check their positions. "The swept channel was narrow and close inshore," which deprived the ships of sufficient maneuvering room; soundings were dangerous to take because of the possibility of drifting mines. In the early-morning darkness, one of the British destroyers "sheered close" to *San Francisco* and warned that she was too close inshore, though sailors on the nearby *Canonicus* claimed not to have picked up the signal. "The squadron turned out, stopped and backed but before headway had been checked, *Roanoke* and *Canonicus* had grounded." The official navy account makes relatively light of the incident, stating that *Canonicus* was able to back off and that only *Roanoke* remained grounded.

It did not seem that way to seaman George Golden, aboard *Canonicus*, another rust bucket dating from the Spanish–American War. Upon grounding, the executive officer ordered all men up from below "if they don't want to drown." Golden was certain that the ship would be abandoned. Fortunately, the sea was calm, and *San Francisco* managed to extricate itself quickly and then helped the other two vessels get unstuck by using every motor- and whaleboat available. Later, *Canonicus*'s skipper complemented his men, saying that "it was the first time he ever saw a ship pulled off of a reef by manpower." The vessels, all only slightly damaged, put in to "Base 17" at Invergordon for a few days to pound out dents, clean and paint ship, and reload with mines before heading back into the North Sea.[15]

As they began to sow their minefields, the layers were in two lines, one ahead of the other on parallel courses five hundred yards apart, since the field would have been widened unnecessarily should all ten vessels be disposed in a line abreast. The field was planted with devilish, if not fiendish, care in three levels so that a U-boat, whether running surfaced or "at ordinary submergence" (sixty to one hundred feet) "or as deep as 250 feet," was in imminent danger for mile after mile. "Only the rear line of ships dropped mines," while the front line stood by to replace any that broke down or suffered any kind of accident. "Steady steaming and steering" were essential for safety as well as for regularity of mine spacing. "God help a ship whose engine broke down or rudder jammed" during its minelaying. The prevalent strong headwinds would cause the hapless craft to drift right into the minefield before any sister ship or guardian destroyer could tow her clear.

"The mines were carried on two of the lower decks," Mannix recalled, "the 'launching deck' and the 'stowage deck.'" The railroad tracks on the launching deck passed through the "barn doors" on *Quinnebaug*'s stern, where an officer in a soundproof booth triggered the dropping of the mines when the flag-ship signaled to begin execution. Every eight seconds an illuminated electri-cal dial illuminated the word *plant*, and a mine was pushed through the open barn door by two crewmen standing next to the tracks. "It was fascinating to watch," Mannix remembered. The mines "would go over with a great splash, bob around in our wake while the box anchor gradually filled with water, then suddenly sink with a dull plop as though a giant hand had reached up from below and pulled them down."

The enlisted men who had to do the scut work understandably found mine-laying less than agreeable. Lester T. Lee, from Jefferson County, Indiana, ap-parently aboard the *Quinnebaug* (which the crew habitually called the "Dizzy Quinne"), thought the quick cruises out to the barrage line "exciting . . . at first," but soon learned the entire enterprise involved "real work, loading mines, steaming." *Quinnebaug's* crew was assured that the mines possessed a "safety device" that prevented them from premature explosion.

On the initial laying run, unmollified sailors saw one go over, then two. Each weapon had been sealed just before drop "with a sal ammoniac plug," designed to slowly melt in saltwater. The third mine went over the side and promptly blew up "with a crash like the Day of Judgement. An enormous column of flames, smoke, mud, and water rose just astern of us." Men five hundred feet away were thrown off their feet, and *Quinnebaug* "quivered and strained" so much that the crew feared she would pop a fatal number of rivets. All in all, "about 6 per cent of the mines exploded prematurely" on that first cruise. The eruptions of the TNT were not like gunpowder. "They would be preceded by a deathly silence, then we would feel a heavy pressure on our chests and all the air in our lungs" would be sucked toward the exploding mine. As the mines left the launching deck, others were raised in elevators from the stowage deck to go overboard in their turn. *Quinnebaug* steamed at full speed, carefully dropping its cargo of eight hundred mines until exhausted. In this way, the ten vessels could sow a field in about three to four hours.

Then it was time to head home through a typically dense North Sea fog often so close that the forecastle disappeared from the view of those on the bridge. At three in the morning, with the fog lifting slightly, the minelayers and their destroyer escorts blundered into a large convoy, and only the most alert seamanship prevented disaster. "Then the whole outfit vanished, leaving us, like the Ancient Mariner, 'all, all alone.'"[16] Continuing through the slowly lifting fog, Mannix was able to take a sun sight shortly after dawn that put his position some thirty miles from Invergordon Harbor. Crawling toward the entrance, he nearly collided with *Baltimore* as she sought safety, and then he narrowly missed several trawlers. Anchoring at last, Mannix wondered if this journey would be his worst. It proved to be only the beginning of many such crises.[17]

All involved either weather, tides, or both, though with minefields still incomplete, the abrupt appearance of an enemy submarine could never be discounted. In Westray Firth one autumn morning, a strong tide against a strong wind created a treacherous cross-sea through which the mining squadron and its escorts had to pass. A British destroyer "broached to," laying for long moments between the columns of American minelayers and "wallowing heavily, as if the next roll would surely take her under." Shortly thereafter, *Quinnebaug*'s rudder quadrant broke, the other arm bending almost to the fracture point. "Had it too gone, she could not have escaped wreck" on the rocky side of the channel. Striving mightily, the crew managed to gain partial shelter, where they made hasty repairs. "Taking after the rest" of the squadron at top speed, the layer arrived at Invergordon only forty-five minutes late.

Officers and men understandably "felt intense pride in their ships" and their mission. "We have been put through a pretty hard pace the last week," George Golden wrote in his diary on August 1, "and while I feel pretty tired I now feel as though we are accomplishing something and doing something to end this war." Pride was intensified by "much favorable comment" as time went on from both the Admiralty and Admiral Mayo, the Atlantic Fleet commander. Ernest King accompanied Mayo on one European inspection junket that included the minelayers' tenth excursion. "The ships went through the Moray Firth, through the Orkney Islands, and then, with particularly exact navigation, to the eastward where the mines were to be laid." The nearby Norwegian coast lay shrouded in fog, and that evening the wardroom dinner was periodically punctuated by the sound of mines exploding prematurely. Crews "spared no effort" to keep their vessels "in regular man-of-war condition." But those so tasked found it no fun. Lester Lee recalled watching coal ships put 300 to 550 tons on board, "and in the bunkers" where it all landed, "the dust is so thick you had to put a handkerchief over your mouth to get your breath; you could not tell your mate working by your side, nor see electric light 10 ft. away." After coaling, "work and more work" was required to clean ship. "Believe me, we realized we were not at home." Unfortunately, there was little else for crews to do in port aside from frequently arranged baseball games ashore.

Officers found the minelayers "comfortable enough to live in while empty," but it was a far different story when the mines came aboard and the ships went to sea, where everyone was subjected to frequent rolling and pitching. Mines contained horns "and other sharp corners" that were "constantly at one's elbow." Together with the "half-knee high" mine tracks, or turntables, they tore clothing, tripped crewmen, and barked their shins. Mess tables were crowded together; only a few men could find room to sling hammocks, while the rest slept on decks or on top of ditty boxes. In late July, aboard *Canonicus*, Golden wrote of airing bedding, which was "quite a joke after sleeping on the decks for two nights."[18]

By late September, bad weather during some parts of an excursion "became the rule." In murky seas, "it was rather ghostly to hear and feel the explosions of the defective mines, yet see nothing—not even the neighboring ship." Marker buoys were also hard to pick up. By the close of the eighth American excursion on September 7, a barrage line had been laid across the entire upper North Sea, and in growing gloom and darkness, the Yankee and British minelayers doubled and trebled the line of mines, while thickening the barrage to as much as thirty-five miles in some places. Only one casualty had occurred, when *Saranac*'s port paravane (a new torpedo-shaped underwater device towed alongside ship, whose attached hydrofoil cables were equipped with serrated blades to foul, then cut, any anchored mines that might be in the way) began to stream wildly and a veteran chief boatswain's mate was swept overboard trying to clear it. Undeterred, the Allied project went ahead, and a total of thirteen American and twelve British mining excursions took place before the Armistice.[19]

The effectiveness of the Northern Barrage—not just its cost-to-kill ratio but its psychological effect—is hard to assess even a century later, since it was never fully completed. British trawler captains in the region of the barrage claimed to hear numerous explosions from mines detonating on their own, and Beatty feared that his Grand Fleet might blunder into floating mines that had become detached. The Admiralty, at least, admitted that some of the American mines had been planted so deep (eighty feet) that a U-boat passing near the surface would merely suffer a mild shakeup if a mine exploded. The incontestable fact, however, was that thanks to the barrage, German U-boat commanders throughout the last months of the war avoided the most convenient (that is, central) navigation lanes of the upper North Sea in passing through to their Atlantic patrol areas. When Kommodore Andreas Michelsen ordered his U-boats home on October 27, 1918, the project was about 85 percent complete.

As conceived and implemented, the barrage consisted of three areas, A, B, and C. The Americans festooned central Area A with more than fifty-six thousand mines; the British more thinly seeded Areas B and C with thirteen-thousand-plus mines. Current consensus is that the Germans lost six or perhaps seven U-boats in the barrage. By the late summer of 1918, it was becoming obvious that they still found it relatively safe to pass through Area C, and they continued to use Norwegian territorial waters for another month until those were closed to them. Beatty bitterly condemned the barrage as "a fearful waste of time and resources," restricting his ships' freedom of movement. Historian John Terraine concludes rather gloomily that "at least" the barrage "was not positively harmful," as was that at Otranto, which after much effort resulted in the confirmed kill of a single U-boat. Dwight Messimer concludes that the barrage was not effective and presents some somber evidence to back his claim. "Had every mine in the barrage been 100 percent effective, a U-boat passing through on the surface or at periscope depth had a theoretical chance of one in three of making the passage safely. Below periscope depth and down to 250 feet, the U-boat had two chances in three of getting through safely. Considering the technical problems the mines suffered, the chances of a U-boat getting through were increased about two times." Professor Halpern finds "something typically American about the Northern barrage that foreshadowed" the country's performance in the greater war a quarter century later. The barrage was a massive, "bold," and costly project, requiring "tremendous effort, great enthusiasm, much money and considerable ingenuity." Yet had the war continued and the barrage been completed, "would the results ever have been in proportion to the effort?"[20]

Probably not. The Northern Barrage never changed Sims's thinking. A month after the war's end, he traveled to Scotland to congratulate the men of the mining force for their "stunt, the like of which has not been done in the world before." The "efficiency" of the barrage, Sims continued, was something that quite properly did not concern the men who laid it down. It had been the "stunt of the fitting out the vessels, learning to handle the mines, planting them, and going through the strenuous work" that had been so impressive, indeed, "really . . . one of the finest stunts the Navy has accomplished on this side."[21]

Dismissing the massive mining barrage as a "stunt" was a conclusion certainly not shared by everyone. Even before the Northern Barrage began to be laid, Allied naval circles in the Mediterranean contemplated laying a series of "grandiose mining barrages" in 1919 across the Sicilian Narrows and several other local choke points as well as a supplement to the existing Otranto Barrage of nets and trawlers.[22] Whatever its intrinsic value as a war weapon, the

Northern Barrage was an impressive feat of industrial engineering, part of the ever-growing and cumulative impact of the United States on world affairs a century ago. In many ways the country led, and would continue to lead, the international community in massive engineering projects until turning to micropower and -processing with equally stunning effect after 1945.

★ ★ ★ ★ ★

The navy's boldness and reach in the use of its many weapons systems during World War I extended to the western front itself. From September 6, 1918, to the Armistice a little more than eight weeks later, five US naval batteries, "each composed of one 14-inch 50 caliber gun carried on a special railway mount attached to ammunition and auxiliary cars," systematically bombarded positions, bases, martialing points, and supply depots "behind enemy lines in France with remarkable efficiency and important results."

The author of this audacious plan was the redoubtable Rear Admiral Ralph Earle. Almost as soon as the war began, the chief of the navy's Bureau of Ordnance faced a dilemma. The service was shifting to sixteen-inch guns for its main battleship batteries, and there was a sudden surplus of the smaller fourteen-inch cannon. Earle was also struck by the efficiency of German long-range heavy artillery in the West, especially the "Big Bertha" that periodically rained shells and terror on Paris, together with slightly smaller guns that bombarded British positions in Flanders as well as the port at Dunkirk. Earle knew that naval batteries had been brought ashore to be used in earlier American wars and that the Italians had for some time been employing mobile, railway-based batteries to fire on Austrian positions and ships up and down the Adriatic. If the Americans could bring into play their gigantic fourteen-inch batteries, they could batter German supply and concentration points far behind the Flanders front, disrupting potential enemy attacks. In the autumn of 1917, "BuOrd" and Admiral Earle began to actively plan for the transfer of guns to France with plans to send more across the Atlantic in 1919. The successful employment of these huge batteries constituted, in the words of one historian, "an unparalleled technological and industrial achievement."[23]

AIR power, too, was having a growing effect on the antisubmarine war. And here as elsewhere, young Americans exerted a growing influence. In 1918, the buildup of US naval aviation in Europe came with a rush characteristic of the entire national effort. It was ensured by an order issued by Secretary of War Newton D. Baker the previous November that "priority be given by the

War Department to naval needs for aviation material necessary to equip and arm seaplane bases."[24] Throughout the final months of that year and well into the next, ever-growing numbers of American sailors streamed off transports at Liverpool, St. Nazaire, and Brest, immediately setting to work (in some cases with German prisoner-of-war labor and what French and English civilian labor was available) constructing airfields, hangars, slipways, barracks, supply depots, receiving and assembly plants, and administration buildings across the British Isles and France. Eventually, the energetic Hutchinson Cone on Sims's staff in London oversaw the creation of twenty-seven naval air stations from Ireland to the Adriatic, exactly half the number of "bases, stations, and other shore facilities" that energetic American construction parties built throughout the British Isles, France, Italy, the Azores, and elsewhere in eighteen months of war.[25]

Pilots from the often beleaguered antisubmarine air station at Dunkirk were responsible for patrolling the northern entrance to the English Channel. "Heavily armed flyingboats" out of Killingholme in Lincolnshire on the English east coast "scouted far and wide across the North Sea." Other American aviators from naval air bases in western England and Ireland flew long hours looking for U-boats and protecting convoys in the Irish Sea and Western Approaches, while flyers from Le Croisic and a half-dozen other airfields on the French Atlantic coast protected the important convoys plying the Bay of Biscay. The (very) young men who flew out of these "aerodromes" had nothing but contempt for the relatively few colleagues assigned to the Italian training station at Lake Balsino and the patrol base at Porto Casini, on the east side of the Adriatic. These four-month assignments were dismissed as little more than a "rest cure."[26]

At Sims's staff at London, Cone's efforts to construct and deploy a comprehensive naval aviation infrastructure were hobbled by significant physical and human constraints. The labor and matériel demands of the western front together with "chaotic" shipment schedules from the States led to frequent breakdowns in construction. Not until the summer of 1918, for example, did the huge assembly and repair facility at Pauillac, on the banks of the Gironde River near Bordeaux, become fully operational, putting together the first American-manufactured engines and aircraft frames in France for both training and combat. Once activities got under way, however, production soared. The same was true at the second American receiving and assembly plant at Brest.[27]

The other constraint on Cone's energetic activities came from elements within American armed forces. Throughout 1917 and into the following winter, Brigadier General Benjamin O. Foulois, chairman of the joint Army-Navy

Aircraft Committee in Paris, did everything in his power to prevent Cone and his naval aviators from playing a major role in the air war both ashore and at sea. The general was especially outraged over navy plans to use land-based aircraft for overwater patrolling. Shortly after the war, he sputtered to Congress that such plans were "contrary to the policies of the American Expeditionary Force." He did "his utmost to deflect resources" away from navy to army channels. Fortunately for the flying sailors, the Aircraft Committee was dissolved in April 1918, and Foulois lost his soapbox. Three months later, however, Marine Corps headquarters in Washington insisted that any future "land flying" that might be done by the navy should be done by the relative handful of Marine Corps aviators then in France. The demand was not frivolous. Naval aviators had flown over the western front in March during the initial German offensive in the West. And at Belleau Wood and Château-Thierry, marines had been playing a major role in successful Allied efforts first to blunt and then to roll back the German thrust.[28]

Probably most of the young men who followed the pioneers of the First Aeronautical Detachment and the Second Yale Unit to Europe during the final year of the war from the burgeoning training schools and airfields that dotted the nation from the University of Washington to Pensacola shared the sentiments of Kenneth MacLeish. The eighteen-year-old Yale flier had been "thrilled," he wrote as his transport approached British waters early in November 1917, to be told by a regular naval officer on board that while the war was going badly and might even be lost if the U-boat menace was not suppressed, "the war might be won in the air. Once the Huns lose that supremacy, they'll tumble." "I have tried hard not to," he confided to himself, "but all the way over I've been wondering whether I'll make a good fighting flier. I need several characteristics, or rather a complete change of attitude. I am fairly sure that as soon as I get busy the change will take place. It's curious, but I wonder if it will change *me* very much. I'm still more or less a boy, and I've always doubted if I'd ever grow up, but I guess my time has come."[29]

Curtis Read, another member of the Yale Unit, caught the tone and rhythms of the time with striking brevity. His transport left New York in convoy shortly after MacLeish sailed and endured three days of "rough seas" and snowstorms in passage until, as the waters calmed, "two destroyers met us" wearing pink and blue camouflage: "They certainly are faithful little boats. Blinking at night." A silver "blimp" soon appeared and escorted the ship to port through a squadron of small fishing vessels. Arriving at Liverpool early in the morning, Read hastened to the consulate to arrange transportation to London. "Interesting talk with British officer" on his way to France: "Fed up on it. Bad business." Liverpool Station was "crowded with troops." In London that night, the aspiring flier found Charing Cross Station "full of wounded" and their ambulances. He walked dark, quiet streets filled with "great numbers of wounded men. Romance all gone. Horrible actuality only thing left." Ambulatory wounded wore blue stripes and could not drink; it was thought alcohol hindered convalescence. Read awoke early his first morning in London, December 3, in a "rotten bed" to confront a "disagreeable maid." Walking to Sims's headquarters at Grosvenor Gardens for further orders, the youngster was again struck with the number of wounded in the streets. Despite their "wonderful uniforms," the English exhibited a "stern coldness," a "no hurry attitude. Almost despair. If only Americans could realize, etc." Sims's people were in "a great hurry to get us over" to France, and Read was promptly packed off to Southampton. "Sad farewells at station. Train crowded with troops. Arrive at Southampton. Dock scene—sadness—pretty effect of lights." His "pacquet boat" soon left for France. "British naval officers—cheers, 'Mud in your eye.' Officer looking for" his "steward. 'Carry on.'"

Recalling similar scenes from his own experience some years later, Ralph Paine added, "There it all is . . . an England that was almost in despair, but stubbornly carried on—a London that was darkened and cold and tired, whose streets were filled with disabled men, but whose pavements echoed to the tramp of fresh battalions bound across the Channel. The sad farewells mingled with the defiant rattle of the drums. . . . It was a long way to Tipperary. Another air raid tonight. This was not the war as Broadway or Pennsylvania Avenue knew it." Into this grim, self-absorbed environment, "these young American aviators wandered with a certain sense of bewilderment. They were like bits of driftwood in the lash of a mighty tide."[30]

Sims's planning staffers also caught the mounting gloom and sense of world crisis. In early February they wrote that the "minds" of both allies and enemies had "reached a condition of acute tension. Civil populations in all the countries at war are beginning to doubt the wisdom of fighting longer. People's wills" had reached a state of "unstable equilibrium." Europe had been rocked by cataclysmic events and mighty endeavors that had produced nothing but bloody stasis. "Faith" in all the armed camps had been "shaken"; "fixity of purpose" had been lost. Now millions simply yearned for a return to an "antebellum condition" of peace.[31]

Fetching up in Paris, many youngsters still required either advanced aviation training or more specialized flying or observational skills and were quickly dispersed to several training schools. But Tours, Hourtin, "and other French stations were incidental to turning up at Moutchic sooner or later." Hastily constructed, Moutchic became the primary training center for American naval aviators. As with so many other aspects of the naval air war, it began slowly and then boomed in size. In December 1917, David Ingalls complained to his father that members of his Yale Unit "and a few older men" were the only naval flyers who had been trained in the United States. The First Air Detachment, composed of apprentice flyers who were beginning to arrive in France, "have had no previous training or practically none. Most of them are men who, on enlisting, were immediately shipped across regardless of their ability or adaptability for aviation. All the flyers here, except us few, have been trained here, first on land machines, then at several French water schools." The situation was not helped by the poor quality of training aircraft. The French FBA flying boats were "cranky, underpowered machines" whose rotary engines created a powerful torque that caused wings to fall off to one side or another, creating "dangerous spins." Their successors, the French "DDs" were no better, nine crashing and burning between December 1917 and the following May, killing a number of student pilots.[32]

By the summer of 1918, however, Moutchic had become a large and efficient facility, averaging 175 to 350 training flights per week. By early autumn, the number had risen to nearly 500, just as the facility at Pauillac came fully on line, dispatching a growing number of assembled Curtiss seaplanes to bases throughout France. Eastleigh performed the same service in England. Each training flight at Moutchic lasted twenty to thirty minutes. "Instruction originally occurred between 4:30 and 10:30 a.m. and then 3:00 and 8:30 p.m. but as many more students arrived lessons were conducted all day long. A new directive encouraged bad weather flying so pilots might know how to deal with such conditions." The need for trained aviators had become acute, especially fighter pilots, or *chasse*, to defend the "lumbering patrol bombers" at Naval Air Station Dunkirk against German fighter aircraft deploying from bases near Ostend and Zeebrugge. Frantic planners reached into the ranks of the Lafayette Flying Corps, the Yale Unit, and the First Aeronautic Detachment to "enlist" (actually, in many cases, draft) the needed aviators.[33]

Kenneth Whiting and his French hosts had originally envisioned three American bases on the north and west coasts of France, at Dunkirk and at the entrances to the rivers Loire and Gironde. Their own fledgling air forces always too thinly spread for the mission responsibilities assigned them, French aviators were delighted to see the Yanks appear: first, because American entry would greatly increase both coastal and deep-sea traffic, necessitating the devotion of ever-greater resources for antisubmarine protection and, second, because the coming of American aviators and equipment allowed the French to transfer squadrons to the nearby western front, which was under perpetual threat. In the event, the number of American pilots and equipment continually increased until November 1918, when "a continuous fringe of United States and French naval air stations for hydro-planes and dirigibles lined the coast from Dunkirk to the Spanish boundary."[34]

French authorities had made the first airfield available to the eager Yanks as early as October 1917. Seaplanes from Le Croisic, near the mouth of the Loire, would "help drive the German submarines further away from the coast and . . . protect the immense amount of transport traffic" in and out of St. Nazaire. On November 18, US Naval Aviation Forces (USNAF)—as they were now designated—officially entered the Great War when a French Tellier seaplane piloted by Yale man Kenneth R. Smith took off on an armed antisubmarine foray into the Bay of Biscay to investigate the reported presence of two U-boats south of Belle Isle.[35]

It proved a disastrous beginning. Lifting off at noon, the young ensign "felt very puffed up" as he and his two crewmen "were the first Americans (either Army or Navy) wholly under the American Government to make an independent war flight on our own resources." In their excitement, they failed to take any survival equipment (though they did carry two pigeons); they were also "too new at the game" to realize that no aircraft should ever be sent out alone. Their commanding officers were equally clueless—or criminally negligent. Smith found no submarines and after flying aimlessly for a time started back to Le Croisic, only to have the engine suddenly die. Slammed down into heavy seas, Smith and his two mates managed to restart the engine several times, but the heaving waters prevented either takeoff or taxiing toward the land that beckoned so tantalizingly in the form of a distant lighthouse. Chronically seasick, their craft slowly filling with water, the three young Americans fought off despair for nearly sixty hours, as Smith released the two birds with guessed position messages some time apart.

Their colleagues, meanwhile, experienced ordeals of their own as they recklessly flew out trying to spot the downed aircraft amid the gray and turbulent seas. "Reg" Toombs and an enlisted pilot named Gillespie with their two-man crews flew so long that they found themselves totally lost somewhere south of La Pallice. Toombs led the way onto the water, and then both pilots carefully maneuvered their craft through the heavy surf onto an empty beach. The pilots and their crewmen had no idea where they were, but a farmer with his cart fortuitously happened by and took Toombs home, where a hot fire and food awaited, along with word that La Pallice was not far. Bringing most of the food back to the men on the beach, Toombs and his colleagues then spent a hard night horsing, hauling, and dragging their planes up the sloping sands to ensure that the wave-battered aircraft were not taken by the waters to drift away to sea. At dawn, the six managed to climb aboard their planes and with some difficulty took off for La Pallice and Le Croisic, where they were met with the disheartening news that despite the messages delivered through rain and fog by the doughty pigeons, Smith and his mates remained missing.

After several days and nights of seasickness and mounting dread, the three aviators in their drifting and slowly sinking aircraft had nearly given up when a French patrol boat, part of an ever-widening search-and-rescue effort, came by and plucked them from the sea just before the stout Tellier at last gave up the struggle and sank from sight.[36]

By the end of 1917, the buildup of American naval aviation in Europe had reached a sufficient, though still low, threshold that through "the inscrutable wisdom of official orders" emanating from Paris—and, soon, London—fliers were "snatched" from Moutchic and nearby Hourtin "to go spinning away to other stations" in France and England either for further, interminable, training courses or—for a lucky few—combat flying. As Ralph Paine later observed, the navy's personnel system regarding its fliers "was like the little round ball that traverses the roulette wheel, and the devil only knows where it will drop next."[37]

For most of the war, pilots, gunners, and observers not only were reduced to flying foreign aircraft, but never flew in recognizable units of their own. Whatever it meant at home, the term "US Naval Aviation Forces" was more a wish than a reality in Europe. Until very late in the war, the eager youngsters of the First Yale Unit, the First Aviation Detachment, and the many hundreds who followed never formed permanent squadrons, their own air groups, or their own patrol wings. For that, they could thank Hutch Cone, who—unlike Pershing—was more concerned with feeding his naval airmen in where they were immediately needed, or could be further trained, than in building up an independent naval air arm. By early 1918, Cone's practice of deferring to Allied needs and wishes resulted in the seeding of ever-greater numbers of US naval aviators on air stations throughout England, Scotland, and France. A fortunate few, including the pilots at Le Croisic and those assigned to Felixstowe, close to Harwich, home port of the Royal Navy's Dover Patrol of light cruiser and destroyers, began combat flying either immediately or after very short courses in the H-12 or F2A flying boats. Most naval pilots, however, continued training in the bewildering arsenal of available French, Italian, and British land and seaplanes. "Scores" of pilots, observers, mechanics, and others engaged in flying, gunnery, and observation at British schools before at last being assigned to frontline air stations. The Royal Flying Corps' School of Special Flying at Gosport, directly on the Channel, proved a special ordeal. Instructors put the handful of American trainees, most from the First Yale Unit, through a brutal regimen of early- and midwinter flying amid clouds, rain, icy fog, and even snowstorms and doubtless did not let up on subsequent cadets as the often abominable weather eased slightly with the coming of spring. A number of the Yalies had become stressed out by fatigue and frustration by the time they reached the School of Advanced Aerial Fighting at Ayre. Their mood was not lightened by encounters with the more numerous members of the First Aeronautic Detachment, composed mainly of those enlisted men whom Ingalls had earlier derided at Moutchic as possessing little training and perhaps less skills. After months of hard training, the enlistees had developed their own shoulder chips. Stung by the condescension of the commissioned pilot-trainees who called them "hard guys" and "roughnecks," the FAD boys sloughed off from drills and wore deliberately nonregulation military attire. In a few cases, the enlisted fliers did fail to develop the abilities necessary for combat; two would later die in crashes at the Dunkirk air station.[38]

Once graduated, the navy boys either flew independently or as part of British or French aircrews from air bases stretching from the upper North Sea to the Channel to the Bay of Biscay. They piloted the various flying boats and seaplanes that escorted convoys to and from France and Holland and down the Biscay coast; they reconnoitered the coasts of Belgium and Germany or patrolled a four-thousand-square-mile "spider's web" centered on the North Hinder Lightship anchored in the North Sea between Britain and Holland. Radio intelligence had long picked up communications between enemy submarines under way through the lower North Sea or Channel and their home bases that revealed favored navigation routes. U-boats could remain submerged for only two or at most three hours at necessarily low speed before declining battery power forced them to the surface to recharge. The trick was to appear on the scene while the U-boats were surfaced somewhere within the web, but in five hours one aircraft could search only "one quarter of the area."[39] So the spider's web became a theater of cat and mouse between U-boat *kapitäns* and British-American flight crews. Mostly, the Germans avoided detection.

The youngsters patrolling the Bay of Biscay made exaggerated claims of U-boat sinkings that postwar records could not substantiate. But their French hosts immediately embraced the enthusiastic claims. In April 1918, two of the earliest trained American aircrews flying French aircraft out of a Breton airfield spied a "suspicious wake" off Pointe Penmarc'h at the northern tip of the Bay of Biscay where the U-boats tended to congregate, awaiting enemy convoys. The first aircraft promptly peeled off and dropped two bombs, one of which landed on the front of the wake, the other ten feet beyond. "The explosion caused a tremendous disturbance that brought up air bubbles and sea growth to the surface." As the second aircraft dropped a phosphorous buoy and loitered, the first, flown by Ken Smith, rushed off to rustle up a destroyer or two. USS *Stewart* and a French gunboat soon arrived to drop depth charges, "which brought more sea growth and oil to the surface." In these early days of antisubmarine warfare, such results were sufficient to confirm a kill, and grateful French authorities awarded Smith and his observer the Croix de Guerre with Palm. In all, "The French credited the Americans with a least three other victories" that could never be proved.[40]

Across the Channel at Felixstowe, patrol flights conformed to the pattern generally followed on stations elsewhere in the area. Two or three aircraft generally flew in loose formations for protection against enemy scout and fighter planes that appeared in growing numbers from the east and fought with increasing ferocity in the final twelve months of the war. An altitude of one thousand feet was deemed optimal for sighting surfaced submarines through the clouds, murk, and sun breaks that characterized most North Sea and Channel days. "In some cases," the British station chief, Commander John C. Porte, "dispatched aircraft to provoke action, believing the machines could defend themselves." In at least two cases, he proved tragically wrong.

Early on the morning of February 15, 1918, Ensign Albert D. Sturtevant and three Royal Naval Air Service enlisted men climbed into their small Curtiss H-12b flying boat, widely known to be poorly designed and on the verge of obsolescence, to take off with another aircraft on a routine convoy-protection flight over the lower North Sea. Shortly after spotting the convoy and beginning patrol maneuvers around it, the two planes were suddenly jumped out of the low cloud cover by five (not ten, as initially reported) swift enemy Hansa-Brandenburg W.29 mono-wing floatplanes. The Germans were delighted to engage in combat; they enjoyed not only superiority of numbers but also speed and maneuverability. Without suffering more than a few bullet holes, the enemy airmen "demolished" Sturtevant's relatively cumbersome flying boat, killing not only the Yale flyer but his three British crewmen as well. When last seen, the aircraft was wobbling toward the Belgian coast, when near Ostend, riddled with machine-gun fire, it crashed in flames into the sea. Sturtevant's wing man, a South African, managed to escape and race back to Felixstowe, where he barely escaped charges of cowardice. The newly arrived Americans were stunned. Sturtevant had been "a very likeable" chap, "clean-cut," who "treated his work here as an absorbing game which he played cheerfully and well." It was an epitaph already widely applicable throughout the Allied aviation communities.

Two months later, Ensign Stephen Potter was copiloting one of two British seaplanes near the North Hinder Lightship when they engaged in action with two similar enemy aircraft, one of which Potter's plane shot down. Five more German floatplanes quickly materialized, and the resulting melee sent Potter's seaplane flaming into the sea. It was obvious, as critics had been insisting for some time, that flying boats were too large and slow to be effectively employed as fighter planes. Naval Air Station Dunkirk was just across the Channel. Fighters from there could provide effective escort for convoy protection and antisubmarine patrols.[41]

Killingholme in Lincolnshire, fronting the North Sea, was the first British base to receive second-generation American pilots and mechanics trained exclusively and intensively in the States. The youngsters had attended schools from Texas to Hampton Roads to the Packard plant in Detroit, where Liberty engines for Curtiss's H-class flying boats were manufactured. The first navy pilot, twenty-year-old Ensign Francis Allen, arrived on February 9 and was soon "worked into the daily routine." Mates who began arriving in large numbers throughout the rest of the month included Ensign George Rumill, who was the first American aloft. By the end of March, more than 350 enlisted personnel had arrived to tend to the big Short floatplanes, with their "enormous wingspan and ungainliness while afloat," and the more popular F2As. After spending time in Washington, Ken Whiting took command of the base in May. Killingholme had originally been conceived as a strategic air base from which to bomb German naval facilities in the Helgoland Bight. The distances were so far beyond the range of existing seaplanes, however, that they would have to be transported at least two hundred miles across the North Sea by lighters before they could take off. They then would conduct their bombing raids and fly back to Killingholme or other nearby bases on their own. Initial trials indicated that the plan was not quite as bizarre as it first seemed. Unfortunately, the Germans got wind of the project, and it had to be abandoned. Thereafter, operations from Killingholme were restricted to both antisubmarine patrolling and convoy escort together with "direct operations against submarines" in the rare instances when they were found.[42] Flight logs from February to July 1918 reflected the steadily growing contribution of American naval aircrews to the U-boat war. Of the 321 patrols conducted, Americans flew 171, "accounting for 596 of the 1,095 total flying hours." Whiting divided mission responsibilities in two: "Convoy Escort Flights" and "War Flights" for antisubmarine and long-range reconnaissance work.[43]

Aircraft from Killingholme safely escorted more than six thousand ships from British ports across the North Sea to France. Shortly after the war, Harald Bartlett, who had commanded the base at Moutchic, observed that there were "almost no cases" of submarines attacking convoys when aircraft were present; just hearing the sound of engines aloft sent U-boats scuttling beneath the waves. Although Bartlett admitted that "dirigibles are more suitable for convoying than planes," due to superior loitering capabilities, "the Dutch and Channel convoys, and, towards the end, the French coastal convoys, were nearly always escorted by planes" as well as dirigibles and surface craft. Bartlett emphasized that the *only* role for aircraft escorting convoys was to get their charges safely through. "There is no excuse," he scolded, for chasing an enemy sighted on the horizon and then have a hostile submarine come up and get several ships."[44]

As pilot Frank Lynch recalled, patrols at Killingholme—and presumably the other stations as well—started at dawn "and sometimes even before the sun came up." Daily activity typically involved two to five patrols in Short floatplanes covering 150 to 250 miles and longer 300-mile patrols in the F2A aircraft. Despite this vigorous activity, "submarine sightings were rare" and often proved to be the tops of sunken ships glimpsed through wind, murk, and cloud. Shortly before turning over his command to Whiting, Porte examined the three years' worth of available flight records and concluded that "the average seaplane on patrol over the North Sea had been compelled to cover an approximate total of twenty-two thousand square miles before sighting an enemy submarine." After sighting the U-boat, the chances of getting within bombing range before the submarine dove for the depths were, at best, "fifty-fifty. And the odds were then one to four against hitting the objective. Compared with all this," finding the proverbial needle in the haystack "was absurdly easy."[45]

Frustration, however, never dampened Yankee enthusiasm. On July 30, while taking pilots up to the British station at South Shields in Yorkshire to ferry two Short aircraft back to Killingholme, Lynch and his flight crew sighted the wake of a submerged submarine about six miles due east of Flamborough Head. "The sub was entirely submerged." Lynch dropped both the bombs he carried on the U-boat's wake and was gratified to observe "large quantities of oil upon the surface." He and his crew were convinced that they had either damaged or sunk the submarine. Later, a member of British naval intelligence informally confirmed the kill, but the American office failed to concur. Lynch had left his wireless set behind to make room for the two supernumeraries and carried no Aldis signaling lamp. Spotting a trawler about five miles away, Lynch landed his aircraft in the usual turbulent sea and reported the enemy's position. "In getting off again in a heaving ground swell, we tore off the step of the boat." Realizing that the next landing would undoubtedly be the damaged aircraft's last, Lynch made posthaste to South Shields, roughly fifty miles up the coast. "The wind was due east and to make a landing close to the beach," it was necessary to cut the engines "while we were still among a lot" of the town's chimneys and smokestacks. Lynch landed the aircraft about fifty yards off the beach, and by the time he was able to turn it around and taxi up the sand, the water aboard the plane was up to a standing man's waist.[46]

Had Lynch sunk, helped sink, or at least badly damaged a submarine? Even a century later, discrepancies exist in the record of German U-boat losses in World War I. Two of the more authoritative sources on the subject agree that no German U-boat was sunk on July 30 or even badly damaged enough to surface and be scuttled. On July 27, UB-107 was destroyed off Scarborough by depth charges from a British trawler and destroyer. Just perhaps Lynch got his dates wrong and at least put the British on to the scent of a damaged U-boat. We shall probably never know.[47]

The final months of the war brought even more frustration to Killingholme. Forty-six new, disassembled H-16s arrived in June aboard the naval supply ship *Jason*, which experienced a "harrowing" twenty-three-day journey across the Atlantic to the north coast of Scotland and then down the North Sea. British and American intelligence were convinced that the Germans had gotten word about the ship and its precious cargo and had "scattered" submarines "along the coast waiting for her." But the Royal Navy provided three destroyers as escorts, and *Jason* reached the Humber safely. The American-designed and -built planes upon which their creators had lavished such care and hope soon exhibited distressing limitations. The Lincoln engines were clearly inferior to the Rolls-Royce power plants that propelled the F2As. "The life of a well-built aeroplane" frame, a contemporary observer wrote, "barring accidents, is about 600 hours of flying. The life of a motor, provided it is run throttled down, is at least 300 hours of running" at one hundred miles an hour. Obviously, the US Navy's aviation mechanics never ran out of work. There were other troubles as well. One pilot complained that the H-16s "were totally unfit for war service." Internally, their fuel tanks had to be shifted, gun mounts had to be built, "bomb gear" had to be installed, and controls required adjustment. Nearly every aircraft suffered from near-fatal torques, probably the result of poorly conceived rotary engines out of sync with the control surfaces they were meant to support, making both wings and tail assemblies heavy, while "imparting a tendency to turn left." British and American flight crews preferred to stick with the F2As, which were much more capable of controlled flight. Unfortunately, these aircraft were flown so incessantly on long-range patrols that unbearable strains were soon put on their capabilities. Thus did Killingholme stagger through the last stages of the war.[48]

Yet public perceptions to the contrary, the U-boat *was* beaten, if not destroyed, a fact that became widely acknowledged as soon as the war ended and records could be compiled and consulted. Initially, death by submarine was a "daily occurrence" among the large convoys that "passed constantly" to and fro between England and the Continent. But "during the five months of aerial patrol in this area, not a single sinking occurred in the presence of airplane patrols except one, and in that case the plane was on the surface of the water, in tow, and obviously unable to take to the air."[49]

Dunkirk air station hosted the headquarters for what was known as the Northern Bombing Squadron, initially manned by Royal Naval Air Service pilots and crews but increasingly leavened with American naval aviators sent from England and other parts of France. The British had been raiding Belgian ports and U-boat bases sporadically since 1916, but with little to show. Both British and, later, American airmen were "frequently diverted to other tasks," and, despite the appearance of four squadrons of the new and impressive Handley-Page night bombers by the end of 1917, together with the lighter D-4 capable of carrying two 230-pound bombs, only 37 percent of the Dover sorties were devoted to attacking Zeebrugge, Bruges, and Ostend. Lines of administration inevitably became more complex as the war transitioned from a relatively static to a fluid state in the spring of 1918. From start to finish, the Bombing Squadron (which would formally become the Northern Bombing Group) was under overall command of the British vice admiral at Dover, who "prescribes the objectives and designates the available free flying time." While frustrated by the nondelivery of their own aircraft, the growing number of Americans took to the skies in whatever was made available to them. Brits and Yanks shared a belief that strategic bombing was on the verge of realization.[50]

By the spring of 1918, impression had hardened into conviction that, despite evidence to the contrary, the U-boats could not be defeated, at least not at sea, nor any time soon. To be sure, transatlantic convoys were getting through with little or no trouble, and enemy submarines were being sunk at a modest rate. But they were still sending Allied ships to the bottom with disheartening, if admittedly reduced, regularity. A host of ships sailing singly, especially after convoys had dispersed near the end of their voyages, remained fair prey. According to a contemporary, "the main point" seemed to be that "Germany could turn out submarines much faster than Allied naval forces could destroy them."[51] In fact, by this stage of the war, German production of all war goods was in dramatic decline, but Allied intelligence apparently was unaware of it.

The prolonged and frustrating nature of the antisubmarine war at last induced planners on both sides of the Atlantic to embrace the long-held convictions of London clubmen that U-boats were far more vulnerable assembled in their bases rather than individually dispersed across several thousand square miles of ocean. If they could be destroyed or seriously damaged in their "nests," the submarine war could be won.[52] Mounting effective air raids across the wide North Sea against the U-boat bases in Germany—Wilhelmshaven and Bremen was clearly impossible, as the Killingholme experience indicated. On the other hand, the majority of the U-boats were based at Bruges, Zeebrugge, and Ostend, on the Flemish coast and were within easy range of aircraft staging out of Dunkirk. In 1915, the first Royal Navy Air Station at Saint Pol had begun operations against German Zeppelin sheds near the Belgian coast that soon expanded to include the enemy's nearby submarine bases as well. Soon, Dunkirk's cramped harbor and nearby airfields were mounting seaplane patrols out into the Channel and bombing raids up the coast. If a heavy and sustained aerial offensive against the U-boats was to be staged, Dunkirk was the obvious place.

The enemy realized this as well and retaliated appropriately. The town soon gained almost as much prominence in the First World War as in the Second. German lines were less than thirty miles away, which allowed the enemy to bring his "Big Berthas" into play. These long-range artillery pieces subjected Dunkirk to unmerciful daily poundings, supplemented by nighttime hit-and-run bomber and destroyer raids. By early 1918 the town had been reduced to a living hell within which its stubborn people hung on grimly. From February on, John Warner Jones, an enlisted navy mechanic, wrote home often of frequent air raids punctuated by shellings "from the land, sea and air." The lad was philosophical. "We lost a little sleep," he told his mother on one occasion, "but as the French say, 'it is all in the war.'" Six months later, he still mentioned "one or two air raids, also a few big shells from land." But by this time, cold and rain affected him more.[53]

In the spring of 1918, the hard-pressed British and French, worn down by years of war in the air as well as on the ground, badly needed reinforcement, no matter how modest. With the enemy clearly poised to mount massive offensives in Flanders and northern France, American naval pilots, among then Ken MacLeish, David Ingalls, Willis Havilland, and "Shorty" Smith, rushed over from Scotland to join the British Royal Flying Corps at Dunkirk. They were later joined by a number of fellow Yale men, including Artemus (Di) Gates. The initial German offensive on the Somme late in March forced Britain's air force to mobilize "every available aviation unit to cover retreating troops, obtain critical intelligence and harass enemy concentrations." The Americans were quickly swept into the British net. The cost to Allied fliers was horrific then and during the remainder of the German trip-hammer assaults. "In one ten-day period in April when fighting in the air reached a crescendo, the RAF [Royal Air Force as it had then become known] lost 478 aircraft." Checked, nonetheless, in his first assault, General Erich von Ludendorff immediately mounted a second massive attack farther north in Flanders, designed to cross the Lys River less than thirty miles from Dunkirk and gain the Channel. Within days, Armentières fell amid fears that the entire coast would have to be abandoned. Haig, the British commander in chief, issued a "backs to the wall" order. The Germans were barely repulsed once again, but the implacable Ludendorff simply shifted the emphasis of attack south to the Aisne. These brutal battles, which cost both sides hundreds of thousands of men, provided a first taste of combat for many of the American flyers.[54]

In the early days of the crisis, Ken MacLeish began engaging in dogfights thousands of feet above the battle lines while a frequent target of German anti-aircraft fire. His reconnaissance flights over the front enthralled the youngster. "Beloved," he wrote his fiancée on April 2, "I went on my first patrol today, and I was full out." He assumed that any "bus" he saw over the battle lines would be German. "We spied some Hun seaplanes off in the distance," obviously on their own patrols out of Zeebrugge. So the Anglo-American formation climbed rapidly toward the sun, reached position, and dove. MacLeish had his target "all picked out," but, focusing on his squadron leader, he lost sight of the enemy momentarily and the target swung quickly away. Chastened, the young flier rejoined his formation as "the old Huns were diving like blazes for shelter." MacLeish managed to fly over one of them. Preparing to attack, he realized with a shock that they were "Allied machines! Do you blame me for feeling cheap?"

The dazzle of being "upstairs" in deep-blue and cloud-flecked skies no less than the prospect of combat together with an unhealthy lack of fear gave the young aviator an enormous kick. "We were quite high this morning, higher than I've ever been before," he wrote three days later. With the distant line of trenches "way below . . . stretching away southward. . . . It was perfectly beautiful too." Four days later, MacLeish found himself "actually on fighting patrols and I actually fly over Hun land." MacLeish's ebullience was in large part due to reaching high altitudes without oxygen. "You know," he wrote to friends, "when you get up real high, about four miles, the air is so rarified that if you move around much or begin to exert yourself, you begin to pant and feel as if you had just run the hundred yard dash. And cold!!!" By this time, Allied and German airmen routinely flew patrols at or even above sixteen thousand feet without oxygen, despite the certainty of hypothermia and hypoxia that could fatally dull senses and reactions. The experience could be exhilarating. "We went way behind Hun lines. You could see the line stretching away in the distance, marked on either side by flecks of smoke from the artillery, and, back aways, the captive" observation balloons tethered to the ground, "mere specks so far down. I had a good look at two of the Hun's biggest bases. It gave me an odd feeling that it was up to me to destroy those cities lying apparently so peacefully, way down there below the clouds." His reverie was quickly interrupted by "Archie's" antiaircraft fire, which "wasn't very friendly, though he wasn't near enough to worry about."

Not every flight was near bliss. On the seventh he wrote his family to apprise them of the "illusions of this flying game. It may be great sport some of the time but when it isn't sport it's positively torture." Ordered to fly in the rain, MacLeish and his mates got "wet, cold, and mad, also frightfully 'Archied' [subject to German antiaircraft fire] as we were low and beautifully silhouetted against the clouds." High-altitude flying "was worse torture than any I had read about." At four thousand feet higher than he had ever flown before, MacLeish froze two fingers, despite heavily layered clothing, while suffering headaches, weakness, and dizziness, though the symptoms disappeared after about a half hour on the ground, except for the headache, which remained "splitting." The veins around his ears "expanded enormously at every heartbeat," entirely shutting down his hearing so that he could hear neither his engine's roar nor the fire from his machine guns "eight or ten inches in front of my face." MacLeish found himself in this "condition" for more than an hour "under some really enterprising" enemy antiaircraft fire.[55]

David Ingalls, who would later become his country's first naval air ace (five confirmed "kills"), was not so fortunate. Although "everyone" worried about the British retreat toward the coast, and thirty-seven of fifty "flights had to move," his diary entries described those days as "dull," "boring," and "dud." "We know little of what is going on." On April 1, he wrote, "Ken went on a patrol today. Lucky bugger." The following day his British mates went on their first "big patrol" without him. Together, George McKay, John Greene, and Maurice Cooper shot down three planes. Following a spot of wretched weather (which obviously did not keep MacLeish grounded), Ingalls at last began flying combat patrols over the Belgian coast. On the eleventh, he wrote laconically of bombing the Zeebrugge docks through heavy antiaircraft fire.

For whatever reasons, in midmonth the RAF abruptly decided it had no further use for the Yankee naval flyers and sent them back to Dunkirk. "Business has been very bad today," MacLeish wrote dolefully on the nineteenth to his fiancée. "The RNAS [Royal Naval Air Service] could use us, but the RAF are too good for us." Di Gates was "way down in the mouth," and Mac-Leish said he and others were "worse." German artillerymen and aviators kept Dunkirk firmly fixed in their sites, requiring officers and men to spend most of their time in underground bunkers. "Sleep became a rare commodity," and boredom again clamped down again tightly. MacLeish, Ingalls, Gates, and the others passed time teaching "the Limeys indoor baseball" and proper ways to play bridge. One day, while starting their "regular afternoon game of baseball" outside, someone hit a high pop fly, and, looking up, the men saw an enemy aircraft through clouds at about seven thousand feet. The boys immediately "grabbed" coats" and "beat it" for their hangars and planes. Ingalls had been in shirtsleeves, and the coat he swiped was thin. Reaching sixteen thousand feet for "about an hour," Ingalls experienced great discomfort with no consoling reward of an enemy kill, "but one fellow, the first one up," caught a Hun "and shot it down, so we feel repaid."[56]

Six weeks later, as the German Flanders offensive ebbed, MacLeish wrote his "Priceless Priscilla" of a "great big project afoot for the USNAF and we'll be in on the ground floor for some cushy jobs soon," unless "they"—meaning Hutch Cone and his ever-inscrutable colleagues on the aviation desks in London and Paris—"live up to their past reputation, or rather their past program of rooking all of us."[57] The project involved an American Northern Bombing Group that would transform the kind of pinprick hit-and-run raids against Ostend and Zeebrugge that Ingalls and others at the Anglo-American air station Dunkirk had been mounting into a massive strategic aerial campaign to end the enemy's Submarine Menace once and for all by bombing his Belgian bases and infrastructure to rubble.

While others contributed to the idea, its most imaginative and successful author was Robert Lovett. Early in 1918, this distinguished member of the

First Yale Unit was in line to command a naval air station in France and, like many others, had concluded that the submarine war was going nowhere. A barrier across the upper North Sea might or might not foil enemy U-boats deploying from German ports, but those operating out of Belgium were simply not being stopped in sufficient numbers. Lovett was an uncommon young man who combined charm, tenacity, courage, and intellect into a powerful character. Once he put his mind to the U-boat problem, Lovett cut through "the welter of schemes and programs some of them plausible, others fantastic" that had begun to appear on aviation desks in Washington, London, and Paris to "present . . . lucid, orderly data" in support of a heavy bombardment campaign. Critical to his success was the bond of trust that he forged with Hutch Cone, who gave him the kind of informal roving commission essential to make his case. Ostensibly preparing for command, Lovett first appeared at Felixstowe, then made a tour of British gunnery and bombing schools, before spending a few weeks with the Royal Naval Air Service intelligence people. Everywhere he went he took copious notes, which he turned into a report upon his return to the Paris Headquarters of the USNAF. Lovett's basic premises were simple enough: "Random" air patrols over the lower North Sea, the English Channel, and the Bay of Biscay had been "a waste of men, time and material." Literally thousands of flight hours had been consumed in fruitless searches for U-boats. When once spotted, wind, clouds, and sea states foiled successful attacks at least half the time. Only "incessant and ferocious bombing" of the Belgian submarine bases "by night and day" could soon make them "untenable."[58]

Lovett believed initially that seaplanes staging out of English and French harbor bases might do the job, but the earlier awkward experiment in strategic bombing from Killingholme seemed to have put paid to that idea. A newfound colleague, US Army lieutenant colonel D. A. Spencer Grey, convinced him that other weapon systems were at hand to do the job in the form of the new British Handley-Page and Italian Caproni heavy bombers, which Lovett soon characterized as "by far the most deadly weapon any of the Allies have yet discovered." In Washington, Marine Corps flyer Albert Cunningham, who had just returned from his European fact-finding mission, joined several navy colleagues to present a different plan to the service's General Board: allow enemy submarines to leave their Belgian ports and then bomb them from seaplanes as they transited "the restricted channels" along the Belgian coast before passing into the English Channel. Killingholme might be too far from German bases across the North Sea, but the naval air stations at Felixstowe and Dunkirk were not far apart and together covered the Channel near its narrowest point. Granted, seaplane operations out of Dunkirk's small, chronically congested harbor would be difficult, but they would be far from impossible and the results gained worth it. Even better would be the use of land-based aircraft staging from fields near the town. A "huge controversy" promptly erupted in both Washington and Europe over the competing proposals and their implications for the war effort.[59]

Shifting from seaplanes to land-based bombers raised numerous issues, from construction of new facilities to the question of daylight versus nighttime bombing, the need to clear the skies of enemy aircraft before a strategic bomber offensive could begin, and so on. With a controversial report from Washington (endorsed by Benson) circulating in both Sims's London headquarters and USNAF Paris, Cone intervened. On March 20, the day before Ludendorff launched his first offensive, Cone ordered Lovett and veteran pilot Eddie McDonnell to Dunkirk "to analyze the entire British bombing operation in Flanders." Over the next days, the two risked their necks flying numerous missions in Royal Naval Air Service Handley-Pages and DH-4s in raids over Bruges. Their accounts read like those of RAF Bomber Command over well-defended German towns and cities a quarter century later.

McDonnell went on his first raid within hours of arrival. The pilot of his Handley-Page, a huge aerial brute for its time, was a Flight Lieutenant Allen, who assigned McDonnell the tail section, manning upper and lower guns. The nighttime raid consisted of four "machines," and Allen brought his bomber across the Bruges docks at fifty-eight hundred feet, dropping his mixed load of 250- and 112-pound missiles "in a line . . . where submarines are housed and repaired and there is much shipping activity." One of the bombs failed to clear and stuck in the bomb bay. McDonnell calmly "shoved this bomb out as we turned and passed over Bruges." German antiaircraft fire was intense and "probably the best in the world." Whenever an aircraft was heard over the dock area at night, enemy gunners let fly a barrage consisting "of a countless number of green luminous balls" extending from near ground level to about ten thousand feet. Allied flyers speculated that the balls were a kind of incendiary designed to inflame enemy marauders when striking canvass wings and fuselages. A "large amount of shrapnel and high explosives" bursting between four and ten thousand feet completed the high-altitude antiaircraft barrage. Those planes flying below four thousand feet could readily be caught in a forest of searchlight beams and "attacked with many large-caliber guns."

Four days later, on March 24, McDonnell went out on a daylight raid in a formation of six smaller DH-9 bombers. His experience anticipated those of the US Eighth and Fifteenth Air Forces over Europe in 1943–44. This time,

McDonnell rode as observer, "which necessitated working the high altitude [bomb] sights and dropping the bombs in addition to fighting the after gun." The bomb load was a far more modest 160 pounds in eight missiles. Rising from the field, the half-dozen planes flew down the coast to Calais and then turned back north at sea, gaining altitude all the way. At fifteen thousand feet, they reached Zeebrugge and turned inland, gliding down to bombing altitude as McDonnell "coached the pilot on a line across the Bruges docks." Dropping his bomb load just before the sight came on, McDonnell and his mates found themselves in the midst of an intense antiaircraft barrage that seemed to lock immediately onto the formation. Rocking and bucking in the turbulent air, several planes were hit; McDonnell's aircraft was holed in one of the wings close to the fuselage, while another "was quite badly shot up, having part of its rudder shot away," a large hole in the side where a shell passed through before exiting the top of the fuselage, and "two machine gun bullets through its forward main spar." The bullets were courtesy of five "German fighting machines" that abruptly materialized as the small bombers exited the scene. Several attacked; one was shot down by another DH-4, while "another came close enough to be engaged by my opposite machine" in the formation "and myself." Placing his gun sights "right on the front" of the attacking German fighter, McDonnell let fly, observing his tracers passing just under the enemy. Since tracers were generally assumed to pass a bit below target, "it is very likely" the enemy fighter was hit. In any case, it broke off "in a steep turn and headed in the opposite direction." Three enemy fighters, however, shadowed the retreating British formation, soon to be joined by a handful of others, all looking to pick off "stragglers" should any motors quit. None did, the enemy at last banked away, and all planes returned safely.[60]

Lovett, too, was determined to gain "practical experience" and flew often over Belgium through "hellish barrage[s] three miles square." He admitted to being more "startled" by the multitude of "flaming onions" that came floating and then rushing up at his plane than of the heavier "Archie" antiaircraft artillery. Later he would admit to being "scared" to look out into the shrapnel- and flame-filled skies. "It wasn't so bad if you were in the first or second machine in the flight formation, but the tail-ender"—*arse-end Charlie* was the term in use by RAF Bomber Command a quarter century later—"caught it where the barrage was well stirred up and going strong. Wow, you were combing those flaming onions out of your hair!"[61]

But Lovett and McDonnell had made the point about strategic bombing, which Cone supported on at least one visit to Dunkirk. Lovett returned to

Paris with definite ideas in mind. Intense and unrelenting night raids yielded ever-greater success; in the final days of an assault, incendiaries should be added to the mix to make the Belgian U-boat bases "untenable, if not stamped off the map." As time passed and the bombing continued, enemy defenses would grow weaker. "Joined with day raids, resistance often grew so feeble that bombing could be accomplished from ever-lower altitudes." Intermittent bombing, on the other hand, was disastrous. Not only did it yield fewer results, but it also allowed the enemy time to rebuild defenses as well as facilities. Finally, relatively large as they were, the Handley-Pages fully loaded "could barely climb to 7000–8000 feet," requiring glide bombing from a thousand feet lower, giving German antiaircraft gunners substantial targets.[62]

Throughout late March and April, intense meetings and conferences took place on both sides of the Atlantic as a northern bombing project took ever-clearer shape. Seaplanes were out. Land-based heavy and light bombers would do the job. In the frustrating absence of suitable American heavy bombers, Sims was forced to reach a barter agreement with Italy to obtain several Caproni aircraft "in exchange for raw materials." Lovett went further than that. Back in December 1917, the Rome government had indicated through its naval attaché in Washington that it would be delighted to have a strong contingent of naval airmen to help patrol the enemy-held upper reaches of the Adriatic with special emphasis on attacking Pola. Upwards of thirty air bases in all would be employed. The request ultimately landed on Cone's London desk, and he sent an experienced subordinate, John Callan, to explore matters. Callan returned convinced that the Italian offer "of training facilities and active stations is so good the Navy should divert men from France," as existing Italian bases "seemed better prepared for combat duties." His idea did not sit well with his old friend Lovett, who was determined that American naval aviators would constitute a substantial component of the emerging Northern Bombing Group. By June, Callan was threatening Lovett with "trouble," suggesting serious bodily harm if Lovett did not stop "butting in my work down here . . . taking away from me the pilots whom I picked to come down here for work." On July 24, 1918, Porto Corsini came on line as the navy's only seaplane patrol station in Italy. It was shortly thereafter that Lovett and his superiors concluded that Caproni bombers were the best aircraft for the Northern Bombing Group and arranged to have some pilots from Dunkirk go down to Italy to fly the planes back across the Alps.[63]

Eddie McDonnell was given command. While the heavies would be used at night, smaller DH-4 aircraft, despite their weak bomb loads, were deemed sufficiently fast and well armed to mount effective daylight raids without fighter escort. The army proved unwilling to provide any training facilities in the United States to assist their navy brethren who turned to the army field at Clermont-Ferrand in France, several facilities in Britain, a Caproni training school in Italy, "and the Marine Corps program in the United States." By May, navy fliers, many from Dunkirk, began drifting into Paris on their way to Clermont-Ferrand to begin work.[64]

There, they found to their dismay that Al Cunningham's zealous lobbying for Marine Corps aviation had paid off. When it materialized, the Northern Bombing Group would be composed of marine pilots bombing by day, with the navy relegated to nighttime raids. Ken MacLeish and his colleagues were devastated. "We saw our dreams of a crack naval squadron that we had striven so hard to obtain and perfect sort of vanishing into thin air," Freddie Beach lamented. "The whole thing—that wonderful dream—is crumbling away under our very eyes," MacLeish added in a letter home. The marines were "childish enough to prevent the navy from fighting side by side in the same cause with them because they know darn well the navy pilots are better than theirs are."[65]

Two weeks earlier, the 82nd Wing, including the 218th Squadron, a composite unit that MacLeish and another navy pilot would soon join, had been attached to the RAF's Fifth Group. By mid-July, MacLeish was part of a thirteen-plane day-bombing group that began pounding the Zeebrugge docks and nearby facilities. Two days later, he undertook a "third and final" raid with the 218th as part of eleven bombers that hit the same area. The next morning he awoke with the Spanish flu. Hospitalized for the next month, the Yale flyer was then assigned a series of frustrating desk jobs in Paris and Eastleigh. Dave Ingalls, meanwhile, flew Sopwith Camels with RAF 213 Squadron patrolling over the front, engaging in frequent strafing runs over enemy infantry and artillery positions and dogfighting with the enemy. Before being recalled in October, the Yale flier shot down the five enemy aircraft required to become an ace.

Di Gates fashioned his own legend. In early August, news came by radio that one of the British Handley-Page bombers pounding the Belgian ports had crashed in the sea off Ostend within range of German guns. "Gates dashed to a moored flying boat" as an escort of Sopwith Camels was quickly organized. The American did not wait for them but took off, flew north, and spotted the wrecked plane, "the downed fliers hanging on to each wing" as enemy shells burst around them. Gates's arrival prompted enemy dispatchers to send out their nearby pontoon-equipped fighter planes, which arrived just as Gates "splashed down" near the Handley-Page. As the Sopwith Camels arrived, they kept the Germans "at bay" while Gates taxied his flying boat around to both pilots, got them aboard, "and was just able to start his plane and lift off for home." Determined to keep flying despite being promoted to commanding officer and winning numerous awards for this action, Gates was shot down later that summer. Captured, he escaped after a time and was literally within feet of reaching the Swiss border when he was caught and sent back to captivity for the few remaining weeks of the war.[66]

Down at Porto Corsini in northern Italy, Ensign C. H. Harmon replicated Gates's rescue with one of his own. During a bombing raid against the enemy port and submarine base across the northern Adriatic at Pola, Harmon landed his shot-up seaplane next to that of downed colleague G. H. Ludlow, who had crashed "just outside the harbor." Harmon took Ludlow aboard and then carefully steered his damaged aircraft through heavy seas, got aloft, and flew the seventy-five miles back to his Italian base. Like Gates, Harmon was highly decorated for his courage.[67]

Barely nineteen at the time, David Ingalls displayed a remarkable coolness and maturity. Apparently unattached and not too close to those at home, he wrote copious diary entries that dramatized the frantic, exhausting air war of the moment when pilots were shuffled from squadron to squadron, place to place, as demand dictated. On October 1, there was "no rest for the wicked," as his squadron was awakened before daylight, given coffee and bread, and sent aloft "to strafe. Everyone expects each trip to be the final one for him"; all prayed to be shot down and taken prisoner, not killed. To prepare for that eventuality, "fellows" took along various keepsakes: a girlfriend's photo in a pocket, gold pieces sown in clothes, razors, toothbrushes. It was all silliness to young Ingalls. "I figured to Hell with the stuff, you couldn't fool the devil's habitat for any appreciable length of time by taking along a few lumps of ice, so I just stuck a box of cartridges in my pocket" for the .32 automatic he always carried. "The gun is to me my rabbit's foot."

Ken MacLeish at last got back in the air when he relieved Ingalls in mid-October. The youngster happily rejoined his old RAF mates in 213 Squadron, flying patrol over enemy lines in Sopwith Camels. "In a wild melee over Belgium," MacLeish bagged his first kill of the war. Taking off again in late afternoon, the boy who had wondered on the way over if he was man enough and mature enough for combat never returned. For months, as the Armistice came and the first American units prepared to head home, nothing was known of MacLeish's fate. Late that December, a Belgian farmer returning to his ruined property discovered the body of "a fully dressed American naval aviator," lying in the yard and nearby his wrecked Sopwith Camel.[68] Shot twice in the head, Ken MacLeish had doubtless died instantly.

By the time MacLeish relieved Ingalls, the Northern Bombing Squadron that had at last begun serious operations found precious little left to fly against. Having absorbed Ludendorff's hammer blows for four and a half months, the Allies and their Yank associates had gone over to the offensive on August 8, a day Ludendorff called the blackest in the history of the German Army. British, French, and American forces assaulted the now exhausted but ever-game German armies with hammer blows of their own. Bounced out of their advanced positions, first in France, then in Flanders, the hard-pressed but undefeated *Soldaten* retreated stubbornly toward a Germany now bitterly divided to the point of revolution by questions of peace or war, social justice, and the economic survival of the home front. The following month, the Northern Bombing Squadron at last became the Northern Bombing Group, as a sufficient number of aircraft were received from factories in Britain and France, from Italy, and from the American assembly plant at Pauillac to allow operations "as a distinct unit." By this time, the British army was chasing the Germans out of Flanders, causing bombing missions to lose much of their strategic value. On October 22, young navy mechanic John Warner Jones wrote his mother from Dunkirk, "We haven't had an air raid for a month. I don't think there will be many more air raids on Dunkerque as the front is too far to bombard us."[69]

Ostend and Zeebrugge were raided early in October, even as the enemy was carrying out mass evacuations of the towns and U-boat bases. For all practical purposes, the air war against the submarine was over. Thereafter, the group turned its attention to day and night raids "on various" enemy "objectives," the first being a raid October 13 on the enemy railroad lines at Thielt. The last of eight similar raids concluded on October 27. Apparently, Captain Hanrahan, or perhaps the naval aviation desk in Paris, then offered the services of the four marine and four navy squadrons to Pershing, who declined, saying that the entire group should maintain its support of the steadily advancing British armies in the North. Within weeks, the war was over. As with the Northern Barrage and the anticipated employment of masses of subchasers at Queenstown, the November Armistice, in the words of one caustic contemporary, "upset a great many plans and spoiled many enterprises."[70]

Despite the Submarine Menace and the promise of aviation, the peoples of 1918 understood what historians would later conclude: that Britain's Grand Fleet was the linchpin of the entire war effort, "the only barrier that lay between a decent earth and a fiendish, Hunnish chaos." This "complex steely fabric of ships" was "the real power behind the anti-submarine campaign." Should it somehow be defeated, Germany would control the sea approaches to Europe; its battle cruisers as well as U-boats would readily starve Britain into submission.[71]

To many in the Admiralty, Washington's grudging and long-delayed decision to bolster a fleet shaken by the near-run victory at Jutland was a matter of too little, if not too late. A month before *Florida, New York, Delaware*, and *Wyoming* braved Atlantic gales to reach Scapa Flow, the Admiralty's director of plans, Rear Admiral Roger Keyes, argued that the entire force of coal-burning Yankee battleships should be induced to come across. Anticipating "considerable development in the naval situation . . . next year," Keyes stated that "various contingencies may arise rendering the presence of the U.S.A. dreadnought battlefleet urgently necessary in the North Sea." From the beginning, the Admiralty, whose intelligence on enemy ship construction and availability was never robust, feared a sudden eruption by a rejuvenated German fleet into the North Sea or Atlantic at a moment when a significant portion of the Grand Fleet was laid up for routine maintenance or refit. During the final two years of the war, the Admiralty believed, erroneously, that the enemy had achieved a "substantial edge" in new battle cruiser construction. Commander in chief of the Grand Fleet, Admiral Sir David Beatty, went so far as to urge the War Cabinet to buy several battle cruisers that were being built in British yards for Japan.

Nonetheless, not everyone at the Admiralty was enamored of an American contribution. Keyes believed that a US battleship force could not operate effectively with the Grand Fleet, "either in a strategical or tactical sense," without months of preparation. For this reason, they must come at once. His frustration with the situation was palpable. "It is difficult to see arguments," including Washington's growing concern with Japanese appetites in the Far Western Pacific, "which keep the American battlefleet immobilized on the other side of the Atlantic." The admiral admitted that the very latest Yankee battlewagons might not fit British needs, since they were oil powered and the U-boat offensive had taken a heavy toll of Britain's precious stocks. But the Americans also had ten modern and rather recently commissioned coal burners that Britain's vast coal reserves could accommodate. If all ten were "sent over" to the Grand Fleet "now," two could be sent back to Norfolk or New York at any one time for upkeep and repair. The continued presence of eight American capital ships would guarantee Allied naval supremacy for as long as the war lasted.[72]

Keyes wrote from ignorance. After April 1917, America's formidable sea power was stretched as badly that of Great Britain to meet an ever-growing number of commitments. In its eighteen months of war, the United States Navy would grow from 70,000 to 538,000 officers and men. Where could it find the personnel to administer steadily growing training camps while providing the professional nucleus for the antisubmarine vessels that were either being hastily built or reconverted in yards all across the nation? As it was, those destroyer sailors who could be spared were being sent home from Queenstown and Brest to man new construction almost as soon as they gained aptitude. In the spring of 1917, an immediate need arose for several hundred experienced gunners to form the nucleus of the armed guards that were being hastily placed aboard as many merchantmen and transports as possible. The need became less urgent thereafter, but it never entirely disappeared. The only source of skilled manpower resided aboard Mayo's Atlantic Fleet battleships, which were stripped "substantially" of their crews to meet the sudden wartime needs of the service. Hundreds of young men had to be trained hastily as replacement crew, even as the big ships added several hundred more men to come up to wartime manning needs. Raw recruits would be sent to the shoreside training centers for a few weeks of preliminary indoctrination, "and then to the battleships in Chesapeake Bay for a finishing course of several weeks, including the actual firing of guns at target practice." Finally, the boys were either kept aboard their particular battleship to fill in the crew or transferred to other ships "in active service at sea."[73]

By the time that *Florida* and her sisters were sent across the Atlantic, this training cycle had been in place for some months, inevitably resulting in less than optimally trained crews. During the first weeks of their sojourn with the Grand Fleet as Battle Squadron Six, the contingent's overall gunnery officer, Commander Husband E. Kimmel, had his hands full bringing his gun teams up to British standards. When *Texas* arrived in early February after a typically stormy winter passage that resulted in the loss of several topmasts and the smashing of lashed-down on-deck gear and small boats, her proficiency proved as woeful as that of her sisters earlier. Steaming at near full speed of nineteen knots down the gunnery range at the western end of Pentland Firth, the battleship fired fifty-five rounds of "reduced" shells from its fourteen-inch guns at a target nearly eleven thousand yards away. The unknown author(s) of the ship's history admitted without further elaboration that results were "poor as the majority of the men were green and many had never seen a 14inch gun until they came aboard and few had ever seen or heard one fired." When the big vessel returned to the range the following week, the gunnery department recorded a "marked improvement."[74]

The general objective of the Grand Fleet and its American contingent was simply to maintain dominance of the North Sea. Within this overall responsibility was the hope of inducing all or a sizable portion the Hochseeflotte into decisive battle.[75] More specific aims were the protection of Allied convoys coming across the three hundred or so miles from Norway to the Orkney bases with critical war supplies. German destroyer and cruiser raids in October and early December 1917 had nearly wiped out two convoys and their escorts. Clearly, some capital ship protection was required, and the reinforcement of the Grand Fleet by American battleships provided the guarantee. Soon enough, Beatty, his men, and the Americans were assigned a third mission—protection for the British and American minelayers setting down the Northern Barrage. With the enemy never making an appearance while they were at sea, America's battleship boys found their frequent sorties defined by tedium and discomfort.[76]

But Beatty never relented in his mission. A controversial leader and seaman possessed of a somewhat unstable if vainglorious personality, he was, nonetheless, a genuine British sea dog and took his ships and people out into the storm-tossed waters of the North Sea as often as possible. To underscore his determination, the commander ordered that no vessel in his Grand Fleet should allow its fuel capacity to fall below 71 percent. Between January and November 1918, the Sixth Battle Squadron made twenty-six separate sorties.[77]

The first was, as so many others would be, a "baiting" cruise, begun in the "black" of a Scapa Flow winter night to avoid the enemy submarines thought to be "laying forever" at the harbor's narrow mouth. Leaving under these conditions had become routine for the British sailor; to his American opposite, it was a "revelation," a triumph of machinery, "a delicate clock, a gyrocompass, a patent log, and a little group of men in each hull," controlling "the destiny of nations." The fleet usually had steam up for relatively quick departure, and when the orders came from the flagship, "blinker lights flashed from scores of British ships," piercing the gloomy scene. "Then the dark hillsides roundabout re-echoed to the harsh clank of chain cables as anchors lifted. After that the black night and silence, and great ships stealing slowly toward the headlands and the fairway, . . . winding through" numerous antisubmarine nets and minefields, past the rocks and shoals of Pentland Firth, masked by its often turbulent waters, and on out to sea. Long before, British sailors had learned to ease the strain of complex maneuvers by great numbers of ships in confined spaces. "In the very center" of Scapa Flow—an almost perfectly round harbor twelve miles in diameter—lay a cluster of rocks called the Barrel of Butter that provided a perfect navigation point for departure. Each vessel—large and small—"always" made a complete turn around the Barrel of Butter in order to straighten out steaming lines and allow each ship to take its proper place in column.[78]

At sea, once a typical wan gray day broke, the majesty of the British Grand Fleet was on display. To awestruck Americans, it was "a veritable cordon of living steel, touching the arc of heaven either way." Here was an enormous "pack in full cry, belching dense volumes of black smoke as" it "sped on defiantly to catch the scent. Millions of dollars and thousands of men!" Then and later, the enemy never appeared, but in the beginning that was a minor point for the Yanks, who, once under way, all too quickly discovered how little they knew, how much they had to learn. A British officer noted that the American battlewagons "dropped out of the skies, plop into the middle" of a Grand Fleet that was the culmination of more than two centuries of naval supremacy, one that fancied itself "the oldest and most conservative—if not the proudest—navy in the world." Now, the Americans were being "grafted on" to this "great parent tree." The experience was initially demoralizing. In training camps across northwestern France, Pershing was slowly fashioning the AEF into an effective fighting force by keeping it from battle for long months, as raw troops drilled and trained, trained and drilled, working out problems as they went. But there was no time for leisurely training on the North Sea. "We found ourselves at once in the enemy's territory, supposedly ready for attack, a new unit of great force which had been drilled to the utmost perfection; operating in formations and deployments entirely new." The signal gangs had to employ a "totally strange system" of flags and codes, forgetting "at once their life's work" to begin all over again. "It was day and night for them, but they stuck to it." During the first cruises, mistakes were made that caused people on every American bridge and chart house to gasp in dismay. Slowly, the mistakes diminished and then "faded completely away." The radiomen found themselves in equal plight, as they encountered changed atmospheres, new sources of interference—"a myriad of them"—different Hertzian wave lengths, and "strange operators to receive from." To men who had long prided themselves on their professionalism, the experience was "disheartening." But here they were at sea with battle impending. There was nothing else to do but "carry on" in the British tradition until they, too, became adept and then could proudly claim a new expertise that the Royal Navy high command never accepted. To the end, Beatty privately confided his belief that the Americans were an "incubus to the Grand Fleet," however much their presence might contribute to Allied morale.[79]

The North Sea proved a harsh mistress. On February 5, 1918, Beatty wrote his wife that he "was sending old Rodman out on an operation of his own. . . . I trust they will come to no harm." The assignment was protection of the Norwegian convoys, and on this their first sortie alone, nature put on a beguiling display that it never repeated. The battleships with an escort of British destroyers and light cruisers slipped out of Scapa Flow on the night of the sixth, the atmosphere "crystal clear, seeming to magnify each star a dozen times." The quiet water glowed with their luster. Then, early in the midwatch (midnight to 4:00 a.m.), the skies suddenly blazed with the green, pulsating streamers of the aurora borealis. Each battlewagon and escort suddenly appeared as distinct, dark silhouette, a perfect target, all agreed uneasily, for lurking U-boats that soon appeared, at least in the hyperimaginations of America's battleship boys. Roughly an hour and a half into the new day, and for nearly fifty minutes thereafter *Florida*, *Delaware*, and *Wyoming* believed they were under U-boat attack. The battleships claimed that they had successfully evaded four torpedoes, fired by one or more enemy submarines, one of whose periscopes lookouts were certain they had spotted.[80]

Such benign weather seems never to have occurred again. Occasionally, a high might slip through the upper North Sea for a few hours, permitting awed sailors to glimpse the snowy mountains of Norway as they lingered outside Bergen or Stavanger after releasing one convoy and waiting for the one homeward bound. But usually, gray winter skies wept snow or sleet while unleashing howling bitter cold gales that occasionally approached hurricane force. The waters were continually roughed up and often came aboard even the biggest ships, either in waves or in bursts of icy spindrift, making topside life always uncomfortable and especially dangerous if one had to on slippery decks, lashing down gear. The continued pitch and roll of great hulls caught in vicious cross- or following seas accentuated the jeopardy, and more than one sailor was abruptly pitched overboard with a scream of dismay to a sudden soaking, freezing death. Spring, summer, and autumn rains were common, and the sea was often wreathed in heavy fog under the customarily gloomy skies. Nature's discomforts and dangers were accentuated by man, for even in 1917–18 the vast majority of the king's ships, large and small, and all of the American battleships attached to the Grand Fleet still burned coal. Two-, three- and four-stack vessels belching the wretched black stuff into the skies added to the murk.

Frustration compounded discomfort. Once the fleet cleared anchorage, and often before, rumors abounded. They were going to bombard Helgoland or Zeebrugge; no, the Hun was out in full force and might be met at any moment.

General Quarters frequently sounded, and once, aboard *Texas*, emergency rations were laid by the primary and secondary batteries in anticipation of imminent battle. The enemy might be ready to fight the entire Anglo-American force. Or perhaps he was waiting to whittle down the Grand Fleet incrementally, pouncing full strength on that portion of it (often the Americans) protecting the Norwegian convoys or the minelayers of the Northern Barrage. Frequent U-boat contacts and a few outright sightings accentuated nervous excitement.[81]

The final abortive thrust of the Hochseeflotte took place during the third week in April 1918. By this time the German surface navy was in dire straits. After nearly two years swinging around the anchor chains at Wilhelmshaven while their own and their country's fortunes slowly declined, the crews were sullen and on the verge of outright mutiny. There had been something of the sort the previous August when four hundred sailors from the battleship *Prinzregent Luitpold* had left their ship and marched through the streets of Wilhelmshaven, demanding an end to the war. Quickly snuffed, the incident revealed an eroding mood within a decaying fleet. Eight months later, with no improvements in sight, Reinhard Scheer realized that something drastic had to be done; some sort of fleet engagement had to be risked. The best opportunity to disrupt Allied supply lines while confronting inferior enemy forces seemed to be the Norwegian convoys. Fall upon one or both, destroy their escorts, and morale might well be restored not only in the fleet but also on the home front. Scheer concealed his plans masterfully, gathering his fleet in the Helgoland Bight by open radio signals but ostensibly for battle practice. At the Admiralty in London, Room 40 was lulled into complacence, concentrating on supporting a desperate and failed naval assault on Zeebrugge. While the Home Fleet, including the American Sixth Battle Squadron, lay temporarily in the Firth of Forth off Edinburgh, the targeted convoys to and from Norway were lightly covered by a single British battle cruiser squadron and a handful of accompanying cruisers and destroyers. The heavy German force, led by Admiral Franz von Hipper's battle cruisers, began to creep into the bight on the night of the twenty-second, followed by the main battle force commanded by Scheer.

Even before the bight could be crossed, however, wretched luck suddenly laid the German plans low. The big, modern battle cruiser *Moltke* suffered a catastrophic engine-room failure, forcing Hipper to turn back toward Scheer's force and, worse, to break radio silence to inform his commander of events. British listening posts immediately picked up the messages, and submarines patrolling off the bight soon informed the Admiralty that the Germans seemed indeed to be coming out in force. Beatty promptly got up steam and left his

Scottish anchorage to intercept. His overwhelming force consisted of thirty-one battleships (including the Americans) and four battle cruisers. Unaware that his scheme had been unmasked, but burdened by the crippled *Moltke*, Scheer decided to put back to port with his main force, including the wretched Moltke , but ordered Hipper to press on and attack the convoys with his remaining battle cruisers. *Moltke* was further damaged by a torpedo from a lurking British submarine, but managed to stagger back to its anchorage. Hipper got within forty-six miles of Stavanger, but further delays caused by the need to slow his ships down in heavy fog caused him to miss both convoys. Prudently, he scuttled back to port before Beatty could catch him. Halpern speculates that had the Sixth Battle Squadron been covering one of the Norwegian convoys at the time and had it met the German fleet alone, the American force probably would have been severely mauled, given its relatively poor gunnery.[82]

While the Grand Fleet's North Sea sorties were frequent (and seldom predictable), they were of brief duration, lasting little more than five or six days, given the short distances between the British Isles and the coasts of Northwest Europe or Scandinavia. But Beatty—like Rodman—was determined to work his sailors hard in order to keep them in fighting trim. Beatty had developed the same kind of pessimism that his predecessor in command of the Grand Fleet had suffered after Jutland: for all his surface confidence and bonhomie, the new fleet commander reposed no more trust in either his ships or his sailors than did the old. It explains why Beatty was at once delighted to see American reinforcements, yet quietly questioned their quality at every turn.

Life at Scapa Flow, and, to a lesser extent in the Firth of Forth where the fleet briefly based itself on two occasions, had its own tensions and stresses, chief among which were the never-ending winds of Scapa Flow. According to the ship's informal history, "It was blowing a hurricane the day the Texas arrived, and from that day on until the day the warship bade the base goodbye for her homeward voyage, the wind never seemed to let up for a minute. Even on those rare occasions when the sun would break through the bleakness of the sky, the wind continued howling—always and forever blowing." Edward Beach Sr., who came over in September 1918 to take command of *New York*, claimed that "not once" in his three months at Scapa Flow or cruising the perpetually stormy waters of the North Sea did he see sunshine. "It was always foggy and rainy. Though the thermometer ranged between 45 and 50 degrees, while I was there I felt colder than in good honest zero weather."[83]

Gunnery drills of all sorts were frequent; so were those involving paravanes. Antisubmarine scares were routine. Personnel and compartment inspections came often. Supplies of stores and ammunition had to be continually replaced, requiring more backbreaking work. Rodman insisted that his ships be spic-and-span at every moment, representing as they did the might of the United States Navy in European waters. Every hours-long coaling was followed by "field days" that could consume as much as another twenty-four hours, as ships—and crews—were returned to pristine physical condition.

Rodman later admitted that "during a whole year no liberty or leave worth mentioning was granted except occasionally for a few hours" at Scapa Flow and especially on the few occasions when the squadron visited the Firth of Forth. New York's refit at Newcastle in February 1918 was an exception. Young Fred Hunter recalled that "for eleven consecutive months," prior to the refit and leave, "with the exception of four nights, the officers and men of the Flagship New York slept aboard their vessel." In World War I, a man's battleship truly was his castle. Initially, the Newcastle refit involved more backbreaking work. No sooner had the great battleship entered drydock than the crew "swarmed" over the side on stage planks hung by lines all around to clean the hull. "With brooms and scrapers they worked in their filthiest clothes, all day, lowering their stages to follow the receding water down the slimy hull." This time in port, however, there would be rewards. While "no one was allowed away from the ships after dark, nor for a period of more than four hours at a time during the day, and then only in the immediate vicinity of the ships," outright leave was another matter. Fully half the crew would obtain it once their cleaning was completed. Hunter is characteristically vague just how far and for how long the enlisted men were let loose, but officers got leave for days and some, including Hunter, went over to France, where their "probative orders" kept them away from "the real front" but allowed them to experience air raids over Boulogne and time to taste "the wild side of Paris," so "fascinating" and "unlike that to be found elsewhere in the world."[84]

Fearing a possible enemy air raid across the North Sea, Rodman also insisted that his five big warships "be completely closed and darkened from sunset to sunrise. In winter," he admitted, "this meant from fifteen to eighteen hours a day. . . in a cold raw climate, when at times it seemed impossible to keep warm." The medical staffs were kept busy preventing major outbreaks of illness. The Spanish flu had yet to break out in the United States, where the first mass cases were not identified until mid-September 1918. But Texas suffered several cases of diphtheria. On one occasion, her executive officer, Commander John W. Timmons, was so stricken that he never returned from the hospital ashore.[85]

Monotony was broken by the usual stratagems that men employ when grim existence forces them back on their own resources. The British had built a crude YMCA hut on Flotta Island, near the Barrel of Butter, and there Yanks and tars put on occasional stage productions for each other. *Texas* hosted a minstrel show complete with blackface actors and "harem girls" in costumes ordered from London. Soon, all of the crews engaged in competitive vaudeville shows, to many of which their British cousins were invited as room allowed. The battleships had also brought across a number of motion pictures, which were shown nightly, as situations allowed. Wherever American soldiers or sailors congregated, however, athletics were the center of entertainment. Boxing "smokers" were held periodically aboard *Texas* and her sisters, and every battlewagon in the Sixth Squadron fielded baseball and football teams. The *Texas* baseball team was so good that Rodman permitted it to travel south to play several army teams in England. While the boys lost, they claimed that their game at Sheffield drew twenty-five thousand, not only American servicemen but also curious Brits.[86]

On the first of two occasions when the entire Grand Fleet anchored in the Firth of Forth, officers were permitted liberty in Edinburgh; the men, however, were restricted to the little town of South Queensbury or Dunfirmline on the firth's north shore, with its "quiet little houses and streets" that the Yanks sought to enliven by meeting and strolling with attractive Scottish lasses. On the second visit, all hands were permitted to visit Edinburgh itself. On July 4–5, the men of the Sixth Battle Squadron were given liberty to go to the "primitive old" Orkney town of Kirkenwall, roughly eight miles from the Flow.[87]

Good fortune smiled on *New York* one last time. Steaming at near full speed through Pentland Firth one night in September, it struck a sharp underwater object. The big craft was clearly damaged, and it promptly steamed south to the Royal Navy dockyard at Rosyth in the Firth of Forth. When the last drop had drained from the dock, the battleship's battered hull stood revealed. "Three blades of the starboard propeller were gone," and several hundred feet forward the hull had been pushed in some twelve to twenty-four inches. Had *New York* hit a submerged U-boat? There was and is some evidence that it had and that the enemy submarine might have sunk as a result. Captain Beach's response then and later was a grunted "maybe."[88]

No other aspect of the American battleship presence in British waters during the final year of the war carried such diplomatic and political importance for the future as did the social function they performed. (Nine eventually served, including *Arkansas*, which replaced *Delaware* in the summer of 1918, plus the three battlewagons that would be assigned to Berehaven late that August). From the arrival of Joe Taussig's destroyer contingent on, the social life of American naval officers in port towns, on airfields, and on and off ships was intense. Whenever duties permitted, they attended teas, dinners, and the occasional ball hosted by their British counterparts and superiors. They golfed and played tennis with their Royal Navy opposites, and they entertained in turn, especially on board the battleships of the Sixth Division. All of the battlewagons—particularly *New York*, which flew Rodman's flag from beginning to end and was thus the showboat of the division—were bombarded with visitors. Despite never-ending prospects of sudden departures to chase the elusive Hun, kings of England and of Belgium with their ladies and impressive retinues appeared on *New York*, *Texas*, and the other vessels. Generals and admirals abounded. Beatty was frequently piped aboard. So was Sims, with Benson in tow, during the frequent times that the chief of naval operations was in Europe. Rodman was forever visiting each of his five ships whenever generally wretched weather permitted. Other senior flag officers of the Royal Navy were always about giving their Yankee cousins a friendly but keen eye. High-level civil officials from Washington (most notably Assistant Navy Secretary Franklin D. Roosevelt) trod the decks as well. Each visitor from European and English courts or nearby British ships wished to see all he could from foretops (seldom) to engine rooms (often). The hosts could afford no mistakes or lapses. Optics had to be absolutely clear, machinery brilliantly bright, and bridges, wardrooms, and all other compartments immaculate.

Here, the great enemy was not the Hun but coal. Thanks to Beatty's insistence on near-full bunkers at all times, coal barges and colliers greeted the Grand Fleet as soon as it anchored, either in Scapa Flow or in the Firth of Forth. Coaling could take place day or night because for most of the year in these high northern latitudes, darkness ruled; the sun was at best a wan and fleeting presence. Duration depended on the size of the ship. Coaling the small destroyers at Queenstown or Brest was a relatively quick affair. For *Florida* and her sisters, the process took hours and when it involved "the unusually dirty Cardiff coal" was always exhausting, vile, and smelly.[89] Dust flew about with every bag deposited on deck. Machinery and optics became begrimed with the stuff; so did desks, officers' bunks, sailors' hammocks, mess decks, and wardroom galleys. No part of a ship, however large or small, could escape. Neither could the several hundred coal-passing deckhands and engine-room personnel who found dark grit ground deep in fingernails, eyelids, and more private parts of their anatomy. Added to the coaling residue from port was that which remained from hard steaming at sea, though much of the deposits above deck were largely washed overboard by rain and seas.

Those not immediately involved in coaling viewed their foreign visitors with awe. "History was being made" on summer days in 1918, one noted, when the great leaders of an alliance in crisis came aboard, turning every battleship into a diplomatic salon. To the ships' crews, the visitors and guests were "irksome," because they caused work and more work "far out of hours" to ensure the ship was in "glistening" condition. In early July, the Grand Fleet patrolled the Jutland area briefly and then returned to port. Aboard *New York*, "a tired, dirty ship and crew dropped anchor in the Firth of Forth" and promptly began the "ordeal" of coaling. Amid "the dirt and exhaustion" came word that the king and queen of Belgium would be visiting the Sixth Battle Squadron the next day and would board *New York* for a formal inspection. A "tired and sea worn" crew completed coaling at midnight and then turned in for five hours and arose to "accomplish the impossible." In nine hours, a thirty-thousand-ton, 580-foot "filthy, sooty, mass of grime" was transformed into "a scoured, holystoned, painted ship manned by a spotless, polished crew" in dress-blue uniforms, "each at his post of inspection." Elitist-minded officers believed the men to be amply rewarded for their brutal labors by a fleeting contact, if contact at all, "with the world's great leaders in the world's most desperate crisis."[90]

The final infusion of American sea power into the Great War of 1914–18 occurred in August, when two of the nation's newest and mightiest battleships— oil burners both—sailed into Bantry Bay under the command of Rear Admiral Thomas S. Rogers. *Oklahoma* and *Nevada* were followed shortly thereafter by *Utah*, *Florida*'s coal-burning sister. The three battlewagons came over to Berehaven in response to stubborn fears in both the Admiralty and Navy Department that, while the Hochseeflotte seemed well and truly beaten, one or more of its battle-cruiser squadrons might undertake a last desperate dash into the Atlantic to destroy convoys bringing thousands of American troops to the western front just as the Allied–American offensive was beginning to roll.[91]

Thinking on this matter, especially in London, presumed a war lasting into 1919. Were that the case, then recollections of the damage done in the world shipping lanes by two modestly armed German merchant cruisers several years before took on new meaning. In the "prolonged darkness" of the coming late-autumn and winter months, "a ship with no lights and a little luck" could readily sneak past—perhaps even pause to destroy—the thin line of British armed merchant cruisers that constituted the ongoing upper North Sea surface patrol. Sailing west, then bending south, a German battle cruiser or two could pass through the Iceland–United Kingdom gap to gain the "high seas and broad Atlantic." While convoys were clearly the best means of frustrating the U-boats, their very concentration of shipping made them prime targets for surface raiders. By midsummer 1918, American troops were crossing the Atlantic by the scores of thousands each month, and the doughboys who had preceded them were already exerting the "most decisive results upon the battlefield." The loss of one or two transports would not have stopped the American juggernaut, but might have improved morale in Germany and depressed that in England and the United States.

"But what exercised" Beatty "the most" was a possible German raid on the Northern Barrage. In that case, three more American battlewagons, even if based some hundreds of miles away, would constitute a further deterrence to whatever designs Reinhard Scheer (who had just taken over as head of the German Admiralty Staff) might have in mind. In the event, Battleship Division Nine left its Bantry Bay anchorage only once, in October for several days, as escort for a convoy of troop transports on false reports that German "cruisers" might be out and about in the Atlantic. "We picked them up in pretty thick weather," one battleship sailor recalled, "and escorted them to somewhere within the English Channel before we turned them over to local escort." Otherwise, the three battlewagons spent their time swinging around their anchor chains while crews drilled frequently, mostly aboard ship. Boredom was rampant, countered as elsewhere by recreational visits to a nearby British YMCA and strenuous rounds of athletics that emphasized sailing competition. Admiral Rogers spent a good bit of time negotiating with Bayly at Queenstown regarding a proper destroyer escort for his big ships if and when they sortied into the Atlantic, while the medical teams aboard *Oklahoma* and *Nevada* at Berehaven fought a serious outbreak of the Spanish flu that carried off a half-dozen of *Oklahoma's* crew, including the gunnery officer, who had been in the midst of a promising career. Olaf Hustvedt, a younger gunnery officer on *Oklahoma*, remembered "caskets being shipped out of our base at Bantry Bay daily for a matter of weeks." Up in Scapa Flow, *Arkansas* suffered 259 cases of the flu by Armistice Day; eleven men died.

The division's most exciting moment came the day after the Armistice, when outraged Sinn Feiners attacked a group of *Oklahoma* sailors as they left the battleship for liberty. "The onslaught backed the unsuspecting sailors toward the end of the dock where several fell off and nearly drowned in the frigid waters." Enraged *Oklahoma* crewmen "took revenge with their fists" the next day in a restaurant that they all but wrecked. Learning of the incident, Rogers ordered his crews to pass the hat and took the money to the mayor "as compensation." Both the division and the Irish were doubtless glad to see the battleship boys get out of town soon after.[92]

★ ★ ★ ★ ★

So went America's ocean war as the final weeks slipped by. Navy fliers patrolled the North Sea and bombed the enemy from Zeebrugge on the Channel to Pola on the Adriatic. The subchasers in their packs of three hunted U-boats off Portsmouth and Queenstown and at Otranto; the Sixth Battle Squadron with the Grand Fleet continued its sweeps and escort work, while American and British minelayers strove to complete the Northern Barrage. At Brest, "forty-one destroyers, some yachts, and mine-sweepers" continued to bring in the transports crowded with doughboys and cargo ships crammed with the stores and sinews of war. At Gibraltar, thirty-five American warships joined their allies in escorting Mediterranean convoys as well as those between the Rock and Great Britain."

To the end, the destroyers and armed yachts carried the brunt of naval operations. Sailing through the stormy waters of the Western Approaches toward the French coast, his majesty's destroyers and those of the "associated power" from across the ocean "gyrate[d] in the slightest sea . . . like maddened switchback cars." Perpetually "grimy with the soot of fuel oil, reeking with oil gasses," they "reeled and plunged at express train speed," even in calm seas. Day and night, sun, cloud, and rain, officers and men alike stood on narrow bridges, "half-choked with frequent backdrafts of gaseous oil smoke" and fumes from the galley stack, while "peer[ing] ahead through a blizzard of flying spray" for any sight of the enemy. Down in the tiny wardrooms aboard American destroyers, "colored" mess attendants "balance[d] like acrobats and with the expertness of long experience" performed "almost impossible feats of juggling with plates and glasses." Officers and men often ate standing up, as perpetually pitching and slanting decks made tables useless. "Even personal cleanliness became impossible" in this "unstable world," where water sloshed out of wash basins slanting at forty-five or fifty degrees. Everything was lashed down, and officers and men alike tumbled into "troubled bunks fully dressed, ready at a moment's notice to appear on deck."

The epitome of early-twentieth-century marine engineering lay below, within the small, narrow hulls where three-eighths of an inch of steel separated the engineering gang from the vicious sea around them. Life was surreal amid the "great turbines with the horsepower of a battleship," throbbing and spinning, "driving . . . whirling screws." There was "not an inch of wasted space. In a swinging and bucking world, crammed like a watch case with a maze of machinery," the engineers moved "like magicians" amid the din and "steel and steam." Winston Churchill, who tended to dismiss the American naval contribution to the Great War at sea, nonetheless paused in his memoirs to pay tribute to the destroyers. "More than a quarter of the whole of the escorts across the Atlantic were provided by American destroyers, and the comradeship of this hard service forms an ineffaceable tradition for the two navies."[93]

Accidents were bound to happen; it is remarkable that more did not and that loss of life was minimal. This was as true of the battleships operating out of Scapa Flow as the small boys working in the Bay of Biscay. After days and nights of sailing at eighteen to twenty knots in "blinding fog," Captain Beach of *New York* found himself "right on top of a great ship." Rodman had told Beach never to worry about the vessels behind him; they would see whatever distress he might encounter and get out of the way. Spying the huge ship suddenly looming out of the fog before him, Beach instinctively ordered "all back full." "The 'collision signals,' with their deafening screams, resounded" throughout the entire five-hundred-plus-foot hull, sending the fifteen-hundred-odd men not on watch tumbling out of hammocks and slamming down coffee cups in the wardroom and mess decks. "On the bridge, we could hear and sense watertight doors throughout our great battleship flying shut." The "suddenly backing engines," thirty thousand horsepower revolving full-speed astern, shook up *New York* as Beach never thought such a monster could be shaken. The battleship had "stumbled" upon *Olympic*, one of Cunard's three great sisters, of whom *Titanic* had been one. As all on *New York*'s bridge held their breath, the monster passenger liner cum troopship slipped past. A shaken Captain Beach suddenly heard a quiet voice beside him: "Beach, you didn't touch her. You missed her by three feet. Good night." It was Rodman, in "pajamas and bare feet," who had rushed to the bridge the moment the collision alarm began to screech. A suddenly deflated but relieved battleship captain realized that his commander belonged to the "'Don't worry' club."[94]

Down in the Bay of Biscay, destroyers *Benham* and *Jarvis* were running at high speed through heavy fog one night off Brest, without lights in "crowded waters," when *Jarvis*'s rudder suddenly jammed and it "sheered quickly toward *Benham*." Before anyone could respond, *Jarvis* slammed into and overrode *Benham* abreast of its bridge, "tearing a great hole" in the ship's side that extended "half way through the wardroom." Incredibly, no one on either vessel was injured. Damage to *Benham* was confined entirely above the waterline, while *Jarvis*'s collision bulkhead held. Both vessels were able to limp into port.[95]

The United States Navy, a thoroughly workmanlike service before the nation went to war, further honed its discipline and focus while retaining somehow that relatively freewheeling and open-minded character that had emerged in the decades before and after the Civil War. Never prior to 1917 had the navy and its sailors been called upon in such vast numbers to develop the raw seamanship required to maintain an enormous oceanic lifeline, while cruising the treacherous waters of the upper North Sea in ships whose size and complexity would have stunned forebears in the Age of Fighting Sail. Photos of the time show the men who manned the destroyers, chasers, and armed yachts dressed in a variety of rough work clothes. "On these sea-whippets," wrote one contemporary admirer, "lived men in dungarees and rubber boots who met the sea and mastered it; men who lived in oil and spray, continuously balanced in a mad unstable world," yet ready in an instant to cast loose depth charges, man guns, and, if necessary, ram U-boats.[96]

No element of American sea power in 1918 better reflected this change than the armed yachts found in every port from Brest to Bordeaux. The formerly "soft white decks" of these once elegant civilian greyhounds had become "torn and dented by hob-nailed boots and the heavy gear which was hauled over them. Long rows" of depth charges "filled the graceful curves" of fantails, while "squat 'Y'-guns crowded the hand-steering gear on the after deck." Repeatedly shattered by heavy seas or the firing of nearby deck guns and depth charges, once graceful windows in formerly grand saloons were boarded up, while belowdecks raw but clean chairs, sofas, and tables—the furnishings of war—had become "worn and battered" by dirty clothing and stained by seawater that perpetually leaked through sprung decks above. Gathered in the Gironde River as 1918 slowly waned, their crews watched as "one by one" America's newest destroyers took over responsibility for shepherding troop convoys up to the northern ports. Assuming the more lowly but critical duties of "storeship" escorts, the yachts were still manned by the same crews, but with "newcomers" in the wardrooms and on the bridges, responsible for their share of the ever "arduous, monotonous and dangerous" work of antisubmarine warfare.

Ensign Walter Ansel had sailed to France in the spring of 1918 and reported aboard the "petit pacquebot" *Rambler*, formerly "one of Tom Lawson's yachts on the Lakes . . . called *Dreamer.*" *Rambler*'s job was to escort convoys composed of British, French, a few American, and even Spanish ships carrying "coal traffic from England out of Bristol" down to the Gironde from Brest. U-boats

were plentiful, and their skippers quickly caught on to the fact that north-
and southbound convoy traffic crossed off the Pointe Penmarc'h. "Penmarche
Pete," as the submarines came to be known by apprehensive Allied seamen,
seemed omnipresent and unmoved by the presence of frequent Allied air patrols
aloft. Ansel recalled that "our hearing gear and our detection gear were very
primitive."

Each coal convoy was composed of between a dozen and a score of ships,
shepherded by a leading yacht, with a second in the middle and a third "bringing up the rear to shoo" stragglers along. An overall escort commander rode
a coal-burning destroyer that "would sashay up and down the line." Ansel and
the other officers of the deck aboard *Rambler* took "fantastic" risks "going up
alongside" big, straggling colliers, shouting through megaphones at their bridge
people, "Get up there where you belong. There's a submarine reported astern."
Rambler lost only one ship in its charge, *Philomel*. More than a half century later,
Ansel remembered the "trail of torpedo bubbles" coming across *Rambler*'s bow,
starboard to port, to smash into the British vessel that "started right down."
Depth-charge attacks proved futile, but the entire ship's company from the
stricken vessel was saved.

Out in the great bay often wracked with violent weather, yacht skippers
clung to handholds on their open bridges "in seas so heavy that they were
constantly drenched with buckets full of spray." Veterans and newcomers endured "interminable nights of anxiety" as they watched the convoys in their
charge plunging and wallowing in sliding seas. "Leviathan" vessels of four thousand tons and more were often "lost to sight behind a cresting wave" and then
"pitched high against the sky, half-bared propellers churning the sea." As wind
and wave scattered the convoys in dark, roiling seascapes, heavily laden ships ran
"wild in a wild sea; invisible, ungovernable . . . careening far out of their course,
liable without warning to loom out of the darkness high above the bridge of a
yacht reeling on the flank or in the rear of the convoy."

The reason for the cargo convoys lay in the ports and docks of the towns
up and down the Gironde that terminated in the great "fan-shaped" city of
Bordeaux. At the river's mouth lay the sheltered roadstead of Le Verdon, where
"fifty and a hundred freighters" gathered at a single time; "coal-burners and
oil-burners" of every type and sort were to be found there. So were the ships
fabricated on America's Great Lakes far from the sea as well as "tramp steamers,
fruit steamers and passenger vessels" that in happier times had touched most of
southern Europe's ports. Two hours upriver from Le Vernon lay Trompeloup,
with its vast nearby training station at Moutchic where American naval aviation

cadets were being graduated at a frantic pace. Another three hours brought ocean traffic to the great docks at Bassin, "where stout freighters" and coal ships discharged their cargoes before dropping back down to Le Verdon for yet other assignments. Bassin embraced not only enormous port facilities, but "miles" of American-laid roads heading north and west toward the steadily advancing and expanding Allied western front. Here, "hundreds of American cars assembled by American mechanics in American shops" received their "innumerable" stores of war matériel and drove off for the front lines. The Yanks were now truly Over There.[97]

Incontestable U-boat kills continued to elude America's sailors during those final weeks and days as they suffered one last tragedy. On the night of September 26, while part of a convoy escort in the Bristol channel, the big US Coast Guard cutter *Tampa* abruptly left her station without informing anyone, apparently thinking it was on the track of a nearby U-boat. Suddenly, everyone in the convoy heard a "huge" explosion in whose aftermath *Tampa*'s absence was quickly noticed. A search was promptly undertaken, but only two bodies were ever recovered, together with a "handful of debris." One hundred thirty-one people perished, including twenty-one passengers from Gibraltar.[98] Even on the cusp of victory, eternal vigilance was essential, and fate could deal the unwary a fatal hand.

As they helped keep critical supplies of men and matériel flowing across the Atlantic and the Channel and up and down the coasts of France and Britain, men in wardrooms and mess spaces on every ship large and small and on every aviation station from Scotland to Italy eagerly devoured news-filled "flimsies" that told of the Allies' remorseless advance toward the German border. Ludendorff collapsed in a nervous fit one day in September, and by early October a deeply divided German government proposed an armistice. In Italy, in the Balkans, in Palestine, and in the Dardenelles, the Allies were pushing and probing, on the march as inexorably as on the western front. Revolutions erupted in Vienna and Budapest; a general strike was called in Berlin; at Kiel and soon at Wilhelmshaven, the Hochseeflotte finally mutinied en masse as word swept decks that its admirals might take it on one final "death ride" against the Grand Fleet. Everywhere, a profusion of democratic, socialist, and communist elements tore imperial Germany and Austria-Hungary apart.

On November 5, a "gray afternoon" at Brest, destroyer *Roe*, a 740-ton "flivver" that had spent the past year in European waters, partly under the command of young Bill Halsey, cleared harbor and headed home, the first US destroyer to be so relieved. Flying a hundred-foot "homeward bound" pennant, *Roe* passed her envious sisters, who signaled mournfully, "Give Our Regards to Broadway." "Good Luck, May You Follow Soon," *Roe's* signalmen replied. But few believed it. Enemy armies were slowly crumbling, but who could say how long they might fight to obtain for their governments the most advantageous surrender terms possible? Six days later, as noontime Brest paused for lunch beneath a "glittering" sun, the old shore battery beneath the ancient fortress suddenly gave off a puff of smoke, followed immediately by a hollow boom. Another gun followed immediately and then another and then a chorus. A big French cruiser broke out the tricolor, letting loose her whistle in a piercing scream. Across the entire harbor, a cacophony of gunfire, whistles, and shrieking sirens broke out as entire crews raced on deck to cheer "madly." The Armistice had come at last. The War to End All Wars was over, ushering in an uncertain peace that would be prologue to more, seemingly endless, wars.[99]

A Navy Second to None

IN THE FIRTH of Forth, a false message of peace on November 7 had sent the Grand Fleet to impromptu celebration until a second message nullifying the first arrived. Two days later, Beatty messaged the fleet, warning that a great naval battle "was more probable than ever before." Down in London, the Admiralty had been convinced for some days that "conditions" on the other side of the North Sea suggested a major sortie by the entire Hochseeflotte. Officers and men should not take rumors of mutiny and peace seriously. But in the early evening of November 11, Beatty informed his charges that the Armistice had begun at 11:00 a.m. and that the "customary method" of celebrating victory in his majesty's ships was to be carried out by each crew—"splicing the main brace," having a tot of rum—at 9:00 p.m. Then, in the time-honored way of celebrating a holiday, the men were ordered to "make and mend clothes."

The anchorage erupted in a cacophony of sound and noise as the entire fleet "went wild with joy." All searchlights, whistles, and sirens were turned on full blast and kept that way; the good citizens of Edinburgh would get little or no sleep that night, not that many really cared. Rockets were fired, and crews taking pots, pans, and tins from their galleys snake-danced around their decks for hours while bands blared and brayed. The Sixth Battle Squadron was, of course, formally "dry." So a group of young officers from *New York* took one of the battleship's boats over to nearby *Renown* for an hour—or more—of "hilarity" in the battle cruiser's wardroom.[1]

Terms of the German naval surrender had been hammered out in the Allied Naval War Council over several weeks as the German and Austro-Hungarian armies continued their retreat and Berlin sought the best terms possible. The

Allied premiers subsequently amended the council's provisions to the extent that all German fleet units could be interned in an Allied port, which opened the way to sequestration at Scapa Flow. On the fifteenth, German admiral Hugo Meuer and staff came aboard HMS *Queen Elizabeth* at Rosyth to receive instructions. When he reached the battleship's quarterdeck, he and his people found no welcoming "by noisy buglers, no marines at 'present h'ahms!' no beating of drums, no band," no committee of senior British naval officers. Rather, a midlevel minion was there to touch his cap lightly and hurry the visitors along to Beatty's cabin, where the admiral and his senior people bowed slightly but refused to shake hands. Once the Germans were told the nature of the surrender and grudgingly approved, Beatty told them that "refreshments" had been arranged. In a nearby cabin, "a bountiful meal had been prepared. A table loaded with hot meats, vegetables, beer and wine." After the Germans had entered, a lowly mess attendant ostentatiously closed the doors. Beatty "was unwilling that any British sailor should act as servant or attendant to the Germans." Upon the humiliated naval party's return to Germany, there was little for the Royal Navy and its American contingent to do but wait for all elements of the High Seas Fleet while maintaining patrols to ensure that every U-boat at sea got the word and was compliant. By the eighteenth, the first submarines were coming out from the Helgoland Bight to surrender, and two days later the High Seas Fleet, with all its elements, battleships, battle cruisers, cruisers, and destroyers, started out to be met in the middle of the North Sea by the British cruiser *Cardiff*. "The Grand Fleet commenced sailing from Scapa Flow at a quarter past two on the morning of November 21 to rendezvous with the enemy off the Firth of Forth."[2]

It should have been a moment of triumph and relief. It was neither. "We of the American Battle Squadron were the only happy ones in that great fleet," *New York*'s captain Beach recalled. The Americans were "full of joy" at the prospect that most would be home for Christmas. Coming aboard *Texas* the evening before the High Seas Fleet surrendered, an American reporter discovered that a "hop" was going on in the wardroom. Expecting to see a group of American and British officers "bunny-hugging" to a piano, he came upon a full-fledged dance party with "a score of pretty Englishwomen, officers' wives and daughters, fox-trotting" with their countrymen and the American hosts "to the strains of a jazz-band," undoubtedly composed of *Texas*'s enlisted musicians, drafted to play light tunes rather than the usual martial music. Over in a corner, the hosts had laid out a spread of "the most ravishing pre-war tea of cream and sugar and butter and white bread and delightful cakes and dainties." And so the victors danced the night away as their vanquished enemies steamed sullenly toward them.[3]

Quite soon, however, British and more than a few of their American cousins changed their minds. The immediate euphoria that a nightmarish prodigality of blood and treasure had at last ended was quickly overtaken by an empty feeling of failure that ironically united both vanquished and victor. On Sunday morning, November 17, "clouds of smoke and soot" lay over the "war harbor" at Wilhelmshaven as the Hochseeflotte prepared to get under way for its final-ever sortie. How often had the smoke risen and soot fallen as the citizens of this premier German naval town sent their sailors off to war with "perfidious Britain." Now, all had changed. "For four years," a young officer wrote in his journal, "I have shared victory and want with my crew, and I won't leave them in the lurch in the end." But going aboard ship for the last time was agonizing. The red flag of revolution still flew at the mainmast, "a sign of all that has collapsed in these last weeks. The crew is serious and quiet; most of them feel how great is the disgrace." Yet the navy refused to believe it had been beaten, and here it shared a mood and attitude not only with its army brethren but also with its enemies across the North Sea. When the High Seas Fleet in all its tattered might came in sight of the victorious Grand Fleet with the caged masts of the five American battlewagons conspicuously present, British officers felt, "strangely enough," that "the German surrender lacked the thrill of victory." There was "the gaping wonder of it all" at the surrender of a great modern industrial fleet steaming alongside its adversaries to its practical death without a gun being fired. That was the problem. In British eyes, the Hochseeflotte had been "conquered but not in the spectacular way that we would have so gladly given our lives to see." The "one prevalent emotion" throughout the Grand Fleet was "pity" that a worthy adversary had not been fought to the death. Speaking to his fleet shortly after the Germans had been ushered into Scapa Flow that would become the cemetery of their splendid ships, Beatty let his hair down with remarkable candor. "It was a most disappointing day," he said, a "pitiful day to see those great ships coming in like sheep being herded by dogs to their fold without an effort on anyone's part."

Sailors aboard at least one American battlewagon shared the sense of general disappointment. Despite the jubilation and partying, despite their captain's assurance to a reporter that he was delighted to bring his men home safely to "mothers and sweethearts," the crew of *Texas* "would have preferred a fight, for they had come thousands of miles from home, suffered uncomplainingly, endured daily hardships just for a chance to get a whack at the Germans," who instead were "coming out" with white flags. "It was unbelievable. It seemed impossible. We felt ashamed for their cowardice. No other Navy had ever been so humiliated." While the Americans viewed the Germans with a mixture of "unconcern" and "contempt," their British cousins generally shared the view that the High Seas Fleet, though not the U-boat arm, had fought honorably and well and deserved a better fate.[4]

It proved a dangerous attitude to embrace. Misplaced sympathy for a stout and unvanquished foe would lead to a fatal acceptance of his rebirth under the most sinister circumstances together with a willingness to accept his psychology of victimhood. In 1935, Beatty, from the House of Lords, would speak out strongly in favor of a treaty that elevated a now Nazified German Navy to within striking distance of parity with its British antagonists in European waters.[5]

Word had come from Washington within a few days of the High Seas Fleet's incarceration at Scapa Flow that Battle Squadron Six, again referred to as Battle Division Nine, US Atlantic Fleet, return home as soon as unneeded stores were off-loaded and other administrative chores completed. The Grand Fleet remained at Rosyth, and there, in the final week of November 1918, the grateful British hosted "dinners, dances and teas and games ashore and afloat" for their departing guess. "We realized more deeply," one young American officer wrote soon after returning to the States, "how fully the bond of comradeship between our forces had been developed.[6]

With words of good wishes and Godspeed in their ears, the American battleships sailed not west but southeast, for orders had come that the trip home should be deferred so that the ships could provide an impressive escort for President Wilson, who was hurrying to the Old World immediately after the Armistice to put it aright for all time, or, at least, conceivable time. The Sixth and Seventh Battle Squadrons from Scapa and Bantry Bay then headed home together, only to be informed at midocean of an impending fleet review at New York City that Secretary Daniels foolishly scheduled for December 26. This one final social obligation required the fleet to noodle along off the Jersey shore on Christmas Day and then drop anchor near the Ambrose Channel Lightship, "thirty miles from Broadway!" "They didn't even send our mail out to us," one disgruntled junior officer recalled. Ships' companies, many of whom had been in the war zone for nearly a year and had counted on being home for the holiday, were outraged, vowing to leave the service as soon as possible rather than reenlist. The review, when it began the following morning, confirmed the sullen mood as the fleet moved through "swirling snow" in the Lower Bay. But as it sailed up the Hudson, the skies cleared, and as the vessels anchored off Riverside Drive, thousands ashore cheered the mighty fleet lustily. To the people aboard and those ashore alike, the United States Navy had confirmed to itself if not the world that it had become the second-mightiest naval power on earth. Within two hours, ten thousand bluejackets had been ferried ashore for a massive parade down Fifth Avenue. Mayo and Rodman with their staffs led the procession "beneath a canopy of bunting," amid "a din of cheers" from scores of thousands of other throats, after which the men were turned loose, "jazzin' around, paintin' the town," enjoying the bars, restaurants, and theaters, where they were given a hero's welcome. How *were* you going "to keep 'em down on the farm after they'd seen" Broadway as well as "Paree"?[7]

While the fleet got its welcome, Gleaves's transport service prepared to bring the AEF home. The true dimension of the army's achievement in France in 1918 would be obscured for many decades by economic depression; another, even greater, world war; and cold war. But those who lived on the western front during its bloody history and thereafter never forgot what the Yanks did, and they passed the word to their progeny. In the summer of 2014, *New York Times* writer Richard Rubin visited those battlefields where Pershing's boys in several weeks accomplished what the French had failed to achieve in four years—driving *les boches* out of seemingly impregnable fixed positions and back toward Germany and defeat.

> In the Argonne, and to the east around St-Mihel, and to the west around Cha-teau Thierry, you will meet any number of French people—guides and farmers, engineers and construction workers, soldiers and environmental scientists—who know much more about the war than you ever will. They grew up with it; sur-rounded by it; they have spent their entire lives looking at those old German for-tifications that have decayed hardly at all over the last century, the ones that make you stare in wonder and ask yourself: How *did* the Germans lose that war? Ask them the same question and, if your experience is anything like mine, they will always—always—give you the same succinct answer: Les Americains.[8]

Like patients in a hospital who never know the number of people working anonymously to save or better their lives, the folks who inhabit the Meuse-Argonne do not realize that they owe the survival of their region to the thou-sands of gallant sailors—British and American—who delivered the saviors to their shores through dark and perilous seas.

Other elements of America's navy deferred homeward voyages to help tidy up the immediate postwar scene. Minesweepers and subchasers worked well into 1919, clearing the Northern Barrage; a handful of other chasers went to Russia that year to show the flag and support the American contingent of the international force that intervened, futilely, in the civil war on the side of the "whites." Perhaps the most exciting homecoming was enjoyed by a half-dozen chasers as they formally raced each other the seven hundred miles from Bermuda to New York Harbor. The Navy Department sanctioned the competition after Ensign Alfred Loomis had convinced his immediate superiors "with a clever concoction of appeals to engineering concerns"—a test of the ships' engines—and public relations. The race was sure to be, and was, well covered by the press, which gave the winners a "big reception" when SC-131 appeared off the Statue of Liberty, including some of the first newsreels ever made. Prominent boating historian John Rousmanier plausibly maintains that the subchasers in general and this race in particular laid the foundations for modern powerboat yachting in the United States.[9]

★ ★ ★ ★ ★

At the beginning of 1917, America's sailors expected to employ their big and reasonably efficient fleet in the kind of line-of-battle combat that had not materially changed since the Age of Fighting Sail. Over the next two years, events forced them to reorient both their thinking and the weapons that they possessed. Time and again, in this context and that, tactical and strategic flexibility was forced upon them, and they responded appropriately. If too many officers, especially those from the battleship squadrons like Husband Kimmel, failed to fully understand the ongoing revolutions in warfare occurring on, under, and above the seas, many others did—young Bill Halsey and Chester Nimitz, to name but two. In World War II, with the glaring exception of the critical coastal trade during the first six months, the United States Navy understood the importance of convoys and antisubmarine warfare. Building on the experience of 1917–18, it rapidly regained its former proficiency.

The navy was determined to exploit what it had achieved and won during the Great War. Throughout 1919 and into the following year, the 120-odd destroyers ordered just before and during the war came off the builders' ways from Bath to Bremerton. Splendid ships for their day, they would constitute the navy's first-line small-ship arsenal for nearly two decades. In January, aircraft began to deploy aboard the battleships chiefly to spot fall of shot during the still-anticipated Mahanian clash of battle lines. Four months later, one of the four big seaplanes that began a planned transatlantic flight from Newfoundland via the Azores and Lisbon to Plymouth, England, completed its hop.

Shortly after, a substantial portion of the battle fleet sailed west. Transiting the Panama Canal, it arrived in Southern California to make San Diego and San Pedro its new home. Thereafter, it began a series of yearly summer maneuvers in Hawaiian waters that projected American power to near midocean. In 1920, the navy commissioned its first aircraft carrier, converting the collier *Jupiter* into *Langley*.

Finally, in the following year, the United States climaxed its remarkable post-war naval surge, as Washington summoned the world's other great sea powers—Britain, France, Japan, and Italy—to a conference designed to freeze naval armaments and the status quo in East Asia for years to come. To the dismay of the British, their cousins had already insisted on equality with what for two centuries past had been the greatest naval power on the globe. At Washington, the Americans formally got their way. Anglo-American naval parity was guaranteed, with Japan obtaining—or relegated to—an inferior but still substantial place of power. In yet another effort to stabilize East Asian affairs, the conference replaced the 1902 Anglo-Japanese Alliance and several prior American-Japanese agreements with a four-power consultative pact between the United States, Britain, France, and Japan. A world war in which the United States Navy had flexed considerable and ever-growing power in European waters was now complemented by a series of international agreements that formally ratified America as a major Pacific power as well, with a formidable fleet to go with it. As the sailors and their diplomatic colleagues left the conference, neither could guess the fate—and, ultimately, the new world—that awaited.[10]

Notes

Introduction

1. William N. Still, *Crisis at Sea: The United States Navy in European Waters in World War I*, is the major source on the subject for this generation. David F. Trask, *Captains and Cabinets: Anglo-American Naval Relations, 1917–1918*, remains a good introduction to the administrative aspects of the Great War at sea. Mary Klachko and David F. Trask, *Admiral William Shepherd Benson: First Chief of Naval Operations*, considers the US naval war from one of its chief administrators. Other general accounts that discuss US naval operations are Paul G. Halpern, *A Naval History of World War I*; Robert K. Massie, *Castles of Steel: Britain, Germany and the Winning of the Great War at Sea*; Arthur J. Marder, *From the Dreadnought to Scapa Flow: The Royal Navy in the Fisher Era, 1904–1919*, HH vols. 4–5; Norman Friedman, *Fighting the Great War at Sea*; and Lawrence Sondhaus, *The Great War at Sea: A Naval History of the First World War*.

2. Lisle A. Rose, *Power at Sea*, 1:289.

Chapter One State of Play

1. William Sowden Sims and Burton J. Hendrick, *The Victory at Sea*, 106–8; Edward N. Hurley, *The Bridge to France*, 232–33; Sondhaus, *Great War at Sea*, 255.

2. Gabriel Voitoux, "The Naval War: Some Light about the *Goeben*'s Escape," 533.

3. Duncan Redford, *The Submarine: A Cultural History from the Great War to Nuclear Combat*, 97; R. H. Gibson and Maurice Prendergast, *The German Submarine War, 1914–1918*, 25.

4. "Ajax," *The German Pirate: His Methods and Record*; William Archer, *The Pirate's Progress: A Short History of the U-boat*; Gerard Fiennes, *Sea Power and Freedom: A Historical Study*; Frank T. Cable, *The Birth and Development of the American Submarine*, 1; Ralph D. Paine, *The Fighting Fleets: Five Months of Active Service with the American Destroyers and Their Allies in the War Zone*, 54; "Naval War Notes" contains a graphic account of a Zeppelin raid over London by its commander that appeared in the *Kölnische Volkszeitung* of August 20, 1918, and was subsequently translated

and republished as "Zeppelin Raids on London." Ian Castle, *London, 1914–17: The Zeppelin Menace*. See also "Zeppelin Raids on London: Mapped," http://londonist. com/2010/07/wwi_airship_attack; "The War in the Air-Bombers: Germany, Zeppelins"; Charles C. Gill, *Naval Power in the War (1914–1918)*, 235–36. The allegedly spiritual nature of the U-boat war was argued by Henry Newbolt, *Submarine and Anti-submarine*, 7–8; Ensign Dole is quoted in Todd A. Woofenden, *Hunters of the Steel Sharks: The Submarine Chasers of World War I*, 36.

5. Barbara Tuchman, *The Zimmerman Telegram*, 107.

6. See Gordon Campbell, *My Mystery Ships*, 1–130 (quote on 3); Harold Auten, *"Q" Boat Adventures: The Exploits of the Famous Mystery Ships by a "Q" Boat Commander*; and E. Keble Chatterton, *Q-Ships and Their Story*.

7. John N. Moore, introduction to *Jane's Fighting Ships of World War I*, 127.

8. The appearance and actions of *Deutschland* and U-53 were fully described in a 1920 report, USisH Department of the Navy, Office of Naval Records and Library Monographs Historical Section, *German Submarine Activities on the Atlantic Coast of the United States and Canada*, 7, 19–22. See also Henry J. James, *German Subs in Yankee Waters: First World War*, xi, 7–9. An authoritative discussion of the navy's prewar and wartime acquisition program together with brief histories of the wartime service of roughly half of the vessels obtained is US Department of the Navy, Naval Historical Center, "Online Library of Selected Images: 'SP's #s and 'ID's #s, World War I Era Patrol Vessels and Other Acquired Ships and Craft." A less comprehensive list is in US Department of the Navy, Naval History and Heritage Command, *Dictionary of American Naval Fighting Ships*, http://www.history.navy.mil./danfs (hereafter cited as *DANFS*). Warship histories, including that of *Benham*, are in ibid. plus designation a-list.htm. See also Norman Friedman, *U.S. Small Combatants Including PT-Boats, Subchasers, and the Brown-Water Navy: An Illustrated Design History*, 24 (caption).

9. The "Red War Plan" is discussed in John B. Hattendorf, "Commonwealth Navies as Seen by the United States Navy, 1910–2010," 161–62. Benson's remarks are quoted in Klachko and Trask, *Admiral William Shepherd Benson*, 58.

10. "America's New Armada," 175.

11. Sims and Hendrick, *The Victory at Sea*, 7; William N. Still, ed., *Joseph Taussig, Queenstown Patrol, 1917*, 19.

12. Holger H. Herwig, *Politics of Frustration: The United States in German Naval Planning*, 26–27, 64–65.

13. George T. Davis, *A Navy Second to None: The Development of Modern American Naval Policy*, 163.

14. Friedman, *Fighting the Great War at Sea*, 246.

15. The rapidly developing revolution in naval power at the close of the nineteenth century is captured in Edward Shippen, *Naval Battles and Our New Navy*, with its grandiose subtitles that include *The Growth, Power and Management of OUR NEW NAVY, in Its Pride and Glory of Swift Cruiser, Impregnable Battle-Ship, Ponderous Engine and Deadly Projectile* . . .

16. Hugh Rodman, *Yarns of a Kentucky Admiral*, 261.

17. James R. Reckner, *Teddy Roosevelt's Great White Fleet*.

18. *Brooklyn*'s service history is in *DANFS*. A summary of the ship's career and a detailed history of its specifications, building, and sea trials are in Ivan Musicant, *U.S. Armored Cruisers*, 45–71.

19. John Alden, *Flush Decks and Four Pipes*, 1–4; Association of United States Navy, "110 Years of Tin Cans."

20. Peter M. Swartz and E. D. McGrady, "U.S. Navy Forward Deployment, 1801–2001"; Seward W. Livermore, "The American Navy as a Factor in World Politics"; Destroyer History Foundation, "Early Destroyers; First Destroyers; *Bainbridge* Class; USS *Bainbridge*."

21. Mark L. Evans, "Performed All Their Duties Well."

22. Kenneth J. Hagan, *This People's Navy: The Making of American Sea Power*, 246; "USNI News Daily Update for 07/02/2014: Maritime News and Analysis," provided by e-mail daily to members by the US Naval Institute.

23. Moore, introduction to *Jane's Fighting Ships*, 133–49.

24. *DANFS, Des Moines* (C-15); Scott Anderson, *Lawrence in Arabia: War, Deceit, Imperial Folly and the Making of the Modern Middle East*, 136.

25. *DANFS*, USS *North Carolina*; Albert Bushnell Hart et al., eds., *The War on the Sea: Battles, Sea Raids and Submarine Campaigns*, 353.

26. J. K. Taussig, "Destroyer Experiences during the Great War" (December 1922): 2015; Francis J. Reynolds, *The United States Navy from the Revolution to Date*, 82.

27. Klachko and Trask, *Admiral William Shepherd Benson*, 50.

28. Frederick S. Harrod, *Manning the New Navy: The Development of a Modern Naval Enlisted Force, 1899–1940*, 57.

29. William S. Sims, "Naval War College"; Elting E. Morison, *Admiral Sims and the Modern American Navy*, 294–95, 304, 312; E. B. Potter, *Bull Halsey*, 101; ough Robert A. Shafter, *Destroyers in Action*, 43, 45.

30. C. S. McDowell, "Naval Research," 897; Linwood S. Howeth, *History of Communications-Electronics in the United States Navy*, 133–52, 167, 227–36.

31. Henry B. Beston, *Full Speed Ahead: Tales from the Log of a Correspondent with Our Navy*, 50–51; Harrod, *Manning the New Navy*, 67.

32. Jeff Phister, Thomas Hone, and Paul Goodyear, *Battleship* Oklahoma, *BB-37*, 15–16; Reynolds, *United States Navy*, 82–86; 114–15, 118; San Diego Naval Historical Association, "Naval Training Center, San Diego Navy History"; "Excerpts from Tegler's Log," note 3, in Todd Woofenden, webmaster, http://subchaser.org/archives-notes/SAN-Vol-2-.

33. Vice Admiral Bernhard Henry Bieri, oral history interview, no. 1, 31.

34. For Saufley, see Adrian O. Van Wyen, "Naval Aviation in World War I: In the Very Beginning," 13; and A. Denis Clift, "The New Navy Prepares for War: The *U.S. Naval Institute Proceedings*, 1910–19," 17.

35. Cable, *Birth and Development of the American Submarine*, 3, 266–78, 285–86; Moore, introduction to *Jane's Fighting Ships*, 151.

36. David Colamaria, "A Sailor's Life in the New Steel Navy: Berthing, Officer-vs-Enlisted."

37. Jonathan G. Utley, *An American Battleship at Peace and War, the U.S.S.* Tennessee, 48–49; Francis T. Hunter, *Beatty, Jellicoe, Sims and Rodman: Yankee Gobs and British Tars*

as Seen by an "Anglomaniac," 62, 119–20, 124, 127; Reynolds, *United States Navy*, 88, 92. The "relic of barbarism" quote is from Vice Admiral Felix L. Johnson, oral history interview, no. 1, 7.

38. Geoffrey L. Rossano, ed., *The Price of Honor: The World War One Letters of Naval Aviator Kenneth MacLeish*, ix.

39. Josephus Daniels, "U.S. Secretary of the Navy Josephus Daniels' Official Report on the U.S. Navy during Wartime"; "Professional Notes: America's Record since Entering the War Two Years Ago"; Harrod, *Manning the New Navy*, 65, 80; Rose, *Power at Sea*, 1:265.

40. Vice Admiral Olaf M. Hustvedt, oral history interview, no. 1, 35.

41. Harold Sprout and Margaret Sprout, *The Rise of American Naval Power, 1776–1918*, 293; John W. Adams, "The Influences Affecting Naval Shipbuilding Legislation, 1910–1916," 55; Wayne P. Hughes, "Bradley Fiske: Leader of Transformation"; Moore, introduction to *Jane's Fighting Ships*, 139–40; H. T. Mayo, introduction to Hart et al., *War on the Sea*.

42. Moore, introduction to *Jane's Fighting Ships*, 56–62, 113–14.

43. Rossano, *Price of Honor*, 1.

44. Sims and Hendrick, *The Victory at Sea*, 96–97; John Jellicoe, *The Submarine Peril: The Admiralty Policy in 1917*, 3; Admiral Lewis Bayly memorandum to US destroyer captains, May 1917, quoted in Taussig, "Destroyer Experiences" (January 1923): 49.

45. Harry Albert Austin, "The United States Unprepared for War."

46. Ernest J. King and Walter Muir Whitehill, *Fleet Admiral King: A Naval Record*, 114–15.

47. On the naval act of 1916, see George Baer, *One Hundred Years of Sea Power: The United States Navy, 1890–1990*, 60. For criticisms of the unbalanced nature of the fleet, see Davis, *Navy Second to None*, 192–95.

48. Leon Wolff, *In Flander's Fields: The 1917 Campaign*, 5–13 (quotes on 6, 13).

49. Sondhaus, *Great War at Sea*, 244–46; Halpern, *Naval History of World War I*, 335. Halpern incorrectly identifies the big new boats as of the UB.II class. In fact, most were the U.93s.

50. Gibson and Prendergast, *German Submarine War*, 205; Klachko and Trask, *Admiral William Shepherd Benson*, 55; Thomas R. Frothingham, "The Strategy of the World War, and the Lessons of the Effort of the United States," 676; Tuchman, *The Zimmerman Telegram*, 161–62. An English-language translation of the complete text of the telegram is at http://history1900s.about.com./od/worldwar1/a/.

51. David M. Kennedy, *Over Here: The First World War and American Society*, 7, 21–22, 158, 159.

52. Gibson and Prendergast, *German Submarine War*, 164–65.

53. Josephus Daniels, *The Navy and the Nation*, 20. The text is reprinted at http://archive.org/stream/navynation00.dani.

54. Taussig, "Destroyer Experiences" (December 1922): 2015–16; Bieri, interview, no. 1, 25.

55. Josephus Daniels, *Our Navy at War*, 1.

56. John Langdon Leighton, *Simsadus: London; The American Navy in Europe*, vi–vii.

57. Geoffrey L. Rossano, *Stalking the U-boat: U.S. Naval Aviation in Europe in World War I*, 3; Albert P. Gleaves, *A History of the Transport Service: Adventures and Experiences of United States Transports and Cruisers in the World War*, 38.

58. See, for example, David F. Trask, *The AEF and Coalition Warfare, 1917–18*.

59. Rossano, *Stalking the U-boat*, 3.

Chapter Two Beat to Quarters

1. USisH Department of the Navy, Office of Naval Records and Library Monographs Historical Section, *The Northern Barrage and Other Mining Activities*, 10.

2. Hart et al., *War on the Sea*, 212–14, 280–324.hereH

3. Lincoln Paine, *The Sea & Civilization: A Maritime History of the World*, 567; "World War 1 at Sea: United States Navy, "British Destroyers."

4. Taussig, "Destroyer Experiences" (December 1922): 2020, 2027; Klachko and Trask, *Admiral William Shepherd Benson*, 62–64.

5. Sims and Hendrick, *The Victory at Sea*, 6; Marder, *From the Dreadnought to Scapa Flow*, vol. 4, *1917: Year of Crisis*, 103.

6. Jellicoe, *Submarine Peril*, 2–3; Julian S. Corbett and Henry Newbolt, *Naval Operations: History of the Great War Based on Official Documents*, 5:11–20; Marder, *From the Dreadnought to Scapa Flow*, 4:127.

7. Jellicoe is quoted in Marder, *From the Dreadnought to Scapa Flow*, 4:108.

8. Ibid., 110; Carson and Geddes quoted in Earl Brassey and John Leyland, eds., *The Naval Annual, 1919*, 15; Corbett and Newbolt, *Naval Operations*, 4:385. The shipowners and insurers' plight is discussed in Hurley, *The Bridge to France*, 233. Antony Preston, *Submarines*, 62–63, discusses the British shipbuilding blunder.

9. Massie, *Castles of Steel*, 716–17, 730 (Lloyd George quotes); Corbett and Newbolt, *Naval Operations*, 5:10–14; Preston, *Submarines*, 63.

10. Sims and Hendrick, *The Victory at Sea*, 8–9; figures on April shipping losses are from Taprell Dorling, *Endless Story: Being an Account of the Work of the Destroyer, Flotilla-Leaders, Torpedo Boats and Patrol Boats in the Great War*, 328.

11. Jellicoe, *Submarine Peril*, 2, 70–71.

12. Leighton, *Simsadus*, 5–6.

13. Sims and Hendrick, *The Victory at Sea*, 26.

14. Ibid., 28–29, 36–38; Gibson and Prendergast, *German Submarine War*, 163; Corbett and Newbolt, *Naval Operations*, 5:2.

15. Halpern, *Naval History of World War I*, 75–76.

16. Sims and Hendrick, *The Victory at Sea*, 88–90, 102–3, 110–11, 113.

17. J. David Perkins, comp. and ed., "German Submarine Losses from All Causes during World War I"; John Terraine, *The U-boat Wars, 1916–1945*, 141.

18. Paul G. Halpern, "The U.S. Navy in the Great War"; Morison, *Admiral Sims*, 345.

19. Jerry W. Jones, *U.S. Battleship Operations in World War I*, 6–8; Jellicoe's comments on the Channel ports are cited in Wolff, *In Flanders Fields*, 112, 116.

20. Norman Friedman, *Seapower as Strategy: Navies and National Interests*, 141–42.

21. Corbett and Newbolt, *Naval Operations*, 5:2–19 ("impressive" quote on 15).

22. Sims and Hendrick, *The Victory at Sea*, 114; Preston, *Submarines*, 63; Hurley, *The Bridge to France*, 233–34.

23. Sims and Hendrick, *The Victory at Sea*, 116; Halpern, "U.S. Navy in the Great War"; Corbett and Newbolt, *Naval Operations*, 5:11–20, 43–44, 48–49.

24. Gleaves, *History of the Transport Service*, 28–29.

25. T. E. Chandler, "American and British Destroyers," 587.

26. Charles Minor Blackford, *Torpedoboat Sailor*, 66.

27. Still, *Queenstown Patrol*, 7–8; Moore, introduction to *Jane's Fighting Ships*, 147.

28. Still, *Queenstown Patrol*, 9.

29. Blackford, *Torpedoboat Sailor*, 71.

30. Still, *Queenstown Patrol*, 10–15.

31. Ibid., 15–16; Taussig, "Destroyer Experiences" (December 1922): 2025.

32. Blackford, *Torpedoboat Sailor*, 66, 71.

33. Taussig, *Queenstown Patrol*, 17–18; Dorling, *Endless Story*, 327; E. B. Potter, *Nimitz*, 129.

34. Massie, *Castles of Steel*, 734, and Blackford, *Torpedoboat Sailor*, 75, describe the American destroyer squadron's arrival at Queenstown; Sims to Secretary of the Navy (Operations), May 11, 1917, reprinted in Michael Simpson, ed., *Anglo-American Naval Relations, 1917–1919*, 220–21; Gleaves, *History of the Transport Service*, 25, 65; Sims and Hendrick, *The Victory at Sea*, 51–2, 55, 77; Wolff, *In Flanders Fields*, 13.

35. Taussig, *Queenstown Patrol*, 17–21; Taussig, "Destroyer Experiences" (January 1923): 41–45.

36. Taussig, "Destroyer Experiences" (January 1923): 39–41.

37. Blackford, *Torpedoboat Sailor*, 76.

38. Quoted in Still, *Crisis at Sea*, 195.

39. Joseph E. Husband, *On the Coast of France: The Story of United States Naval Forces in French Waters*, 6–9.

40. Society of the First Division, *History of the First Division during the World War, 1917–1919*, 1–2.

41. Gleaves, *History of the Transport Service*, 68–69.

42. Ibid., 25, 26, 28, 32; King and Whitehill, *Fleet Admiral King*, 115; Josephus Daniels, *Our Navy at War*, 71.

43. Gleaves, *History of the Transport Service*, 36.

44. Ibid., 34–35; Moore, introduction to *Jane's Fighting Ships*, 139–40. A summary of *Shaw's* operations in World War I is in US Department of the Navy, Naval History and Heritage Command, *Dictionary of American Naval Fighting Ships* (hereafter cited as *DANFS*).

45. The orders are printed in full in "All Hands," ed., *U.S.S. Seattle during the War*, 27–30; the varied speeds of each convoy group are in ibid., 37.

46. Moore, introduction to *Jane's Fighting Ships*, 147–48.

47. Gleaves, *History of the Transport Service*, 36; *Maumee's* history is in *DANFS*.

48. The undated order is in "All Hands," *U.S.S. Seattle during the War*, 31, 33–35.

49. Gleaves's orders of June 7, 1917, reprinted in ibid., 30; summary wartime histories of *Aphrodite*, *Kanawha*, and *Corsair* are in *DANFS*.

50. Laurence Stallings, *The Doughboys: The Story of the AEF, 1917–1918*, 23; Society of the First Division, *History of the First Division*, 6; "All Hands," *U.S.S.* Seattle *during the War*, 37–39; Gleaves, *History of the Transport Service*, 55–56.

51. "All Hands," *U.S.S.* Seattle *during the War*, 37.

52. Ibid., 39.

53. Ibid., 39, 41; Gleaves, *History of the Transport Service*, 46; *DANFS*, "*Davis* II."

54. "All Hands," *U.S.S.* Seattle *during the War*, 41; Gleaves, *History of the Transport Service*, 41–47; Society of the First Division, *History of the First Division*, 6.

55. Newspaper clipping, "Cruiser Crew Plans Reunion," no source; "World War I file, folder "The *South Dakota* Cruiser," Puget Sound Maritime Historical Society, Seattle; *DANFS, South Dakota*.

56. Stallings, *Doughboys*, 213; Still, *Crisis at Sea*, 302–3.

57. Still, *Crisis at Sea*, 304.

58. Diary of Searcy B. Dysart, US Navy, May 30, October 9–17, 1918, National World War I Museum, 2003.8.1, Kansas City, MO; diary of CPO Leroy V. Collins, USN, no specific dates, 2005.30.5, ibid.

59. Stallings, *Doughboys*, 38.

60. Evans's role and heroics are summarized in Dorling, *Endless Story*, 327. See also Sims and Hendrick, *The Victory at Sea*, 74.

61. Taussig, "Destroyer Experiences" (January 1923): 48. The description of Bantry Bay is by destroyer *McDougal* crewman Charles Minor Blackford (*Torpedoboat Sailor*, 78).

62. Blackford, *Torpedoboat Sailor*, 49.

63. Ibid., 53–54.

64. Ibid., 54–56; Taussig, *Queenstown Patrol*, 30–31.

65. Taussig, "Destroyer Experiences" (January 1923): 55.

66. Ibid., 56.

67. Taussig, *Queenstown Patrol*, 31.

68. Morison, *Admiral Sims*, 355.

69. Dorling, *Endless Story*, 329; G. S. Knox, "The United States Navy," in *The Naval Annual, 1919*, edited by Brassey and Leyland, 69. See also Taussig, *Queenstown Patrol*, 66; Taussig, "Destroyer Experiences" (January 1923): 57; *DANFS*, "*Conyngham* I" and "*Downes* I." *Jenkins's* experiences are related in "U.S.S. *Jenkins*, DD-42"; "Troopships, Battleships, Subs, Cruisers, Destroyers: A History of How the United States Navy Moved the Army to the War in Europe during WWI."

70. Preston, *Submarines*, 66–67; Sims and Hendrick, *The Victory at Sea*, 160–61; Corbett and Newbolt, *Naval Operations*, 5:76–77; Destroyer History Foundation, "Early Destroyers; First Destroyers; *Bainbridge* Class; USS *Bainbridge*."

71. Morison, *Admiral Sims*, 368–70, 375.

Chapter Three Aloft

1. "Aviators Attempt London–Paris Return Flight," *International Herald Tribune*, June 9, 1914, reprinted in *New York Times* online, July 13, 2014; Hart et al., *War on the Sea*, 288.

2. The inventory is in Roy Grossnick et al., *United States Naval Aviation, 1910–1995*, 447. See also Arthur Hezlet, *Aircraft and Sea Power*, 91; Rossano, *Price of Honor*, 1; Rossano, *Stalking the U-boat*, 6; Edward Arpee, *From Frigates to Flat-Tops: The Story of the Life and Achievements of Rear Admiral William Adger Moffett, U.S.N., "the Father of Naval Aviation,"* 82.

3. Perkins, "German Submarine Losses"; Hezlet, *Aircraft and Sea Power*, 92; Hart et al., *War on the Sea*, 286–87; Dwight R. Messimer, *Find and Destroy: Anti-submarine Warfare in World War I*, 138.

4. Van Wyen, "Naval Aviation in World War I," 13; Grossnick et al., *United States Naval Aviation*, 26.

5. Rossano, *Stalking the U-boat*, 7–8, 149, 150.

6. Ibid., 8–15; Geoffrey L. Rossano, ed., *Hero of the Angry Sky: The World War I Diary and Letters of David S. Ingalls, America's First Naval Ace*, 5; Joe G. Cline, "Naval Aviation in World War I: First Naval Aviation Unit in France," 10–12; Hezlet, *Aircraft and Sea Power*, 95–96.

7. Cline, "First Naval Aviation Unit," 12–13.

8. Ibid., 12.

9. Ibid.

10. Kennedy, *Over Here*, 147; Rossano, *Hero of the Angry Sky*, 11, 14.

11. Rossano, *Price of Honor*, 3–4, 9 (MacLeish quote); Ralph D. Paine, *The First Yale Unit*, 1:11. The two-volume work is online at various sources. I have used the Hathi Trust Digital Library version, http://Catalogue.hathitrust.org/Record/000403341, based on the holding at the University of California Library.

12. Rossano, *Price of Honor*, 16–17; Rossano, *Hero of the Angry Sky*, 21, 27, 31n, 34, 35 (captions); Sims and Hendrick, *The Victory at Sea*, 328–29; R. Paine, *The First Yale Unit*, 1:1–36, 158–60, 164–65, which recounts in detail the stories of Vorys, Wells, and Davison; Amy Athey McDonald, "Defending Allied Skies: Yale's Pioneering Pilots Form First Naval Aviation Unit."

13. Rossano, *Stalking the U-boat*, 17.

14. Grossnick et al., *United States Naval Aviation*, 27.

15. Rossano, *Stalking the U-boat*, 22–23, 81.

16. Grossnick et al., *United States Naval Aviation*, 29.

17. David Langley, "The Life and Times of Glenn Hammond Curtiss"; R. Paine, *The First Yale Unit*, 2:76.

18. Izette Winter Robb, "Naval Aviation in World War I: The Navy Builds an Aircraft Factory," 34–35.

19. J. Sterling Halstead, "Naval Aviation in World War I: Trained by the Royal Flying Corps"; Grossnick et al., *United States Naval Aviation*, 27.

20. Michael D. Roberts, *Dictionary of American Naval Aviation Squadrons*, vol. 2, *The History of VP, VPB, VP (HL) and VP (AM) Squadrons*, chap. 1; "World War I Era Naval Aviation Stations"; Grossnick et al., *United States Naval Aviation*, 27–28; Sims and Hendrick, *The Victory at Sea*, 327–29.

21. Robb, "Navy Builds a Factory," 35.

22. Sims and Hendrick, *The Victory at Sea*, 247–48; Geddes is quoted in Hart et al., *War on the Sea*, 359.

23. Rossano, *Stalking the U-boat*, 27.

24. Grossnick et al., *United States Naval Aviation*, 30; Cone is quoted in Rossano, *Stalking the U-boat*, 26.

Chapter Four "Drab Efficiency"

1. Charles C. Gill, "Role of the U.S. Navy's Transport Service during World War 1, November 1918," n.p.

2. Corbett and Newbolt, *Naval Operations*, 5:50–51.

3. Gleaves, *History of the Transport Service*, 52, 61–65; Gill, "Role of the U.S. Navy's Transport Service."

4. Hurley, *The Bridge to France*, 46–47.

5. Ibid., 42–45; information on the fifty-eight *West* cargo vessels is in a memorandum by Gene Harrower titled "'West' Ships of World War I," Austen Hemion Collection, Puget Sound Maritime Historical Society, Seattle.

6. Gleaves, *History of the Transport Service*, 62–74. The portion of Daniels's report referring to the electrical repairs to ex-German ships is quoted in Hart et al., *War on the Sea*, 319–20.

7. H. W. McCurdy, *Maritime History of the Pacific Northwest*, 1:271.

8. Hurley, *The Bridge to France*, 51–52.

9. Bill Durham, "The Shipping Board Ships," 25; Bill Durham, "The Last Boom: Wooden Shipbuilding in World War I."

10. Dorling, *Endless Story*, 331; Gill, "Role of the U.S. Navy's Transport Service." See also "Josephus Daniels' Official Report"; and US Department of the Navy, Naval Historical Center, "Online Library of Selected Images: World War I Era Transports."

11. Sims and Hendrick, *The Victory at Sea*, 130–31, 140.

12. Ibid., 130–32; Corbett and Newbolt, *Naval Operations*, 5:48–49.

13. Sims and Hendrick, *The Victory at Sea*, 163, 361–62; Gleaves, *History of the Transport Service*, 241; Rossano, *Stalking the U-boat*, 52.

14. Sims and Hendrick, *The Victory at Sea*, 122–23.

15. Ibid., 123, 124, 129.

16. Howeth, *History of Communications-Electronics*, 253, 258, 264.

17. The Admiralty's assertion is quoted in US Department of the Navy, Office of Naval Records and Library Monographs Historical Section, *German Submarine Activities*, 9; Sims and Hendrick, *The Victory at Sea*, 124–25.

18. Ibid., 125, 129; Carroll Storrs Alden, "American Submarine Operations in the War," 1017.

19. Corbett and Newbolt, *Naval Operations*, 5:135.

20. USisH Department of the Navy, Office of Naval Records and Library Monographs Historical Section, *German Submarine Activities*, 8–12, 23. The cruises of U-151, 156, 140, 117, 155, and 106 and their activities are detailed on 23–134. For U-151's suspected cable-cutting operations, see 119–23. The navy's conclusions about the U-boat war in the western Atlantic are in ibid., 141, following a series of quite confusing charts and tables. For an early postwar list of losses to submarine operations off

the American coast, including mining and gunfire, see US Department of the Navy, Office of Naval Records and Library Monographs Historical Section, *American Ship Casualties of the World War: Including Naval Vessels, Merchant Ships, Sailing Vessels and Fishing Craft*; and Terraine, *U-boat Wars*, 133. The chaotic state of America's antisubmarine war in coastal waters a quarter century later is ably recounted in Michael Gannon, *Operation Drumbeat: The Dramatic True Story of Germany's First U-boat Attacks along the American Coast in World War II*. The frequent frustrations and limitations of submarine warfare seem to produce a measure of barbarism in its practitioners, no matter their nationality. See Michael Sturma, *Surface and Destroy: The Submarine Gun War in the Pacific*.

21. Sims and Hendrick, *The Victory at Sea*, 59–60.

22. Ibid., 362.

23. Halpern, *Naval History of World War I*, 364.

24. Sims and Hendrick, *The Victory at Sea*, 136.

25. R. Paine, *Fighting Fleets*, 1–2, 35–37; Blackford, *Torpedoboat Sailor*, 90.

26. By this time, nearly every merchantman and warship on the Atlantic wore similar paint schemes. The author was Royal Navy lieutenant Norman Wilkinson. Following months of study and examination of various color schemes from a variety of angles and conditions of light and through both direct and periscope observation, Wilkinson recommended a "dazzle" pattern of ship painting that was taken up enthusiastically in May 1917 by both the British and the American maritime communities. The objective was not to hide a vessel but to confuse and deceive U-boat commanders attempting to set up a line of attack. Some Allied sources dismissed camouflage as of little consequence. A British submarine commander argued that visibility at sea was "more a matter of mass than of colour." In 1931, naval historians R. H. Gibson and Maurice Prendergast agreed: "It is doubtful whether these dazzle-painted ships caused many submarine commanders at the periscope to mis-estimate the target's course and speed." More recent scholarship, however, asserts that camouflage did have a disruptive effect on U-boat captains as they prepared to attack. Some commanders "were so bothered by the lurid emerald greens, pinks and purples used in ships' color-schemes that they had the eye-pieces of their periscopes fitted with color-filters." Whether camouflage was effective or not, it became "the fad of the hour" during the last eighteen months of the war. Journalist Henry Beston observed that hundreds of "one colour boats" plying the perilous Atlantic from the New World to the Old and back again "have been docked to make a cubist holiday; the futurists are saving democracy." Gibson and Prendergast, *German Submarine War*, 177; Beston, *Full Speed Ahead*, 123; Preston, *Submarines*, 62, 63.

27. Diary . . . from the Service of Leonard C. Kenyon, May 8–November 9, 1918, National World War I Museum, Kansas City, MO.

28. Samuel E. Avery, "Soldier's Mail: Letters Home from a New England Soldier, 1916–1918."

29. "Johnny Arthur Didway"; Diary of Stephen W. Ostrander, National World War I Museum, Kansas City, MO; Blackford, *Torpedoboat Sailor*, 98–99.

30. R. Paine, *Fighting Fleets*, 36–38.

31. Horace Taylor Diaries, 1917–18 "Green Journal" ("To France and Back"), National World War I Museum Archives, Kansas City, MO; Canadian Broadcasting Company [CBC] News, "Halifax Explosion."

32. R. Paine, *Fighting Fleets*, 36–38.

33. Blackford, *Torpedoboat Sailor*, 114, 137.

34. Ibid., 111–12.

35. G. S. Knox, "The United States Navy," in *The Naval Annual, 1919*, edited by Brassey and Leyland, 72; J. K. Taussig, "Destroyer Experiences" (February 1923): 237–41; Sims and Hendrick, *The Victory at Sea*, 138.

36. William F. Halsey and J. Bryan III, *Admiral Halsey's Story*, 29.

37. Ray Millholland, *The Splinter Fleet of the Otranto Barrage*, 72–73; Blackford, *Torpedoboat Sailor*, 128–33; Still, *Queenstown Patrol*, 92–94; Still, *Crisis at Sea*, 359, 403.

38. Halsey and Bryan, *Admiral Halsey's Story*, 36.

39. Ibid., 27.

40. Taussig, "Destroyer Experiences" (February 1923): 227, 234.

41. Ibid., 235; Blackford, *Torpedoboat Sailor*, 84; Sims and Hendrick, *The Victory at Sea*, 83–85; R. Paine, *Fighting Fleets*, 85.

42. R. Paine, *Fighting Fleets*, 84–88.

43. Blackford, *Torpedoboat Sailor*, 84, 88.

44. Sims and Hendrick, *The Victory at Sea*, 119, 143, 154.

45. "Marine Flyer in France: The Diary of Captain Alfred A. Cunningham, November 1917–January 1918."

46. R. Paine, *Fighting Fleets*, 24–25.

47. Trask, *Captains and Cabinets*, 80–81.

48. Corbett and Newbolt, *Naval Operations*, 5:120–42 (quote on 136).

49. Perkins, "German Submarine Losses"; Still, *Crisis at Sea*, 187.

50. Corbett and Newbolt, *Naval Operations*, 5:136–39; Preston, *Submarines*, 62; Hezlet, *Aircraft and Sea Power*, 100–101.

51. Quoted in Klachko and Trask, *Admiral William Shepherd Benson*, 77.

52. Sims to Opnav, July 21, 1917, reprinted in Simpson, *Anglo-American Naval Relations*, 330; Jones, *U.S. Battleship Operations*, 6–10.

53. Wilson is quoted in Klachko and Trask, *Admiral William Shepherd Benson*, 80–81; Morison, *Admiral Sims*, 362.

54. Klachko and Trask, *Admiral William Shepherd Benson*, 78–79.

55. Corbett and Newbolt, *Naval Operations*, 5:130–33; Bacon's 1916 plan is discussed in Sondhaus, *Great War at Sea*, 268–69.

56. Ibid., 134; Klachko and Trask, *Admiral William Shepherd Benson*, 83; Jones, *U.S. Battleship Operations*, 12–13.

57. Dudley W. Knox, *American Naval Participation in the Great War (with Special Reference to the European Theater of Operations)*, unpaginated, source: US Congress, House Committee on Naval Affairs, *Hearings Before Committee on Naval Affairs of the House of Representatives on Sundry Legislation Affecting the Naval Establishment, 1927–1928* (70th Cong., 1st sess.). The Benson-Sims exchange and its background are in Klachko and Trask, *Admiral William Shepherd Benson*, 71, 108–9.

58. Knox, *American Naval Participation*.

59. Klachko and Trask, *Admiral William Shepherd Benson*, 108–9.

60. Throughout late 1917 and early into the following year, the armed-yacht flotilla at Brest was strengthened by a small but steady stream of naval units, either direct from the United States or from Ireland. Husband, *On the Coast of France*, 12–13, 16–17.

61. Knox, *American Naval Participation*; Halpern, "U.S. Navy in the Great War."

62. "Professional Notes: Convoy System's Success"; Gleaves, *History of the Transport Service*, 30; Sims and Hendrick, *The Victory at Sea*, 33–34 (quote). A brief account of the loss of the *Antilles*, *Covington*, and *President Lincoln* is in Knox, *American Naval Participation*. Additional information on the *President Lincoln* can be found at US Department of the Navy, Naval Historical Center, "Online Library of Selected Images: U.S.S. *President Lincoln* (1917–1918)." For *Covington*, see "Troopships, Battleships, Subs, Cruisers, Destroyers."

63. "The Sinking of the *Tuscania*," including Cobb's account "When the Sea-Asp Stings" that appeared in the March 9, 1918, issue of the *Saturday Evening Post*, is in "Doughboy Center: The Story of the American Expeditionary Force." Most of a lengthy, unpaginated, and untitled article incorporating survivors' stories and impressions of the *Tuscania* sinking is in US Army Twentieth Engineers, "World War 1: The Sixth Engineers." A note indicates that the article was taken almost verbatim from "Twentieth Engineers—France—1917–1918–1919."

64. The most complete contemporary account of *Cassin*'s ordeal is Secretary Daniels's wartime report excerpted in Hart et al., *War on the Sea*, 343–46. See also Dorling, *Endless Story*, 333–34; R. Paine, *Fighting Fleets*, 69–70; *Cassin* entry in US Department of the Navy, Naval History and Heritage Command, *Dictionary of American Naval Fighting Ships* (hereafter cited as *DANFS*); and NavSource Naval History, Destroyer Archive, *Cassin* http://www.navsource.org/archives/05/043.htm.

65. *DANFS*, *Alcedo*.

66. The scarcely mentioned and barely remembered loss of *Chauncey* is briefly recounted in US Department of the Navy, Naval Historical Center, "Online Library of Selected Images: US Navy Ships, USS *Chauncey*"; and Brock Yates, *Destroyers and Destroyermen: The Story of Our "Tin-Can" Navy*, 25. *Jones*'s ordeal is amply recounted in Hart et al., *War on the Sea*, 346–49; R. Paine, *Fighting Fleets*, 62–69; Dorling, *Endless Story*, 335–37; and for Kalk's heroics and death, Still, *Crisis at Sea*. A recent account of the loss of the *Jones* is Worth Bagley, "Torpedoed in the Celtic Sea." For Hans Rose, see Sims, *The Victory at Sea*, 127–28.

67. Sims's characteristically dramatic story is in Sims and Hendrick, *The Victory at Sea*, 155–60. Dorling tells essentially the same tale with a slight variation in details in *Endless Story*, 334. A cursory account is in *DANFS*, *Fanning*.

68. Klachko and Trask, *Admiral William Shepherd Benson*, 86.

69. "Memorandum by Benson, London, November 1917," reprinted in Simpson, *Anglo-American Naval Relations*, 333–34. See also Jones, *U.S. Battleship Operations*, 15–17.

70. Leighton, *Simsadus*, 60–61; Rossano, *Stalking the U-boat*, 51–52, 314, 319. For the origins of the Planning Staff in Sims's headquarters, see William Benson (CNO) to the Navy Department, November 19, 1917, and Planning Staff Memoranda No.

45 ("Organization of a Plans Division for the Navy Department," August 10, 1918) and Memorandum No. 71 ("History of the Planning Section London," December 30, 1918).The admission by planning staffers that they knew relatively little about the technical side of naval aviation is Memorandum No. 12 ("United States Naval Air Effort in European Waters," February 15, 1918). All documents published in US Department of the Navy, Office of Naval Intelligence, Historical Section, *The American Naval Planning Section London*, 10, 61, 311, 489–91.

Chapter Five **Sending the Hunters**

1. Dwight R. Messimer, *Find and Destroy: Antisubmarine Warfare in World War I*, 141 (quote), 146.

2. C. Alden, "American Submarine Operations," 814; Edward C. Whitman, "The School of War: U.S. Submarines in World War I."

3. Whitman, "School of War."

4. Ibid. Journalist Henry B. Beston recounted the young sub skipper's story in *Full Speed Ahead*, 4–9. A more comprehensive and authoritative account is C. Alden, "American Submarine Operations," 1013–14.

5. John Rousmanier, "The Romance of the Subchasers," 44.

6. Stephen D. Regan, "Gilded Men and the Suicide Fleet," 60.

7. Rousmanier, "Romance of the Subchasers," 43, 44 (caption); Michael D. Hull, "The Navy's Gallant Sentries"; Woofenden, *Hunters of the Steel Sharks*, 10–25.

8. Vernon I. Lucas, "The Battle of Alaska."

9. G. S. Knox, "The United States Navy," in *The Naval Annual, 1919*, edited by Brassey and Leyland, 73; Delaware Military History, "The SC-1 Class Submarine Chaser." The listing of all 448 World War I subchasers with some entries including captioned photos can be found at Paul R. Yarnall, webmaster, "Patrol Vessels, Gunboats, Submarine Chasers and Section Patrol Craft Index: 'SC-1 Class 110' Submarine Chaser (SC-1 to SC-448)."

10. Dole is quoted in Woofenden, *Hunters of the Steel Sharks*, 14; Rousmanier, "Romance of the Subchasers," 43.

11. Woofenden, *Hunters of the Steel Sharks*, 28.

12. Alexander W. Moffat, *Maverick Navy*, 35–38.

13. Ibid., 38–40.

14. Rousmanier, "Romance of the Subchasers," 44; Woofenden, *Hunters of the Steel Sharks*, 61; "International Notes: U-boat Chasers Crossing the Atlantic."

15. Moffat, *Maverick Navy*, 45; Millholland, *Splinter Fleet*, 19–20, 37–40.

16. Millholland, *Splinter Fleet*, 50–55.

17. Leighton, *Simsadus*, 78.

18. Moffat, *Maverick Navy*, 49–56; Millholland, *Splinter Fleet*, 55; Rousmanier, "Romance of the Subchasers," 43; Woofenden, *Hunters of the Steel Sharks*, 61–63; Hilary Ranald Chambers Jr., *United States Submarine Chasers in the Mediterranean, Adriatic and the Attack on Durazzo*, chaps. 3–4.

19. Millholland, *Splinter Fleet*, 57, 61–62.

20. Woofenden, *Hunters of the Steel Sharks*, 70–73; Moffat, *Maverick Navy*, 66–70; Rousmanier, "Romance of the Subchasers," 44.

21. Leighton, *Simsadus*, 30.

Chapter Six **Battleship Boys**

1. Daniels to Benson, November 13, 1917, reprinted in Simpson, *Anglo-American Naval Relations*, 335; Jones, *U.S. Battleship Operations*, 17.

2. Hugh Power, *Battleship Texas*, 12; Bieri, oral history interview, no. 1, 27–28.

3. Hunter, *Jellicoe, Beatty, Sims and Rodman*, 5–6.

4. Moore, introduction to *Jane's Fighting Ships*, 134–36.

5. The following account of Battleship Division Nine's ordeal off the Newfoundland Banks is from Hunter, *Jellicoe, Beatty, Sims and Rodman*, 6–14.

6. Rodman's remark is quoted in Jones, *U.S. Battleship Operations*, 26–27.

7. Ibid., 28; Rodman, *Yarns of a Kentucky Admiral*, 268–69.

8. Rodman, *Yarns of a Kentucky Admiral*, 274; Still, *Crisis at Sea*, 203; Jones, *U.S. Battleship Operations*, 29–32.

9. Hunter, *Beatty, Jellicoe, Sims and Rodman*, 18–22; Rodman, *Yarns of a Kentucky Admiral*, 275–80.

10. Sims to Benson, February 15, 1918, reprinted in Simpson, *Anglo-American Naval Relations*, 343.

11. "America's New Armada," 176; H. T. Mayo, introduction to *War on the Sea*, edited by Hart et al., vii.

Chapter Seven **Keeping the Seas**

1. Hew Strachan, *The First World War*, 296; Max Hastings, "The Necessary War."

2. Memoranda Nos. 1–8 are published in US Department of the Navy, Office of Naval Intelligence, Historical Section, *American Naval Planning Section*, 14–58. Memorandum No. 45 ("Organization of a Plans Division for the Navy Department," August 10, 1918) stressed the concentration of the London Planning Staff on its main mission, not administrative work. Ibid., 311.

3. Memoranda Nos. 9 and 18, in ibid., 67–68, 171.

4. Gleaves, *History of the Transport Service*, appx. table B, "Report by Months of Transport and Escort Duty Performed by U.S. and Foreign Navies Up to Signing of the Armistice," 241; Knox, *American Naval Participation*.

5. Blackford, *Torpedoboat Sailor*, 101.

6. Husband, *On the Coast of France*, 13–14, 15.

7. Ibid., 20–22.

8. Ibid., 23.

9. US Department of the Navy: Naval History and Heritage Command, *Dictionary of American Naval Fighting Ships* (hereafter cited as *DANFS*), *Manley* II, http://www.history.navy.mil/danfs/m3/manley.

10. Dorling, *Endless Story*, 337–38; semiofficial histories of *Stewart*, *Whipple*, and *Truxton* are in *DANFS*; US Department of the Navy, Naval History and Heritage Command, "Navy Medal of Honor, World War 1."

11. Dorling, *Endless Story*, 340–42; *DANFS, Shaw*.

12. Blackford, *Torpedoboat Sailor*, 141.

13. R. Paine, *Fighting Fleets*, 72–73.

14. Ibid., 210; Still, *Crisis at Sea*, 369.

15. R. Paine, *Fighting Fleets*, 211–15.

16. *Corsair's* history is in *DANFS*. Further information and photos can be found at "Remo," "Naval Warfare: Examining Ships That Have Made an Impact on Naval Warfare and Naval History."

17. Sims and Hendrick, *The Victory at Sea*, 152–54.

18. *DANFS, Lydonia*. The fates of UB-70 and UB-39 are listed in Perkins, "German Submarine Losses." See also Sims and Hendrick, *The Victory at Sea*, 163.

19. Beston, *Full Speed Ahead*, 125–29.

20. R. Paine, *Fighting Fleets*, 99; Whitman, "School of War."

21. Whitman, "School of War."

22. Ibid.; R. Paine, *Fighting Fleets*, 101–7.

23. Whitman, "School of War"; C. Alden, "American Submarine Operations," 1016–18.

24. C. Alden, "American Submarine Operations," 1015; Messimer, *Find and Destroy*, 140–41.

25. C. Alden, "American Submarine Operations," 1019.

26. Ibid., 1020.

27. Ibid., 1021–22.

28. Ibid., 1025.

29. Ibid., 1033.

30. Ibid., 1027–30.

31. Ibid., 1035–39; Whitman, "School of War."

32. C. Alden, "American Submarine Operations," 1023.

33. Ibid., 1025.

34. Ibid., 1043; Whitman, "School of War"; "L4" history in *DANFS*.

35. See entries for K-3, K-4, and E-1 in *DANFS*.

Chapter Eight Chasers

1. Sims and Hendrick, *The Victory at Sea*, 287.

2. Diana Schroeder, *The History of the Sea Mine and Its Continued Importance in Today's Navy*, 1.

3. Leighton, *Simsadus*, 68; Sims and Hendrick, *The Victory at Sea*, 290; Knox, *American Naval Participation*; Messimer, *Find and Destroy*, 26.

4. "Summary of Memoranda No. 29, 32, and 34 of May 25, May 30, June 7; "Memorandum No. 41 ("Anti-submarine Tactics," July 13, 1918), in US Department of the Navy, Office of Naval Intelligence, Historical Section, *American Naval Planning Section*, 273, 513 (hereafter cited as Memorandum No. [title and date], in *American Naval Planning Section*).

5. "Summary of Memoranda 29, 32 and 34 . . ."; Sims and Hendrick, *The Victory at Sea*, 211–13 (quotes), 256; Chambers, *United States Submarine Chasers*, chaps. 1–2 (with editorial note).

6. Memoranda No. 29 ("Submarine Chaser Bases," May 25, 1918); Memorandum No. 36 ("Depth Charge Equipment of Submarine Chasers," June 12, 1918), in *American Naval Planning Section*, 227, 243.

7. Sims and Hendrick, *The Victory at Sea*, 215. For Keyes's innovations, see Leighton, *Simsadus*, 68–69. See also Woofenden, "Rough Seas." The *Subchaser Archives Notes* are published online monthly. They are found at http://www.subchaser.org/SAN-Vol-No.

8. Moffat, *Maverick Navy*, 89–90, discusses the C-tube, Woofenden, *Hunters of the Steel Sharks*, 40–43, the K-tube. See also Sims and Hendrick, *The Victory at Sea*, 204, 216–20. Cotten's instructions are reprinted in Todd Woofenden, webmaster, "Cotten: Instructions and Doctrine."

9. Leighton, *Simsadus*, 79; Todd Woofenden, "SC 254"; Dole is quoted in Woofenden, *Hunters of the Steel Sharks*, 93.

10. Sims and Hendrick, *The Victory at Sea*, 217.

11. Millholland, *Splinter Fleet*, 180.

12. "Cotten: Instructions and Doctrine."

13. Todd Woofenden has published the eighteen incident reports filed by subchaser captains on the Ottranto Barrage line between June 15 and October 24, 1918; while several report ambiguous evidence at best of some possible damage to submarines, none claims a clear-cut kill. Woofenden, *Hunters of the Steel Sharks*, 95–98. See also Chambers, *United States Submarine Chasers*, chap. 10, notes 1–3.

14. M. S. Brown, "Life Overseas on the Yankee Sub-Chasers," 3, 6.

15. Ibid., 7; John Ford, director, Darryl F. Zanuck producer, *Submarine Patrol*. The snappy dialogue was in part due to occasional screenwriter William Faulkner.

16. US Department of the Navy, Office of Naval Records and Library Monographs Historical Section, *Northern Barrage*, 9.

17. Paul G. Halpern, *The Naval War in the Mediterranean, 1914–1918*, 288, 358–63.

18. Sims and Hendrick, *The Victory at Sea*, 213–14; Halpern, *Naval History of World War I*, 160–61, 171–72.

19. Woofenden, *Hunters of the Steel Sharks*, 77–82; Leighton, *Simsadus*, 78; Sims and Hendrick, *The Victory at Sea*, 214.

20. Halpern, *Naval War in the Mediterranean*, 504–5.

21. Chambers, *U.S. Submarine Chasers*, chap. 8.

22. Halpern, *Naval War in the Mediterranean*, 506.

23. Alfred F. Loomis, "What Were the Faults of the Sub-Chasers?"; Millholland, *Splinter Fleet*, 221.

24. Chambers, *U.S. Submarine Chasers*, chap. 9.

25. D. J. Williams, "A Brief Diary of My Cruise in Foreign Waters on the USSC 227"; John M. Berry, *The Great Influenza: The Epic Story of the Deadliest Plague in History*, 2–3.

26. Halpern, *Naval History of World War I*, 175–76.

27. Unless otherwise cited, this account of the Durazzo Raid is from Chambers, *U.S. Submarine Chasers*, chap. 10, notes 1–3. Woofenden contributes supplementary information in *Hunters of the Steel Sharks*, 98–106. Millholland, *Splinter Fleet*, 227–39, provides a somewhat over-the-top account that needs to be read with care (quote on 227).

Chapter Nine **Barrages, Batteries, Bombers, and Battleships**

1. USisH Department of the Navy, Office of Naval Records and Library Monographs Historical Section, *Northern Barrage*, 12 (hereafter cited as *Northern Barrage*).

2. Ibid., 13; Morison, *Admiral Sims*, 414–15.

3. *Northern Barrage*, 13, 14.

4. Sims and Hendrick, *The Victory at Sea*, 293; Knox, *American Naval Participation*. A detailed discussion of the numerous approaches and decision-making processes that lay behind the development of the Mark VI mine is in *Northern Barrage*, 16–19.

5. Those portions of Earle's reports of July 18 and 30, 1917, quoted herein are reprinted in *Northern Barrage*, 19–22. Description of the complex manufacture and assembly procedure is in Hart et al., *War on the Sea*, 325–26.

6. *Northern Barrage*, 28.

7. Ibid., 31.

8. Ibid., 51–52, 70–71; Knox, *American Naval Participation*.

9. Daniel P. Mannix III, "The Great North Sea Mine Barrage," 1–2.

10. *Northern Barrage*, 93–94.

11. Memorandum Number 17 ("Review of Mining Policy," March 12, 1918), British Comment, in US Department of the Navy, Office of Naval Intelligence, Historical Section, *American Naval Planning Section*, 157, 163 (hereafter cited as Memorandum No. [title and date], in *American Naval Planning Section*).

12. Memorandum Number 18 ("Anti-submarine Policy," March 28, 1918), in ibid., 177; *Northern Barrage*, 91–103 (quotes on 100, 103).

13. Mannix, "Great North Sea Mine Barrage," 3; Paul Ottenstein Diary, November 12, 1918, National World War I Museum, 84.66.5, Kansas City, MO.

14. Mannix, "Great North Sea Mine Barrage," 4; Reginald R. Belknap, "The Yankee Mining Squadron; or, Laying the North Sea Mine Barrage," 13. Commander Belknap was officer in overall charge of the American minelaying expedition. Knox, *American Naval Participation*.

15. *Northern Barrage*, 110; George L. Golden, diary, "7/16–20/18," National World War I Museum, Kansas City, MO.

16. Belknap, "Yankee Mining Squadron," 14–16; Mannix, "Great North Sea Mine Barrage," 3, 4; Lester T. Lee, "Navy"; Knox, *American Naval Participation*.

17. Mannix, "Great North Sea Mine Barrage," 5. The sal ammoniac seal is discussed in King and Whitehill, *Fleet Admiral King*, 135.

18. Lee, "Navy"; Golden, diary, "7/25, 27"; Belknap, "Yankee Mining Squadron," 5–6, 30–31.

19. Belknap, "Yankee Mining Squadron," 21, 28; Halpern, *Naval History of World War I*, 440.

20. Corbett and Newbolt, *Naval Operations*, 5:334–35, 342–43; Terraine, *U-boat Wars*, 89; Messimer, *Find and Destroy*, 186–87; Halpern, *Naval History of World War I*, 440–41.

21. Sims is quoted in Morison, *Admiral Sims*, 416.

22. Halpern, *Naval War in the Mediterranean*, 513.

23. E. R. Lewis, "The 14-Inch Naval Railway Batteries"; US Department of the Navy, Office of Naval Records and Library Monographs Historical Section, *The United States Naval Railway Batteries in France*, esp. 1–2.

24. Grossnick et al., *United States Naval Aviation*, 30.

25. Still, *Crisis at Sea*, 143; Rossano, *Price of Honor*, 2–3.

26. Rossano, *Price of Honor*, 144.

27. Rossano, *Stalking the U-boat*, 128–30; Grossnick et al., *United States Naval Aviation*, 27, 35 (caption).

28. Roberts, *American Naval Aviation Squadrons*, vol. 2, chap. 1 (unpaginated); R. Paine, *The First Yale Unit*, 2:31.

29. Rossano, *Price of Honor*, 33.

30. R. Paine, *The First Yale Unit*, 2:3–5.

31. Memorandum No. 11 ("Morale: Allied and Enemy," February 13, 1918), in *American Naval Planning Section*, 84.

32. Rossano, *Hero of the Angry Sky*, 81, 136.

33. Rossano, *Stalking the U-boat*, 85–87, 88–89, 150.

34. Husband, *On the Coast of France*, 109.

35. Rossano, *Stalking the U-boat*, 88, 123, 150, 186–88; Rossano, *Hero of the Angry Sky*, 81, 135 (caption); R. Paine, *The First Yale Unit*, 2:31; Grossnick et al., *United States Naval Aviation*, 31.

36. There are a number of accounts of this incident. The most detailed is R. Paine, *The First Yale Unit*, 2:35–45 (quotes on 36, 41).

37. Ibid., 31.

38. Rossano, *Stalking the U-boat*, 150–53.

39. Ibid., 159.

40. Messimer, *Find and Destroy*, 137–38.

41. Roberts, *American Naval Aviation Squadrons*, 8; "Casualties of the United States Navy: Naval Aviation by Date and Base"; Rossano, *Stalking the U-boat*, 159; R. Paine, *The First Yale Unit*, 2:92–96; R. Paine, *Fighting Fleets*, 152–53.

42. Knox, *American Naval Participation*.

43. Rossano, *Stalking the U-boat*, 172.

44. Knox, *American Naval Participation*; Rossano, *Stalking the U-boat*, 86; H. T. Bartlett, "Mission of Aircraft with the Fleet," 741. For a brief discussion of the overall naval uses of dirigibles, see R. G. Pennoyer, "Rigid Airships in the United States Navy," 526–27.

45. Rossano, *Stalking the U-boat*, 178; R. Paine, *The First Yale Unit*, 2:169–70, 298.

46. R. Paine, *The First Yale Unit*, 2:298–300.

47. Perkins, "German Submarine Losses"; "U-boat Fates: U-boat Losses, 1914–1918."

48. Henry Woodhouse, "The Aircraft's Part in Beating the U-boat," 2738; Rossano, *Stalking the U-boat*, 178–79; R. Paine, *The First Yale Unit*, 2:300.

49. D. E. Cummings, "Use of Aircraft in Naval Warfare," 1682.

50. Hezlet, *Aircraft and Sea Power*, 97–98; Leighton, *Simsadus*, 90–99; Hart et al., *War on the Sea*, 359.

51. R. Paine, *The First Yale Unit*, 2:170.

52. Ibid.

53. Ralph Paine devoted an entire chapter to "the sublime spirit of Dunkirk" in *Fighting Fleets*, 236–67. For additional materials, see his *First Yale Unit*, 2:140–42. John Warner Jones Correspondence, March 31, August 2, 1918, and passim, National World War I Museum, Kansas City, MO.

54. Rossano, *Stalking the U-boat*, 64; Rossano, *Hero of the Angry Sky*, 141–42, 151n22; Strachan, *The First World War*, 296–98.

55. Rossano, *Price of Honor*, 131–34.

56. Rossano, *Hero of the Angry Sky*, 144–63 (quotes on 150, 155, 161, 162); Rossano, *Price of Honor*, 144, 147.

57. Rossano, *Price of Honor*, 160.

58. R. Paine, *The First Yale Unit*, 2:169–71; Rossano, *Stalking the U-boat*, 315.

59. Rossano, *Stalking the U-boat*, 315–16.

60. R. Paine, *The First Yale Unit*, 2:180–83.

61. Ibid., 175.

62. Rossano, *Stalking the U-boat*, 320–21.

63. Ibid., 286–91 (quote on 290).

64. Ibid., 325–26; Sims and Hendrick, *The Victory at Sea*, 331. Sims misspells McDonnell's name, erroneously adding an *a*. Paine and Rossano, however, concur.

65. Rossano, *Price of Honor*, 176–77; Hart et al., *War on the Sea,* 359.

66. Gates's exploits are fully recounted in R. Paine, *The First Yale Unit*, 2:315–49, and more recently in the online comments accompanying the documentary film *The Millionaires Unit*, released in 2014 and based on the 2007 book by Marc Wortman, *The Millionaire's Unit: The Aristocratic Flyboys Who Fought the Great War and Invented American Air Power*. The entry is at http://www.millionairesunit.org/home/php.

67. Harmon's heroics are summarized in Sims and Hendrick, *The Victory at Sea*, 334.

68. Rossano, *Price of Honor*, 184, 186, 191, 207, 221, 229; Rossano, *Hero of the Angry Sky*, 269.

69. John Warner Jones Correspondence, October 22, 1918, National World War I Memorial, 84.108.10, Kansas City, MO.

70. Leighton, *Simsadus*, 91; Knox, *American Naval Participation*.

71. Jones, *U.S. Battleship Operations*, 22; Hunter, *Jellicoe, Beatty, Sims and Rodman*, 94.

72. "Memorandum by Director of Plans, 19 November 1917: Co-operation of the British and American Battlefleets and Suggested Redistribution of Forces," reprinted in Simpson, *Anglo-American Naval Relations*, 335–36; Norman Friedman, *U.S. Battleships: An Illustrated Design History*, 171–72.

73. Knox, *American Naval Participation*.

74. *North Sea Days: A Brief History of the U.S.S.* Texas *and Life Generally in the North Sea during a War*, 36, 41. Despite vile weather and destructive seas, *Texas* was able to maintain fifteen knots through the worst of the storm. A brief description of the voyage is in Bieri, oral history interview, no. 1, 29–30. Bieri was a junior gunnery officer aboard *Texas*.

75. Bieri, oral history interview, no. 1, 30.

76. Massie, *Castles of Steel*, 747, briefly recounts the German surface attacks on the Norwegian convoys.

77. *North Sea Days*, 34; Jones, *U.S. Battleship Operations*, viii.

78. *North Sea Days*, 26–28; Hunter, *Jellicoe, Beatty, Sims and Rodman*, 95; R. Paine, *Fighting Fleets*, 295.

79. Hunter, *Jellicoe, Beatty, Sims and Rodman*, 96–98; Massie, *Castles of Steel*, 759.

80. Hunter, *Jellicoe, Beatty, Sims and Rodman*, 102–3; Knox, *American Naval Participation*; Massie, *Castles of Steel*, 759.

81. *North Sea Days*, 31–41; R. Paine, *Fighting Fleets*, 289–303; Hunter, *Jellicoe, Beatty, Sims and Rodman*, 93–141; Bieri, oral history interview, no. 1, 31.

82. Corbett and Newbolt, *Naval Operations*, 5:230–38; Halpern, *Naval History of World War I*, 419–21.

83. *North Sea Days*, 24–25; Edward L. Beach Sr. and Edward L. Beach Jr., *From Annapolis to Scapa Flow: The Autobiography of Edward L. Beach, Sr.*, 279.

84. Hunter, *Jellicoe, Beatty, Sims and Rodman*, 72, 75–87 (quotes on 75, 83); Rodman, *Yarns of a Kentucky Admiral*, 273.

85. Rodman, *Yarns of a Kentucky Admiral*, 273; *North Sea Days*, 25, 41, 70; John Berry, *Great Influenza*, 1–3.

86. *North Sea Days*, 42–43, 64–67; Still, *Crisis at Sea*, 261–62.

87. *North Sea Days*, 46, 60.

88. Beach and Beach, *From Annapolis to Scapa Flow*, 281–82.

89. *North Sea Days*, 44.

90. Ibid., 28–74; Hunter, *Jellicoe, Beatty, Sims and Rodman*, 62.

91. Hustvedt, oral history interview, no. 2, 56–57, 60–61; Phister, Hone, and Goodyear, *Battleship Oklahoma, BB-37*, 24–25.

92. Ibid., 24–25; Marder, *From the Dreadnought to Scapa Flow*, vol. 5, *Victory and Aftermath, January 1918–June 1919*, 167; Jones, *U.S. Battleship Operations*, 100–106; Sims and Hendrick, *The Victory at Sea*, 354; Leighton, *Simsadus*, 64–65.

93. Husband, *On the Coast of France*, 86–88; Winston S. Churchill, *The World Crisis, 1911–1918*, 2:1227.

94. Beach and Beach, *From Annapolis to Scapa Flow*, 282–83.

95. Remarkably, neither the *Benham* nor the *Jarvis* entries in US Department of the Navy, Naval History and Heritage Command, *Dictionary of American Naval Fighting Ships* (hereafter cited as *DANFS*), makes any mention of this incident, though Husband published photos of the damaged ships (*On the Coast of France*, between 96–97). Sims, Dorling, Leighton, and other contemporary sources are also silent.

96. Husband, *On the Coast of France*, 87–88.

97. The list of American warships based at Brest and Gibraltar during the final months of the war is in Leighton, *Simsadus*, 144. Information on destroyer and yacht operations off Brest and in the Bay of Biscay is in Husband, *On the Coast of France*, 61–66, 97. Ansel recounts his experiences in Rear Admiral Walter C. W. Ansel, oral history interview, no. 1, 15–18.

98. Still, *Crisis at Sea*, 399.

99. The final weeks of the war are summarized in Strachan, *The First World War*, 320–25; Husband, *On the Coast of France*, 127–29; *DANFS*, "*Roe* I."

Chapter Ten **A Navy Second to None**

1. Corbett and Newbolt, *Naval Operations*, 5:369; *North Sea Days*, 84; Hunter, *Beatty, Jellicoe, Sims and Rodman*, 167–69.

2. Corbett and Newbolt, *Naval Operations*, 5:371–76, 378–81.

3. Beach and Beach, *From Annapolis to Scapa Flow*, 285; Hart et al., *War on the Sea*, 396.

4. Ibid., 385–86, 388, 394; *North Sea Days*, 93.

5. Rose, *Power at Sea*, 2:90.

6. Hunter, *Beatty, Jellicoe, Sims and Rodman*, 180.

7. Bieri, oral history interview, no. 1, 33–34; Hunter, *Beatty, Jellicoe, Sims and Rodman*, 194–96.

8. Richard Rubin, "Where the Great War Ended," *New York Times*, December 28, 2014.

9. Woofenden, *Hunters of the Steel Sharks*, 121–64; Rousmanier, "Romance of the Subchasers," 44–45.

10. Harold Sprout and Margaret Sprout, *Toward a New Order of Sea Power: American Naval Policy and the World Scene, 1918–1922*.

Bibliography

Manuscript Collections

National World War I Museum, Kansas City, MO
Diary of CPO Leroy V. Collins
Diary of Searcy B. Dysart, no. 2003.8.1
Diary of George L. Golden Jr., no. 2004.97.1a, b
John Warner Jones Correspondence, no. 84.108
Diary from the Service of Leonard C. Kenyon
Diary of Stephen W. Ostrander, no. 2003.9.3
Horace Taylor Diaries, "Green" and "Tan" Journals
Puget Sound Historical Society, Seattle
Austen Hemion Collection
World War I Files: folders "USS *South Dakota*"; Emergency Shipping Corporation

Oral Histories

Naval Institute Oral History Program
Rear Admiral Walter C. W. Ansel
Vice Admiral Bernhard Henry Bieri
Vice Admiral Olaf M. Hustvedt
Vice Admiral Felix L. Johnson

Government Publications

US Department of the Navy. Naval Historical Center. "Online Library of Selected
    Images: 'SP's #s and 'ID's #s, World War I Era Patrol Vessels and Other Acquired
    Ships and Craft." http://www.history.navy.mil/photos/shusn-no/s.
————. "Online Library of Selected Images: U.S.S. *President Lincoln* (1917–1918)."
    http://www.history.navy.mil/photos/sh-usn/usn.
————. "Online Library of Selected Images: World War I Era Transports." http://
    www.history.navy.mil/photos/usnshtp/ap.

US Department of the Navy. Naval History and Heritage Command. *Dictionary of American Naval Fighting Ships*. http://www.history.navy.mil./danfs.

———. "Navy Medal of Honor, World War 1." http://www.history.navy.mil/faqs /moh/moh-1.

US Department of the Navy. Office of Naval Intelligence, Historical Section. *The American Naval Planning Section London*. Publication Number 7. Washington, DC: US Government Printing Office, 1923.

US Department of the Navy. Office of Naval Records and Library Monographs Historical Section. *American Ship Casualties of the World War: Including Naval Vessels, Merchant Ships, Sailing Vessels and Fishing Craft*. Washington, DC: US Government Printing Office, 1923. https://archives.org/stream/americanshipscasuOO/unit. djvu.txt.

———. *German Submarine Activities on the Atlantic Coast of the United States and Canada*. Publication Number 1. Washington, DC: US Government Printing Office, 1920. http://archives.org/stream/germansubmarinea00unitrich_djvu.txt.

———. *The Northern Barrage and Other Mining Activities*. Publication Number 2. Washington, DC: US Government Printing Office, 1920. https://archive.org/stream/ northernbarrageOO.unitrich.

———. *The United States Railway Batteries in France*. Publication Number 6. Washington, DC: US Government Printing Office, 1922. https://archives.org/details/ unitedstatesnavalOO.unitrich.

Other Sources

Adams, John W. "The Influences Affecting Naval Shipbuilding Legislation, 1910– 1916." *Naval War College Review* 22 (December 1969): 41–70.

"Ajax." *The German Pirate: His Methods and Record*. New York: George H. Doran, 1918.

Alden, Carroll Storrs. "American Submarine Operations in the War." *United States Naval Institute Proceedings* 46 (July 1920): 811–50, 1013–48.

Alden, John. *Flush Decks and Four Pipes*. Annapolis, MD: Naval Institute Press, 1965.

"All Hands," ed. *U.S.S.* Seattle *during the War*. Brooklyn: Brooklyn Daily Eagle, 1919.

"America's New Armada." In *The Navy League Annual*, by Robert Yerburgh, Archibald Hurd, and Gerard Fiennes. London: John Murray, 1916.

Anderson, Scott. *Lawrence in Arabia: War, Deceit, Imperial Folly and the Making of the Modern Middle East*. New York: Random House Anchor Books, 2014.

Archer, William. *The Pirate's Progress: A Short History of the U–boat*. New York: Harper & Brothers, 1918.

Arpee, Edward. *From Frigates to Flat-Tops: The Story of the Life and Achievements of Rear Admiral William Adger Moffett, U.S.N., "the Father of Naval Aviation."* Printed and distributed by the author.

Association of United States Navy. "110 Years of Tin Cans." http://asun.org/News Publications/NavyMagazine/MagazineArticles/tabid/2170/ID/34672/110 -years-of-Tin-Cans.aspx.

Austin, Harry Albert. "The United States Unprepared for War." *Forum* 51 (April 1914): 526–33.

Auten, Harold. *"Q" Boat Adventures: The Exploits of the Famous Mystery Ships by a "Q" Boat Commander.* London: Herbert Jenkins, 1919.

Avery, Samuel E. "Soldier's Mail: Letters Home from a New England Soldier, 1916–1918." *WW1: Memoirs and Reminiscences.* http://www.lib.byu.edu/index.php /Diaries_Memo.

Baer, George. *One Hundred Years of Sea Power: The United States Navy, 1890–1990.* Stanford, CA: Stanford University Press, 1993.

Bagley, Worth. "Torpedoed in the Celtic Sea." *Naval History* 11 (May–June 1997): 36–40.

Barry, John M. *The Great Influenza: The Epic Story of the Deadliest Plague in History.* New York: Penguin Books, 2005.

Bartlett, H. T. "Mission of Aircraft with the Fleet." *United States Naval Institute Proceedings* 43 (May 1919): 729–41.

Beach, Edward L., Sr., and Edward L. Beach Jr. *From Annapolis to Scapa Flow: The Autobiography of Edward L. Beach, Sr.* Annapolis, MD: Naval Institute Press, 2003.

Belknap, Reginald R. "The Yankee Mining Squadron; or, Laying the North Sea Mine Barrage." *United States Naval Institute Proceedings* 46 (January 1920): 5–32.

Berry, John M. *The Great Influenza: The Epic Story of the Deadliest Plague in History.* New York: Penguin Books, 2005.

Beston, Henry B. *Full Speed Ahead: Tales from the Log of a Correspondent with Our Navy.* Garden City, NY: Doubleday, Page, 1919.

Blackford, Charles Minor. *Torpedoboat Sailor.* Annapolis, MD: US Naval Institute, 1968.

Brassey, Earl, and John Leyland, eds., *The Naval Annual, 1919.* London: William Clowes and Sons, 1919.

Brown, M. S. "Life Overseas on the Yankee Sub-Chasers." *Pacific Motor Boat* 12 (April 1920): 3–9.

Cable, Frank T. *The Birth and Development of the American Submarine.* New York: Harper & Brothers, 1924.

Campbell, Gordon. *My Mystery Ships.* London: Hodder and Stoughton, 1928.

Canadian Broadcasting Company [CBC] News. "Halifax Explosion." N.d. http://cbc .ca/halifaxexplosion.

Castle, Ian. *London, 1914–17: The Zeppelin Menace.* Oxford: Osprey, 2008.

"Casualties of the United States Navy: Naval Aviation by Date and Base." http:// www.naval-history.net/WWI.NavyUS-C.

Chambers, Hilary Ranald, Jr. *United States Submarine Chasers in the Mediterranean, Adriatic and the Attack on Durazzo.* New York: Knickerbocker Press, 1920. Reprinted unpaginated in Todd A. Woofenden, webmaster, *Subchaser Archives Notes* 9, no. 12 (2013). "Subchaser Stories, Chambers, *U.S. Submarine Chasers.*" http://www. subchaser.org/chambers.

Chandler, T. E. "American and British Destroyers." *United States Naval Institute Proceedings* 48 (April 1922): 581–95.

Chatterton, E. Keble. *Q-Ships and Their Story.* London: Sidgwick and Jackson, 1922.

Churchill, Winston S. *The World Crisis, 1911–1918.* 2 vols. New York: Barnes and Noble Books, 1993.

Clift, A. Denis. "The New Navy Prepares for War: The *U.S. Naval Institute Proceedings*, 1910–19." *United States Naval Institute Proceedings* 140 (September 2014): 17–19.

Cline, Joe G. "Naval Aviation in World War I: First Naval Aviation Unit in France." *Naval Aviation News* (June 1967).

Colamaria, David. "A Sailor's Life in the New Steel Navy: Berthing, Officer-vs-Enlisted." 2010. http://www.steelnavy.org/history/berthing.

Corbett, Julian S., and Henry Newbolt. *Naval Operations: History of the Great War Based on Official Documents.* 5 vols. London: Imperial War Museum and Naval and Military Press, n.d. Vols. 4–5 originally published 1928, 1931.

Cummings, D. E. "Use of Aircraft in Naval Warfare." *United States Naval Institute Proceedings* 47 (November 1921): 1677–88.

Daniels, Josephus. *The Navy and the Nation.* New York: George H. Doran, 1919. http://archive.org/stream/navynation00.dani.

———. *Our Navy at War.* New York: George H. Doran, 1922. https://archives.org/details/cu3192409731.

———. "U.S. Secretary of the Navy Josephus Daniels' Official Report on the U.S. Navy during Wartime." http://www.firstworldwar.com/sources/usnavy.

Davis, George T. *A Navy Second to None: The Development of Modern American Naval Policy.* New York: Harcourt, Brace, 1940.

Delaware Military History. "The SC-1 Class Submarine Chaser." http://www.militaryhistory.org/index.html.

Destroyer History Foundation. "Early Destroyers; First Destroyers; *Bainbridge* Class; USS *Bainbridge*." http://destroyerhistory.org/early/ussbainbridge.

Dönitz, Karl. *Memoirs: Ten Years and Twenty Days.* Translated by R. H. Stevens. Cleveland: World, 1959.

Dorling, Taprell [Taffrail]. *Endless Story: Being an Account of the Work of the Destroyer, Flotilla-Leaders, Torpedo Boats and Patrol Boats in the Great War.* London: Hodder and Stoughton, 1931.

"Doughboy Center: The Story of the American Expeditionary Force." http://www.worldwar1.com/dbc/tuscania.htm.

Durham, Bill. "The Last Boom: Wooden Shipbuilding in World War I." Copy in World War 1 Files, folder: Emergency Fleet Corporation, Puget Sound Maritime Historical Society, Seattle.

———. "The Shipping Board Ships." *Seaways: Journal of Maritime History and Research* 1 (July–August 1990): 22–31.

Evans, Mark L. "Performed All Their Duties Well." *Naval History* 23 (October 2009): 42–53.

Fahey, James C. *The Ships and Aircraft of the United States Fleet, 1939.* Falls Church, VA: Ships and Aircraft, 1939.

Fayle, C. Ernest. *History of the Great War: Seaborne Trade.* 3 vols. London: Historical Section of the Committee of Imperial Defence, 1920–24.

Fiennes, Gerard. *Sea Power and Freedom: A Historical Study.* New York: G. P. Putnam's Sons, 1918.

Ford, John, director. Darryl F. Zanuck, producer. *Submarine Patrol*. Fox Films, 1938.

Friedman, Norman. *Fighting the Great War at Sea*. Annapolis, MD: Naval Institute Press, 2014.

———. *Seapower as Strategy: Navies and National Interests*. Annapolis, MD: Naval Institute Press, 2001.

———. *U.S. Battleships: An Illustrated Design History*. Annapolis, MD: Naval Institute Press, 1985.

———. *U.S. Small Combatants Including PT-Boats, Subchasers, and the Brown-Water Navy: An Illustrated Design History*. Annapolis, MD: Naval Institute Press, 1987.

Frothingham, Thomas R. "The Strategy of the World War, and the Lessons of the Effort of the United States." *United States Naval Institute Proceedings* 47 (May 1921): 669–83.

Gannon, Michael. *Operation Drumbeat: The Dramatic True Story of Germany's First U-boat Attacks along the American Coast in World War II*. New York: Harper Perennial Books, 1991.

Gibson, R. H., and Maurice Prendergast. *The German Submarine War, 1914–1918*. London: Constable, 1931.

Gill, Charles C. *Naval Power in the War (1914–1918)*. New York: George H. Doran, 1919.

———. "Role of the U.S. Navy's Transport Service during World War 1, November 1918." http://www.firstworldwar.com./sources/usnavy_gi.

Gleaves, Albert P. *A History of the Transport Service: Adventures and Experiences of United States Transports and Cruisers in the World War*. New York: George H. Doran, 1921. https://archives.org/stream/historyofthetranspo00.

Gravatt, Brent L. "On the Back of the Fleet." *Naval History* 4 (Spring 1990): 15–18.

Grossnick, Roy, et al. *United States Naval Aviation, 1910–1995*. Washington, DC: Naval Historical Center, 1997.

Hadley, Michael J. *Count Not the Dead: The Popular Image of the German Submarine*. Annapolis, MD: Naval Institute Press, 1995.

Hagan, Kenneth J. *This People's Navy: The Making of American Sea Power*. New York: Free Press, 1991.

Halpern, Paul G. *A Naval History of World War I*. Annapolis, MD: Naval Institute Press, 1994.

———. *The Naval War in the Mediterranean, 1914–1918*. Annapolis, MD: Naval Institute Press, 1987.

———. "The U.S. Navy in the Great War." *Relevance: The Quarterly Journal of the Great War Society* 13 (Spring 2004). http://www.worldwar1.com/tgws/usnw wone.htr.

Halsey, William F., and J. Bryan III. *Admiral Halsey's Story*. New York: Whittlesey House, 1947.

Halstead, J. Sterling. "Naval Aviation in World War I: Trained by the Royal Flying Corps." *Naval Aviation News* (August 1967): 24–26.

Harrod, Frederick S. *Manning the New Navy: The Development of a Modern Naval Enlisted Force, 1899–1940*. Westport, CT: Greenwood Press, 1978.

Hart, Albert Bushnell, et al., eds. *The War at Sea: Battles, Sea Raids and Submarine Campaigns.* Harper's Pictorial Library of the World War, vol. 4. New York: Harper & Brothers, 1920.

Hastings, Max. "The Necessary War." BBC2 Television, February 24, 2014. http:// www.youtube.com/watch?v=Pg5LWHO.

Hattendorf, John B. "Commonwealth Navies as Seen by the United States Navy, 1910–2010." *Northern Mariner/Le Marin du Nord* 24 (July–October 2014): 157–75.

———. *Naval History and Maritime Strategy: Collected Essays.* Malabar, FL: Kreiger, 2000.

Herwig, Holger H. *Politics of Frustration: The United States in German Naval Planning.* Boston: Little, Brown, 1976.

Hezlet, Arthur. *Aircraft and Sea Power.* New York: Stein and Day, 1970.

Howarth, Stephen. *To Shining Sea: A History of the United States Navy, 1776–1991.* New York: Random House, 1991.

Howeth, Linwood S. *History of Communications-Electronics in the United States Navy.* Washington, DC: Bureau of Ships, Office of Naval History, 1963.

Hughes, Wayne P. "Bradley Fiske: Leader of Transformation." *Naval History* 18 (April 2004): 28–29.

Hull, Michael D. "The Navy's Gallant Sentries." *Naval History* 28 (October 2014): 44.

Humanus Documentary Film Foundation. "The Millionaires Unit." 2014. http:// www.millionairesunit.org/intro.php.

Hunter, Francis T. *Beatty, Jellicoe, Sims and Rodman: Yankee Gobs and British Tars as Seen by an "Anglomaniac."* Garden City, NY: Doubleday, Page, 1919. http://babel .hathitrust.org/cgi/pt?=id.loc.ark/13960/t12n5n13w;view+1up;seq=9.

Hurley, Edward N. *The Bridge to France.* Philadelphia: J. B. Lippincott, 1927.

Husband, Joseph E. *On the Coast of France: The Story of United States Naval Forces in French Waters.* Chicago: A. C. McClurg, 1919. http://babel.hathitrust.org/cgi /pt?id+uc2.ark.

Hynes, Samuel. *The Unsubstantial Air: American Fliers in the First World War.* New York: Farrar, Straus, and Giroux, 2014.

"International Notes: U-boat Chasers Crossing the Atlantic." *United States Naval Institute Proceedings* 44 (December 1918): 2860.

James, Henry J. enryH*German Subs in Yankee Waters: First World War.* New York: Gotham House, 1940.

Jellicoe, John. *The Submarine Peril: The Admiralty Policy in 1917.* London: Cassel, 1934.

"Johnny Arthur Didway." In *World War 1 Vets: USS [sic] Navy.* http://www.wwvets .com/navy.

Jones, Jerry W. *U.S. Battleship Operations in World War I.* Annapolis, MD: Naval Institute Press, 1998.

Jordan, David. *Wolfpack: The U-boat War and the Allied Counter-attack, 1939–1945.* New York: Barnes and Noble Books, 2002.

Keegan, John. *The First World War.* New York: Random House, 1998.

———. *The Price of Admiralty: The Evolution of Naval Warfare.* New York: Penguin Books, 1988.

Kennedy, David M. *Over Here: The First World War and American Society*. New York: Oxford University Press, 2004.

King, Ernest J., and Walter Muir Whitehill. *Fleet Admiral King: A Naval Record*. New York: W. W. Norton, 1952.

Kittredge, Tracy Barrett. *Naval Lessons of the Great War: A Review of the Senate Naval Investigation of the Criticisms by Admiral Sims of the Policies and Methods of Josephus Daniels*. 1921. Reprint, London: Forgotten Books, 2015.

Klachko, Mary, and David F. Trask. *Admiral William Shepherd Benson: First Chief of Naval Operations*. Annapolis, MD: Naval Institute Press, 1987.

Knox, Dudley W. *American Naval Participation in the Great War (with Special Reference to the European Theater of Operations)*. Washington, DC: US Navy Department, Naval History and Heritage Command, the Navy Department Library, n.d.

Langley, David. "The Life and Times of Glenn Hammond Curtiss." http://aviation-history.com/early/curtiss.htm.

Lee, Lester T. "Navy." Recollections at "World War I Vets.com, 'Navy.'" No pagination. http://www.wwvets.com/Navy.html.

Le Fleming, H. M. *Warships of World War I* [combined vol.]. London: Ian Allen, 1961.

Leighton, John Langdon. *Simsadus: London; The American Navy in Europe*. New York: Henry Holt, 1920. http://catalog.hathitrust.org/Record/009561809.

Lewis, E. R. "The 14-Inch Naval Railway Batteries." *Naval History* 5 (Spring 1991): 41–45.

Linn, Brian McAllister. "America's Expeditionary War Transformation." *Naval History* 19 (October 2005): 56–61.

Livermore, Seward W. "The American Navy as a Factor in World Politics." *American Historical Review* 63 (July 1958): 863–79.

"Londonist." July 29, 2010. http://londonist.com/2019/07/wwi.

Loomis, Alfred F. "What Were the Faults of the Sub-Chasers?" *Motor Boating*, December 1919. Reprinted in Todd A. Woofenden, webmaster, Subchaser Archives. "Subchaser Stories—Published." http://www.subchasers.org.stories.

Lucas, Vernon I. "The Battle of Alaska." *Pacific Motor Boat* 12 (October 1919): 20–34.

Mannix, Daniel P., III. "The Great North Sea Mine Barrage." *American Heritage* 34 (April–May 1983): 1–5.

Marder, Arthur J. *From the Dreadnought to Scapa Flow: The Royal Navy in the Fisher Era, 1904–1919*. 5 vols. London: Oxford University Press, 1961–70. Vol. 4, *1917: Year of Crisis*. Vol. 5, *Victory and Aftermath, January 1918–June 1919*.

"Marine Flyer in France: The Diary of Captain Alfred A. Cunningham, November 1917–January 1918." WW1: Memoirs and Reminiscences. http://www.lib.byu.edu/index.php/Diaries_Memo.

Massie, Robert K. *Castles of Steel: Britain, Germany and the Winning of the Great War at Sea*. New York: Ballantine Books, 2003.

McCurdy, H. W. *Maritime History of the Pacific Northwest*. 2 vols. Seattle: Superior, 1966, 1977.

McDowell, C. S. "Naval Research." *United States Naval Institute Proceedings* 45 (June 1919): 895–908.

McDonald, Amy Athey. "Defending Allies Skies: Yale's Pioneering Pilots Form First Naval Aviation Unit." *Yale News*, August 17, 2014. http://news.yale.edu/2014 /08/17/defending-allied-skies-yale-s-pioneering-pilots-form-first-naval-aviation -unit.

Messimer, Dwight R. *Find and Destroy: Anti-submarine Warfare in World War I*. Annapolis, MD: Naval Institute Press, 2001.

Millholland, Ray. *The Splinter Fleet of the Otranto Barrage*. New York: Readers' League of America, 1936.

Moffat, Alexander W. *Maverick Navy*. Middletown, CT: Wesleyan University Press, 1976.

Moore, John N. Introduction to *Jane's Fighting Ships of World War I*. London: Random House Group, 2001.

Morison, Elting E. *Admiral Sims and the Modern American Navy*. Boston: Houghton Mifflin, 1942.

Musicant, Ivan. *U.S. Armored Cruisers*. Annapolis, MD: Naval Institute Press, 1985.

"Naval War Notes." *United States Naval Institute Proceedings* 44 (December 1918): 2860–70.

Newbolt, Henry. *Submarine and Anti-submarine*. London: Longmans, Green, 1918.

North Sea Days: A Brief History of the U.S.S. Texas and Life Generally in the North Sea during a War. Austin: Texas Parks and Wildlife Department, n.d. http://www. gwpda.org/naval/txnseady.htm.

O'Brien, Phillips Payson, ed. *Technology and Naval Combat in the Twentieth Century and Beyond*. London: Frank Cass, 2001.

Paine, Lincoln. *The Sea & Civilization: A Maritime History of the World*. New York: Alfred A. Knopf, 2013.

Paine, Ralph D. *The Fighting Fleets: Five Months of Active Service with the American Destroyers and Their Allies in the War Zone*. Boston: Houghton Mifflin, 1918.

———. *The First Yale Unit*. 2 vols. Cambridge, MA: Riverside Press, 1925. http://catalogue.hathitrust.org/Record/000403341.

Pennoyer, R. G. "Rigid Airships in the United States Navy." *United States Naval Institute Proceedings* 48 (April 1922): 517–29.

Perkins, J. David, comp. and ed. "German Submarine Losses from All Causes during World War I." http://www.gwpda.org/naval/sm100001.htn.

Phister, Jeff, Thomas Hone, and Paul Goodyear. *Battleship* Oklahoma, *BB-37*. Norman: University of Oklahoma Press, 2008.

Potter, E. B. *Bull Halsey*. Annapolis, MD: Naval Institute Press, 1988.

———. *Nimitz*. Annapolis, MD: Naval Institute Press, 1982.

Power, Hugh. *Battleship* Texas. College Station: Texas A&M University Press, 1992.

Preston, Antony. *Submarines*. New York: Gallery Books, 1982.

"Professional Notes: America's Record since Entering the War Two Years Ago." *United States Naval Institute Proceedings* 45 (May 1919): 846–47.

"Professional Notes: Convoy System's Success." *United States Naval Institute Proceedings* 45 (January 1919): 146–47.

Reckner, James R. *Teddy Roosevelt's Great White Fleet*. Annapolis, MD: Naval Institute Press, 1988.

Redford, Duncan. *The Submarine: A Cultural History from the Great War to Nuclear Combat.* London: Taurus Academic Studies, 2010.

Regan, Stephen D. "Gilded Men and the Suicide Fleet." *Naval History* 29 (June 2015): 58–63.

"Remo." "Naval Warfare: Examining Ships That Have Made an Impact on Naval Warfare and Naval History." May 25, 2010. http://navalwarfare.blogspot.com/2010/05/us.

Reynolds, Francis J. *The United States Navy from the Revolution to Date.* New York: P. F. Collier & Son, 1915.

Robb, Izette Winter. "Naval Aviation in World War I: The Navy Builds an Aircraft Factory." *Naval Aviation News* (October 1967): 22–24.

Roberts, Michael D. *Dictionary of American Naval Aviation Squadrons.* 2 vols. Washington, DC: US Department of the Navy, Naval Historical Center, 1995, 2000. Vol. 2, *The History of VP, VPB, VP (HL) and VP (AM) Squadrons.* http://www.history.navy.mil/research/histories/naval-aviation-history/dictionary-of-american-naval-aviation-squadrons-volume-2.html.

Rodman, Hugh. *Yarns of a Kentucky Admiral.* Indianapolis: Bobbs-Merrill, 1928.

Rose, Lisle A. *Power at Sea.* 3 vols. Columbia: University of Missouri Press, 2006. Vol. 2, *The Age of Navalism.* Vol. 2, *The Breaking Storm, 1919–1945.*

Rossano, Geoffrey L., ed. *Hero of the Angry Sky: The World War I Diary and Letters of David S. Ingalls, America's First Naval Ace.* Athens: Ohio University Press, 2013.

———, ed. *The Price of Honor: The World War One Letters of Naval Aviator Kenneth MacLeish.* Annapolis, MD: Naval Institute Press, 1991.

———. *Stalking the U-boat: U.S. Naval Aviation in Europe in World War I.* Gainesville: University Press of Florida, 2010.

Rousmanier, John. "The Romance of the Subchasers." *Naval History* 6 (Summer 1992): 42–45.

San Diego Naval Historical Association. "Naval Training Center, San Diego Navy History." http://www.quarterdeck.org/AreaBases/NTC%20History_filesntc_history.

Schroeder, Diana. *The History of the Sea Mine and Its Continued Importance in Today's Navy.* Washington, DC: US Department of the Navy, Naval History and Heritage Command. http://www.history.navy.mil/museums/keyport.

Shafter, Robert A. *Destroyers in Action.* New York: Cornell Maritime Press, 1945.

Shippen, Edward. *Naval Battles and Our New Navy. . . .* Philadelphia: P. W. Ziegler, 1894.

Simpson, Michael, ed. *Anglo-American Naval Relations, 1917–1919.* London: Scolar Press for the Navy Records Society, 1991.

Sims, William S. "Naval War College." *United States Naval Institute Proceedings* 47 (May 1921): 709–10.

Sims, William Sowden, and Burton J. Hendrick. *The Victory at Sea.* Garden City, NY: Doubleday, Page, 1921.

Society of the First Division. *History of the First Division during the World War, 1917–1919.* Philadelphia: John C. Winston, 1922.

Sondhaus, Lawrence. *The Great War at Sea: A Naval History of the First World War.* Cambridge: Cambridge University Press, 2014.

Sprout, Harold, and Margaret Sprout. *The Rise of American Naval Power, 1776–1918.* 3rd ed. Princeton, NJ: Princeton University Press, 1944.

———. *Toward a New Order of Sea Power: American Naval Policy and the World Scene, 1918–1922.* Princeton, NJ: Princeton University Press, 1940.

Stallings, Laurence. *Doughboys: The Story of the AEF, 1917–1918.* New York: Popular Library, 1964.

Sterner, Eric. "Bradley Fiske, Reformer." *Naval History* 7 (Spring 1993): 21–25.

Stevens, William Oliver, and Allan Westcott. *A History of Sea Power.* New York: George H. Doran, 1920.

Still, William N., ed. *Crisis at Sea: The United States Navy in European Waters in World War I.* Gainesville: University Press of Florida, 2006.

———, ed. *Joseph Taussig, Queenstown Patrol, 1917.* Newport, RI: Naval War College Press, 1996.

Strachan, Hew. *The First World War.* New York: Penguin Books, 2003.

Sturma, Michael. *Surface and Destroy: The Submarine Gun War in the Pacific.* Lexington: University Press of Kentucky, 2011.

"Subchasers of World War I." http://www.splinterfleet.org/sfww1.php.

Swartz, Peter M., and E. D. McGrady. "U.S. Navy Forward Deployment, 1801–2001." Navy Department Library. http://www.history.navy.mil/library/online/forward.

Taussig, Joseph K. "Destroyer Experiences during the Great War." Pts. 1–2. *United States Naval Institute Proceedings* 48, no. 12 (1922): 2015–40; 49, nos. 1–3 (January, February, March 1923): 1, 39–69; 2, 221–48; 3, 383–408.

Terraine, John. *The U-boat Wars, 1916–1945.* New York: G. P. Putnam's Sons, 1989.

Trask, David F. *The AEF and Coalition Warfare, 1917–18.* Lawrence: University Press of Kansas 1993.

———. *Captains and Cabinets: Anglo-American Naval Relations, 1917–1918.* Columbia: University of Missouri Press, 1972.

"Troopships, Battleships, Subs, Cruisers, Destroyers: A History of How the United States Navy Moved the Army to the War in Europe during WWI." http://freepages.military.rootsweb.ancestry.com.

Tuchman, Barbara. *The Zimmerman Telegram.* New York: Dell, 1965.

"U-boat Fates: U-boat Losses, 1914–1918." http://uboat.net/wwi/fates/losses.html.

Uhlig, Frank, Jr. *How Navies Fight: The U.S. Navy and Its Allies.* Annapolis, MD: Naval Institute Press, 1994.

US Army Twentieth Engineers. "World War 1: The Sixth Engineers." http://www.20thengineers.com/ww1-bmo6.html.

"U.S.S. *Jenkins,* DD-42." *McDougal's.* In "U.S.S. *McDougal,* DD-54." http://freepages.military.rootsweb.ancestry.com.

Utley, Jonathan G. *An American Battleship at Peace and War, the U.S.S.* Tennessee. Lawrence: University Press of Kansas, 1991.

Van Wyen, Adrian O. "Naval Aviation in World War I: In the Very Beginning." *Naval Aviation News* (April 1967): 12–13. Naval Heritage and History Command. http://www./history.navy.mil/nan/backissues/1960's/1967/April67.pdt.

Voitoux, Gabriel. "The Naval War: Some Light about the *Goeben*'s Escape." *United States Naval Institute Proceedings* 48 (April 1922): 531–45.

"The War in the Air–Bombers: Germany, Zeppelins." http://www.firstworldwar.com/airwar/bombers.

Wegener, Wolfgang. *The Naval Strategy of the World War*. Translated by Holger H. Herwig. 1929. Reprint, Annapolis, MD: Naval Institute Press, 1989.

Whitman, Edward C. "The School of War: U.S. Submarines in World War I." *Undersea Warfare: The Official Magazine of the U.S. Submarine Force* (Spring 2004). http://www.navy.mil/navydata/cno/n87/usw/iss.

Williams, D. J. "A Brief Diary of My Cruise in Foreign Waters on the USSC 227." In Todd A. Woofenden, webmaster, Subchaser Archives. "Subchaser Stories—Unpublished." *SAN* 3, no. 9 (2007).

Wolff, Leon. *In Flander's Fields: The 1917 Campaign*. London: Penguin Classics, 2001.

Woodhouse, Henry. "The Aircraft's Part in Beating the U-boat." *United States Naval Institute Proceedings* 44 (December 1918): 2727–39.

Woofenden, Todd A., webmaster. "Cotten: Instructions and Doctrine." Subchaser Archives. "Document Archives—Tactics." N.d. http://subchaser.org/Cotten-03.

———. *Hunters of the Steel Sharks: The Submarine Chasers of World War I*. Bowdoinham, ME: Signal Light Books, 2006.

———, webmaster. "Rough Seas." *Subchaser Archives Notes*. *SAN* 2, no. 12 (2006): unit 21, coll. 14. http://www.subchaser.org/SAN-Vol-No.

———. "SC 254." *Subchaser Archives Notes* 2, no. 12 (2006).

———, webmaster. Subchaser Archives. http://subchaser.org/archives-notes/SAN.

Wooldridge, E. T. "Milestones in Naval Aviation: Flight from the Sea." *Naval History* 17 (December 2003): 20–26.

"World War 1 at Sea: United States Navy, British Destroyers." Pt. 1. http://www.naval-history.net/WW1/Navy.BritishDi.

"World War I Era Naval Aviation Stations." Bluejacket.com. http://bluejacket.com/usn-usmc_avi_ww1_air_field.

Yarnall, Paul R., webmaster. "Patrol Vessels, Gunboats, Submarine Chasers and Section Patrol Craft Index: 'SC-1 Class 110' Submarine Chaser (SC-1 to SC-448)." NavSource Photo Archives. http://www.navsource.org.

Yates, Brock. *Destroyers and Destroyermen: The Story of Our "Tin-Can" Navy*. New York: Harper & Brothers, 1959.

Index

313

Porte, John C., 236, 238
Porter, J. C., 80, 90
postwar work of US naval forces, 275–76
Potter, Stephen, 237
Prendergast, Maurice, 288n26
Preston, Antony, 124–25
Princeton, aviation corps at, 84
Proceedings (periodical), 26
progressive movement, and US social
    disruption, 36

Q ships, 12, 44, 72
Queen Elizabeth (British battleship), 272
Queenstown, Ireland: enlisted men's
    clubhouse in, 120; officers' social life
    in, 118; sailors' life ashore in, 114–15,
    119–20; ships sunk near, 10
Queenstown, US naval forces at, 58, 62,
    70, 71, 72, 73, 103, 118–19, 122, 129,
    130, 136; arrival of, 56–57, 62, 72, 155;
    and debate on best use of escorts, 129;
    facilities for, 50; subchasers, 201, 202. *See
    also* Destroyer Division 8, US Atlantic
    Fleet

radio communications: Allied interception
    and analysis of, 103–4; development of,
    24; German advances in, 34; and tracking
    of U-boats, 102–4, 190, 235; types of
    transmitters, 102; of US Navy, quality of,
    102–3, 173; US operations with British
    Fleet and, 255
radio direction finders (RDFs), and
    tracking of U-boats, 103–4
Rambler (US armed yacht), 266–67
Ransom, Philip, 195
Rathenau, Walther, 123
Rayals, P., 195
Read, Curtis, 230–31
refueling underway: first US ships to
    accomplish, 56; by subchasers, 154
reservists, and Navy prewar expansion, 29

Richards, J. K., 135
Rodman, Hugh, *161*; as commander of
    Battleship Division 6, 169, 258–59,
    260, 261, 265; on Navy's technological
    improvements, 16–17; relations with
    British officers, 173, 174, 175, 256; and
    return of US forces, 275
Roe (US destroyer), 268–69
Rogers, Thomas S., 262, 263–64
Rood, G. A., 191
Room 40, 103–4, 257
Roosevelt, Franklin D., 145–46, 216, 261
Roosevelt, Theodore "Teddy," 15
Rose, Hans, 12–13, 78, 105, 135
Rousmanier, John, 276
Royal Yacht Club (Cork, Ireland), 118
Rubin, Richard, 275
Rumill, George, 237
Russia: revolution in, 276; withdrawal from
    war, 34, 35, 177

sailors, US: adaptation to new warfare, 4–5;
    calls to sea duty, 120; on destroyers, stress
    on, 182–83; dislike of merchant sailors,
    114–15, 179; living conditions for, 26–29;
    and military discipline, 38; morale of,
    119–20; and new warship technology, 16,
    24, 27; recruitment of, 24; shore leaves,
    118, 119–20, 259, 260, 263; subchasers
    crews, 147, 150, 201; on submarines,
    stress on, 196–97; training and education
    of, 17, 24–25, 253
St. Paul (passenger ship), 120–22
sanitation, aboard ship, 28, 29, 61
Saufley, Richard, 20, 25–26
Scheer, Reinhard, 257, 263
sea, mastery of, as key to Allied victory, 41
sealift capacity, US: prewar deficiency of,
    33, 53. *See also* transport and cargo ships;
    troop ships for AEF transport
Sexton, W. R., 75
Shanks, D. C., 96